Composing
Ethnography

ETHNOGRAPHIC ALTERNATIVES BOOK SERIES

Series Editors

Carolyn Ellis
Arthur P. Bochner
(both at the University of South Florida)

About the Series:

Ethnographic Alternatives will emphasize experimental forms of qualitative writing that blur the boundaries between social sciences and humanities.

The editors encourage submissions that experiment with novel forms of expressing lived experience, including literary, poetic, autobiographical, multi-voiced, conversational, critical, visual, performative, and co-constructed representations. Emphasis should be on expressing concrete lived experience through narrative modes of writing.

We are interested in ethnographic alternatives that promote narration of local stories; literary modes of descriptive scene setting, dialogue, and unfolding action; and inclusion of the author's subjective reactions, involvement in the research process, and strategies for practicing reflexive fieldwork.

Please send proposals to:

Carolyn Ellis and Arthur P. Bochner
College of Arts and Sciences
Department of Communication
University of South Florida
4202 East Fowler Avenue, CIS 1040
Tampa, FL 33620-7800

Books in the series:

Volume 1, *Composing Ethnography: Alternative Forms of Qualitative Writing*, Carolyn Ellis and Arthur P. Bochner, editors.

Composing Ethnography

Alternative Forms of Qualitative Writing

Carolyn Ellis
Arthur P. Bochner

EDITORS

Ethnographic Alternatives Series
Volume 1

ALTAMIRA
PRESS

A Division of Sage Publications, Inc.
Walnut Creek ■ London ■ New Delhi

For information contact:

AltaMira Press
A Division of Sage Publications, Inc.
1630 North Main Street, Suite 367
Walnut Creek, California 94596 U.S.A.

Sage Publications Ltd.
6 Bonhill Street
London EC2A 4PU United Kingdom

Sage Publications India Pvt. Ltd.
M-32 Market
Greater Kailash 1
New Delhi, 110 048 India

PRINTED IN THE UNITED STATES OF AMERICA

Library of Congress Cataloging-in-Publication Data

Composing ethnography : alternative forms of qualitative writing / Carolyn Ellis and Arthur P. Bochner, editors.
     p.   cm. — (Ethnographic alternatives ; vol. 1)
     Includes bibliographical references and index.
     ISBN 0-7619-9163-8 (cloth : alk. paper). — ISBN 0-7619-9164-6 (pbk. : alk. paper)
     1. Ethnology—Authorship.   2. Social sciences—Authorship. I. Ellis, Carolyn, 1950– . II. Bochner, Arthur P. III. Series.
GN307.7.C66   1996
305.8—dc20

                                      96-23079
                                          CIP

Production Services: Strawberry Field Publishing
Editorial Management: Denise M. Santoro
Cover and Text Design: Paula Goldstein
Cover art created by Clay Bodenhammer

p. 228–229   "Aunt Sue's Stories" from *Selected Poems* by Langston Hughes © 1926 by Alfred A. Knopf, Inc. and renewed in 1954 by Langston Hughes. Reprinted by permission of the publisher and Harold Ober Associates.

Contents

About the Editors

Arthur P. Bochner (Professor of Communication) is Chair of the Department of Communication at the University of South Florida. He lives in Tampa with Carolyn Ellis, his partner *par excellence,* and their four kindred dogs. He is the author of more than 40 articles and monographs that focus mainly on communication in close relationships. Art enjoys experimenting with reflexive and narrative modes of teaching, hiking in the mountains, white-water rafting, and games of chance.

Carolyn Ellis (Professor of Communication and Sociology, University of South Florida) lives in Tampa with her soul mate, Arthur Bochner, and their four dogs, who seduce her into "dog reality" several times each day. She is the author of *Final Negotiations: A Story of Love, Loss, and Chronic Illness* (Temple) and coeditor of *Investigating Subjectivity: Research on Lived Experience* (Sage). In her work on narrative, subjectivity, and illness, she seeks to write evocative texts that remind readers of the complexity of their social worlds. Writing autoethnographic texts has intensified her life experience; she hopes these stories also contribute meaningfully to the lives of readers.

For each other

Preface

In August 1993, Donileen Loseke and Spencer Cahill invited us to serve as guest editors of a special issue of the *Journal of Contemporary Ethnography* that would focus on "experimental approaches" to ethnography. We accepted their offer and, in the summer of 1994, we issued a call for manuscripts that would blur the boundaries between social sciences and humanities. We invited submissions that covered a wide range of topics, including strategies for practicing reflexivity, subjectivity in the research process, ethnography as a morally and politically engaged subject, ethnographers as storytellers, intertextuality and voice, writing as inquiry, the participatory side of fieldwork, experimental genres of ethnographic narration, and ethnography as performance.

Within a few months, we literally were swamped with manuscripts. Apparently we had touched a hot nerve extending across the fields of social science that practice ethnography and qualitative research methods. Manuscripts came from anthropologists, sociologists, and psychologists, as well as scholars in cultural studies, American studies, education, and communication. Many of these scholars expressed a hunger for alternatives to mainstream social science writing and a desire to break down the walls between social science and literature. Quickly, we appointed an editorial board to handle the initial flow of more than 70 manuscripts in a timely way. And the papers kept coming for months, as did the phone calls, e-mails, and letters. Soon it became obvious that we had too many good manuscripts to limit our publication to a single special issue.

In June 1995, Mitch Allen contacted us about the possibility of expanding our conception of the special issue, "Taking Ethnography into the Twenty-First Century," into an interdisciplinary book series for AltaMira Press called *Ethnographic Alternatives*. We are grateful to Mitch for nurturing the development of this project, which is the first book in the series.

All of the manuscripts published in this book were refereed by external reviewers. We acknowledge the extraordinary work of all of our reviewers. Their perceptive and probing evaluations substantially improved all of the chapters. Many authors commented positively on the helpful criticism they received from readers. In particular, we are indebted to our deputy editors, Elizabeth Bell, Norman Denzin, Eric Eisenberg, Mark Neumann, David Payne, Laurel Richardson, and Allen Shelton, whom we called on for advice frequently and with little fore-warning. Their work authenticates the meaning of the term "colleague and friend."

Finally, there is our home base, The University of South Florida, where we enjoy a unique and supportive environment in which to take risks and experiment with unorthodox styles of teaching and research. No words can aptly express the extraordinary thrill and inspiration we get from the passionate and validating commitments of our students at USF.

Acknowledgments

Deputy Editors

We wish to thank Elizabeth Bell; Norman Denzin; Eric Eisenberg; Mark Neumann; David Payne; Laurel Richardson; and Allen Shelton.

Reviewers

We wish to thank Patricia Adler, Peter Adler, David Altheide, Michael Angrosino, Amber Ault, Deborah Austin, Howard Becker, Edward Bruner, Dan Carbaugh, Susan Chase, Keith Cherry, Adele Clarke,

Patricia Clough, F. Michael Connelly, Peter Conrad, Arlene Kaplan Daniels, Marjorie DeVault, Bernard Downs, Mitchell Duneier, David Eason, Michael Flaherty, Andy Fontana, Karen Fox, Arthur Frank, Jennifer Friedman, Patricia Geist, John Giancola, H.L. Goodall, Simon Gottschalk, Bill Gourd, Laurel Graham, Judith Hamera, Douglas Harper, Regina Hewitt, Mark Hutter, Chris Inman, Jean Jackson, John Johnson, Jane Jorgenson, David Karp, Donna Lee King, Jim King, Sherryl Kleinman, Joe Kotarba, Cheris Kramarae, Susan Krieger, Kristin Langellier, Patti Lather, Niza Licuanan, Yvonna Lincoln, Ruth Linden, Donileen Loseke, David Maines, Peter Manning, Michal McCall, Sheila McNamee, C. David Mortensen, Dennis Mumby, Lois Nixon, Judy Perry, Christy Ponticelli, Trevor Purcell, Nancy Ramsey, William Rawlins, Shulamit Reinharz, Bill Rodman, Gil Rodman, Carol Rambo Ronai, Laura Sells, Herb Simons, Tim Simpson, Fred Steier, Paul Stoller, Mary Strine, Bryan Taylor, John Van Maanen, and Janet Yerby.

Talking Over Ethnography

Arthur P. Bochner
Carolyn Ellis

Scene: The living room of a middle-class home. A brick fireplace, reaching through the 25-foot-tall beamed cathedral ceiling, separates the rustic, cedar living area from a newly remodeled kitchen. In view behind the fireplace is a second-floor loft cluttered with piles of disheveled books and papers surrounding a computer, bearing the unmistakable stamp of a professor's office.

On a wooden cabinet built into the side of the fireplace sits a CD player and amplifier connected to four speakers surrounding the room. Loose CDs hide an old turntable that looks to be rarely used. Above five short windows on the side wall are framed drawings of four dogs. Martina, a German shepherd who died recently, towers over Ande, a Jack Russell terrier, and Likker and Traf, two rat terriers. The other side wall is covered with windows, abstract art, and stained glass.

Facing the fireplace is a large, round, tan couch. Behind the couch stands a mahogany bookcase in which novels, cookbooks, travel guides, photo albums and loose pictures, pet and gardening books, and health and sex manuals are spread haphazardly across the shelves.

A winding stairway leads to an upstairs landing that faces the fireplace and loft across the room. Off the landing are entrances to a library and a second professor's office. Hidden from view are the piles of books, a computer, printer, fax, and copier in that office, and floor-to-ceiling bookcases in the library. The journals on the top shelves—Social Forces, American Sociological Review, Human Communication Research—*are reachable only by a step ladder that leans against the wall. At eye level are* Journal of Contemporary Ethnography, Journal of Narrative and Life History, Qualitative Inquiry, The Sociological Quarterly, Text and Performance Quarterly, Qualitative Sociology, Symbolic Interaction, *and* Feminist Studies.

It is early February 1996. Art enters the living room from outside carrying a large bag of groceries and some books and papers. Four dogs greet him at the door—including Sunya, the 10-week-old Australian shepherd puppy—all jumping up and down, barking, and sniffing the grocery bag. Hearing the commotion, Carolyn walks out of her upstairs office to the landing that looks down on the scene below.

Art: (*Shouting above the barking dogs*) Hi. I brought dinner.

Carolyn: (*Running down the steps and following the dogs and Art toward the kitchen*) Oh, good. But can we talk for a while before we eat? I've got some news to tell you about our book.

Art: (*He calms the dogs affectionately, giving them biscuits, and reenters the living room. He approaches Carolyn, who now is reclining on the round couch and cuddling Likker, who lies with his head on her shoulder.*) Tell me the news. Did you hear from Mitch Allen at AltaMira? (*Art sits down next to Carolyn; Sunya, Ande, and Traf follow, still chewing on biscuits, and curl up on the couch between Art and Carolyn.*)

Carolyn: Yes, Mitch e-mailed me. He wants to get our project to press as soon as possible . . .

Art: (*Interrupting*) Did you tell him we have received all the revised chapters and can send the whole package immediately? We're ready to go to press.

Carolyn: Hold on a second. Yes, he knows the papers are done, but he told me there was one task he still wants us to complete.

Art: What's that?

Carolyn: Mitch wants us to write a standard introduction to the book. He thinks the chapters need to be situated and contextualized for readers. We need to say why we developed this project, who will benefit from reading it, what themes run through the chapters, how each chapter can be read and understood. You know, what the point of the whole project is.

Art: (*Showing irritation*) What? Are you kidding? (*Art stands up and begins pacing back and forth across the room. After a reflective pause, he continues.*) Mitch knows our book is not intended to be a received text where we pose as the experts on how to read and interpret each study, doesn't he?

Carolyn: Sit down here, would you! (*Carolyn reaches out for Art's hand, gently tugging him toward her on the couch, as she continues.*) Mitch knows we're trying to change the reading practices of social scientists, but he's speaking from a publisher's perspective. He's afraid that if we don't provide a framework for the volume, we may lose the opportunity to reach a wider audience.

Art: (*Facing Carolyn and seated on the couch*) Look, I just don't want to be stuck saying, in one breath, "We promote the idea of a plural text, open to many interpretations"; then, in the next breath, declare, "Here's how to read and interpret each chapter."

Carolyn: I don't see it that way, Art. As editors, we do have a perspective on ethnographic practices that guided our selection of papers. Can't we discuss this perspective and help readers connect themselves to these essays and studies without necessarily privileging our voices? I think it's dishonest to pretend we're invisible. We've left traces of our convictions all over this text. Instead of masking our presence, leaving it at the margins, we should make ourselves more personally accountable for our perspective.

Art: Why am I not surprised by your resistance to camouflaging the "I"?

Carolyn: For the same reason I'm not surprised you don't want to write the kind of dull and generic introduction that typifies edited volumes.

Art: Am I really that predictable?

Carolyn: (*Smiles and nods her head*) Both of us are.

Art: Well, I guess we do have to be sensitive to the marketing problem.

Carolyn: Especially since the ethnographic studies in our book are not unique to any one discipline.

Art: Yes, we're trying to reach across the disciplinary boundaries of sociology, anthropology, communication, cultural studies, race and gender studies, aging, education, nursing, and medicine.

Carolyn: Most of our readers already understand that boundaries between academic disciplines have been dissolving for a long time. To a large extent, academic departments are only budgetary conveniences for universities and a means of crafting a professional identity for faculty.

Art: But universities continue to function as if knowledge could be divided neatly into separate domains. Course offerings, degree requirements, student credit-hour calculations, institutionalized evaluation standards—all these things make it difficult to break away from the habit of insulating ourselves from conversation and collaboration with colleagues in other fields.

Carolyn: So you can understand Mitch's problem as a publisher of an interdisciplinary series. He's trying to surmount these considerable obstacles so that books like ours can open traffic across the borders of social sciences and humanities disciplines. He wants us to let readers know in the introduction that they've come to the right place, that we've got something useful and different for them to read.

Art: That's hard to argue against. Our main problem is how to reach people who are looking for alternatives, who want to write differently, and who see an opportunity to expand the boundaries of ethnographic research. What is ethnography anyway? It's not the name of a discipline.

Carolyn: Ethnography is what ethnographers *do*. It's an activity. Ethnographers inscribe patterns of cultural experience; they give perspective on life. They interact, they take note, they photograph, moralize, and write.

Art: And most ethnographers eventually turn to some form of cultural analysis.

Carolyn: Anthropology used to be the discipline most closely associated with cultural analysis, but that's no longer true. Today, the boundaries of cultural analysis are diffuse and uncontained.

Art: Clifford Geertz deserves a lot of the credit. He opened up the concept of culture by equating it with Weber's idea of "the webs of significance" we spin ourselves. The goals of ethnography were transformed from the search for laws to the search for meanings. Now we just assume that where there is meaning, there is culture.

Carolyn: Some of the most interesting dialogues about "culture" now take place outside anthropology, among scholars focusing on media, technology, history, literature, pedagogy, and politics. All of these scholars talk about the forms of common sense that shape everyday life—the practices, texts, and representations of culture that circulate and mediate lived experience.

Art: Yes, and they write and speak about culture not only for the purpose of analysis but also for critique, intervention, and inspiration . . . *(A phone rings, interrupting the conversation.)*

Carolyn: Is that my phone or yours?

Art: It's yours. Let the answering machine get it. I'm having fun talking through these issues.

Carolyn: Shh! Let me hear who it is. *(There's a click and the phone shuts off.)* Oh, good, a hang up. I was afraid it was one of my doctoral students. I've got a committee meeting in Sociology and one in Education tomorrow. And the study group in Communication meets tomorrow at 5:00. Sometimes I think my academic life was much easier before we became so committed to interdisciplinary work. It's hard to keep up. *(Another phone rings.)*

Art: That's my line. Be quiet for a second.

Carolyn: You're not going to answer, are you?

Art: Only if it's about the faculty search in Interdisciplinary Social Sciences. Their new faculty member may want to be appointed in Communication and add support to the Institute for Interpretive Human Studies. The politics of the hire are pretty complicated. *(Art listens closely to the message his office manager is leaving about the time for a meeting the next morning.)*

Carolyn: I'll be glad when you're not department chair anymore and don't have to juggle all these worlds.

Art: I think we'll always be juggling these worlds.

Carolyn: Let's get back to what we were talking about. Where were we? *(A few seconds go by.)* Oh, yes, culture. You know, we need to think about the culture of the university too. I don't think the humanities and social sciences are really that different in what they are trying to do.

Art: Neither do I. Ethnography tries to deepen and enlarge our sense of a human community. Literature does this too.

Carolyn: That's our starting point for this book. The walls between social sciences and humanities have crumbled. In the 1970s and 1980s postmodernists, poststructuralists, and feminists challenged us to contemplate how social science may be closer to literature than to physics. These critiques helped draw ethnographers who thought of themselves as sociologists and anthropologists closer to colleagues in history, women's studies, folklore, media studies, and communication. We not only began to question the usefulness of boundaries between disciplines, but some of us became downright hostile toward our own disciplines.

Art: Strange isn't it? How so many of us were brought together by our discontent. We were disgruntled about the state of our own fields and wanted to set a different research agenda. I guess you could say we were united by our alienation and liminality.

Carolyn: Maybe that's why "new ethnography" appealed so strongly to women, people of color, marginal voices.

Art: And to all of us who weren't buying the party line, who wanted to come to grips with the predicaments of the scholar as an involved, situated, and integral part of the research and writing process.

Carolyn: It appealed to people like me who didn't want to stay stuck at the level of data. I wanted to be a storyteller, someone who used narrative strategies to transport readers into experiences and make them feel as well as think.

Art: The "crisis of representation" created an opening to explore new styles of research and writing. That's where *Composing Ethnography* enters. It addresses the need to show some of the different possibilities for ethnographic expression. We highlight a number of genres of writing that express the way the world can be perceived, felt, and lived. Our goal is to open ethnography to a wider audience, not just academics but all people who can benefit from thinking about their own lives in terms of other people's experiences.

Carolyn: The title of our book series, *Ethnographic Alternatives,* really has a double meaning for us. Books in the series will explore experimental styles of writing. Ethnographic writing thus is understood as a choice among numerous alternatives. And all of these alternatives, to some extent, breach the received genre of realist writing that construes the author as a neutral, authoritative, and scientific voice.

Art: In fact, our project begins with the assumption that ethnographers cannot stand above and outside what they study. When we produce what we call ethnography, our product can never be an accurate map because the processes of production make transparent representation impossible.

Carolyn: Like what happens when we turn our observations into field notes and our field notes into stories.

Art: That's why we need to see what we do not so much as representation but as *communication.* Eventually we transform "data" into an ethnographic text. Language sits in for life. We use words. We write. We take our audience into account. We worry about how our readers will interpret what we write, what they may think, and how they will feel.

Carolyn: And our writing is constrained by the writing conventions of our discipline.

Art: Dan Rose observes that what we read teaches us how we are supposed to write. We expect to write the way our predecessors wrote.

Carolyn: I learned the hard way that if you resist conforming to the accepted genres of writing, you'll have a difficult time getting your work published.

Art: But *Composing Ethnography* wants to reform those practices. Ethnography's attachment to the correspondence theory of truth—you know, the idea that we could describe objects in the world out there apart from and independent of our activity as language users—well, that illusion was pretty thoroughly shattered over the past three decades by historians of science such as Thomas Kuhn; philosophers such as Rorty, Derrida, Lyotard, and Foucault; culture critics such as Marcus, de Certeau, and Tyler; and feminists such as Haraway and Harding.

Carolyn: *(Interrupting)* Get to the point, would you?

Art: OK, OK. The point is that language cannot be a neutral means of communicating what exists in the world. We have no assurance that if the world could talk she would say the same things we say when we write our sentences about her.

Carolyn: So when we say that ethnographers can't stand above or outside language, we mean that the world as we "know" it cannot be separated from the language we use to explain, understand, or describe it.

Art: Sorry to say, but ethnographers are stuck with language. The positivist idea that applying rigorous scientific method could give us a place to stand apart, remove us from the intrusions of our own experience and subjectivity—that's nonsense! We can't extricate ourselves from language.

Carolyn: When ethnographers like me make texts, try as we may to report and represent accurately, we necessarily invent and construct the cultures we write about. We cannot help but read something into what is there, because we are there with it.

Art: Your utterances in language cannot express anything completely independent of what you're doing there. When we give up the notion of an unmediated reality, we forgo the scientist's strong claim that he is discovering something completely outside himself.

Carolyn: But when you say words like *invent* or *construct,* orthodox social scientists get very upset.

Art: Yes, they think we're giving license to turn serious, systematic inquiry into frivolous relativism where anything goes; that we've lost all respect for facts.

Carolyn: Well, I've never been happy about these polarities. Why can't I be committed to careful, systematic research and still admit that the scientist cannot see with a naked eye?

Art: I think there's a fear that we cannot trust ourselves. Science has given us a lot of comfort. It is comforting to believe there is Truth to be found and criteria that do not depend on our utterances or modes of inscription. It's the same kind of solace many people find within formalized religion. If we lose faith in scientific method as a path to Truth beyond human subjectivity, then we have to rely on ourselves to decide what to believe.

Carolyn: And that scares people who were educated to treat human subjectivity as a threat to rationality and to believe that differences of opinion could be arbitrated by objective criteria beyond dispute. They were taught that objective truth has to be given priority over emotion and opinion.

Art: But that's what is important and liberating about the so-called crisis of representation. It allows a more sober understanding of words like *truth, knowledge,* and *reality.* We can become more comfortable with contingencies of language and human experience. We no longer have to see social science as a culture that is distinct from literature—you know, either you write literature or you write scientific reports.

Carolyn: Before we can merge these worlds, though, I think we need to appreciate the differences between making something and making it up. The idea of blurring genres of inquiry may help obscure the boundaries between science and literature, but it doesn't obliterate the responsibility to try to be faithful to our experiences in the field.

Art: That reminds me of what Gregory Bateson used to say. He stressed the importance of deliberate, careful, empirical work, though he recognized it could never produce unmediated objective knowledge. Bateson knew there was no way to guarantee objective truth, but he didn't think that meant the end result had to be make-believe.

Carolyn: Yeah, that's the danger of going too far with the notion of ethnographic fiction. We ought to treat our ethnographies as partial, situated, and selective productions, but this should not be seen as license to exclude details that don't fit the story we want to tell. I want to retain a distinction between saying our work is selective, partial, and contestable, and saying that the impossibility of telling the whole truth means you can lie. If we unquestioningly accept

the depiction of the ethnographer as a trickster, a sophist,
and a politician, we aren't far from seeing her as a liar.

Art: I think we can break free from the quagmire of these messy
distinctions by becoming more pragmatist. We need to ask,
"What do we want ethnography to do? How can other
people use our work?" Michael Jackson urges ethnographers to see the binaries science/art and fact/fiction as
mutually necessary and inextricably connected. If we tie
ourselves down to rigid rules, we lose the flexibility of
adopting different discursive strategies depending upon
our circumstances and purposes. Jackson's emphasis on the
rhetorical demands of ethnographic research helps avoid
the temptation to trivialize important differences between
art and science. To make science more artful doesn't mean
art and science become one and the same activity. (*A phone
rings, interrupting the conversation.*)

Carolyn and Art (*Together*): Don't answer! (*Both laugh and ignore the
voice in the background.*)

Carolyn: I love what Jackson says in *At Home in the World*—that "we
need to replace our craving to know how to know with a
desire to know how to live." That's how I hope people will
read *Composing Ethnography.* Try to put yourself in the
place of the Other; to feel what it feels like to engage in the
self-destructive culture of bulimia (Tillmann-Healy), to
confront the double messages of growing up with a mentally retarded mother (Ronai), of being sexually abused as a
child but remembering your abuser as someone you felt
love for (Fox), of doing factory work that dislocates body
from self (Payne), of learning that you have inflammatory
breast cancer at midlife and midcareer (Kolker). How do
people live and cope with these circumstances?

Art: Jackson's focus on "coping" instead of "controlling" keeps
our attention on the pragmatism of ethnography. It
replaces the question "how is it true?" with the question
"how is it useful?" One of the uses of autoethnography is to
allow another person's world of experience to inspire critical reflection on your own. Richard Rorty calls this "the

inspirational value of reading." You recontextualize what you knew already in light of your encounter with someone else's life or culture.

Carolyn: But useful doesn't necessarily mean pleasant. When autoethnography strikes a chord in readers, it may change them, and the direction of change can't be predicted perfectly. A lot depends on the reader's subjectivity and emotions. If you want to restrict yourself to pleasurable experiences, much of autoethnography may disappoint or intimidate you. I recall the comments of one of our colleagues who told me her material life had been profoundly and negatively affected by the raw depictions of sexual abuse in an autoethnography I asked her to read. She apologized for not being a typical reader who tries to keep her professional distance from what she reads.

Art: She should be congratulated for not being the kind of "good" academic reader who keeps what she reads at a critical distance. Not many people say they're profoundly affected by the social science they read. Too many people say they're so bored they can't get through it.

Carolyn: Yes, but she felt too exposed. She couldn't protect herself from the pain and horror of child abuse. She couldn't pull away from the text, you know, stand outside it.

Art: I don't know if this is a problem with the text or with the reader. If a text makes you want to scream, is it due to a quality of the text or a quality of the reader, who may have a readiness to scream under some provocation?

Carolyn: All this talk about screaming makes me want to scream. (*Both laugh.*) We aren't claiming that all autoethnography should be primal. Most of life is commonplace, so a lot of autoethnography will focus on details of everyday life that won't provoke these raw emotions.

Art: Of course. But let's not forget that one of the points of first-person accounts is to help us understand how we've been constructed traditionally by social science texts as passive and unengaged readers. We haven't been asked to care about the *particular* people whose lives are depicted by ethnography. A good account can inspire a different way of reading. It isn't meant to be consumed as "knowledge" or received passively, you know, as an object of contemplation.

Carolyn: Maybe it's good to worry about the impact social science can have on your life. It makes the concern some critics have raised about the self-indulgence of autoethnographers seem absurd. If autoethnography doesn't touch a world beyond the self of the writer, then there's no need to worry about its potentially profound impact on one's material existence.

Art: The self-indulgence charge seems like only another way to try to reinscribe ethnographic orthodoxy. If culture circulates through all of us, how can autoethnography be free of connection to a world beyond the self?

Carolyn: It can't. And the concern about material effects only reinforces how this work can inspire further connection through engaged readings. On the whole, autoethnographers don't want you to sit back as spectators; they want readers to feel and care and desire. I guess if that's a criticism—that it may affect your life; may even dredge up feelings you're not prepared to deal with now—well, maybe that's a sign it's making a difference.

Art: Maybe there needs to be more screaming about the atrocities people experience. We admit that education can hurt, especially when it makes you question your values and behavior. The way I look at it, well, some of these personal narratives are written by people who have suffered in silence for too long. I mean, our polyglot world includes child abusers, and drug pushers, and homeless people, and harassers, and racists, and wife beaters, and people with HIV and Alzheimer's and on life support. Many people live in a world where death is just around the corner and life feels worse than the alternative. Hey, there's a hell of a lot to scream about even in polite society.

Carolyn: *(Stands abruptly and looks around the room)* Where did Sunya go? I'm going to scream if Sunya is peeing on the floor again. Sunya! *(Suddenly Sunya bounds into the living room from the hallway, water dripping from her face. The other dogs awaken and start looking for toys.)*

Art: Not now, dogs. This is work time. *(Sunya and Traf start to play their game of "keep away," taking turns keeping a ball from each other.)*

Carolyn: *(Smiling in admiration)* Notice the definite rules they follow. One dog can't bully the ball from the other. She has to wait until the other one drops it. Turn-taking keeps the game going.

Art: I knew the conversation analysts were on to something. Maybe they should study dogs.

Carolyn: Maybe we should. It would keep us away from some of the sad and terrifying topics we tend to get into.

Art: Someday perhaps. Where were we?

Carolyn: We were talking about personal narratives. *(She sits down on the couch as the dogs settle back in. After a momentary pause, she continues.)* A lot of people have expressed gratitude for being exposed to stories that historically have been shrouded in secrecy. They think of these stories as gifts.

Art: They are gifts, at least to the extent they make it possible to converse about previously silenced and unspeakable topics and prepare us to appreciate and deal more humanely with the diversity of human experience.

Carolyn: Well, OK, I agree our main purpose isn't to make readers suffer but to help them learn how to converse with and use these stories. But that's not so easy, is it?

Art: No, it's not. And some stories aren't intended to encourage dialogue. But we can learn from these stories too. We can understand better what new directions to take, when alienating our readers works against our purposes, and when it may be necessary in order to challenge the assumptions they take for granted.

Carolyn: Now you've shifted to the critical and analytical dimension, which focuses attention more directly on how readers use and respond to these stories. After students read these works in my classes, their conversations sometimes become emotionally charged and antagonistic. Students feel the tensions between the comfort of fixed and canonical meanings, on the one hand, and the contradictions, gaps, and ambiguities of multiple and conflicting interpretations, on the other.

Art: These discussions can be tense, but they help students understand that meanings are contested and diverse.

Carolyn: And that their own ways of understanding the world are cultural and political productions tied to and influenced by the discourses of class, race, ethnicity, and sexual orientation.

Art: Confronting some of the more disturbing accounts is dangerous and may feel threatening, but I think it would be more dangerous not to do it, to go on imagining people don't live and feel and suffer these things, that they are not vulnerable to relations of power, and that we don't have a responsibility to try to find a way to talk about and care about them.

Carolyn: But let's be fair. My colleague didn't object to the subject matter. Her main complaint was that ethnographers don't measure up as writers. They don't give enough aesthetic distance. Great literature allows room to breathe.

Art: Well, I can think of some great novels and films that took my breath away . . .

Carolyn: *(Interrupting)* That's how I felt about the movie *Dead Man Walking.*

Art: I know what you mean. But what our colleague is expressing seems more like a personal taste than a universal standard. Granted, some of the newer genres of ethnographies aspire to higher literary and aesthetic standards, but it's not as if we're competing for space in literary magazines. Not many of us think of ourselves primarily as writers and only secondarily as ethnographers.

Carolyn: But we are more aware of our craft now. We recognize that ethnography is a game played with words, and we know that written reality is a second-order reality that reshapes the events it depicts.

Art: But as far as I'm concerned, the main question still is, what consequences are created by what we write? Ethnography should broaden our horizons, awaken our capacity to care about people different from us, help us know how to converse with them, feel connected. If that's what good literature does, then the comparison is meaningful, but it's not so we can impress people with our eloquence and literary style.

Carolyn: I wish we could somehow dodge this whole issue, you know, change the terms of the discussion. But I guess we're always working within a set of traditions and conventions, and it's threatening to people who have conducted research and written articles a certain way for a long time and felt pretty successful doing so. Suddenly they hear postmodernists saying that what they've been doing all these years needs to be changed. How do you expect them to react?

Art: So there's a lot at stake when they defend the orthodoxy. Tacking back and forth between fact and fiction, that's a tough pill for traditional social scientists to swallow.

Carolyn: It may take some time before most of us can be at peace with our location in the spaces between reality and make-believe. And what you said earlier about being pragmatic, well, that sure wasn't one of the legacies of my graduate education.

Art: No, we were taught that winning the respect of our peers and colleagues was what was really important. Heck, I don't remember ever being asked who was going to use our research.

Carolyn: Nor was I. Looking back, I can see that I learned to write in a way that severely limited who could read what I wrote.

Art: I remember one professor who made such a big deal out of Eric Berne's popularity after he wrote *Games People Play*. The point seemed to be that if your work was popular, if "common people" could read and understand it, then it probably wasn't very good—you know, not very deep, or profound, or theoretical.

Carolyn: But suddenly social science is becoming accountable to the public. Users are talking back. They tell us that too often we're boring, esoteric, and parochial. They want to know why what we do matters, and to whom. How can it help people live better lives?

Art: If we think we can avoid responding to these questions, we are going to be in deep trouble. That's why I think we need to see the knowledge we're seeking in ethnography as the kind that helps readers use other people's sorrows and triumphs as a way to reflect on or recontextualize their own, enhancing their capacity to cope with life's contingencies.

Carolyn: *Composing Ethnograpy* is a modest attempt to do this. What we're trying to do is enlarge the space to practice ethnographic writing as a form of creative nonfiction, to take certain expressive liberties associated with the arts, but to feel the ethical pull of converting data into experiences readers can use.

Art: And to reach a wider audience, not only to write *about* families, organizations, communities, and institutions, but to write *to* them as well.

Carolyn: We encourage ethnographers to open their imaginations and take risks. What falls under the rubric "ethnographic alternatives" is diverse, multiple, and noncanonical. There are no hard-and-fast rules to follow, no set categories to embrace.

Art: I wonder what readers would think if they knew that only this morning we were still discussing what to call the different sections of the book and arguing about which papers should go in which sections.

Carolyn: Seems like we've been discussing that for weeks, as if there was a coherent and natural order to be discovered and named.

Art: Well, there isn't and we didn't. I'm reminded of Jules Henry's observation that human phenomena don't arrange themselves obligingly into types. The borders between autoethnography, sociopoetics, and reflexivity are pretty fuzzy. Most of the chapters could easily be moved from one section to another. In fact, to a large extent the entire book is an argument for self-conscious reflexivity. Many of our authors are struggling with the dilemma of how to position themselves within their research projects to reveal aspects of their own tacit world, challenge their own assumptions, locate themselves through the eyes of the Other, and observe themselves observing.

Carolyn: Many of these issues are associated closely with work classified as "new ethnography."

Art: We should point out that some of our colleagues resist the idea of new ethnography. They say that these so-called

experimental genres of writing have been around a long
time. They're really not new.

Carolyn: Yes, Mark Neumann makes that point in his chapter, even
as he recommends adopting the style of New Journalism as
a way of illustrating the experiential contradictions that
cast doubt on consensual versions of reality.

Art: But, as Mark aptly notes, what made these genres "experimental" and "new" was the attempt to legitimate genres of
writing responsive to the calls for self-conscious reflexivity,
dialogue, and multiple voices within disciplinary sensibilities tied to orthodox scientific traditions. It's the struggle to
gain legitimacy for alternative modes of expression, however long they've been around, that warrants their classification as experimental and new.

Carolyn: I don't think the question of what should be considered
new or experimental has been an essential issue for us.

Art: No, it hasn't been. When I was a young Assistant Professor,
I recall my older colleagues' conditioned responses to suggestions by younger faculty like me to innovate or reform
the curriculum: "Tried it, done it, won't work!" they
replied. I guess claims about what's new or experimental
are always contestable.

Carolyn: So the issue for us wasn't whether the terms we chose for
our unit headings were new, but whether they helped open
discussion about alternative genres of ethnography. When I
teach "Qualitative Methods," "Ethnography," or "Fieldwork
Practicum," and the students read and discuss works like
Myerhoff's *Number Our Days,* Jackson's *At Home in the
World,* Brown's *Mama Lola,* and Butler and Rosenblum's
Cancer in Two Voices, they get excited about issues revolving
around voice, literary genres, and dialectics of self and culture. Our discussions frequently center on vexing questions about personal narrative, how to use the first-person
voice, and the turn toward autobiography as a source of
origins and connection precipitated by the blurring of categorical distinctions between self and culture.

Art: And in my seminar on "Narrative Inquiry," students feel
challenged as writers to experiment with ways of dis-
placing the notion of language as representation with

language as a mode of communication, using creative
genres of writing that can help mobilize social action or
evoke participatory experiences through imagination, performance art, and storytelling

Carolyn: So all we claim is that *autoethnography, sociopoetics,* and
reflexivity are terms we find useful for promoting
edifying discussions about ethnographic alternatives.
The essays and studies that fall under these headings
explore the use of the first-person voice, the appropriation of literary modes of writing for utilitarian ends, and
the complications of being positioned within what one
is studying.

Art: I think we've dwelled more than enough on the arbitrariness of the unit headings.

Carolyn: But we still need to emphasize that these aren't exclusively
methodological issues.

Art: I don't like the theory/methodology distinction.

Carolyn: I wasn't going in that direction. I only wanted to point out
that many of these chapters are critical, even subversive.
And they range across a wide array of issues, encompassing
ethnicity, race, family, community, emotions, adolescence,
violence, embodiment, sexual abuse, work, memory,
gender, health, illness, and stigma.

Art: Do you think we could talk about the specific chapters one
last time, just to make sure the order works?

Carolyn: Oh, not again! Promise me, this will be the last time.

Art: I promise. Let's start with David Payne's "Autobiology."
David's work dissolves the standard frames for theoretical,
critical, and autobiographical writing. He bridges the
philosophical and the evocative, alternating the "cool" for-
matting frames of philosophical discourse with the "hot"
evocative stories of first-person accounts. David vividly
shows the power that accrues from how a text is put
together as he covertly releases the reader from the confines of conventional modes of academic specification in
order to draw out the tensions provoked by juxtaposing
analysis and emotion.

Carolyn: You know, sometimes I think analysis becomes an unnecessary diversion from the emotional experience of the story.

But in David's case, the analytical sections orchestrate an experiential atmosphere rather than a focused explanation of how our bodies are institutionalized and memory is embodied. Attempting to express his personal story from the site of his body, David uses theoretical abstractions as a means, however limited, of extricating his body from its ideologically institutionalized inscriptions.

Art: One of our reviewers, Allen Shelton, called it a "musical essay." Rarely have I heard social science texts classified this way, but it makes sense. The reader has to give in to the tonal effects.

Carolyn: Quite a contrast to Lisa Tillmann-Healy's "A Secret Life in a Culture of Thinness: Reflections on Body, Food, and Bulimia." As Lisa once invited bulimia to live with her, now she invites readers into her secret life as a bulimic woman. Resisting the tyranny of the pathologizing voices of medical and clinical authorities, Lisa searches for the meanings of a bulimic lifestyle in the particularity of her own experience—how she lives, what she does, how it feels. She shows in startling detail, through episodic stories and poems, how she learned over 19 years to relate bulimically to food and her body. The grip of bulimia is graphically portrayed as a sensible response to the cultural contradictions of abundance and thinness.

Art: Lisa gives us a sensual text and a humble one. She doesn't pose as a heroine. She knows she's taking a risk. There's no victory here; the battle isn't over. She refuses to hide the multiplicity of her identity as woman, scholar, bulimic, and culture critic. Bulimia is Other and "I."

Carolyn: Carol Rambo Ronai's "My Mother Is Mentally Retarded" focuses on pathologizing discourses. Returning to her origins as a child of a mentally retarded mother, Carol uses the resources of memory and story to sort through her lingering ambivalence between the desire to love a stigmatized mother and the anger and frustration characteristic of the patterns that connect them. Beginning with the memories of her childhood, Carol recalls concrete instances in which she had to cope with extraordinary ambiguity before knowing her mother was retarded.

Art: But once she learns of her mother's limitations, new ques-
           tions arise that are no less unsettling: "Am I retarded too?
           How much of who I am is my mother? What is my legacy?"
           Living through an unending spiral of secrecy, double mes-
           sages, betrayal, and shame, Carol reaches troubling conclu-
           sions that she expresses in spirited emotional detail.

Carolyn: Her story extends beyond herself, to the backstage of dis-
           turbed families. These families are not so much different in
           the issues they confront as in the extremes to which they
           go when confronting them. Carol uses narrative to show a
           world normally hidden from view in clinical literature and
           to explore interpretive possibilities that can extend her
           family history in a positive direction.

Art: Payne, Tillmann-Healy, and Ronai bring their bodies into
           the texts they write in ways that challenge writing conven-
           tions and the polarities of self/other and subject/object.

Carolyn: That's what Ruth Linden says about Aliza Kolker's paper,
           "Thrown Overboard: The Human Costs of Health Care
           Rationing," that "she dares to bring her body into the text"
           in "bold and risky ways."

Art: Aliza certainly does that.

Carolyn: She uses the story of her personal battle against inflamma-
           tory breast cancer to reveal inequities in health care
           rationing by insurance companies. Her personal narrative
           raises troubling questions about the fairness of health
           rationing in the context of her illness.

Art: But Aliza's story can be read in many different ways.
           Whereas Aliza vilifies insurance companies, Ruth Linden's
           response, "The Life Boat Is Fraught: Reflections on 'Thrown
           Overboard'," blames the for-profit health sector for
           exploiting patients who feel desperate. Aliza's interpretation
           warns readers that their lives may depend on capricious
           and arbitrary reimbursement policies, while Ruth cautions
           women that they may only be able to save their lives by
           becoming as conversant as the official "experts" on a broad
           range of scientific, clinical, and policy issues.

Carolyn: One outcome of this dialogue is that we understand better
           the situated meanings of a story. Each interpretation makes
           different claims.

Art: Yes, viewed within her own life circumstances, Aliza's vulnerability to arbitrary reimbursement policies seems grossly unfair.

Carolyn: And viewed from within Ruth's life circumstances—her involvement in breast cancer activism in California—the different issues she sees at stake in Aliza's story make sense.

Art: One thing that strikes me as important is how Aliza's personal narrative gives way either to analysis of the insurance companies or to scientific/technical evidence about bone marrow transplants. Aliza's subjectivity and emotion get transferred to these other issues.

Carolyn: But not completely. Her story really evoked strong feelings in me. I was shaken by her statement about being interrupted by cancer at midlife and midcareer, a mother of young children and a productive member of society.

Art: It told me how hard she was struggling to make sense of her illness and reminded me how unprepared any of us may be to face such blows of fate. I read Aliza as a person searching for narrative coherence and continuity. "I'm not supposed to be struck down at the peak of my powers as an academic, a woman, and a mother," she seems to be saying. It hurts, it's senseless, it doesn't fit. Stanley Hauerwas's book, *Naming the Silences,* discusses how difficult it is to interpret serious and life-threatening illnesses within a framework of meaning already in place, a context that cannot make sense of pointless suffering. Aliza's illness, for example, is not part of the narrative unity of her life story. There does not seem to be a point to her suffering. If we can't invent or locate a narrative for coping with the unpleasant contingencies of life, we have no recourse but to rely on overcoming or controlling them.

Carolyn: I think of Aliza's story as a helpful reminder about how we use narrative to make sense of our lives. While she is using narrative to offer a critical analysis of health care rationing, she is also using it to make sense of her experiences. She shows the multiple meanings and uses of qualitative writing.

Art: All of these autoethnographies extend outward from the self to others and culture. The dialectic self/culture is Mark

Neumann's point of departure in "Collecting Ourselves at the End of the Century." Refusing the temptation to embrace new ethnography uncritically, Mark returns to ethnography's historical quest "to find oneself in a broken world." The puzzles of self and culture do not go away, Mark observes, but "perpetually return to us in modern life." He urges a renewed respect for the traditions and history of ethnography that have inspired our concern and appreciation for worlds different from and outside our own.

Carolyn: Mark's use of *collection* as a metaphor for how ethnography connects culture to self—we "collect ourselves by carrying back stories and artifacts," finding and losing and finding ourselves through the objects and images we gather around us—augments the dialectical and self-reflexive qualities of ethnographic inquiry. These are qualities that Judith Hamera portrays in her elegant and poetic essay, "Reconstructing Asparas from Memory: Six Thoughts."

Art: Yes, I thought her experimental, lyrical, performative style was very moving. It expresses the "incommensurable choreography" of the ethnographic dance between her and the Sam family, refugees from Cambodia who survived the genocide of the Khmer Rouge. Judith writes a highly personal, self-reflexive text that interrogates the political and personal stakes of ethnography by confronting the haunting incommensurability between her needs and desires and those of the Sam family. She boldly requires readers to fill in the gaps about Khmer Rouge genocide and the failure of her own research strategies to produce ethnographic "knowledge" that would frame the account if it were written in a more conventional format.

Carolyn: Some researchers undoubtedly will read this as a story of ethnographic failure. In important respects, though, Judith's account of collaborative "failure" is a stunning success, at least insofar as she teaches us valuable lessons about celebrating and respecting the Other and recontextualizing ourselves and the meaning of our work. She gently helps us challenge the ethnographic fictions of affinity, empathy, and mutuality, and also helps us imagine how ethnography might accommodate the more tentative and austere fictions of quiet, distance, and insularity.

Art: Judith notes how the web of differences makes duets between cultures hard to perform and how difficult it can be to recognize that the voice of the Other truly is not one's own. How do we hear the voice of the Other, and to what extent does it intersect ours?

Carolyn: Deborah Austin shows another side of the issue of difference in "Kaleidoscope: The Same and Different," using narrative poetry to perform the intersecting subjectivities of two African women, one born in Zaire, the other from North Carolina. In Deborah's poem, the qualitative interview becomes a dialogue in which what transpires *between* Deborah and Annie is a jointly enacted meeting of cultural discourses where each can probe the Other's worldview. Their dialogue is an attempt to speak to and with one another, and the double-voiced character of the poem, though written by Deborah alone, reflects the dialogic commitment to open-endedness, diversity, and pluralism.

Art: Yes, and there's also a sense of movement in the poem as Deborah alternates between outward expression and inward reflection.

Carolyn: Deborah calls attention to the sensual dimensions of life and invites readers to consider how qualitative research can express the sounds, feel, and taste of lived experiences.

Art: Dwight Conquergood says that the performance paradigm in ethnography shifts attention from products to processes. Deborah's poem reinforces this emphasis on process by inviting readers to enter and experience her conversations with Annie and bear witness to her attempts to make sense of their differences.

Carolyn: Performance is also a theme of "Speech Lessons," in which Laurel Richardson links biography to sociology, giving her personal account of "the parts she learned to play" and those she became unwilling to play over the course of her private and academic life. The seeds for Laurel's patterns of speaking, love of writing, and attraction to a sociological perspective are firmly planted in childhood experiences.

Art: Her story made me aware of the ways universities construct roles for us to play, as well as the local politics associated with the performances we call "education" or "social
scientist."

Carolyn: You know, it's odd how we so willingly accept the role of
obliging critic when it comes to examining institutional life
except when it's the institutional practices in which we ourselves are embedded. We spend most of our life in a university, but rarely do we ever focus our ethnographic and
critical eye on our own practices.

Art: When I was on the faculty at Temple University, there was
an M.A. student who was studying group process. She
wanted to attend faculty meetings as an observer for a year
and use her field notes from meetings as "data" for her
thesis. You wouldn't believe how threatening this idea was to
faculty—that we would become the subjects and expose our
performances of faculty decision making to studied scrutiny.

Carolyn: Yes, I would. Remember how disarming it was when Laurel
Richardson gave a paper at a conference in which she
incorporated colleagues' responses to her poem, some who
were there in the room.

Art: And I'm sure you haven't forgotten that incident with *Final
Negotiations*. Remember how upset that reviewer got when
you quoted parts of his first review in a subsequent draft of
your book. He acted as though he had no accountability
for what he said.

Carolyn: Yeah, he returned the manuscript to the editor without
reviewing it, he was so mad.

Art: Unfortunately, I think these sorts of responses are typical of
the way many people react to the first-person accounts of
sociologists.

Carolyn: Yes, we're not supposed to use our own life as primary
data. Sociology is about everyone else's life.

Art: "Maternal Connections" joins "Speech Lessons" in
breaching these conventions. You use your own participation in the world and your feelings to express the
dilemmas of middle-age connections between mothers and
daughters.

Carolyn: I've been interested in exploring the evocative possibilities of the episodic form of ethnographic short stories. A lot of people our age have to come to grips with a different kind of parental obligation, becoming parents to our parents. Concrete episodes that depict how we engage and respond to these epiphanies give us an opportunity to understand the circular connectedness of life. In my particular case, I was facing the need to become a mother to my mother at the same time I was facing the imminent possibility that I would never have my own child.

Art: You mean our child, don't you?

Carolyn: Yes, ours. (*There's a pregnant pause. Art and Carolyn instinctively hug each other, then reach out and stroke the dogs one by one.*)

(*Continues*) The connections go in several directions. I think the short story form enables me to perform this episode in a contextualized way, showing the connections among the seasons of a woman's life and encouraging readers to sense what I am feeling as well as hear what I am thinking. And to express their own feelings and think about their own experiences too.

Art: So we have examples of lyrical, poetic, autobiographical, and episodic forms of narrating lived experience, each moving ethnography away from realism and toward genres of writing more closely associated with literature, the humanities, and the arts.

Carolyn: Jim Mienczakowski's "An Ethnographic Act: The Construction of Consensual Theatre" also links ethnography with the arts.

Art: Yes, it does. He discusses two research projects in which he used ethnographically based theatrical performances to create a context for producing social change. He configures ethnographic fieldwork as a collaboratively produced play intended to be used as a teaching tool and an agent for transforming social practices. The play is a consensual production involving numerous sectors of the health system, including student nurses, health consumers, caregivers, medical students, and patients. Based on participant observation and interviewing sessions, these collaboratively developed scripts become potentially empowering "ethnodramas" that can act back reflexively on health care providers, making them more knowledgeable about and accountable to their consumers' needs and experiences.

Carolyn: Some readers may not be completely at ease with Jim's emphasis on the accuracy and validity of the ethno-drama process, but I admire the way he bridges the traditional concerns of conventional ethnography with the subversive goals of critical theory.

Art: I think his project really takes the idea of interactive ethnography seriously. The dramas are public performances heard and responded to by a wide and diverse population of people who have something at stake in the issues addressed by the plays. Fieldwork is transformed into dramas that are explicitly political and public. Although ethnodrama seeks a closer approximation to an "accurate" portrayal of reality, its incomplete, ongoing, and emergent qualities, and its strong commitment to democratic co-construction, separate it from conventional modes of realist ethnography.

Carolyn: The self-consciously reflexive goals of Jim's research, in which those participating in the system of health care present concrete experiences of their health and social oppression to themselves, is a good segue to the final section of the book. The chapters on reflexivity explicitly focus on how ethnographic research acts back on the ethnographer— what we can learn about ourselves from studying "them."

Art: In "Devil, Not-Quite-White, Rootless Cosmopolitan: *Tsuris* in Latin America, the Bronx, and the USSR," Marc Edelman turns reflexivity inward, using his own fieldwork experiences to tackle disturbing and neglected questions about how ethnographers respond to bigotry and racism when they confront it in the field. Specifically, Marc concentrates on the question of how his Jewishness entered into his fieldwork among non-Jews, how he presented himself, what he disclosed and concealed about himself, when he was silent and why. With rare candor, Marc assumes responsibility for his own tactics of "sanitizing" ethnographic experience and "managing" his Jewishness, and he questions whether the failure to contest racism or anti-Semitism in the field is a disturbing form of tacit collusion in the production of racist politics and bigotry.

Carolyn: I was startled by Marc's statement about his "almost willful obtuseness in not recognizing anti-Jewish prejudice or in putting a benign gloss on it." It made me think about times when I held something back that bothered me because I thought it might disturb my relationship with my informants.

Art: I hope other ethnographers will think seriously about these crucial ethical issues. Marc draws attention to the impulses that may prevent ethnographers from confronting racism and bigotry more directly—our desire to be accepted by our community, anxiety about our own ethnic, racial, or sexual identity, and the norms of maintaining reciprocally positive feelings.

Carolyn: I agree with Marc that we really need to consider the differences between our responsibilities as scholars and our responsibilities as human beings. This means we must interrogate ourselves and openly confront some of the "undiscussables" of fieldwork relationships.

Art: Whereas Marc Edelman uses his field experiences to understand why he and other ethnographers don't do more to change ethnic and racist behavior when they experience it, Tanice Foltz and Wendy Griffin's "'She Changes Everything She Touches': Ethnographic Journeys of Self-Discovery," examines how their attitudes toward a coven of Dianic witches were radically transformed by participation in the practices and rituals of the coven, a feminist religious group that professes to be an agent of empowerment and change. Over the course of their "research journey," Tanice and Wendy move gradually from hesitant, skeptical outsiders to accepting, participating insiders.

Carolyn: While it was interesting to see how these researchers were converted, I also learned some fascinating details about the witches—their equinox and solstice ritual celebrations

with chanting, altered states, spells, visualizations, oint-
ments, and priestess initiations; their feminist politics,
meditative techniques, and concept of "Goddess"—an
autonomous female divinity who also stands metaphorically for earth interconnections among living things. They
shattered my stereotype of witches.

Art: Tanice and Wendy give readers pause to consider the multiple consequences of ethnography. Certainly, not all of us
will be as radically transformed by our fieldwork journeys
as they were. But at least we can ask, how were we
changed? What differences did the Others make on our
lives? If I'm no different as a human being or as an ethnographer after returning from the field, then what can I say I
learned?

Carolyn: In "Silent Voices: A Subversive Reading of Child Sexual
Abuse," Karen Fox shows that the consequences of qualitative research can extend in both directions. By considering
the perspective of child sex offenders and survivors, Karen
challenges her own ways of thinking about child sexual
abuse, and she contests how child sexual abuse researchers
traditionally have thought about the bodies and agency of
children. Her unusual form of storytelling interjects the
researcher's story between the accounts of an offender and
survivor. This three-person account complexifies the more
simplified canonical version of sex abuse that typically
denies the possibility of child agency and neatly divides the
world into a dichotomous world of offenders and victims.

Art: Karen's "subversive reading" rocks the boat. It is difficult to
deny the possibility that children potentially can exert
some agency, even in regard to sexual relations with adults.
But if we admit this thought, we may lose the comfort of
categorical distinctions between victims and victimizers. To
maintain such clear distinctions, Fox argues, is to refuse to
understand child sex abuse as the outcome of interactional
dynamics and thus to prevent the possibility that changes
in patterns of interaction could conceivably change the
outcomes.

Carolyn: Somehow Karen is able to be disgusted by the offender she interviews without falling back on simple solutions and categorical distinctions. Her own experiences as a sexually abused child help her understand that she has to live with the ambiguities and contradictions that make simplistic explanations untenable. Writing from the authority of her personal experience, she pushes us to appreciate this complexity as well.

Art: Readers seeking some relief from exposure to the violent and sickening details of child sexual abuse may find solace in Richard Quinney's restful tale, "Once My Father Traveled West to California," in which he tells the story of a trip his father took in the early 1920s. Richard reconstructs the trip from old photographs his father took and letters his father sent back home during the journey. The photographs show what caught his father's eye; the letters detail his adventures, note his interpretation of the pictures, and express his worries about friends, family, and chores back home. As the tale unfolds, revealing how some lives were lived and thought about at that time and place, Richard tells not only about his father but also about himself. The son and the ethnographer seek connection to the father, family history, and the old days of farm life in southern Wisconsin.

Carolyn: Richard shows the richness of mundane, everyday life. His story is a gentle, reflexive tale of attachment and loss. Richard is there, like his father, traveling around the country, then coming home. His homecoming is a loose metaphor for return—back to his roots, to a place, to a family, to a way of seeing and experiencing the world. Photographs, written texts, and reflections bring Richard back to his childhood, to his father, and to the meanings of ethnography.

Art: Ethnography becomes a form of mourning, coping with loss through the sense-making activities that give new meanings to a trip taken long ago, for other reasons, but which now lives on in the effects of recollection that linger within Richard.

Carolyn: But Richard observes that neither ethnography nor photography can replace a life that was lived and is gone; they
can only help us prepare a little better to face death.

Art: And he recommends a broader humanistic vision of the
wondrous and wild possibilities of ethnography, the trips
we can take if we do not restrict ourselves to the strictures
of rigid disciplinary boundaries.

Carolyn: Quinney returns us to where we started and the goals of
our project. Readers are encouraged to loosen the boundaries of ethnography. Don't be afraid to make ethnography
dangerous, political, and personal. Take risks. Write from
the heart as well as the head. Turn the field back on yourself. Turn yourself against canonical stories. Closely
examine the production of your texts and theirs. Give
respect to empathy and solidarity, but try to hear Others
speaking back. These are our themes.

Art: I'm tired and I'm starving. *(He looks at his watch.)* Wow, it's
after 10:00. *(He begins to get up from the couch slowly.)*

Carolyn: Geez, another late dinner. But, after all these months of
putting this project together, it was fun to sit and reflect on
the whole book and where ethnography might be heading.
Too bad we didn't tape the conversation.

Art: Who'd believe it anyway? They'd still think we made it up.
*(The dogs are awakened by the movements and begin to nip at
each other playfully.)*

Carolyn: Didn't we? Would they? *(Her attention is now drawn to the
dogs.)* You heat up the Thai food, and I'll feed the dogs. *(As
Carolyn gathers the dogs and exits the room, she barely hears
Art's response.)*

Art: *(Shouting over the excited barking of hungry dogs.)* I enjoyed
talking over ethnography, but I haven't changed my mind.
Call Mitch in the morning and tell him we're not going to
write an introduction. The readers should get the last word.

References

Bateson, G. 1972. *Steps to an Ecology of Mind.* New York: Ballantine.
Benson, P., ed. 1993. *Anthropology and Literature.* Urbana: University of
Illinois Press.

Berne, E. 1964. *Games People Play*. New York: Grove Press.

Bochner, A. P. 1994. "Perspectives on Inquiry II: Theories and Stories." In *Handbook of Interpersonal Communication*. 2nd ed. edited by M. Knapp and G. Miller. (Newbury Park, CA: Sage): 21–41.

Bochner, A. P., and J. Waugh. 1995. "Talking with as a Model for Writing about: Implications of Rortian Pragmatism for Communication Theory." In *Recovering Pragmatism's Voice: The Classical Tradition and the Philosophy of Communication*, edited by L. Langsdorf and A. Smith. (Albany: SUNY Press): 211–233.

Brown, K. M. 1991. *Mama Lola: A Voodoo Priestess in Brooklyn*. Berkeley: University of California Press.

Brown, R. H. 1977. *A Poetic for Sociology*. Cambridge, UK: Cambridge University Press.

Bruner, E. 1993. "Introduction: The Ethnographic Self and the Personal Self." In *Anthropology and Literature*, edited by P. Benson. (Urbana: University of Illinois Press): 1–26.

Bruner, J. 1990. *Acts of Meaning*. Cambridge, MA: Harvard University Press.

Butler, S., and B. Rosenblum. 1991. *Cancer in Two Voices*. San Francisco: Spinsters Book Company.

Clifford, J., and G. Marcus. eds. 1986. *Writing Culture: The Poetics and Politics of Ethnography*. Berkeley: University of California Press.

Conquergood, D. 1986. "Between Experience and Meaning: Performance as a Paradigm for Meaningful Action." In *Renewal and Revision: The Future of Interpretation*, edited by T. Colson. (Denton, TX: Omega): 26–57.

de Certeau, M. 1984. *The Practices of Everyday Life*. Los Angeles: University of California Press.

Denzin, N. K. 1992. *Symbolic Interactionism and Cultural Studies: The Politics of Interpretation*. Oxford: Basil Blackwell.

Denzin, N. K., and Y. Lincoln. eds. 1994. *Handbook of Qualitative Research*. Thousand Oaks, CA: Sage.

Derrida, J. 1978. *Writing and Difference*. London: Routledge & Kegan.

——. 1981. *Positions*. Chicago: University of Chicago Press.

Ellis, C. 1995a. *Final Negotiations: A Story of Love, Loss, and Chronic Illness*. Philadelphia: Temple University Press.

——. 1995b. "Emotional and Ethical Quagmires in Returning to the Field." *Journal of Contemporary Ethnography* 24: 68–96.

Ellis, C., and M. Flaherty. eds. 1992. *Investigating Subjectivity: Research on Lived Experience*. Newbury Park, CA: Sage.

Foucault, M. 1970. *The Order of Things: An Archaeology of the Human Sciences*. New York: Random House.

Geertz, C. 1973. *The Interpretation of Cultures*. New York: Basic Books.

Gergen, K. 1982. *Towards Transformation in Social Knowledge*. New York: Springer-Verlag.

Grossberg, L., C. Nelson, and P. A. Treichler. eds. 1992. *Cultural Studies*. New York: Routledge.

Haraway, D. J. 1988. "Situated Knowledges: The Science Questions in Feminism and the Privilege." *Feminist Studies* 14: 75–99.

———. 1989. *Primate Visions: Gender, Race, and Nature in the World of Modern Science*. New York: Routledge.

Harding, S. 1986. *The Science Question in Feminism*. Milton Keynes, UK: Open University Press.

Hauerwas, S. 1990. *Naming the Silences: God, Medicine, and the Problem of Suffering*. Grand Rapids, MI: William B. Eermans.

Henry, J. 1971. *Pathways to Madness*. New York: Vintage Books.

Jackson, M. 1989. *Paths Toward a Clearing: Radical Empiricism and Ethnographic Inquiry*. Bloomington: Indiana University Press.

———. 1995. *At Home in the World*. Durham, NC: Duke University Press.

Kiesinger, C. 1995. "The Anorexic and Bulimic Self: Making Sense of Food and Eating." Ph.D. dissertation, University of South Florida.

Kuhn, T. 1962. *The Structure of Scientific Revolutions*. Chicago: University of Chicago Press.

Lyotard, J. 1984. *The Postmodern Condition: A Report on Knowledge*. Minneapolis: University of Minnesota Press.

Mairs, N. 1989. *Remembering the Bone House: An Erotics of Place and Space*. New York: Harper Row.

Marcus, G. E. 1994. "What Comes (Just) After "post"? The Case of Ethnography." In *Handbook of Qualitative Research*, edited by N. K. Denzin and Y. S. Lincoln. (Thousand Oaks, CA: Sage): 563–574.

Myerhoff, B. 1978. *Number Our Days*. New York: Simon & Schuster.

Mykhalovskiy, E. 1996. "Reconsidering Table Talk: Critical Thoughts on the Relationship Between Sociology, Autobiography and Self-Indulgence." *Qualitative Sociology* 19: 131–151.

Richardson, L. 1993. "The Case of the Skipped Line: Poetics, Dramatics and Transgressive Validity. *Sociological Quarterly* 34: 695–710.

———. 1994. "Writing As a Method of Inquiry." In *Handbook of Qualitative Research*, edited by N. K. Denzin and Y. S. Lincoln. (Thousand Oaks, CA: Sage): 516–529.

Rorty, R. 1982. *Consequences of Pragmatism (Essays 1972–1980)*. Minneapolis: University of Minnesota Press.

———. 1989. *Contingency, Irony, and Solidarity*. Cambridge, UK: Cambridge University Press.

———. 1996. "The Necessity of Inspired Reading." *The Chronicle of Higher Education*, XLII, 22: A48.

Rosaldo, R. 1989. *Culture and Truth: The Remaking of Social Analysis*. Boston: Beacon.

Rose, D. 1990. *Living the Ethnographic Life*. Newbury Park, CA: Sage.

———. 1993. "Ethnography as a Form of Life: The Written Word and the Work of the World." In *Anthropology and Literature*, edited by P. Benson. (Urbana: University of Illinois Press): 192–224.

Rosenau, P. M. 1991. *Postmodernism and Social Sciences: Insights, Inroads, and Instructions*. Princeton, NJ: Princeton University Press.

Rosenwald, G. C., and R. L. Ochberg. eds. 1992. *Storied Lives: The Cultural Politics of Self-Understanding*. New Haven, CT: Yale University Press.

Spence, D. 1982. *Narrative Truth and Historical Truth*. New York: W. W. Norton.

Steier, F., ed. 1991. *Research on Reflexivity*. London: Sage.

Turner, E. 1993. "Experience and Poetics in Anthropological Writing." In *Anthropology and Literature*, edited by P. Benson. (Urbana: University of Illinois Press): 27–47.

Turner, V., and E. Bruner. 1986. *The Anthropology of Experience*. Urbana: University of Illinois Press.

Tyler, S. 1986. "Post-modern Ethnography: From Document of the Occult to Occult Document." In *Writing Culture: The Poetics and Politics of Culture*, edited by J. Clifford and G. Marcus. (Berkeley: University of California Press): 122–140.

The authors acknowledge the helpful comments of Eric Eisenberg and Denise Santoro.

PART ONE

Autoethnography

CHAPTER ONE

Autobiology
David Payne

Just how science "gets at" the world remains far from resolved.
What does seem resolved, however, is that science grows from and
enables concrete ways of life, including particular constructions of
love, knowledge, and power.

—Donna Haraway (1989, 8)

Love, Knowledge, Authority: three basic ideals, variously embodied
in structures of power, and all liable to such transformations as
make of them a mockery. As translated into the terms of social
organization, they are necessarily somewhat at odds. But in
moments of exaltation, ideally, we may think of them as a trinity,
standing to one another in a relation of mutual reenforcement.

—Kenneth Burke ([1945] 1969,
124)

Introduction

<hr />

The ideas and stories of this essay are concerned with the location of the
body in the productions of our discourse. Our various discourses of
power and control do in fact *locate* the body within symbolic, mythic
worlds that *dislocate* the body and its ownership from the self. The consequences of this phenomenon are a central concern of contemporary
feminist, ideological, and ethical research.

Autobiology takes its inspiration from primate biologist Donna
Haraway and her insight that the discourse of biological science in this
century narrates the lives of primates, including humans, in ways
convenient to the moral, ideological, and material hierarchies of

Western culture. Women and other primates are thereby dispossessed of authority over their bodies and the meanings of their experiences. As Haraway suggests in the passage cited at the beginning of the chapter, collusion among the rhetorics of scientific discourses "enables concrete ways of life," ways of life sustained through relationships we name and represent as "love, knowledge, and power."

What follows are two stories told in tandem: a personal narrative of my experience working at a factory over 20 years ago and a theoretical discussion woven around my contemplation of that experience. The personal narrative attempts to write from the site of my body—where it was, what it was doing, what was done to it. The theoretical text is also a story, but one told through my intellectual exploration of the themes and ideological critiques of contemporary scholarship. Even so, this theory also renarrates the site of my body in an ideological universe.

"Autobiology" revisits a "concrete way of life," a past site of my own personal experience, and asks (as well as I am able) what ways "love, knowledge, and power" were constructed for me, through me, and by me, in this particular episode. How was my body located in this situation? What biology was practiced by the ideology of this industrial complex? What are the possibilities for an autobiology? Can I somehow reclaim the site of my body and renarrate my experience on my own terms? Let me emphasize: *It is not at all clear to me that I can. The discursive structures associated with the fact that I am sitting at this computer producing these words may not be altogether different from those that kept me at my workstation producing lantern parts 20 years ago.* I claim no heroics for liberating myself or others through the theoretical understanding that has allowed me to revisit and renarrate this story of what happened to my body one summer in 1972.

I organize my ideas and stories under the three headings of "Love," "Knowledge," and "Authority." In this demarcation I intend only that the reader contemplate these important topics, attempting to glean Haraway's insight that our academic and scientific discourses, the stories they tell, create the possibilities and limitations for our experiences of these meaningful relationships. Or, as Burke suggests in the opening passage, these "ideals" of human relations are essential terms to which the "structures of power" may be reduced, giving us both unities for which to strive and conflicts that we necessarily experience in living by and through the mechanisms of social organization.

"Love" here refers to our relationships with each other and how we regard self and other—in my case, family, friends, and workmates. "Knowledge" concerns how we come to represent and understand our experience and how ideas manipulate the sites and qualities of experience—examined here in the micropolitics of an organization. "Authority" is here considered as a problem of ownership and self-control, a realization that our stories are "authored" by social discourses with the designs of power. The interrelationships among these three ideals are far more remarkable than their distinctiveness.

Love

◆

In the summer of 1972, between my sophomore and junior years in college, I found myself walking into the personnel office of the Coleman Company in Wichita, Kansas, looking for work. True summer work was scarce, and I wasn't telling Coleman or my other potential employers about the "summer" part of my application.

They've surely remodeled the personnel office in the 20 years since, and they've surely sharpened their public relations skills. The office was not a particularly nice decor or a friendly place. I filled out an application and was asked to wait. I was then invited to a small, cheaply paneled and fluorescently lit office where some man said virtually nothing to me, but asked if I could start the next day. With surprise I said yes and was told to report tomorrow to this locale for a physical and then to the downtown plant for work.

Believe me, I didn't want to do factory work that summer, or ever. My folks worked for Boeing, and I thought it a fate equivalent to death to trudge off to any of the many large factories in Wichita for a living. My parents had done so, Mother more happily than Father, as had most of the parents of my school friends. Those friends who had not gone away to college—nearly all of them—were doing manual labor of one sort or another, but with few exceptions had avoided the several large factories in Wichita. I was attending the prestige college in the state, Kansas University, and some relatively upper-crust expectations had worn off on me. Besides that, Coleman was strictly the bottom of the barrel in the hierarchy of factory futures. Boeing was tops, then Lear, then Beach or Cessna, but only the real no-talents worked at Coleman for a living. Those other places were difficult to get on at, impossible for the summer, and I wasn't interested in a future. I needed a job and I needed to get my mother off my back about earning money for college. She was persistent, and I was resistant, about applying to Coleman.

I passed through the doors at Coleman into the strange world of industrial production. Most people know that Coleman manufactures a large range of camping gear and now, air conditioning and heating equipment. The origin, and at this time still the heart of, the Coleman line was the famous Coleman gas lantern. I did not know it when I walked in—I was told virtually nothing about the job—but I was to work on an assembly line making the large double-burner lantern.

There are reasons why Coleman was considered the bottom of the barrel as far as factory work goes. I don't recall how I located my workplace that first day, but friendly helpfulness had no part in it. The downtown plant had two old decrepit buildings along the rail line, large buildings separated by a brick alley between them. I soon found out this alley was where lunch and air would be taken. My shop was part of the second story of one of the large buildings and was easily as large as a football field. The anterooms to the shop were clean, with blond brick and linoleum, and there I was shown the nurse's station. But beyond the double doors into the shop, I entered a deeply depressing place. The floor was concrete, the walls were old brick with paint peeling, the windows were metal-encased panes that folded out, so frosted with age they scarcely admitted light, but so necessary because there was no air conditioning. The lighting was eerie, and continued to strike me so; it had that mercury-vapor quality even though it wasn't. I think it was just the entire space that seemed so bright-yet-dingy. Around the room there were oddly shaped tables and work spaces, and dozens of large and strange machines operated by perhaps 100 employees. The machines were all painted a dull institutional green, with a uniform patina of grease and grime covering them. The people were all ages and races, and they weren't by and large a pretty group. The older ones seemed well worn by their lives.

My supervisor was youthful, nicely groomed, and by these standards noticeably good looking. He wore neat slacks, shirt, and comfortable shoes. He was clean. I immediately associated his status with his looks and demeanor. They said something obvious about the distinction between management and employee, what was promotable material and what was not. Even though I had grown up in a factory family in a factory town, this was a class phenomenon for me.

The supervisor didn't say much to me. We probably shook hands but that is all. He took me to a group of people who were stooping on the floor in what appeared to be a big pile of junk, using channel-lock pliers on parts of something. He introduced me to a very cool reception, then left. I had the feeling that these people had been laughing and joking before I came, but now were quiet and somewhat studied in ignoring me. There were two men and a woman. The younger of the men, maybe 30 years old, gave me a pair of channel-locks and reluctantly explained that they were doing re-work. As it turned out, they did re-work when their machines were down. They were taking badly made parts and disassembling them for remaking into good parts. The parts were lantern burners, which I later found out I would be assembling.

Nowhere in my orientation to the job (there was none) or introduction to the shop had anyone shown me a completed lantern, or explained what I would be doing as a small part in the larger scheme. There was no tour of the plant, and I would have been horrified had I seen then what I later saw.

The Coleman lantern is a classic, and as far as I knew was the only gas-fueled camping lantern people bought. My father had one of the old red (single-burner) units from as far back as I could remember, and it was yet hanging in our garage in working condition. We had used it on dozens of campouts and fishing trips throughout my childhood. Although they still made this lantern, the larger, green, double-burner lantern was the more popular product. I had seen them in stores, but had never used one.

That afternoon whatever was wrong over at the line had been fixed and I was introduced to my assembly line. The four of us had a table about 15 feet long with bar-height stools to sit on. My job involved inserting a generator into the lantern burner. A generator is a little brass tube about 5 inches long and a quarter-inch in diameter, with a long needle running through it. The needle seats in the end of the tube and is used to regulate the gas flow to the burners. I was shown how to take a generator, tap it against the table to get the end of the needle out, and dip it into a bowl of brass nuts with holes in them. When the generator is inserted in the burner, the nut screws the base of the generator to the regulating handle.

John was the younger man who spoke to me at first. Jack was somewhat older and never said much. The woman on our team was named Rita. Sometime I found out, by asking I suppose, that I wasn't replacing anyone on this assembly line, that the three of them had performed these operations efficiently until I was placed there. This information connected immediately to the fact that they were not especially pleased to have me join the team, but were trying very hard not to make it personal.

I don't know when it all fell into place, but it goes like this. One of the reasons Coleman was an undesirable place to work was that employees were paid by piecework. This means a quota for operations was placed on your job, and you should manufacture a certain number of parts or pieces during an eight-hour shift. If you surpass that quota, you are paid a bonus that is prorated to the number of parts you produce and how long it took you. It is an outdated system and nearly universally despised by employees. It is, or used to be, favored by management because it keeps pay low and works employees harder. The old factory folklore is that if you overproduced your quota, then management would simply raise your quota, though that did not happen to me or anyone there as far as I know. The upshot of the folklore is "don't work too fast" and "don't mess with the system."

Our assembly line was placed together as a whole unit for the figuring of quotas and for the paying of bonuses. What I quickly became sure of, although no one told me, is that this three-person line had been overproducing their quota quite regularly and earning a relatively decent wage at it. They were hard workers and smart, especially compared to the other employees, and they had a nice little team going that was beating the system by some small margin. I had been put in their line to reduce their productivity. By putting a new employee in the line, their quota would be increased by another 500 parts per day, even though there would be no significant increase in parts produced by the line. This is true because operations were not changed greatly by another set of hands, and because the new employee could be counted on to slow them down. This, I'm sure, is what my coworkers feared would be the result of my joining them. Whatever else is true, what happened to me convinces me that I wasn't there because the company had said, "We need to make more lantern burners, hire another assembler for this line."

I'm good with my hands, and fast, and I love to concentrate on a single task and lose myself in it. Over the first week I was there, my coworkers gradually became warmer and warmer to me. This was partly human nature, but also because they were surprised that I wasn't a complete loss. Rita softened first, because I was working as fast as she after only two days. John had been friendly in tone from the beginning, but started to include me in joking and break time. Jack never said anything much, just ran his machine with amazing speed, but he, too, softened.

Sometime early in the second week of the job I figured out a new way of doing it. I found that I could insert the generator with my right hand, and then by holding the part against my side with my left hand, screw the nut down with the left hand while my right hand was getting the next generator and nut ready. For the first time, the generator/nut tightening end of the line could keep up with the two guys on the machines. I could produce enough complete parts to keep Rita busy tightening in a steady flow, eliminating the back-up from the machines. Everyone was amazed. They were my best friends. Their bonuses were back.

For eight hours each day I focused on the parts in front of me and was oblivious to everything else. During breaks I just rested and smoked cigarettes, and had lunch by myself. My back hurt from sitting on the stools.

I came home very tired each afternoon and usually napped. At night my hands and arms ached from the distorted routine I put them through some 3000 times each day (enough for a good bonus). My shirts all developed this grease spot where I held the parts against my side (my mother suggested sewing a leather patch on an apron at that spot). Closing my eyes to sleep I would visualize the bowl of brass nuts gleaming in the stark lights of the shop. Sometimes I would wake up, having been dreaming about inserting generators and screwing down nuts.

I don't know why I bothered to work so hard. I guess because there was nothing else to do to make the time go. We developed the team feeling they had shared, that we were beating the company at something (measured in not terribly significant bonuses on payday).

In order for any principle of social organization to operate it must control the bodies of that society's members. This is axiomatic, since uncontrolled bodies are by definition not organized socially. In the "open" systems of "normal" society, bodies are controlled through ideas, as with the discourses of shame, guilt, and anxiety that mark the history of Western societies (Riesman et al. 1950).

Discourses that construct and maintain principles of social organization must represent the body in some ways rather than others. The binary and oppositional dualisms of Western culture represent the body as subordinate and opposed to the principles of governance set forth in our ideas of moral order. Thus the system of representations itself denies its origins in the body and takes the form of opposition to the body as it naturally occurs. That is, our discourses objectify the body and assert the authority of the organizational principle as somehow logically, temporally, and/or morally prior to the experiences of embodiment.

Elaine Scarry has observed that physical pain is simply not expressible in language. We can sign pain, signal its presence in an environment, but we cannot really express it or represent it as experience. "Physical pain does not simply resist language," she writes, "but actively destroys it, bringing about an immediate reversion to a state anterior to language" (1985, 4). Representations of pain then are all misrepresentations. Pain cannot be confirmed or disconfirmed, objectively; thus its objectification provides a peculiar distancing from any knowledge of its actual experience—a state of affairs crucial to the conduct of violence and war. We can be in an environment where someone is in pain and not know it; further, the impenetrable linguistic space that separates us from others' pain allows us to inflict it.

Perhaps the dramatic political consequences of pain's inexpressibility draw our attention to it as a case, but one wonders whether the boundaries of language are any more true of pain than in any other physical, bodily experience. What words do not abstract (in the sense of "drawing from"), objectify, reify, and thus misrepresent interior experience? Thus the problem is not just pain as a singular case of inexpressibility, but is, of course, the entire issue of representational language. Vision, the appearance of the outside world inside the mind's eye, is technically a bodily experience, but has been torn from that context. Vision is the most likely candidate for objective description, seeming to hold the greatest possibility for the shareability of bodily experience with others. Science, attempting to perfect this objective reflexivity, is intimately bound up with the visual act. Yet this is perhaps a trick played on us by vision and by language, one deeply exploited by the scientific attitude. Because of its potential for shareability, the practice of visual observation came to specialize in the cultivation of the objective "gaze," even before science, but certainly as part and product of science.

Bob was a young, thirtyish, smart, clean-cut guy with a bit of a beer belly—and some obvious status here. The fellow he worked with was Carl, a black man about the same age. Bob and Carl ran two large machines set perpendicular to the head of our table, where our assembly began.

I had met these guys hanging out at breaks and downtimes. They would come over and joke. Carl didn't say much, but laughed a lot and was friendly.

Bob was an extrovert, kind of a clown, and he teased Rita mercilessly in a way that more than suggested mutual sexual attraction. This attraction was held in check by the workplace and by the fact that Bob was married. I soon discovered he was a group leader and friendly with the supervisor.

Bob tells us that he has had a meeting with the supervisor and that their line was to be merged with our line. Again the quota system and way of figuring bonuses would change, with both lines' productivity measured together. Bob was the foreman, or team leader or kingpin or something, of this new team. I could tell by the cool reception to the idea that this was another attempt to quell the bonuses we had been getting. No one said this out loud, at least not to me. Bob was upbeat and gave some advice about how to deal with the new system. The only change I could see was that when their machines went down, which was often enough, they didn't go down until our line ran out of parts. When they finished their work they would come over and tighten nuts with Rita. When a machine went down there was always a race to get the most parts finished in the least time, because your quota was figured against actual operating time. If you ran out of parts from the line in front of you, then you went down. The counting and ciphering of bonuses was a mystery to me, but Bob kept close track and did the paperwork.

Bob was a smart guy and smooth talker and obviously had the supervisor fooled about his loyalties. It didn't take him long to regear this new system to our advantage. By manipulating the downtimes and helping out on our line, the damage to the system was minimized. I'm not sure exactly how it worked, but Bob and Carl had a couple of barrels of re-work parts over by their machines. One day their machines went down, so Bob clocked the whole line on downtime. Carl goes over to the rework barrels and pulled the first six inches of stacked-up burners off. This reveals some shop rags that had been laid over the rest of the parts in the barrel, which, as it turned out, were new parts that Bob and Carl had finished but hadn't sent along. Carl gave this funny look when he pulled the shop rags off and revealed the extra parts, like the barrel was filled with bourbon or something. Everyone laughed and honked approval, except me because I had no idea what was happening. So we six continue to produce completed burners even though we were "down" on the clock. For an entire week we slipped these two barrels full of burners into the flow of our output, all on downtime that was not counted against us on our quota. The result was a check that contained about $100 in bonus the following week.

The camaraderie was high on this new team and I was part of it. Bob constantly praised me on my speed and really folded me into the new group. The original threesome had been clannish but not very talkative. Bob was a real spark plug who gave the group a sense of itself as a group. One day at break Bob was slamming Rita with insults, and I cracked off a good one at her expense. Bob laughed hard, slapped me on the back, and proclaimed me one of them. Rita turned bright red at this unexpected betrayal and hit me on the arm, yelling, "I thought you were on my side!" My silence was broken, I was a member, but I felt badly about Rita. She had been nice to me and I was a little attracted to her.

The play, although heavily constrained, was important. I was to finish my summer at Coleman working on the conveyor belt, something I will get into later. In front of our work area, across the conveyor belt, was a whole other shop of workers. These workers had nothing to do with our shop, I think, because, unlike us, their time clock was conveniently located right around the corner.

Anyway, we never spoke to these workers but had to watch them all day long, as they were in our direct line of vision. These workers were all older by my standards then, 45–55, and they looked as though they had been there or someplace like it for many years. They were noticeably happier than the younger folk I knew upstairs, more playful, and more completely adjusted to the work routine and the discipline it required.

I really remember only one of these workers. He had a machine right across the conveyor belt, 10 feet away from where we spent our days. He was Mexican American almost surely, or at least of Latin American descent, and he operated his machine with the most amazing speed and consistency. His machine punched holes in the base of the lantern, a round steel part about the size of a small mixing bowl. I nicknamed this guy "Manuel Dexterity," more for its pun value than for racism, and I did admire his work. His machine would hammer down, stamping two different holes in two lantern bases. Each base was stamped twice. With his right hand he could remove the finished base and stack it, and with his left, simultaneously lift the one stamped only once, turn it around, and place it in the next position. Then he would quickly grab an unstamped base and place it where the old one had been. Hands clear, the machine would wham down and stamp the two holes. His work and his machine set a rhythm for the whole area. It was marvelously consistent—and fast.

I watched Manuel every day for the weeks I was on the conveyor belt. He stood, repeating his operation thousands of times all day every one of those days, yet he was always smiling when he stopped for break or lunch. The curious thing, and it seems grotesque here out of context, was the play. A fellow Manuel had obviously known for years would come into the area, walk up behind him, put his hands around Manuel's waist, and thrust his pelvis against Manuel's rear. This can only be described as a "butt hump." They would laugh and Manuel would always exaggerate surprise and pleasure on his face. Other times, Manuel would leave his machine and walk to where another one of these older fellows stood, and do the same to him. Again they would laugh and make some remark. It was an all-male shop here by the conveyor belt. There were many women on the assembly lines upstairs, but now that I think about it, none on the big machines. I wonder now why it didn't seem offensive when I was watching it all go on—maybe just because it was so playful and human.

Knowledge
◆

Donna Haraway's work, *Primate Visions* (1989), details the ways in which the field of primatology reflects the ideological enterprises of scientific epistemology. Early in the book, Haraway focuses on the ironic mission of the taxidermist-scientist, Carl Akeley, a pioneer in the practice of stuffing scientific specimens and re-creating them in natural habitats—those dioramic displays we see in museums of natural history. In the name of science, and out of love for vanishing nature, Akeley would laboriously seek out the wild animal in perfect pose, kill the animal to preserve it in its noble stature, and re-create with perfect realism his encounter with the animal in its natural surround.

Ironically, what Akeley re-created was the moment of the animal's encounter with its killer, the moment of its death at the hands of man-in-charge-of science (or the other way?). In this way, Akeley "preserved" nature for humankind, so that we might, in our encounter with the museum piece, come to know and love nature as he did. This is literally true, as in our encounter with this re-created moment, we are in the position of the man killing the animal. We, too, kill it.

In each diorama of stuffed animals, Haraway notes, there is one animal that catches your gaze, one that seems to be looking at you. There is a moment of startlement and fixation, as the animal holds your gaze, as you encounter this other, as the animal informs you about you in a way no live animal could. The reflexive trick is that you cannot help but think the animal is aware of your gaze and, unlike a live animal, holds it transfixed. The rhetorical magic worked by this trick is that your piety is enriched by killing the animal anew with this gaze just as the original scientist killed it; guilt and mystery about self, other, and nature, abound in that moment of contact. The animal, you keep thinking, is dead, and you confront your own death in its gaze.

Akeley called his stuffed animals *facts*. To him, the realistic depiction and display, the re-creation of the moment when science stopped this animal's world, was the meaning of a fact. When we gaze at the animal in our encounter, we are confronted with our own *facticity*, our death. This encounter, Akeley and the other scientists believed, would at once sponsor the scientific attitude, make us aware of our special role in nature, and facilitate our maturity into manhood. The gaze kills the story of our bodies, causing us to embrace the stories of science and culture. "Culture originates in the denial of life and the body" (Brown, cited in Jackson 1989, 205, fn. 9).

I really did not meet or associate with anyone in the plant other than my five coworkers. Occasionally someone they knew would stop by for a joke or howdy during break, but I was seldom introduced and never engaged in any conversation. There just wasn't much affiliation or communication between the cogs in this human machine at all.

But there was this one guy who seemed to make the rounds. He was a dumpy fortyish fellow who ran a machine all by himself. That is, he was not part of any assembly line or group operation. His machine stood by the entrance to the shop.

Who this fellow was or what he did was never explained to me. But he frequently stopped by and was always very chipper and full of hellos. He was much too happy, and much too friendly, not to stick out in this place. He didn't have the same look in his eye as the others. It was never clear to me whether he was just some simpish, not very bright type who had decided to be happy here, or whether he had a reason to be so happy and well adjusted. I noticed that my group didn't spend any time talking to him beyond the "howzit-goin" level, although he often came up to talk. Weeks into this job I still pretty much watched others' reactions to figure out who was who and what to say—I mostly didn't say much at all and just smiled when spoken to.

I was suspicious of the dumpy guy probably based purely on the guarded and trivial reactions my teammates had toward him, and because he was the only one who ever tried to talk to me when they weren't around. He had approached me in the lunchroom one day and invited me to join his table where he was sitting with some older female employees. I must have seemed strange to them, since I was pretty reluctant to say much. This was the kind of social-izing one would expect as common, but here it seemed totally out of place and threatening to me. He looked like a company man through and through and I was suspicious of his come-on, but perhaps he had just appointed himself the social director for this completely antisocial environment. All I know is that I instinctively remained cool toward him whenever he approached.

After the week of our "huge" bonus this fellow comes up to me while I'm by myself and says, "I hear you guys got a big paycheck this week."

I looked down and mumbled, "It was OK . . . we had some from last week they forgot to give us," which was the truth but not the whole truth.

He seemed to be expecting me to tell him more about what apparently was a legendary paycheck. I didn't believe for a minute that my coworkers had bragged to him about it, and if not them, then who? I wondered if this toady was a spy for the management and he was looking for some information. His gaze hung on for a good deal longer than I thought reasonable, and he kept looking at me and I away from him. More paranoia.

On Wednesday of the week following the large paycheck I was sitting on my workstool inserting generators and fastening nuts with the cultivated oblivion that got me through each of these days. The supervisor, with whom I had never spoken past the first day and seldom seen, came up behind me and put his hand on my shoulder. I was startled.

"I want you to come with me."

I looked at my coworkers, who shared my puzzled look for a second and then looked at their work. I went with the supervisor down some stairs and then across the brick alley toward some very large garagelike doors. He didn't say much except that they needed me to "work over here" today.

We entered a very large strange room and walked toward some fellows standing around this desk. It was a small, school-like, slanted desktop elevated to standing height with some papers on it, attached to a pole that went to the ceiling. The time clock was nearby, so I gathered this was the official workstation or something. He introduced me to someone and said I would be theirs for the day. Then he left.

It is difficult to describe the feeling of entering this place. The first thing I noticed was the heat, about 120 degrees I guessed. I was the only white person in the room. All were male, all, obviously, soaked with sweat. One fellow didn't have a shirt on, the others were unbuttoned or nearly so.

Large racks hung in about four rows, the rows being about 6 feet high and 20 feet long. The racks had long spiny points and were made of a rubber-coated metal. The rows of racks were suspended from large bars that in turn were suspended by chains so that they could be moved along the tracks on the ceiling. Behind the racks were large rust-covered metal vats, rectangular and maybe 10 feet high and 30 feet wide. There were several vats in two rows headed back to the rear of the room. Smoke and a strange chemical smell arose from the vats. These were the chrome-plating vats, and the pointed spikes on the racks held different parts that were dipped in the succession of vats lined up there. Again, no one explained this to me.

No one was working yet. After the supervisor left, the fellows continued what they were doing standing by the workstation. One guy opened the desktop and pulled out this huge knife that seemed to just keep coming out of the desk as my eyes grew wider. They were laughing and looking at the door, completely unconcerned about my being there. The knife was about 20 inches long and the blade 4 inches wide at its widest point—gargantuan. Although I had a moment of fear when he pulled it out, I soon surmised that he was making the knife and was going to chrome-plate it with the other parts.

The job here was to put parts on the spikes on the racks for dipping into the vats and to take parts off the spikes when they came out of the vats. The huge racks were lifted up mechanically by the chains and lowered into the vats in a sequence. I don't recall doing anything but removing parts with one other guy, who was friendly enough. I got the impression that people who worked here didn't show up a lot and the turnover was pretty heavy, and I could imagine why. It was hot and it stunk and the work was about as debasing as anything I had done. It looked dangerous, as though those racks could impale a person, and the hot chemicals didn't help the feeling. For eight hours I worked in this heat, careful not to stab my hands with the racks, and wondered what the point of all this was.

Perhaps it was the class descent into the hell of this company that alarmed me, but I didn't believe that this was just some temporary personnel shift. Our end of things was too distant from this end of things for me just to be a friendly loan to another supervisor—whoever he was. I still don't think this likely, that someone just said, "Boy, we need someone today over in the chrome-plating vats, have you got a spare assembler?"

No. Not at all. I spent the entire day reviewing the politics of my stay there and what point this could have. I tended to take it personally, and why not, I was the one chosen for this treatment. I wondered, and still do, if the supervisor was just showing me how bad it could be and making me value my position there in a way I never had. It surely had that effect, imbuing my assembly job with a new status I hadn't imagined possible. Even though I had in fact taken my job for granted and had felt myself superior to everyone else in the place, I couldn't recall any instance of when I let that show, or had said anything at all about the job, or done anything to warrant this punishment.

Except, maybe, being cool toward the dumpy guy who tried to get me to talk about the paycheck. Or, maybe, just earning such a large paycheck while being a new employee, when most of these people had been there for years and were still just making quota. Maybe this was some social leveling tactic; some way of letting off jealousy created by what must be some public rumoring about my paycheck. It seemed too complex, too paranoid for even this place, and presumed that people would know that the new guy got sent over to "chrome plating" for a day and what an awful thing that was—like Cool Hand Luke spending the night in "the box."

Hèléne Cixous notes Freud's contention that the birth of patriarchy represents a moment that established the superiority of ideas over the physical senses, and that this epistemological "victory" signifies a "step forward in culture," a "declaration in favor of the thought-process" (1986, 100).

The idea, as I get it, is that maternity is a natural relationship, grounded in biological and sensate experience, giving rise to an ordering process of dependence and nurturance. As a principle of social organization, matriarchy thus has natural grounds in the experiences of the senses and the biological survival of the organism. Patriarchy, on the other hand, is a principle of organization composed of sheer mythos, sociopolitical authority, the hegemony and empowerment of an idea about order and control that is not itself a biological reality. Once the father has spread his seed, as it were, his participation in the process is, for all physical purposes, ended. He dies unto the reality of birth and nurturance of the offspring. Completion of the sex act is, as far as nature's purposes are concerned, his death.

Fatherhood, then, is entirely an invention of a symbolic order, an invasion of the family for dominance and control by the male, a testimony to the alternative ordering principles of temporal priority and causality. This story of when patriarchy overthrew matriarchy represents what Kenneth Burke calls a "temporizing of essence," in which the logical priority of the male's power and authority is interpreted as the *cause* of the event of birth, establishing his ownership (family as private property) and hence governance of the social order ([1945] 1969, 430). This manipulation was a victory for ideological rules of governance over those of natural order; ideas over senses; *culture* over *nature*. Civilization, as we know it or call it, for better or worse, is then founded upon the elevation of symbolic organization over and above natural organization. With the master trope of "fatherhood" at the helm, ideas could rule the senses, as Judeo-Christian religion has demonstrated, a position that science has been reluctant to yield.

Norman O. Brown (1966, 3–31) adds an idea that is potentially helpful. Brown suggests that patriarchy is only one of two patterns of male organization, the other being fraternity. The organization of Athens, Brown argues, is that of patriarchy, found developed and perpetuated in Aristotle. The minority view, that of fraternity, was the principle of Sparta, to which Plato ascribed. The primary enterprise of fraternity is to overthrow the patriarchy; the primary enterprise of patriarchy is to punish the son for his disobedience and rivalry—to cast out the son so that the father can continue his dominance.

Brown posits that there are cultural sites and epochs in which one or another of these two principles prevail. The American Revolution, for instance, seems a clear instance of fraternity, while the era of industrialism seems an unmitigated victory for patriarchy and the punishment of brothers. One implication is that not all men are admitted to the patriarchy. Indeed, very few achieve the ideal of this manhood and transactionally, this creates a situation in which this threatened manhood is compensated by increased domination of the female.

Brown notes that times of increased fraternity are times in which female freedom and inclusion are greater. The dialectics of this are puzzling. Fraternity seems to draw upon exclusion of women. The basis for patriarchy is dominion, including males in those dominated. In one sense, unmitigated patriarchy should provide a greater identification among men and women so dominated. That doesn't appear to be the case. The script for maturity and manhood provides that the excluded and dominated male achieve masculinity through further subjugation and control of the female, in other words, repressed masculinity localizing itself in situations apart from the patriarchal domination of the male. Fraternity, on the other hand, essentially a homosexual enterprise, provides some basis for identification with the female, especially insofar as male and female alike are the objects of patriarchy's domination.

Perhaps something is to be gained by not seeing patriarchy as a universal fraternity and the birthright of males. Men have also been forced to deal with a Christian terminology that has a "way of so merging concepts of servitude and freedom, of obligation and privilege, of obedience and rule, that the free man can be defined in terms of service, and the servant in terms of liberty" (Burke [1945] 1969, 122). Patriarchy is privilege of males, and a script for male domination, but for most men a privilege gained at the expense of servitude.

One thing going on at Coleman that summer was the controversial vote on the union. Coleman had no union, and management, obviously, did not want one. Some of the employees did. Perhaps the people in favor of a union knew who each other were, but I did not. I recall almost no talk with my teammates about the issue. As the vote approached, there was more and more tension about it, but I did not ask any questions about it and no answers were volunteered. There was enough free-floating paranoia about the vote that I detached myself completely. I was generally paranoid about this place, and I was a short-timer.

For a while some printed flyer or another was handed out as we exited the long alley for the parking lot each Friday (payday). These were on different colored papers. As the vote approached, these became more frequent, sometimes both sides handing out flyers on opposite sides of the alley. Both the company's and the union's flyers were pretty basic propaganda, focusing on character and slogans rather than any of the issues, of which I knew no specifics. I wish I could recall the drawings and claims made about the evils of the company or the union, but their basic themes involved outrage at the company and scandal about the union.

Sitting here now I can say that if ever employees needed a union, then these people did. I think my coworkers were probably in favor but I don't really know. I had been raised in a non-union household. My parents had never joined a union and I sensed they mostly thought unions were corrupt. I had no real disposition on the matter at all, except the union literature seemed pretty outrageous and deceptive, and I didn't care one way or another about the company. I was sure I was there for a summer and out.

As the vote approached, more and more talk was made about it, but surprisingly little and none of it to me. I do remember some horror story circulated about the last place this particular union had taken over. People stood together in groups during break and didn't seem to be telling jokes as they usually did. A few days before the vote, it came up in our small group, and I volunteered to John that I hadn't been there long enough to know much about it, so I wasn't going to vote.

"I don't think they're going to let you," he responded.

John was referring to the fact that I was still a probationary employee. I was happy that he and the others saw me as separated from this conflict, although I wasn't sure he was accurate about my voting rights. Every employee was probationary for the first 90 days, and the rules for infractions and dismissal were different for these employees. In other words, they had virtually no rights or protection in the job. What this had to do with the union vote I didn't know and didn't ask.

The day of the big union vote was growing near, and the activity surrounding it continued to grow more lively. For me it was just something in the air—a comment here and there, the increasing number and emotionalism of the handouts in the alley, observing people talking in groups. But that is not to say that there was any open campaigning going on among the employees. I suspect they were mostly talking with people who they knew were on the same side as they. What behind-the-scenes campaigning was going on was never revealed to me and was not public. The pro-union forces that were in this shop were decidedly underground.

The day before the vote there was a bit of a buzz around the shop. At 10:00 a.m. one of the company owners was going to speak to us. He evidently was making a stump campaign through all of the factory areas to try to dissuade people from voting in the union. All I can remember are impressions.

The owner entered the shop with a suited entourage and, smiling, walked briskly to the center of the shop by the supervisor's glassed-in office. His name was Coleman, one of the sons of the founder. They had created a little platform which he mounted. Then he turned toward the group of employees, who closed in behind the entourage. He motioned for us to gather closer and began a very smooth motivational speech. Its content amounted to a testimonial about how much the company cares and what it is doing and future prospects and what not. Quite likely he repeated some of the negative stories about this particular union.

What I do recall is the incredible class discrepancy I felt. The owner had that trim, shiny, CEO look—tailored gray suit, neat hair, stylish glasses. The crowd to whom he spoke, and the entire environment, were mangy by comparison. He was organized, polished, and smooth. This stuff, I thought, works. The darker-suited bigwigs standing behind him added something—here was a glimpse of the corporate image, I noticed, and today we were finally getting a piece of it in our dingy sweatshop.

The short speech ended with an appeal to vote down the union for our own good and that of the company, and then as quickly as he had come the boss and his suits were off down the runway again. There were no challenges or hard questions from the floor—I don't recall that any were invited—and the crowd more or less quietly went back to their job stations without comment. One would expect some eye rolling or head shaking by those who strongly favored the union, some cynicism or anger. If those people were there, and they were, they were tightly controlled in their responses. I suspect that my coworkers were among them.

The next day around 10 in the morning we had the big vote. I don't know who started the official move, but almost on cue everyone left their stations to head to the voting booths that had been set up by the supervisor's glass office. My coworkers looked at me with a moment of awkwardness as I did not leave my seat. Clearly I was invited, since no one told me not to come. Walking by me, John said with a verbal shrug, "Hmm. I guess I was wrong." There was no judgment in his tone at all.

I put my head down on the long bench and closed my eyes, but not for long. It was quite strange to be in that large room with no people and no noisy machinery clanging. I felt odd and conspicuous. The supervisor walked by at one point and asked, "Aren't you going to vote?" "No," I said, "I don't know that much about it." "Oh," he said, without really signaling that he understood, and walked on. I felt like I was doing something wrong. Just to be noticed, just to stand apart from the crowd, can give you that feeling.

As I sat I wondered whether I might be punished, by coworkers or the supervisor, for not participating. In such a heated conflict, I thought, it might be worse not to vote than to be on one side or another. I still wonder whether that might be true, but I never found out. Nothing was said between my friends and me; no ill feeling was ever displayed.

I don't remember when it was announced—that day, the next, or the Monday following. The union lost the vote by a close margin. There were no tears of joy or sighs of anguish. Things just went right on as they had.

Authority

◆

"*Vis a Tergo* causality," Burke writes, came to "be applied to the biological, anthropological, and sociological spheres" as grounds to construct the relationship between organism and environment as one of conflict: The organism is seen as "a separate unit more or less at odds with its environmental context—and to this context it [seeks] with varying degrees of success to adapt itself" ([1935] 1984, 232). Something like this route led those biologists who were loving the body to death to define human intelligence and superiority as "adaptability" (Haraway 1989, 73–79).

Scientific thinking managed to turn this description into a principle of dominance and authority: If the environment has control over the organism, then control over the environment is the quickest vehicle to dominance. Burke attempted to reverse this logic, outlining a method of "metabiology" wherein we recognize that "any living genus possesses an authority of its own, since different genera manifest totally different 'laws' of growth and action" ([1935] 1984, 232–233). Haraway resounds this metabiological theme—she seeks to discover ways that primates, including humans, "author" their own stories and how we can recognize the essential authority of their modes of being (1989, 8).

This essential separation of the organism from the environment, the cleavage of culture from nature, would seem to be a chief target for coming to any description of the role of the body. As Michael Jackson argues, "the self cannot . . . be treated as a thing among things; it is a function of our involvement with others in a world of diverse and ever-altering interests and situations" (1989, 3). And, as Brown offers, "The split of self from environment, of self into both self and environment, is also the split of self or soul from body" (1966, 51). Progressively, our idea of culture has come to be set over and against environment, as a spiritual achievement rather than a material and productive relationship to context and environment. Culture is our moral elevation over the animals, to be encountered quite like those stuffed animals in the Museum of Natural History—to have culture stare back at us and allow it to diminish, elevate, and thus moralize us in its gaze.

The birth of patriarchy as a "temporized essence" contains the seed of this faulty dualism between nature and culture. This event established the dominance of ideas over nature. When God (The Father) said no, and was disobeyed, humankind was separated from nature and set over against it. Yet, curiously, the punishment was a moral victory. As Mark Twain put it, when man fell from grace he rose above the animals—it was a "falling up." In becoming the object of patriarchal wrath, then, one is made moral. One is sentenced to death, and in the sentencing one is given the potential for obedience, for salvation. In one's role as dominated, one becomes included. One is shown the way.

Evolutionary science did not alter but extended the authority of culture, for man no longer knew whether he was a fallen angel or a risen ape. The father of the modern biological classification system, Linnaeus, literally thought that he was the second Adam, giving the correct names to animals that had heretofore been misnamed (Haraway 1989, 9). Culture, taken over by science, seemed to be that which ultimately would render the environment under control. Science thus perfected the religious technology for mortification of the body and further entrenched the divided self of industrial man. In one's participation in the great mind, the human conspiracy, one must punish oneself and further subjugate the body. The dualities became sharper; the technology whereby correct ideas dominate the body became certified. Haraway writes: "Nature/culture and sex/gender are not loosely related pairs of terms; their specific form of relation is hierarchical appropriation, connected as Aristotle taught, by the logic of active/passive, form/matter, achieved form/resource, man/animal, final/material cause. Symbolically, nature and culture, as well as sex and gender, mutually (but not equally) construct each other; one pole of a dualism cannot exist without the other" (1989, 7).

Having been aligned with nature, there indeed seems to be little room for woman *as controller* in the divided scientific identity. Thus the feminist desire to leave the museum where culture has embalmed her, to rewrite the body, to discover that *author*ity whereby her genus exercises its peculiar laws-in-relation-to nature, appears a logical rhetorical answer. Yet there is little room for the male, either, at least so far as he retains his body; certainly so far as he cherishes fraternity. The recovery of his body, his authority, from patriarchy may potentially be an even more difficult task.

It wasn't long after the union vote, perhaps as much as a week, that I sat down at my stool one morning to begin work. The supervisor again came up behind me and caught my attention by laying his clipboard against my arm. "Come with me," he said in his low-key and official way. I remember Bob almost yelling, "Hey, we need David."

"No. I have a job for David," the Super said over his shoulder as we walked out.

At first I was prepared for some other unknown adventure like my day at the chrome-plating vats. As we walked he told me that I would be doing a different job from now on. We went downstairs to the first floor. We were in a room full of shipping flats next to a big door that opened to the alley. We were at the end of the conveyor belt where finished, boxed lanterns came rumbling down from upstairs, one every eight feet or so. He introduced me to a clean-looking young guy about my age. I noticed the lack of grease immediately. The new job was to stack lantern boxes on these flats in a particular order and tie them up for shipping. The Super told me that this job carried no bonuses, that it was a strict hourly wage. The job normally would pay less per hour than my base rate as an assembler, but they wouldn't lower my hourly rate. Hmm.

The job was OK. Mindless, without pressure, and without supervision. We were nearly all alone down at the end of the line. Sometimes the boxes came fast and furious, but much of the time the line was slow or completely down. At those times we could lay on the empty flats and catch a rest, and no one important would notice. There wasn't anything else to do but sweep up, and I took it that no one expected us to do anything. I was curious about why I had been shifted, and remained curious about everything that had happened to me, but on the whole I rather preferred the new job. What I didn't like was the sense of being singled out and "demoted" with no apparent reason.

I didn't see my old coworkers much. The new fellow, Brad, and I had to go up to the old shop to punch in and out, so I saw them then. There were "Hi's" of recognition, but not much talk. I remember once, after I had been gone a few weeks, Bob said he had been talking to the Super about getting me back, that no one could do it as fast as I could. That's the whole point, I thought, and I wondered if Bob really didn't know that. "We need you up here," he said in his enthusiastic way that had always made me feel good.

The days and weeks ticked off pretty quickly and uneventfully. Brad told me that the guy who had been doing my job was an older hippie who had left and just never came back to work. Brad was a real nice guy and we talked and joked in ways that never had happened on the line, although we really had little in common.

From the first day or two of my move to the new job, Brad had introduced me to a new practice. Since we were a long way off from the time clock, at punch-out time we would take turns going up there and punching each other's time card. This was evidently what he and the old guy had done, and I really thought nothing of it. I should say that sometimes we were loaded with boxes coming down, and we often stayed a few minutes late to finish stacking them. But often enough we were finished at quitting time, and then one of us could leave a few seconds early and get out to the parking lot before the onrushing hordes. People were always in a dangerous hurry when the whistle blew.

One day the supervisor shows up around lunchtime with some fellow in a suit I hadn't seen before. I don't know what if anything he had to do with all this. The supervisor asked me if I had left early on Friday. I said, "Yes, a few seconds." "Who punched your time card?" he asked. Not thinking too quickly, I pointed at Brad—"He did." "Is that true?" he asked Brad. Brad nodded. The supervisor didn't even frown, but sort of nodded as he walked away with the guy in the suit.

At 2:30 that afternoon, the supervisor came and got Brad and took him upstairs. About 15 minutes later Brad came back and said the Super wanted to see me. "What happened?" I asked. "Not much," he said, "I got a one-day suspension." That didn't seem too rough, so I wasn't very worried.

Once in the glass office, the supervisor motioned for me to sit down across from his desk. His assistant, a much older fellow, got up and left. The supervisor drew a breath and gave his speech:

"Now you may have done this before or you may have seen this done, but it is a violation of the rules to clock other people's cards, and we can't have that going on here. If you weren't a probationary employee, it would just be a suspension, but since you haven't been here for 90 days, I have to fire you. No one likes to fire people and I hope this doesn't cause you hardship. If you would like to use me as a reference, you've done a good job for me and that will be the first thing I say. As far as getting back on here . . . you can try." He delivered this last line with a rising intonation and a "who knows?" tone. I read it very closely—not because there was any chance I would apply here again—but for some sign of a personal clue about what he thought amidst his otherwise official speech.

I've noticed this kind of gripping tense feeling, one of fear and tight self-control, whenever I'm in a confrontation—like when you might have to fight someone or someone starts yelling at you with anger. I felt this then. "Look," I said, summoning up some courage, "I swear I left here less than 30 seconds early."

"It doesn't matter whether it was 30 seconds or 3 hours, you can't do that." He stated this with unarguable conviction.

"Is my termination effective immediately?" I asked. I wasn't calm but very controlled.

"Yes. You are terminated immediately." This was crisp and final, but not mean.

It was the last week in July and I had been planning to quit in a few weeks anyway to go back to school. Other than the kind of official embarrassment at having been fired, I was on the whole unaffected by the event. I wasn't angry with the system or upset at having lost the job. It pretty much fit my basic picture of factories and work, so if anything, I guess I was affirmed in the whole matter. Brad apologized profusely when I went to pick up my things. I told him not to worry about it, that I was sorry I hadn't made up some story about who punched my time card. I really hadn't realized we were doing anything criminal, I guess because he had been so nonchalant about it.

I told my folks about what happened and they weren't too upset either. But when I made my counter-arguments they were vocally on the side of the company. "No, David," I remember my mother saying, "it doesn't matter. No one can punch anyone else's time card." Clearly this was a cardinal rule of factory work, part of the basic factory morality to which their entire lives had been testament. This, evidently, was the lesson to be learned here—the absolute about which there were no shades of gray, the singular fact that made everything else about unions, quotas, bonuses, and quality working conditions completely irrelevant. And, I had to admit, these issues really were completely aside from what had happened, which made the firing a less than satisfying symbol of the conflicts and tensions I had felt during my two months at the factory. They just didn't really matter. Had I not broken the rules, I could have stayed on indefinitely. None of what had happened or why would have made the least difference to my future there, so long as I took whatever job they gave me.

The fact that I had no intention of staying on also made my experiences there somewhat irrelevant to me personally. But if I had been an employee looking for a future, certain facts seem clear: I had been taken from a job with relative status and benefits and put into one with no future and lower pay, and this, I assume, because I had been doing a good job. Why I had been delivered to the chrome-plating vats was still a great curiosity to me. Why, and whether, my detachment from the union vote was a factor in my treatment was unknown. Basically, everything that had happened was mysterious, and I think probably would have remained so no matter what my behavior or intentions with the job. I suppose I would have just kept on stacking boxes until I made some move to get a better job there. I don't know much about how people move up in such environments, but my guess is it takes a long time and has little to do with their talents or aspirations, and much more to do with accidents and random decision making.

Conclusion
◆

I did not go back to Wichita for summer work again. I didn't return there to live until after I graduated and spent a few months traveling. But when I did return, I once again found myself applying at local institutions for work. Again at my mother's persistence I applied at the factories—but certainly not Coleman. She was most persistent about Boeing, where she and Dad worked for 10 and 20 years, respectively. I was most resistant about Boeing. My father had always buried his resentment against leaving the farm for this life, but not too deeply for me to share. I had always found my mother's "company woman" ambitions objectionable, for she saw this life as a perfect medium for leaving her depression-era shame.

Just as I had been mysteriously hired at Coleman that summer, I walked out of the Boeing personnel office with a job, by all local standards, a very good job. I was to be an industrial engineer. Obviously all that was required was a college degree for this job, membership in the managerial class. The other thing required was that one wear slacks to work rather than jeans.

At Coleman the job of industrial engineer would have meant studying the work operations and setting the quotas for individual production, and this irony did not escape me when I accepted the job. At Boeing, it meant organizing operations for whichever of thousands of areas one could be sent. In my case, I was to make bar charts that scheduled the work done in commercial modification, which was refurbishing commercial aircraft after so many cycles of use.

I never really learned to do that job. I didn't do anything for three months, but I did make more money than either of my parents. "Here comes 100% company overhead," the shop workers would say when I came around. That was true. "Hemorrhoids and heart attacks," I would say of the job, because we sat doing nothing all day, and a few men in their 50s died at their desks during my short stay there.

After three months, one of the higher-ups decided that since we had no work to do, several in my office would perform a productivity study. This involved each of us identifying 20 workers and sampling their activity on random trips through the shop. This practice terrorized the workers, because they were sure we identified them by name (which we didn't). Their rule during these studies was "if you go to the bathroom, take a tool with you," since carrying a tool would identify them as engaged in "productive activity."

Doing this was lousy enough, especially given my identifications with the shop workers, of which my father had been one. After a few weeks, however, it came down from the higher-up that the study wasn't showing the results he wanted, so on our random trips through the shop areas we were now to go into the bathrooms and count the number of workers there. I had enough.

I told my lead-man that I thought this was truly chicken-shit, and that it wasn't a study, and it wasn't related to productivity (imagine, as I did, rating their "productivity" in the bathrooms).

This angered my boss. "This is just a quirk in your head," he said with anger and frustration. "Studying anything that affects the productivity of the shop is our responsibility."

"I just don't think I want to do this," I answered.

"So don't do it," he said with abruptness and finality.

This episode created a lot of tension in the shop, because I didn't do it, and others did. The next day it was announced that the study was over. Within three days I had located another job and told my lead-man.

"I want to give two weeks notice."

"One week is enough."

"Who do I notify?"

"I'll take care of it."

The whole office breathed a huge sigh of relief when I walked out the next Friday. I wore jeans that day.

My mother went on to become one of the first woman supervisors in the Boeing organization. My father was made supervisor for a short period of time, but didn't care for it. After almost 30 years, someone recognized that he knew more about fixing airplanes than anyone else around, and he was given a lush position in research and development. He retired a year later, at age 55—a retirement age that was almost unheard of among his cohorts. What happened to me is a whole other set of stories.

My parents visited recently. They have been retired for 15 years now. They related an experience that perhaps captures a central point of my story and the core idea of autobiology. They say that they still dream about being at work sometimes. And when they do, they are still workers—not management as they were during the last years of their employment. And in these dreams, they both have the same crisis: they panic because they suddenly realize they have forgotten to punch the time clock.

Over the last 20 years I have thought about these encounters with the factory world, both at Coleman and at Boeing, but much more about Coleman. I was never bitter about Coleman, but I surely was about Boeing.

I occasionally visualize that gleaming bowl of brass nuts I stared at for weeks. I most often think about and can even smell the chrome-plating vats, as though that day were the complete nadir of my working life. I have told the story of walking in, with those guys pulling out the huge knife, on several occasions. I have had occasion to remember the union flyers or the president's speech, in the same vague way I have described them here. I think with regret about the day I insulted Rita—I remember very clearly what my coworkers looked like. Most crisply, though, I remember sitting in the supervisor's office and my physical feeling of being trapped or held while he delivered his speech about the "rule." And I surely remember shedding that tension from my body as I walked past my old assembly line and out of the factory that last day.

It seems as though I remember the Boeing experience mostly with my mind. It fits into some ideological scheme in my outlooks, and has narrative significance as a kind of turning point in my life story. I think the reason I return to these images from Coleman is that I remember them mostly with my body. The whole episode is some strange dis-lodged chunk, something I did or went through, sitting all by itself and unrelated to any life changes or choices or basic beliefs I hold. None of it ever made a great deal of sense, or any apparent difference; it is a strange and extreme experience as far as my work history goes, but seemingly a normal one for the world that I visited that summer. Unlike my stint in management at Boeing, I had not authored it into my story until now.

References

Brown, N. O. 1966. *Love's Body*. New York: Random House.

Burke, K. [1945] 1969. *A Grammar of Motives*. Berkeley: University of California Press.

Burke, K. [1935] 1984. *Permanence and Change*. Berkeley: University of California Press.

Cixous, H. and C. Clement. 1986. *Newly Born Woman*, translated by B. Wing. Minneapolis: University of Minnesota Press.

Haraway, D. 1989. *Primate Visions: Gender and Nature in the World of Modern Science*. New York: Routledge.

Jackson, M. 1989. *Paths Toward a Clearing: Radical Empiricism and Ethnographic Inquiry*. Bloomington: Indiana University Press.

Riesman, D., et al. 1950. *The Lonely Crowd*. New Haven, CT: Yale University Press.

Scarry, E. 1985. *The Body in Pain*. New York: Oxford University Press.

◆————————

David Payne is Associate Professor of Communication at the University of South Florida in Tampa. He lives in a middle-class suburban home with his wife, who is also a professor, and two children. He believes that universities are becoming more and more like the factory he writes about in this essay, and he hopes that this publication will help to fill his quota.

CHAPTER TWO

A Secret Life
in a Culture of Thinness
Reflections on Body, Food, and Bulimia
Lisa M. Tillmann-Healy

In the spring of 1986, at the age of 15, I invited bulimia to come live with me. She never moved out. Sometimes I tuck her deep in my closet, behind forgotten dresses and old shoes. Then one day, I'll come across her—as if by accident—and experience genuine surprise that she remains with me. Other times, for a few days or perhaps a week or month, she'll emerge from that closet to sleep at my side, closer than a sister or lover would.

This is our story.

An Afternoon with Cherry Garcia

A pint of Ben and Jerry's Cherry Garcia sits next to me in the passenger seat. Tossing the plastic grocery bag aside, I stare at the container for a moment.

Soon, I think to myself.

The car behind me honks. Embarrassed, I wave apologetically, put my Nissan in gear, and pull into the intersection.

The half mile home feels much longer than usual. I keep glancing at the round pint. Unable to resist, I reach over and take it into my palm. The container sweats from the heat of my touch. I place it between my legs and lift the top. The lid descends onto my waiting tongue. Slowly, I lick the sweet cherry ice cream until none remains. With a sigh of anticipation, I replace the cover.

At last, I make my way into the apartment complex. I scoot around the car, toss the pint back into the shopping bag (so no one will catch me), and rush up the two flights of stairs leading to my apartment.

I unlock the door and move swiftly to the kitchen. *I'm on a mission.* The last clean spoon glistens when I open the utensil drawer.

I sink into the overstuffed sofa and pause for a moment, preparing for the experience to come. Taking a deep breath, I open the container once more. I glide my stainless steel friend across the soft frozen matter. My mouth waters in response to the pink cream, half black cherry, and chocolate chunk captured by my spoon. I bring the first bite to my lips and slide it around in my mouth. The cream melts on my tongue while I leisurely chew the added treats. I swallow and feel the coolness move down my throat.

"Oh . . . yes," I say aloud.

I remove my pinching pumps, tuck my thankful feet under a woven stadium blanket, and turn on *Days of Our Lives*. As John tries to win Kristen back, Kate's plane crashes into the ocean, and Austin decides whether or not to tell Carrie that he slept with her sister, I smile with a rare contentment.

My spoon enters the carton again, more determined this time. I dig deeper, stabbing left and right, in search of many chocolate chunks. Four on my spoon, I bring them to my mouth. I move my tongue over these to melt the surrounding ice cream. When all chunks are positioned correctly, I apply just enough pressure to melt the chocolate as well.

Again and again, my spoon meets the pint, scraping across one edge, then the other, then the center. My nose takes in the sweet aroma while the luscious tastes and perfect blend of textures further arouse my insatiable appetite.

Turning the label, my eyes meet a grainy black-and-white photograph of Ben and Jerry. They look plump and happy.

"You're good men," I tell them.

I turn further for the nutrition information—20 grams of fat per serving, four servings in the meager carton on my lap.

"You should have gotten the frozen yogurt," I admonish myself. "Then you wouldn't have to do it."

The container empty, I wait for a commercial break, then stride to the bathroom, close the door, lift the toilet seat, and vomit.

I am 24 years old.

◆ ◆ ◆

"Bulimia nervosa," according to Goldbloom et al. (1992, 171), "is an eating disorder characterized by episodes of binge eating and various attempts to counteract the effect of the ingested calories." Counteractions may include vomiting, dieting, exercise, and the use of diuretics and laxatives (see Tobin, Johnson, and Dennis 1992).

More young women engage in bulimic behaviors—and more often—than ever before (Rosenzweig and Spruill 1987). It is estimated that 46% of adolescent girls have binged, and over 11% have purged at least once (Crowther, Post, and Zaynor 1985). By the time they reach college, 10% will fit the criteria for bulimia (Gray and Ford 1985).

Though the term *bulimia* (literally meaning "ox hunger") has been used for centuries (Parry-Jones and Parry-Jones 1991), the medical community considered it a subsyndrome of anorexia until 1979 (Russell 1979). Since then, it has been extensively studied as a separate "disorder." Most research on bulimia has been conducted by physicians and therapists.

Here is their story.

◆ ◆ ◆

Physicians and therapists focus mainly on medical and psychological aspects of bulimia. The bulimic's home environment, psychological traits, behavioral tendencies, physical health, and treatment options have been thoroughly discussed in the literature.

Many studies suggest that an "unhealthy" home predisposes one to bulimia. Researchers believe that circumstances such as abuse (Pitts and Waller 1993), high parental conflict (Lacey, Coker, and Birtchnell 1986), and alcohol misuse (Chandy et al. 1995) occur more frequently in bulimics' families than in families of nonbulimics.

In addition to common environmental factors, therapists indicate that bulimics share psychological characteristics. Those mentioned most often include: body dissatisfaction (Thompson, Berg, and Shatford 1987), low self-esteem (Pertschuk et al. 1986), self-directed hostility (Williams et al. 1993), and attachment and separation problems (Armstrong and Roth 1989). Some research even links bulimia to depression (Greenberg 1986) and borderline personality disorder (Skodol et al. 1993).

Therapists also associate bulimia with certain behavioral tendencies. They suggest that bulimics demonstrate overall impulsivity (Heilbrun and Bloomfield 1986) and perfectionism (Thompson et al. 1987) as well as problems with drinking (Striegel-Moore and Huydic 1993) and drugs (Bulik et al. 1992).

Physicians claim that bulimia threatens physical health. They connect binging and purging to insufficient levels of vitamins (Philipp et al. 1988), enamel erosion (Philipp et al. 1991), migraine headaches (Brewerton and George 1993), ulcers (Neil 1980), pregnancy complications (Franko and Walton 1993), bowel disorders (Neil 1980), spontaneous stomach rupture (Breslow, Yates, and Shisslak 1986), frontal lobe lesions (Erb et al. 1989), heart failure (Kohn 1987), and even death (Neil 1980).

In response to the apparent consequences of bulimia, several treatments have been developed. Health care professionals have experimented with self-help (Huon 1985); drugs—particularly anticonvulsants (Mitchell 1988) and antidepressants (Crane et al. 1987); progressive relaxation (Mizes and Fleece 1986); hypnotherapy (Vanderlinden and Vandereycken 1988), behavior therapy (Cooper, Cooper, and Hill 1989); cognitive-behavior therapy (Lee and Rush 1986); nutritional counseling (O'Connor, Touyz, and Beumont 1988); and group therapy (Stuber and Strober 1987).

In the medical and psychological literature on bulimia, the voices of physicians and therapists speak. First they tell me about my "troubled childhood."

"Wait a minute," I say. "I grew up in a stable and loving home."

Then they tell me about my "psychological and behavioral problems."

"But I'm a functioning, well-adjusted adult," I insist.

I want their story to help me understand my participation in the dark, secret world of bulimia. But it doesn't. According to the story they tell, I have no reason (indeed no *right*) to be bulimic. But I am, and I know I'm not alone.

For almost a decade, I have moved through this covert culture of young women, and I can take you there. I am not an "authority" on bulimia, but I can show you a view no physician or therapist can, because, in the midst of an otherwise "normal" life, I experience how a bulimic *lives* and *feels.*

This renders my account different from theirs in a number of ways. Physicians and therapists study bulimia with laboratory experiments, surveys, and patient interviews. I examine bulimia through systematic introspection (Ellis 1991), treating my own lived experience as the "primary data" (Jackson 1989). They move toward general conclusions. I move *through* what Baumeister and Newman (1994, 676) call "experiential particularity." Physicians and therapists use terms such as *causes, effects,* and *associations* to try to explain, predict, and control bulimia. I use evocative narratives to try to understand bulimia and to help others see and sense it more fully. They write from a dispassionate third-person stance that preserves their position as "experts." I write from an emotional first-person stance that highlights my multiple interpretive positions. Physicians and therapists keep readers at a distance. I invite you to come close and experience this world for yourself.

You won't find such an account anywhere else—not in the case studies in which the lives of women (hidden behind guises such as "Miss A" and "Patient 2") count for little more than "evidence" in support of the author's hypothesis; not on the talk shows, where women's "disordered" experiences become public spectacles; not in popular magazines, where most of the attention focuses on celebrities who have "overcome" bulimia; and not on TV dramas (such as *Days of Our Lives* and *Beverly Hills 90210*), where bulimia becomes a storyline for a few episodes, then magically disappears.

I don't doubt the good intentions of physicians, therapists, and even producers of popular culture. But these sources focus on "deviant" behavior, medical diagnosis, and treatment directed toward the ultimate end: "cure" of the "disease." While stopping bulimic behaviors is an admirable goal, directing our attention there obscures the emotional intensity of bulimic experiences and fails to help us understand what bulimia *means* to those who live with it every day and what it *says* about our culture.

Unlike most accounts, my story reveals the irony of living simultaneously in a culture of abundance and a culture of thinness—a culture in which 80% of fourth-grade girls are on self-imposed diets, a culture in which the same percentage of women believe they are overweight, a culture in which between 3 and 8 million of those women turn to bulimia (Bernstein 1986).

In short, my story implicates the family and cultural stories (see Yerby, Buerkel-Rothfuss, and Bochner 1995) that encourage young women (and, increasingly, young men as well) to relate pathologically to food and to their own bodies. I take the emotional/professional risk of sharing the darkest, most painful secret of my life in order to expose some of the lived, felt consequences of these stories and to open dialogues aimed at writing new and better ones.

They Lied
When I was

a
lit
tle
girl

they said that getting

B I G

was a good thing.

Teach Your Children Well

◆

I lie on my stomach across the patchwork quilt that covers my parents' bed. Wearing only a cream lace bra and panties, my mother styles the chestnut locks that fall freely across her shoulders and down her back. The brush whooshes softly as it rolls off the ends. She stands in front of the mirror attached to the pine dresser her father made. I look up at Mom's reflection, and she smiles at me.

When her gaze returns to her own image, a different expression washes over my mother's face. She sets the brush down. Turning to the side, she squeezes the skin beneath her rib cage.

Back to center, Mom's hand sweeps over her slightly rounded middle. Her eyebrows curl and her lips purse as she watches herself intently.

Mom turns away and dresses hurriedly. While she dons baggy sweatpants and a long shirt, I reach underneath my sweater and feel for excess flesh.

I am 4 years old.

Sixty Pounds
◆

I enter the upstairs bathroom and flick on the light. The door closes behind me, and I turn to push the lock.

I slide the digital scale back from the peach-papered wall. Stepping on, I watch the glowing numbers roll. I imagine myself to be a contestant on *The Price Is Right*. Today, the "big wheel" stops on . . . 60. "That can't be right," I think to myself as I step off.

"I'd like to spin again, Bob," I say to my imaginary host.

Once more, the whirling digits come to rest on 60. I kick off my sandals—no change. I shed my long-sleeved T-shirt—nope. My corduroy pants and underwear—still 60 pounds. I dress quickly and bolt out of the bathroom.

"Grilled cheese and tomato soup okay for lunch?" my mother asks as I pass her in the hall.

"I don't want any lunch, Mom," I say, exiting through the back door.

I run laps around the house until I can no longer breathe.

I am 7 years old.

Cellulite
◆

"You have cellulite," Samantha tells me.

"What?" I ask, trying to negotiate last year's bathing suit over my hips.

"Cell-yoo-lite," she repeats.

"What's that?"

"Those fatty dimples on the back of your legs."

"Where?" I ask, turning my butt toward the mirror.

"*There*," Samantha says, pointing.

"I don't see anything."

"Look," she orders, moving me closer to the mirror. "See how your skin back here is bumpy."

"I guess so."

"That's cellulite," Samantha says.

"Yuck. What can I do?"

"Diet and exercise," she suggests. "For now, you might want to wear a towel around your waist."

"Yeah. I wouldn't want anyone else to see my cellulite."

"My sister says it makes a woman's thighs look like cottage cheese," Samantha tells me.

"Great, and I'm not even a woman yet."

I am 10 years old.

Weighing In

◆

"Who's first?" my sixth-grade gym teacher calls.

Nobody steps forward, so Mr. Turner checks his roster. "Collins!"

"Lucky me," Kelly says, dropping her chin.

Mr. Turner instructs the rest of us to form a line in alphabetical order, then turns to his assistant, who records the results. "Collins . . . 99 pounds!"

This is met with some hushed "oohs" and "aahs."

"Dankins," he says as the next girl steps on, "87 pounds!"

I sneak off to the locker room. Once inside, I enter the far stall and close the door. Hoping a miracle of nature will send 10 pounds of liquid weight rushing out of my body, I push on my stomach and bear down. Only a few ounces spill into the toilet.

Through several concrete walls, I can still hear the gym teacher booming. "Frank . . . 84 pounds!"

I flush and wash my hands.

As I exit the locker room, Becky shoots me a pained look from the front of the line. She crosses her fingers behind her back.

"Kirkland . . . 97 pounds!" I can hear her groan.

I pass Sharon, who is running in place.

"What are you doing?" I ask her.

"Burning calories," she answers matter-of-factly.

"You have to burn 3,500 to lose a pound," I tell her. With a disappointed look, she stops.

"Mason . . . 103 pounds!"

"I wish he'd shut up!" someone behind me shouts. I wish the same thing.

The line's moving quickly now. One after the other, names and numbers echo off the walls. "Nichols . . . 86 pounds!" "O'Reiley . . . 89 pounds!"

Faster and faster, closer and closer. I feel myself perspiring.

"Sellers . . . 90 pounds!"

As she exits, Sharon puts her hands over her throat, as if to say she choked. She joins me in line.

"Want me to wait?" Sharon asks.

"That's OK. Go on ahead," I tell her.

"I'll wait," she offers again.

"No, I'd rather you didn't."

"But I *want to*," Sharon says. She's so competitive.

Only Tannen and Thermon to go. Then me.

"Tannen . . . 81 pounds!" Mr. Turner calls.

"What I wouldn't give . . . " I say to Sharon.

"No shit," she responds. Only Sharon uses such words.

I'm outside the office door. My joints feel frozen in place, and I find it difficult to swallow.

"Thermon . . . 82 pounds!" Jessica breathes a sigh of relief.

As I enter, Mr. Turner says to his assistant, "Two scrawny gals in a row." I know there won't be a third.

He turns to me. "Ah, Tillmann. Get on the scale, please."

"Can I take off my shoes?" I ask him.

"Just get on it, will you?"

"Tillmann . . . " he begins. It seems like an eternity. I can't look. I can't breathe. "94 pounds!"

I cringe.

I am 12 years old.

The Spaghetti Feed (and Other Meals)

◆

I'm standing in line at the yacht club's annual spaghetti dinner. Surrounded by Izod polos and the latest ensembles from Dayton's, I glance down at my faded navy sweatshirt, borrowed shorts, and soiled tennis shoes. "What the hell am I doing here?" I wonder to myself.

"Lis? Hey!" From the look on my boyfriend's face, I assume he has been talking for some time. "You eating today?"

"Yeah," I say reluctantly, taking my plate out of Brad's hand. "But let me get it."

The food looks wonderful—piles of fresh, slippery noodles, alfredo, bolognese, and basil-tomato sauces, oregano-sprinkled French bread with and without melted mozzarella, Caesar salad, and spumoni for dessert. My mouth waters.

With the serving fork, I move a helping of spaghetti the size of a dollop of mashed potatoes onto my plate. I top this with a small scoop of tomato sauce (but no parmesan sprinkles), take one slice of no-cheese bread, and skip the ice cream.

Brad finds an empty table. "They call it a spaghetti *feed* for a reason," he teases. "You never eat a damn thing."

"I'm not very hungry I guess," I tell him.

Just then, my stomach growls loudly. Brad gives me a knowing smile as he digs into the first of three helpings.

I tear off a small piece of bread and put it in my mouth. Brad scrutinizes my every move; in the two months we've been together, he has never seen me eat. I shoot him a coy smile, hoping he'll turn away, but of course, he doesn't.

Shifting in my seat, I cut my spaghetti into tiny pieces. I wait a spell, then take a small bite into my mouth, chew several times, and swallow. Though my eyes focus on my plate, I can feel Brad looking at me, so I wait some more. Another bite. Wait. Another. Wait. Another. He's still staring. I put my fork down. "You want something?" I ask.

"Gonna eat that?" Brad responds, his mouth full of spumoni.

"Nah, I had a big lunch."

"Do you mind?" he asks, eyeing my leftovers.

"Not at all," I answer, and Brad scrapes what remains on my plate onto his. When he finishes, we bring our dishes inside and say our obligatory farewells.

I walk him to the dock. "I'll drop by your house when the regatta is over," Brad says, planting a kiss on my cheek.

"See you then."

As I make my way home, I am met by a succession of honks. My father's brown Zephyr pulls off the road.

Dad rolls down his window. "We're goin' to the Root Beer Stand for dinner," he calls. "Wanna come?"

"Sure," I say, getting in. "I'm *famished.*"
I am 14 years old.

A Symbolic Purge

♦

I read these stories aloud and feel conflicted. As a feminist, I'm embarrassed by the amount of attention I've paid to my body. As a daughter, I worry that these revelations will hurt my parents. As a scholar, I'm concerned that fellow academics will dismiss my work as self-absorbed.

One after the other, over and over, I take these in. I swallow the words and feel them waddle down my throat. More voices, new doubts, I ingest them all.

At last, my stomach tumbles and churns, twisting, sloshing. In a mass eruption, the words rush out of my mouth—a symbolic purge. On the page, my insides lay bare for everyone to read. Perhaps I should be ashamed, but somehow, I feel only relief.

The First Time

♦

I kneel in front of the toilet bowl, afraid yet strangely fascinated. As I stare at my rippling reflection in the pool of Saniflush-blue water, my thoughts turn to an article in the latest *Teen Magazine* about a young woman who induced vomiting to control her weight. It sounds repulsive in light of my experiences with the flu and hangovers. Still, I want to try it, to see if I can do it.

I place the shaking index finger of my right hand to the back of my throat. I hold it there for five or six seconds, but nothing happens. I push it down further. Still nothing. Further. Nothing. Frustrated, I move it around in circular motions. At last, I feel my stomach contract, and this encourages me to continue. Just then, I gag loudly.

Shhh.

Footsteps clonk on the linoleum outside the bathroom door, and I immediately pull my finger out of my mouth.

"Lis?" my father calls. "You OK?"

"I'm fine, Dad," I answer. "Playing basketball tonight?"

"Yeah, and I'm late."

I hear him pass through the dining room and ascend the stairs.

Listening closely for other intruders, I gaze into the commode, determined to see this through. The front door slams as my father exits, and I return to my crude technique. Again my stomach contracts. When I feel my body rejecting the food, I move my hand aside to allow the smooth, still-cold liquid to pour out of me—a once perfect Dairy Queen turtle sundae emerges as a brown swirl of soft-serve ice cream, hot fudge and butterscotch, and minute fragments of chopped pecans.

Again and again, 20 times or more, I repeat this until I know by pushing on my stomach that it is satisfactorily empty. My pulse races.

I am 15 years old.

Dangerous Dips

Peppermint bonbon and vanilla wafer.
  We have almost any flavor.
Rum raisin and pralines with cream.
  Thirty-one varieties is a dream.

Lime sherbet and butterscotch chip.
  Can I scoop you one more dip?
Peach melba and raspberry truffle.
  "Oh hell, make it a double."

This is the best job in the world.

Fresh strawberries and pineapple from Dole.
  Too many choices, too little control.
A spoonful here, a spoonful there.
  Such working conditions are most unfair.

Hot fudge running down your chin.
  "How do you work here and stay so thin?"
Bananas foster in a cone or cup.
  Excuse me a moment, I need to throw up.

This is the worst job in the world.

Help Arrives in Time . . . For Someone Else
◆

I set down the receiver and dash out the door. Failing to acknowledge the whips of Minnesota wind, I jog briskly to the back entrance of the local hospital.

My boots clop on cement stairs as I climb to the second floor. Pushing open the heavy metal door, I note Elaine's room on the right. I hesitate before entering.

As I walk in, faded avocado curtains block afternoon sunlight. They speak of sickness and decay.

Elaine stares at me for a moment, then smiles. Rushing over to give her a hug, I tell her she looks good. It is a lie.

A thin, pink gown highlights Elaine's weary body. Pale, blotchy skin covers her long legs and arms, and Elaine's usually glossy amber tresses lay brittle and limp. Once crystal gray-blue eyes appear sunken. "I'm so tired," she manages.

"Do they know?" I ask her.

"Yeah. They're sending me to St. Peter's to see someone," Elaine tells me. I don't like the way she says "*see someone.*"

A nurse enters and replaces the now empty bag of IV fluid.

"What are they giving you?" I ask.

"Nothing with calories, I hope," she answers.

"Listen, I'll swing by later, okay? Love you."

As I exit, I try to define what I'm feeling. Is it concern? Definitely. Elaine collapsed yesterday while pouring herself a glass of water. I wonder how she'll come through all this. Is it shame? Perhaps. It could easily have been me lying in that bed. And what is this—this little twinge? Could it be *envy*?

I am 15 years old.

One Careful Day
Three o'clock this Monday morning,
   I tiptoe past my sleeping brothers
   and slink down the creaky wooden stairs.

Rest now . . .
   You mustn't hear the sounds,
   the grotesque choking sounds.

On this Monday afternoon,
  I discover my fix hiding
  deep within the refrigerator—
  a bulimic's liquor cabinet.

But don't worry . . .
  I won't let you see it—
  I'll swiftly flush the evidence away.

After this Monday evening's dinner,
  I escape from the table
  and prance upstairs to undo
  what has been done.

I'll be careful . . . so careful.
  I'll run the tap.
  I'll listen for you.
  I'll keep the secret down.

Later this Monday night,
  I hear bath water being drawn
  beside my primary destination,
  the shuffling pages of *Sports Illustrated*
  atop option number two.

No matter . . .
  the gas station toilet,
  the restroom at Hillside Park,
  an open field at the end of a dirt road—

I can hide it from you . . .
　　　　　　　　. . . anywhere.

Clicks

◆

I'm in the basement watching *Little House on the Prairie* and eating Lucky
Charms. I don't think about anything in particular, except that I'm
enjoying the quiet time alone.

During a tearful scene in which Laura trades her beloved horse to the dreadful Nellie Olson in exchange for the stove Mrs. Ingalls wants for Christmas, it suddenly "clicks." My mood changes instantly, and my full attention focuses on the bowl of sugar-coated wheat puffs, soft marshmallows, and pastel milk that sits in my lap. I watch as my hand directs the spoon to move quickly from bowl to mouth and to pick up larger quantities each time. I eat ravenously, greedily. Twenty seconds later, I have consumed the entire portion. For a moment, I stare perplexed at the empty bowl, then scurry upstairs to pour myself another.

I am 16 years old.

The Last Time

♦

I pull out the drain stopper and set it atop the sink. As I'm turning the faucet, I notice the skin just above my first knuckle. A small, purplish patch there reminds me of the wounds I used to incur playing soccer in the yard with our beagle, Sparky. Of course, I didn't get this bite from a dog.

I start to put that finger in my mouth, but I worry that the mark will become too visible. I know that my friend, Patti, uses a toothbrush to induce vomiting, so I decide to try that. It works well enough, but I hate how it feels. I then switch to the index finger of my left hand, but the angle seems so foreign that I can't relax enough to release the food.

I decide to do it the usual way. I vomit in four sets of five. A set happens like this: I slip my right index finger down my throat, wiggle it around, move my hand, and vomit; down, wiggle, move, vomit; down, wiggle, move, vomit; down, wiggle, move, vomit; down, wiggle, move, vomit. The further along in the set, the easier the food comes up.

After the first set, I meet my gaze in the mirror above the sink. As if touching my face, I run wet, sticky fingers over the place in my reflection where mascara and eyeliner run in murky brown streaks and fresh lipstick swirls with foundation. From my mouth flow orange saliva, bile, and tiny remnants of macaroni.

I cup my hand under the tap and splash my mouth and cheeks with warm water, taking some in to rinse my teeth. I worry about them a lot, these four-years-of-braces, three-thousand-dollar teeth. They've already turned a bit yellow, and I've seen pictures of bulimic women whose enamel wore off. Disgusting!

Seeing that I'm short on time, I decide to do one long set of 15 to save the in-between clean-up time. I'm counting off in my head—one, two, three, four, five, six . . . Oh, god!

What is this? Rocked by the crescendo of a wrenching, stabbing pain in my chest, I feel my stomach tighten, and my lungs seem to cave in. Struggling to breathe, I lower myself to the floor. With the same hand I used to vomit just moments before, I pound violently on my breast bone. *Make it stop.*

Laying my forehead on the cool tiles, I clutch my heart. I start to cry but the contractions only intensify the pain.

I imagine the headlines: "Local Girl Dead at 17," or worse, "Bulimic Dies of Heart Attack." *No, god. Please no.*

What a way to go—crumpled here with vomit dripping from my mouth, running down my arm. Who will find my body? My mom should be home from work in an hour. She'll have to call my father at the office. Will she tell him over the phone or wait until he can see for himself what has become of his only daughter? Perhaps my 10-year-old brother will find me first.

How did I get here? How could I become so out of control?

The pain begins to taper off, and I'm able to sit up. After a minute or so, it's over.

I'll never do it again. I swear I'll never do it again.

Promises, promises.

I am 17 years old.

If I could, I would make those heartbreaking animal sounds that reach the deepest places of the soul to express my longing (Butler and Rosenblum 1991, 43).

Hear Me
Why don't you hear me?
  The after-meal ritual—
  15 or 30 times over,
  5 or 10 labored minutes.
  It doesn't matter.
  You just don't hear.
How many would be enough? How long sufficient?

Doesn't it seem even a little odd, one bit suspicious?
How can you look at me with those wide, admiring eyes?
Don't you know who I am?

Why can't you hear me?
   I've stopped leaving the house.
   I've stopped waiting to be alone.
   I've stopped going upstairs.
   I've stopped turning the fan on.
   I've stopped running the tap.
   I've become almost *cavalier.*

Why won't you hear me?
   Ten little paces outside the door,
   I hear you talking and laughing,
   the supper plates clanking as
   you rack them in place.
   So near . . . yet so completely unreachable.

Why don't you hear me?
   How loud must I say these things
   before you force me to speak them?

Please, god.
   If only this once,
   just let them hear me.

An Open Door

◆

A shadow unfolds across springtime floral wallpaper and hinges squeak as my bedroom door opens. My mother speaks in an unusually hesitant voice. "Honey?"

Lying in bed with my back to her, I glance at the alarm clock—10 minutes after 4. Quietly sucking air through my mouth, I hope that Mom will think me asleep and leave me alone.

"Lisa?" she calls out, more purposefully this time.

"Whaaaht?" I respond, as if just regaining consciousness.

"Something's wrong, isn't it?"

Oh, my god. She knows.

"What do you mean?" I say, trying to postpone the impact.

"Something's not right with you."

Maybe she doesn't.

"Like what?" I ask her.

"I just know it's something. Something's definitely wrong with you." She's trying not to cry.

She doesn't know.

"Go back to bed, Mom."

"You've always been able to talk to me," she says.

Jesus, maybe you should tell her.

"Lisa?"

Face it, it's no longer an experiment.

"Please tell me, Lisa."

The door's open. Just walk through it. Just walk through. She can help you. You need her to help you.

"There's nothing to tell," I hear myself say.

Damn you! Take that back. Take it back now!

She doesn't give up. "Nothing?"

Another chance. This is it, Lisa. Tell her about it. Please just tell her. Don't let her leave!

"Nothing, Mom."

Stupid girl!

The shadow recedes across springtime floral wallpaper and hinges squeak as my bedroom door closes behind her. It never opens in this way again.

I am 18 years old.

Common Bathroom
◆

I chew the last Dorito and take a swig of Diet Coke. Without bothering to lock up, I head down the hall.

I stride to the common bath—the worst feature of dormitory living. When Gloria from the west wing exits, the swinging door nearly hits me in the face.

"Sorry," she says with a sniffle. Her red eyes, filled with tears, give her away.

"You OK?" I ask.

"Never better," she responds, and I don't push.

I move to the corner stall and lift the toilet seat. Fresh vomit sprays cover the rim. "You're getting indiscreet, Gloria," I say softly.

I lean over and push my finger down my throat. The Doritos and Diet Coke come up stubbornly in thick clumps. "Bad idea," I scold myself.

The swinging door opens again, so I pull my finger out, quietly put the seat back, and sit on the toilet, waiting. Someone enters the stall two down from me. She slides the lock into place. Instead of the expected bathroom sounds, I hear the toilet seat being lifted, then a flush. Over the whirl of suction, I can still make out gagging and splashing. I take a peek under the divider and recognize the black suede boots that Carrie wore to history class this morning.

I flush and move to the sink. As I wash my hands, Carrie's toilet flushes again, and she emerges sheepishly from the stall.

"I didn't know anyone was here," she says as our eyes meet in the mirror. "No one can know about this. Do you understand?"

"I understand," I tell her.

We lock gazes for a few seconds before Carrie quietly goes off to her room.

I am 19 years old.

The Perfect Evening

◆

I take a shopping basket from the floor as I enter Lofton's Market on the upper east side. The round face of a young man unpacking oranges from a wooden crate brightens when he sees me.

"Can I help you?" he asks pleasantly.

"I'll let you know," I answer, returning his smile.

From the exquisite spread of produce, I painstakingly select three plum tomatoes, a bulb of garlic, a handful of shitake mushrooms, and a bundle each of fresh basil and thyme.

At the counter, I request a half pound of lemon-pepper pasta, a dozen tiger shrimp, a loaf of sourdough bread, and directions to the closest liquor store. "Take a right out the front door," the matronly clerk says. "It's about three blocks down on the other side of the street."

I head down the boulevard debating between Cabernet and champagne. In Campus Liquor's window, I spot an ad for my favorite brand of Asti. Finding the display, I grab a bottle and walk swiftly to the cashier.

I stop next outside Fawnridge Mall. Rushing past the usual Friday afternoon crowds, I find my destination. As I cross the threshold, I am struck by the sensual mixture of English garden body lotions, strawberry and vanilla sachets, and flowery perfumes. "Welcome to Victoria's Secret," a saleswoman beams.

"Thanks. I'm looking for something special for tonight."

She first brings out a red push-up bra and matching panties.

"Overstated," I say, shaking my head.

"How about this?" the saleswoman asks, pointing to a long peach nightgown.

"Too innocent."

"I have another idea," she says, taking me to the adjoining room. "What about *this*?" On a satin hanger, the saleswoman presents a deep violet camisole set, silk with lace overlay.

"Perfect," I say. "Now, do you have tapered candles?"

An hour later, I slip into a leisurely bubble bath. I wash my hair twice, apply a deep conditioner, shave my legs, and cleanse every inch with a soapy sponge.

After drying off, I dust myself with Obsession powder and dot cologne behind my ears, down my neck, and across my wrists. I curl, tease, and spray my hair into place. Just the right shade of brown on my eyelids, precise lines of coral blush on my cheekbones, and two swoops of Amber Blaze lipstick—I feel attractive and inviting. Under a dangerously low-cut black dress, I hide the Victorian secret.

My kitchen awakens to scents of olive oil, dry cooking wine, and Italian spices. The roommates have been chased out; the table has been set.

I greet Michael at the door with a kiss. Taking his coat, I show him to his seat and serve the candle-lit dinner. I watch hungrily for expressions on his face but find none. "He must be tired," I think to myself. After the meal, I direct him to the bedroom as I finish the dishes.

A few minutes later, I find him lying on the bed reading a magazine. I close the door behind me, and my heart pounds with anticipation. "Stay there," I say.

I toss my shoes aside and unzip the back of my dress. Sliding it slowly, deliberately down my body, I uncover the violet number. With a "tah-dah" gesture, I smile at him.

He sits up on the bed. "Is that all?" he asks.

"What do you mean *all?*"

"I mean I'm not an adolescent boy who gets excited just by looking at you."

Silence.

I grab a robe from the closet. Opening the bedroom door, I pause, wanting to say something. But I don't. I stride across the hall and into the bathroom. The bolt clicks as I turn it.

I lift the toilet seat and kneel on the floor. Choking back tears, I push my finger deep in my throat. I watch as the remains of fresh plum tomatoes, shitake mushrooms, and lemon-pepper pasta descend from my mouth into the water below.

I am 20 years old.

Alternate Endings
◆

I dislike the ending of that story, so I've written two alternate versions. In the first, I, the heroine, slap Michael's stupid face. It feels surprisingly good (but I know I'd never do it). In the second, I, the heroine, bounce back with a seething comment of my own. I tell him, "Lots of other men get excited when they look at me, and I think it's time I dated them."

This latter version seems consistent with the strong, intelligent woman I hope I am. What the hell was wrong with me then? Why did I walk out of the bedroom instead of out of that relationship? Why did I punish myself instead of him?

◆ ◆ ◆

How do I disclose and to whom? Under what conditions does disclosure become relevant? Give it language, it becomes exposed to air. It breathes, it's alive: to tell is to make real (Butler and Rosenblum 1991, 39).

The deepest wound was the hunger to be seen. To be heard. To be understood (Butler and Rosenblum 1991, 71).

My First Confession
◆

My cheek presses against his chest. His breathing shifts over from consciousness to sleep.

Do it, Lisa. Don't wait.

"Douglas?" my strained voice calls out.

"Umhmm . . . "

"There's something I need to tell you."

Probably not a good opening line.

"What's that?" he asks.

"I know I should have told you this before, and I hope you won't be upset that I didn't." Deep breath. Swallow.

It's okay. You're doing fine.

"What is it?" he asks, more insistent this time.

Loooong pause. "Lisa, what is it?"

He's getting nervous. Spit it out.

"Oh, god, Douglas. I don't . . . I . . . shit!"

You've come too far. Don't fall apart. Just say it, Lisa. Say the words.

"To one degree or another . . . I have been . . . bulimic . . .

Fuck! I hate the sound of that word.

. . . since I was 15."

It's out there. You said it.

He pulls me closer. "Who knows about this?"

"A few old friends and some people I go to school with."

"Your family?"

Oh god. Here we go.

"No . . . I haven't told them."

Boom!

"Jesus," he says.

No kidding.

"Well, how bad is it now?"

"It has been much worse."
"That's not what I asked."
"It's not that bad."
Liar.
"Have you done it since you met me?"
If you only knew.
"A couple of times, but I don't want you to be concerned."
Oh, please. Please be concerned.
"You must know what that does to your body."
Believe me, I know. I know everything.
"I'm really glad you told me," he says as I start to cry.
"I love you, Lisa. Tell me how I can help you. Please."
You just did. You can't imagine how much.
He pulls me close, stroking my hair until I go to sleep.
I am 22 years old.

Peanut Butter Cookies

This ordinary summer morning,
   you say,
      "I will bake some peanut butter cookies.
      I will use the extra creamy peanut butter
      to make them smooth . . .
                        . . . so smooth.
      And we will eat them soft and warm."

I watch closely as you whip the honey
   and brown sugar
   into the extra creamy peanut butter.

The mixing complete, your gentle caress
   rolls spoonfuls of dough
   into tiny, sweet balls.

I crisscross these with a fork,
   then sprinkle them lightly
   with Hawaiian cane sugar.

Tray after tray,
    we prepare our morning treats
    in this way.

A few moments pass,
    and the scent of
    extra creamy peanut butter creations

                air.
            the
        into
    escapes

I peer through the oven window
    like some Pavlovian dog,
    waiting . . . wanting.

After nine long minutes,
    we serve them with milk
    and eat them soft and warm.

In and out the baking sheets go,
    until, at last,
    our cookie jar sits full.

We smile in culinary delight.

When you leave to take your shower,
    a little girl sneaks two more
    and feels rather devilish.

At twenty-five minutes to one,
    I see you putting on a tie.

"What are you doing?" I ask,
    trying to conceal my brewing panic.
    "I thought you had the day off."

"No, baby,"
  you tell me,
  "that's tomorrow."

Tomorrow.

  Oh . . . oh . . . nooo.
  No, no not tomorrow.
  I need you here . . .
                    . . . today.

  I need you because . . .
               . . . because . . . I . . .

Don't you see
  I can't be alone with them?

There are so many.
  So many,
  so soft,
  so warm,
  so. . .
      . . . over
        whelming.

As you kiss me goodbye
  I want to scream,
  "No! Please stay here
  and protect me from them. . .
               . . . from myself."

But I don't.

I can't speak the words because
  you won't understand.
  After all, they're
    so little,
    so. . . innocuous.

The door closes behind you
  with a resolute   thud!
  and I am left alone. . .
         . . . alone with five dozen
         soft and warm
         extra creamy
         peanut butter
         cookies.

Poetic Interactions
◆

In January of 1995, I sobbed through the construction of "Peanut Butter Cookies." I felt as out of control writing about the incident as I did living it six months before. For several weeks, I pressed the Page Down key when I came to the place in my manuscript where the poem appeared. For whatever reason, that piece hit me hard. Between January and June, I gained some distance from it. More and more, I found myself able to examine "Peanut Butter Cookies" critically, to make revisions, and eventually to read it aloud.

Today is June 10, and I see "Peanut Butter Cookies" quite differently. As I read about mixing ingredients and ponder "soft and warm" cookies, I feel unadulterated hunger. The words on the blue screen blur as I mentally scan the refrigerator and cupboards. "There's nothing here to binge on," I think to myself. So I compare the distances between my house and the nearest bakery, McDonald's, and the corner grocery. . . "No!" I scream, pounding the keyboard. I force myself to read on.

Holiday Pies
I received the photograph you sent, Mom—
a Norman Rockwell sort of family (our family),
surrounded by holiday pies.
  The season is upon us, Mom.
  Upon us.

I'm sorry I'm not in this picture, Mom.
I know how your heart longs for me
in these weeks nestled
between Thanksgiving and New Year's.
    But I can't get away, Mom.
    I can't.

I hold dear a memory of a Christmas long ago, Mom,
when I sat in our old kitchen
admiring how your hands kneaded and braided
special crusts for holiday pies.
    I remember, Mom.
    I remember.

I wanted the photo to hang on my refrigerator, Mom.
But you had written so clearly in red ink,
"Incomplete without Lisa."
    You have no idea, Mom.
    No idea.

I'm sorry *I'm not in this picture,* Mom.
But I no longer smile at holiday pies.
In fact, I'm now rather afraid of them.
    Why is that, Mom?
    Why?

I'm not the person you think I am, Mom.
I fear I've lost so much
since those blessed childhood Christmases.
    But I'm trying to find my way again, Mom.
    I'm trying.

I read the note hiding behind the photograph, Mom.
You said you wished we could share
a cup of Christmas tea and a slice of holiday pie,
like mothers and daughters should.
    Some day, Mom.
    Some day.

A Private Celebration
◆

I sit down to Christmas dinner at Andy's apartment. It feels strange to be here, among colleagues, instead of at my parents' house in Minnesota, surrounded by quirky relatives.

The food covers Andy's small table and kitchen counter. Pretty much the usual—a roasted turkey, mashed potatoes, candied yams, two salads, homemade bread, relishes, and, of course, pumpkin and pecan pies. I wait for the feeling of alarm to come over me, the sweat to bead at the base of my neck. To my surprise, it doesn't.

I take a little of everything onto my plate. I pepper my turkey, dress my salad, and butter my potatoes and bread. It all tastes very familiar—delicious—and scary.

After the meal, we laugh, drink, and assemble a puzzle. An hour passes, and Andy serves the pie.

"Pecan or pumpkin?" he asks me.

"A little of both please," I request.

Ten minutes later, I get up from the table. When I excuse myself, Doug looks at me with narrowing eyes. "Don't do it," they seem to plead.

I close the bathroom door and move toward the toilet. Automatically, I put my finger in my mouth. I hold it there for several seconds, then slowly slide it out. I turn to my reflection in the mirror above the sink and watch myself for a long time. Washing my hands, I can't believe what I'm about to do—walk away.

When I rejoin the men at the table, I smile at Doug. With what might be relief, he smiles back. Maybe later I'll tell him that this is the first holiday dinner I haven't purged since 1986.

I am 23 years old.

Epilogue
◆

If my paper were a medical or psychological report, this section would contain the author's definitive conclusions aimed at explaining, predicting, and controlling bulimia. If it were a TV drama, the "cured" protagonist would be moving on to a normal life. But this is my story, and it is a story without resolution. Unlike popular culture depictions, mine isn't a tale of fighting my eating disorder, overcoming it, and living happily, healthily ever after. Bulimia is not a one-time battle I have won; it is an ongoing struggle with food, body, self, and meaning.

It may frustrate some that I close without revealing "what it all means." But, as Robert Coles (1989, 47) tells us, "the beauty of a good story is its openness—the way you or I or anyone reading it can take it in, and use it for ourselves."

At the same time, I purposefully told my story *this way*. I wrote a sensual text to pull you away from the abstractions and categories that fill traditional research on eating disorders and into the *experience* (Parry 1991, 42), to help you engage how bulimia *feels*. I used multiple forms to mimic the complex and multilayered nature of food addiction. Wanting the action to unfold before your eyes, I wrote most episodes in present tense. Later, (with the exception of the opening piece) I arranged these chronologically to guide you along my nine-year journey. I then interjected three experiences I had *as a reader* of my own work to show you that I continue to "experience the experiences" (Ellis and Bochner 1992) in new and different ways.

Originally, "Holiday Pies" closed the narrative section, but I felt uncomfortable leaving you (and me!) there. I added "A Private Celebration" recently, an ending that seems quite appropriate. It does not offer the tidy conclusion that some might want. But it does suggest movement toward a new and better place, a place of self-acceptance and empowerment. I suppose my "narrative challenge" (Bochner 1994, 31) will be to live more fully as the kind of character I became at the end of my story.

Before I began this project, I couldn't understand why "someone like me"—bright, educated, feminist—would binge and purge. I have since looked long and hard at the family and cultural stories that surround(ed) me. In the context of those stories—stories that teach all of us to relate pathologically to food and to our bodies, stories told and repeated at home, at school, and in the media—bulimia no longer seems an illogical "choice."

Often, I'll admit, the personal and professional risks of writing about my relationship with bulimia have overwhelmed me. Did I really want you to know this? What would you think of my work? How would you feel about *me*?

Still, I knew I had something to say that wasn't being said. I knew I could show you in detail how a bulimic *lives*, and I wanted you to know.

Perhaps you already knew; if so, I offer this account as comfort and companionship. If you didn't, I offer it as instruction. I hope that my lived experience helps maintain a critical attitude toward many of our culture's stories of body and food and helps create new and better stories that direct us toward healthier bodies and more contented hearts.

References

Armstrong, J. G., and D. M. Roth. 1989. "Attachment and Separation Difficulties in Eating Disorders: A Preliminary Investigation." *International Journal of Eating Disorders* 8: 141–155.

Baumeister, R. F., and L. S. Newman. 1994. "How Stories Make Sense of Personal Experiences: Motives that Shape Autobiographical Narratives." *Personality and Social Psychology Bulletin* 20: 676–690.

Bernstein, F. 1986. "Bulimia: A Woman's Terror." *People Weekly* 26: 36–41.

Bochner, A. P. 1994. "Perspectives on Inquiry II: Theories and Stories." In *Handbook of Interpersonal Communication*, edited by M. L. Knapp and G. R. Miller. Thousand Oaks, CA: Sage.

Breslow, M., A. Yates, and C. Shisslak. 1986. "Spontaneous Rupture of the Stomach: A Complication of Bulimia." *International Journal of Eating Disorders* 5: 137–142.

Brewerton, T. D., and M. S. George. 1993. "Is Migraine Related to the Eating Disorders?" *International Journal of Eating Disorders* 14: 75–79.

Bulik, C. M., P. F. Sullivan, L. H. Epstein, M. McKee, W. H. Kaye, R. E. Dahl, and T. E. Weltzin. 1992. "Drug Use in Women with Anorexia and Bulimia Nervosa." *International Journal of Eating Disorders* 11: 213–225.

Butler, S., and B. Rosenblum. 1991. *Cancer in Two Voices*. San Francisco: spinsters book company.

Chandy, J. M., L. Harris, R. W. Blum, and M. D. Resnick. 1995. "Female Adolescents of Alcohol Misusers: Disordered Eating Features." *International Journal of Eating Disorders* 17: 283–289.

Coles, R. 1989. *The Call of Stories: Teaching and the Moral Imagination*. Boston: Houghton Mifflin.

Cooper, P. J., Z. Cooper, and C. Hill. 1989. "Behavioral Treatment of Bulimia Nervosa." *International Journal of Eating Disorders* 8: 87–92.

Crane, R. A., V. Raskin, M. Weiler, J. Perri, T. H. Jobe, J. Anderson, and B. Burg. 1987. "Nomifensine Treatment of Bulimia: Results of an Open Trial." *International Journal of Eating Disorders* 6: 427–430.

Crowther, J. H., G. Post, and L. Zaynor. 1985. "The Prevalence of Bulimia and Binge Eating in Adolescent Girls." *International Journal of Eating Disorders* 4: 29–42.

Ellis, C. 1991. "Sociological Introspection and Emotional Experience." *Symbolic Interaction* 14: 23–50.

Ellis, C., and A. P. Bochner. 1992. "Telling and Performing Personal Stories: The Constraints of Choice in Abortion." In *Investigating Subjectivity*, edited by C. Ellis and M. G. Flaherty. Newbury Park, CA: Sage.

Erb, J. L., H. E. Gwirtsman, J. M. Fuster, and S. H. Richeimer. 1989. "Bulimia Associated with Frontal Lobe Lesions." *International Journal of Eating Disorders* 8: 117–121.

Franko, D. L., and B. E. Walton. 1993. "Pregnancy and Eating Disorders: A Review and Clinical Implications." *International Journal of Eating Disorders* 13: 41–48.

Goldbloom, D. S., B. Zinman, L. K. Hicks, and P. E. Garfinkel. 1992. "The Baseline Metabolic State in Bulimia Nervosa: Abnormality and Adaptation." *International Journal of Eating Disorders* 12: 171–178.

Gray, J. J., and K. Ford. 1985. "The Incidence of Bulimia in a College Sample." *International Journal of Eating Disorders* 4: 201–210.

Greenberg, B. R. 1986. "Predictors of Binge Eating in Bulimic and Nonbulimic Women." *International Journal of Eating Disorders* 5: 269–284.

Heilbrun, A. B., and D. L. Bloomfield. 1986. "Cognitive Differences Between Bulimic and Anorexic Females: Self-Control Deficits in Bulimia." *International Journal of Eating Disorders* 5: 209–222.

Huon, G. F. 1985. "An Initial Validation of a Self-Help Program for Bulimia." *International Journal of Eating Disorders* 4: 573–588.

Jackson, M. 1989. *Paths Toward a Clearing: Radical Empiricism and Ethnographic Inquiry*. Bloomington: Indiana University Press.

Kohn, V. 1987. "The Body Prison: A Bulimic's Compulsion to Eat More, Eat Less, Add Muscle, Get Thinner." *Life* 10: 44.

Lacey, J. H., S. Coker, and S. A. Birtchnell. 1986. "Bulimia: Factors Associated with its Etiology and Maintenance." *International Journal of Eating Disorders* 5: 475–487.

Lee, N. F., and A. J. Rush. 1986. "Cognitive-Behavioral Group Therapy For Bulimia." *International Journal of Eating Disorders* 5: 599–615.

Mitchell, P. B. 1988. "The Pharmacological Management of Bulimia Nervosa: A Critical Review." *International Journal of Eating Disorders* 7: 29–41.

Mizes, J. S., and E. L. Fleece. 1986. "On the Use of Progressive Relaxation in the Treatment of Bulimia: A Single-Subject Design Study." *International Journal of Eating Disorders* 5: 169–176.

Neil, J. 1980. "Eating Their Cake and Heaving it Too." *MacLean's* 93: 51–52.

O'Connor, M., S. Touyz, and P. Beumont. 1988. "Nutritional Management and Dietary Counseling in Bulimia Nervosa: Some Preliminary Observations." *International Journal of Eating Disorders* 7: 657–662.

Parry, A. 1991. "A Universe of Stories." *Family Process* 30: 37–54.

Parry-Jones, B., and W. L. Parry-Jones. 1991. "Bulimia: An Archival Review of Its History in Psychosomatic Medicine." *International Journal of Eating Disorders* 10: 129–143.

Pertschuk, M., M. Collins, J. Kreisberg, and S. S. Fager. 1986. "Psychiatric Symptoms Associated with Eating Disorder in a College Population." *International Journal of Eating Disorders* 5: 563–568.

Philipp, E., K. M. Pirke, M. Seidl, R. J. Tuschl, M. M. Fichter, M. Eckert, and G. Wolfram. 1988. "Vitamin Status in Patients with Anorexia Nervosa and Bulimia Nervosa." *International Journal of Eating Disorders* 8: 209–218.

Philipp, E., B. Willershausen-Zonnchen, G. Hamm, and K. M. Pirke. 1991. "Oral and Dental Characteristics in Bulimic and Anoretic Patients." *International Journal of Eating Disorders* 10: 423–431.

Pitts, C., and G. Waller. 1993. "Self-Denigratory Beliefs Following Sexual Abuse: Association with the Symptomology of Bulimic Disorders. *International Journal of Eating Disorders* 13: 407–410.

Rosenzweig, M., and J. Spruill. 1987. "Twenty Years After Twiggy: A Retrospective Investigation of Bulimic-Like Behaviors." *International Journal of Eating Disorders* 6: 59–65.

Russell, G. 1979. "Bulimia Nervosa: An Ominous Variant of Anorexia Nervosa." *Psychological Medicine* 9: 429–448.

Skodol, A. E., J. M. Oldham, S. E. Hyler, H. D. Kellman, N. Doidge, and M. Davies. 1993. "Comorbidity of DSM-III-R Eating Disorders and Personality Disorders." *International Journal of Eating Disorders* 14: 403–416.

Striegel-Moore, R. H., and E. S. Huydic. 1993. "Problem Drinking and Symptoms of Disordered Eating in Female High School Students." *International Journal of Eating Disorders* 14: 417–425.

Stuber, M., and M. Strober. 1987. "Group Therapy in the Treatment of Adolescents with Bulimia: Some Preliminary Observations." *International Journal of Eating Disorders* 6: 125–131.

Thompson, D. A., K. M. Berg, and L. A. Shatford. 1987. "The Heterogeneity of Bulimic Symptomology: Cognitive and Behavioral Dimensions." *International Journal of Eating Disorders* 6: 215–234.

Tobin, D. L., C. L. Johnson, and A. B. Dennis. 1992. "Divergent Forms of Purging Behavior in Bulimia Nervosa Patients." *International Journal of Eating Disorders* 11: 17–24.

Vanderlinden, J., and W. Vandereycken. 1988. "The Use of Hynotherapy in the Treatment of Eating Disorders." *International Journal of Eating Disorders* 7: 673–679.

Williams, G. J., K. G. Power, H. R. Millar, C. P. Freeman, A. Yellowlees, T. Dowds, M. Walker, L. Campsie, F. MacPherson, and M. A. Jackson. 1993. "Comparison of Eating Disorders and Other Dietary/Weight Groups on Measures of Perceived Control, Assertiveness, Self-Esteem, and Self-Directed Hostility." *International Journal of Eating Disorders* 14: 27–32.

Yerby, J., N. Buerkel-Rothfuss, and A. P. Bochner. 1995. *Understanding Family Communication* Scottsdale, AZ: Gorsuch Scarisbrick, Publishers.

◆───────────

Lisa M. Tillmann-Healy moved to Tampa, Florida in 1993 to join the Ph.D. program in communication at the University of South Florida, where she developed interests in relationship, interpretive, and narrative studies. When she breaks from scholarship, Lisa takes long walks and plays with her husband, Doug, whom she married on New Year's Eve, 1995.

The author wishes to thank Art Bochner, Carolyn Ellis, Eric Eisenberg, Larry Wright, Linda Andrews, and Jennifer Pickman for their many careful readings of this text.

CHAPTER THREE

My Mother Is Mentally Retarded

Carol Rambo Ronai

In her 20s, my mother, Suzanne, was a full-figured, green-eyed blonde who tanned easily as she strolled the streets on her daily walks. Frequently, she evoked catcalls from the men who drove by. Now she is 60 years old, stands 5 feet 4 inches, weighs 200 pounds, and has the emotional maturity of a 7-year-old.

With a few exceptions, Suzanne is generally harmless. When I was a child, she was the one who yelled and stamped her feet in the store if she did not get her way. I was the one who gave in, hoping to calm her and avoid further embarrassment. One Thanksgiving she locked the entire family out of the house because, as she put it, "Everyone is ignoring me." On other occasions, she ruined holiday meals by pouting, yelling, or otherwise making a scene at the dinner table. Once she rolled up a newspaper and beat my grandmother so hard that she ripped the skin off the surface of my grandmother's forearm.

My mother's intelligence quotient score has been estimated by several psychologists in social service capacities to range from 65 to 80. Reading at a second- or third-grade level, she stumbles over the text and makes up phrases when she cannot identify words. Although she has no math ability, she possesses a wide repertoire of television and movie trivia.

When people first meet Suzanne, they don't know anything is "off" until they have spoken with her for a while. She monopolizes the conversation with talk of television and her life. Those who are patient find a way to leave politely after a few minutes; others bolt immediately. She is the butt of many jokes which, mercifully, are told behind her back or go over her head.

Suzanne enjoys hanging around malls and talking to salespeople, store managers, or anyone who shows an interest in her. On occasion she has been asked by nervous clerks to leave their store because they were concerned that she was shoplifting or driving away customers. She also watches a great deal of television, avidly reads children's books, colors in coloring books, paints by numbers, assembles simple crafts, and sings in the church choir. Giving the appearance of living a full life, she stays alone in an apartment paid for by a trust fund set up by my grandmother.

There is no sociological literature on mentally retarded parenting. The research that exists has been published by psychiatrists and social workers. Their work usually conforms to the medical model in which having a mentally retarded parent is equated with having a pathological condition that must be evaluated (Tymchuk 1991; Stoneman 1989; Feldman et. al. 1986; Robinson 1978) and treated (Whitman, Graves, and Accardo 1989; Heighway, Kidd-Webster, and Snodgrass 1988; Peterson, Robinson, and Littman 1983).

The mentally retarded parents in these studies were evaluated by researchers using psychometric questionnaires. As participants in social service culture, they were readily available subjects, accustomed to answering surveys. None was empowered by this methodology to define their lives using any other categories except those presented by their caseworkers. Similar to Ellis and Bochner's (1992, 97) discussion on abortion research, mentally retarded parenting is "a subject so steeped in political ideology and indignation that its experiential side can be forgotten and neglected." Specifically, the literature has ignored the lived experience of children of mentally retarded parents. Because little is known about the relationship of mentally retarded parents and their children, few guidelines exist for how to act in various social situations, and identity construction becomes problematic.

In this paper, I use the format of a layered account (Ronai 1995, 1992) and a method called sociological introspection (Ellis 1991) to present my own experience of being the daughter of a mentally retarded mother. Following Ellis and Bochner (1992, 97), I explore issues such as "What is one's point of reference for knowing how to act?" and "What is it like to live through an experience that potentially places you in a muddle of uncertainty, doubt, contradiction, and ambivalence?"

According to a 1994 broadcast of *48 Hours,* roughly 90% of all mentally retarded people are thought to be victims of sexual abuse. I often wonder, was my mother raped or coerced? Did she agree to have sex with my father? Did he attack her as he attacked both of us when we lived with him? Can a retarded person give consent if she does not fully understand human sexuality? Why do these thoughts occupy my consciousness? Wanted, unwanted, the result of a sexual assault—why do I care?

To understand my mother and me, you need to know that our relationship was embedded within the context of our relationships with my grandmother and father.

When I was 8 years old, my father left us on Grandmother's (my mother's mother) doorstep. Shortly thereafter, he was arrested for indecent exposure. When news of his arrest appeared in the local newspaper, all of Grandmother's friends called to offer their "condolences." Although Grandmother was not wealthy, she came from a well-to-do family and had pretensions of being a socialite. My father's arrest humiliated her. In her anger, Grandmother informed me, "Don't expect much from me. I have to take care of you, but I don't have to like it. I told your mother to have an abortion, but she wouldn't. You shouldn't be here. You shouldn't be alive. You just shouldn't be, given the way Suzanne and your father are."

I shrunk inside when Grandmother said this. I had fantasized about living like a regular little girl, in a regular house, attending a regular school. I wanted normalcy so badly, trusted the situation too much, and from the great heights of hope I plunged into new depths of betrayal. I really was a scummy little girl. I really wasn't ever going to be allowed to be regular, happy, and safe. It was stupid to think it could all work out, since it never had before. I just assumed everything was going to be all right. Now, I feared something was wrong with me and it had to do with who my mother and father were. My new existence was to be one of walking on eggshells, just like my old existence; except now, instead of avoiding beatings and sex with my father, I had to avoid the furnace blast of my grandmother's blatant hatred of me.

The entire time I lived with my grandmother, she never cuddled, comforted, nor offered affection. She received my hugs, but never gave them. If she purchased a Christmas present for me (actually, she gave Aunt Kathy a small sum to buy everyone a gift, but Kathy added money of her own because she was embarrassed by Grandmother's penury), I had to approach her chair, reach out and down, and put my arms around her bony body and hug her. I was careful not to hug too hard, because she was fragile. I was careful not to hug too lightly, because the hug might seem insincere. She always told us that we took it for granted that she was financially supporting us. A fake hug would be a sure sign she was right.

If I brought her flowers, she would put them in a glass of water and say nothing. One evening, when I was a third grader, I created a "Greatest Grandmother of the Year" award for her using construction paper, tape, and crayons and awarded it to her in front of her friends. I asked her, "What do you think of your award?" She responded, "What do you expect me to do with that? Wear it to work?"

Grandmother daily told mother and me what an enormous favor she was doing by taking us in, describing as she did a life of bridge, cocktail parties, and social events she could not take part in. It was clear that we owed her a debt we could never repay. We brought the roaches with us (according to Grandmother) and we had destroyed her life.

None of this gives me a clear reason to be angry at my mother. This was Grandmother's interpretation of my existence, not my mother's. So why is it that when I am with my mother I am just barely able to keep my anger in check and unable to restrain myself from correcting her speech and behavior? I can't stand the way Suzanne breathes: how she huffs when she doesn't get her way; how she puffs when she is out of breath from walking because she has let herself get weak and fat; the way her outward affect is often so melodramatic that I can't tell what her emotions or needs "really" are because I'm forced to second-guess them through her obvious attempts to get attention. I can only last a few hours around her before I am enraged and making everyone's life miserable. Why?

My mother stood nearby as he grabbed my small arm, practically pulling it out of the socket. "No," I said, planting my feet and pulling away, "I don't want to." "You know you like it," he said, pulling me toward the bed. "I don't like it today," I said, flinging all my weight in the opposite direction in an effort to counterbalance his pulling on me. If I put up enough resistance, sometimes he would give up, regarding the whole matter as not worth the effort. This time the strategy wasn't working. My feet were dragging across the multicolored shag rug of the efficiency apartment, burning from the friction. "No," I screamed, flinging my bottom to the floor as he continued to drag me. When I kicked at him and missed, he laughed affectionately, as if reacting to something "cute" I might have done.

Upon seeing the violence I was willing to employ, my mother intervened and pulled on my other arm. "It's her bedtime, Frank, let her be," my mother stated. "Since when?" he asked, dubious of my mother's motives, forgetting to pull me for a second. "It has always been 8:00, 'cause she has to get up to go to school in the morning," my mother replied, yanking my right arm, pulling me away from him. He thought about this for a moment, then pulled my left arm and stated, "That can't be right; it's too long to sleep." My mother and father pulled on me back and forth like this for several rounds.

Each time my mother pulled I leaned into her direction, hoping to break his grasp and run. Ultimately "logic" won out. "I'm her father and I'm setting a new bedtime, 8:30." I flashed a desperate look to my mother as she let go. "There's nothing I can do," she said, as she turned her back and left for the bathroom. "NO!" I screamed, vibrating from the effort to keep the word airborne. "No, no, no," I whimpered as he dragged me to the bed, raking my panties down my legs, scratching long red welts with his nails. "No," escaped from my lips, now barely a whispered sigh as he parted my legs and descended, face first, between them. "You always like this once we get started," he said. "Not today," I replied, watching my mother watch from the bathroom doorway.

I resent having to take care of her when she did such a poor job of taking care of me. She not only let my father beat me and sexually abuse me, sometimes even delivering me to him for that purpose, but she sexually abused me herself (see Ronai 1995, 415–416). According to Finkelhor and Hotaling (1984), 81% of incest occurs with the male alone, 11% with the female alone, and 9% with both. When both are involved:

> the abuse occurs on the initiative and at the direction of the male . . . when a female is a participant in such a situation, it is usually only in the sense of being an observer or being directed by the male to participate (1984, 27).

Similarly, Tymchuck (1992, 167) notes of mentally retarded mothers:

> Where purposeful abuse does occur, often it is a result of another person associated with the mother rather than the mother herself, including a husband or partner (either male or female) who is emotionally disturbed.

Reading this, I tell myself, "Remember she is retarded, didn't know better, was abused by my father also, and is as much a victim as I am." I see the words. I understand that others may think I should get over it, but I can't let her off the hook. I know she knew better.

In the third grade I was exposed to an antidrug and crime program called Junior Deputies, sponsored by the sheriff's department. While participating in the program, I ran across the term *sexual molestation* in a pamphlet. I showed it to my grandmother who defined the term for me. Knowing these words described what my parents had done to me, I took the pamphlet to my mother and asked her the meaning of sexual molestation. She looked up at me, her eyes huge, as if caught in the glare of oncoming traffic with no escape, and said, "Something parents should never do to their children." I said, "Oh, you mean like what you and Frank did to me?" She turned away and said, "Yes." Nothing more was ever mentioned about this topic.

I resent the imperative to pretend that all is normal with my family, an imperative that is enforced by silence, secrecy, and "you don't talk about this to anyone" rhetoric. Our pretense is designed to make events flow smoothly, but it doesn't work. Everyone is plastic and fake around my mother, including me. Why? Because no one has told her to her face that she is retarded. We say we don't want to upset her. I don't think we are ready to deal with her reaction to the truth. Something inside me longs to tell her so that she finally will be able to explain to herself the events in her life, yet I don't know if she would be able to understand this information.

Because of Suzanne, and because of how the family as a unit has chosen to deal with the problem, I have compartmentalized a whole segment of my life into a lie. It is not fair to blame my mother, but part of me cries out to her, "How dare you passively sit back while everyone takes care of you?" and "Why don't you demand to know what is going on around you?" and "Why does there always seem to be something everyone else knows that you don't, as if there is an inside joke circulating that no one will tell you because no one thinks you will get it?"

The government has contributed to the pretense that everything is normal. They won't certify her as too retarded to hold a job, but they will provide her job training. I worked many hours, on three separate occasions over an eight-year period, to get her vocational rehabilitation. Each time she stopped the counseling and vocational training the moment my back was turned. Since social service workers cannot force services on anyone, and since Suzanne has to want the help, no one can do anything about it. And so we go on protecting her from the truth, lying, keeping silent and pretending everything is perfectly normal. In a sense we are complicit agents in her failure. If she did not have us, if she did not have the trust fund, if she could not go on living this fiction, she would be forced to go out and get job training. When I was 5 years old, my father went to prison for a year and a half for sexually assaulting someone. During that time my mother obtained federal housing, food stamps, and other Aid to Families with Dependent

Children by following the social workers' instructions to the letter. When survival was problematic, Suzanne came through for us. So where is her fighting spirit now? Somewhere in my gut, I just *know* she is being lazy.

Klein (1990) notes that children of mentally disturbed parents tend to develop coping strategies that exhibit exaggerated independence, autonomy, and self-reliance relative to their developmental stage. When I was 10, Grandmother said she was sick of supporting us and we had to find a way to contribute or she was going to kick us out. My mother and I applied for welfare, which included Aid to Families with Dependent Children (AFDC) and food stamps. When my mother and I met with the social worker, my mother threw a temper tantrum, refused to answer questions or fill out any forms, and stormed out of the AFDC office. I panicked, asked the social worker to wait, ran after my mother, and begged her to come back. When she returned, I filled out the forms and answered the social worker's questions. Later, when my mother went to the bathroom, the social worker came to me with tears in her eyes, hugged me, and said, "God, this must be awful for you."

I saw myself through her eyes and realized what a spectacle my mother and I must have made, and yet it was OK. I was the kid here; it was not my fault. Someone finally understood how hard this was for me. Self-consciousness and relief swept over me, simultaneously flushing my face and filling my eyes with tears that I fought to control. "Poor baby," she said maternally, motioning to two of the other workers. The concern and sympathy on all of their faces were too much. My body went limp in her arms as the dam burst and tears flowed. I shouldn't have been doing this, but it felt so good. Crying was not allowed at home. When it occurred, it was handled much like masturbation—you do it in private and hope you don't get caught.

My mother came out of the bathroom, saw me crying, screwed her face up, and said, "What's she acting like that for?" The other two workers led her away from me, telling her that everything was going to be all right. Our caseworker took me aside and showed me how to answer the questions differently so that she could approve us for aid. It was important that these questions were answered the same way every year. I understood that I was going to be responsible for this process from now on.

I went from tears to elation. I had gotten us the welfare. It was only $1,400 a year, $120 a month in food stamps, plus Medicaid, but that was substantial enough to impress Grandmother. Later, I explained the process to Grandmother, the amount of money we were to expect, and how I would have to stand in line each month to pick up the food stamps. She stared at me and said nothing.

From that moment on, I was the designated deal with government aid hitter. I ended up applying for Social Security for Suzanne (which she was not disabled enough to get), I arranged for her to go to vocational rehabilitation, and each year, I applied for welfare with my mother in tow.

As time wore on, my grandmother depended on me to run her errands at the Social Security office, buy her liquor and cigarettes (by 14 I already looked the legal drinking and smoking age of 18, so no one ever carded me), purchase certificates of deposit, balance her checkbook, and make out the checks to pay the bills.

I look at what I just wrote. All of it is true, yet I haven't told you the worst of it. I am disgusted that this creature, Suzanne, is my mother. She is horrifying, vile, potentially defective genetic material, someone I or my child might take after. Half of all I am came from her, and the rest from Frank, the friendly neighborhood sexual psychopath. Most of my childhood training was placed in their capable hands. How do I explain this to myself? Are they who I am? Like it or not, their identities, their biographies, partially shape who I am.

I cannot let my thoughts dwell here for very long because none of this makes sense. There is no "right" answer to find. The meta-narratives on child rearing handed to me by psychologists and other child care experts do not match my experience. I am an assistant professor with a Ph.D. I have a good relationship with my husband. I have a healthy, happy baby. So why is it I often feel as if I am missing something? Am I missing something because my mother was retarded and my father a sexual psychopath? Or am I letting the idea that I am supposed to be missing something structure my discourse on my identity and my emotions? Or is it that everyone feels as if they are missing something? How do I know when my feelings are normal?

In *Newsweek*, a woman named Betty Graves, program director of "Parents Learning Together," said that none of the children of mentally retarded parents "is going to reach the potential they might have reached" (Kantrowitz, King, and Witherspoon 1986, 62). Reading this is a slam in the gut. I suspect many people worry about whether or not they have reached their potential. As I sit here typing this, I doubt my own abilities. I don't speed-read, my writing needs work, and I did not graduate from an Ivy League school. Always, I can hunt down deficiencies in my abilities and my biography that instill self-doubt.

This, in turn, makes me angry. How dare this woman tell me I am not going to realize my potential. Aren't retarded people and their children everywhere grateful for her existence? I hope her repressive discourse doesn't hinder her from realizing all her potential as program director. If she doesn't expect much from the children of her clients, she will not get much and she will burden them with cumbersome labels and a doubtful self-identity. Never mind that her remark in *Newsweek* has contributed negative discourse to the stock of knowledge about children of mentally retarded parents.

Blowing off steam like that felt good. I was self-righteous, indignant, sure of myself. My ambivalence was held at bay. Getting angry is an excellent form of self-defense. I bring both Graves's selfhood and her potential discourse about my self into question. It allows me to dismiss the possibility that I will not reach my "potential," or at least it shields me for now from internalizing this idea into my identity.

According to researchers, I don't have a good reason to bring my own genetic status into question: "90% of the known causes of retardation have nothing to do with heredity; many cases are the result of problems during pregnancy and childbirth" (Kantrowitz, King, and Witherspoon 1986, 62). Individuals throughout my life have reassured me of this point.

I was styling my Barbie doll's hair one Christmas when my uncle asked me what I wanted to be when I grew up. I answered, "A hairdresser." My uncle took me aside and said, "My worst nightmare for you is that you grow up to be a hairdresser and marry some truck driver. Take a look at your family. All of us except your mother have college degrees. You come from a great gene pool. Even your grandmother had a degree at a time when women didn't get degrees. You can do so much better than being a hairdresser." I will always adore my aunt and uncle. They had a very positive impact on my life. But what they could not understand is that, for me, assurance that I was "normal" implicitly called my normality into question.

Often my status was brought into question in more direct ways. I rarely invited friends over to play. If I told a friend about my mother's retardation, I considered it a major disclosure, a juncture in our relationship when either I would be rejected or the relationship would deepen. Sometimes I was rejected, particularly when I was younger, because my mother tried to play with us as if she were a little girl. One girl said, "Your mom thinks she is one of us but she's not. She's weird and so are you."

At other times it was the parents of other children who brought my status into question. Lisa's mother, for instance, liked having me around because she thought I was polite and a good influence on her childrens' manners. Starved for approval, I always washed dishes and said, "may I," "please," and "thank you," very diligently. When Lisa's mother finally met my mother, I was not allowed to play at Lisa's house again. Debbi's mother, on the other hand, let me play with Debbi, but only when Debbi's father was away. On the one occasion he came home early, I was asked to sneak out the back door.

I told these stories to my aunt and uncle when they visited. They informed me, "Anyone who would treat a little girl like that, because of her mother or for any reason, is not worth having as a friend." It made sense, but the sentiments still hurt.

◆ ◆ ◆

One evening, when I was around 8 years old, I came home from my friend's house at 6:00 instead of the agreed upon 5:30 curfew. Earlier, around 3:30, I had called my mother to ask her if I could go to the mall with Cheryl and her mother. Cheryl's mom said that she could not get me home until 6:00. Having been interrupted from a television show, my mother quickly agreed I could stay out and hung up the phone. When I got home, my mother screamed at me, demanding to know why I was late. My grandmother, who occasionally acted as referee in these matters, calmly asked me why I was late. I said, "I called from Cheryl's and got Mom's permission." My Mom said, "She's lying, she never called." Stunned and afraid, not sure what my mother was up to, I said, "Did too and I'll prove it. Cheryl was there when I called you, you just don't remember." With her open palm, my mother slapped me, boxing my right ear into a temporary deafness that sent stars across my vision. I cannot show weakness, I thought to myself, because Grandmother'll think I'm lying. I held my ground and yelled at the top of my lungs, over and over, "Call Cheryl's and see, call Cheryl's and see." My mother grabbed me by the hair and pulled me into the bedroom, slamming the door behind her. I looked into her face as she beat me and realized she was enjoying it.

Three years earlier, I was in the first grade. On the particular day in question, I had lied and told my mother that school was canceled so I could play hookey. It had worked one other time. She did not know I was lying until Collete, who lived downstairs in the same apartment building, informed her that her son had attended school that day. My mother called me in to hear Collete's accusation. I admitted I had lied and Collete looked at me and said, "Boy are you gonna get a whoopin'. If you were my little boy I'd whoop the tar outta' you." I looked up at my mother and she had a peculiar mask stretched across her face, something twisted, a cross between a rictus and a grin of anticipatory pleasure. She dragged me up the stairs of the apartment building, shoved me into our apartment, and slammed the door behind us. As if to excuse her from what was to come next, she said, "You know I have to punish you don't you?" She then proceeded to beat me, pounding me with her fists while I screamed out over and over, "I'm sorry, I'm sorry, I won't do it again." I fell to the ground in a fetal position to protect my face, gut, and head. She kicked me in the back, arms, and head, then leaned over and grabbed at my arms and legs to unfold me, so that she could land some kicks to my more vulnerable insides. After two kicks landed on my chest, I scrambled up off the floor and ran. She chased me around the living room, swung at me, landed an occasional slap and tripped me to the floor.

When I got up, I looked into her face. There was no rage. There was no stern parent trying her loving best to discipline her child. She was having fun playing out this melodrama at my expense. Her role was the deceived parent, and deceived parents, according to Collete, "whoop" their children. I decided at this point to stop reacting to her. Maybe if I stopped playing, so would she. I passively stood in front of her and watched her face as I accepted five more slaps. As I took each blow, her face made me angrier and angrier. I had already paid for skipping school. This was beyond. Then I made a mistake. I yelled at her, "You like doing this just like Frank likes kicking you."

My father, Frank Gross (no lie, pronounced "Graas") Rambo, had a police record as a child molester, a rapist, and an exhibitionist. He was also violent. Even though we were on public assistance, our lives were much calmer during the time he was in prison. Her beating me was an enormous betrayal. Yes, I needed to be disciplined, but this was not a spanking. This was the kind of beating Frank dished out.

My mother's eyes lit up and caught fire. She balled up both fists and swung them together like a baseball bat and landed them on the right side of my head. The force knocked me to the floor. She screamed incoherently at me, enraged that I had missed school, that I thought I could fool her, that I had said she enjoyed doing this, and that I said she was acting like Frank. She kicked at me on the floor and stormed out of the apartment.

Later in the day, she was sitting with several neighbors on the porch, bragging about how she had given me what I had coming, sounding just like Collete. Collete praised her for acting like a "real mother." When I appeared on the porch, everyone became quiet and Collete shot me a smug, knowing look.

Earlier that week Collete had swept the porch while I played outside quietly. Collete came up behind me and pretended to sweep me up. I giggled. She sat on a chair and said, "You know Carol, you're OK." I giggled in pleasure at the attention. Collete had a reputation for being dangerous and dishonest and her saying something nice to me was somehow flattering. "No," she said, "I mean you are all right, but your momma ain't. No, indeed, your momma ain't right in the head at all, is she?" I said, "I don't know," frightened at this new line of questioning. She was tapping into all my secret fears, that something was wrong with all of us—my mother, my father, and me. "Yes, you do know child, that look on your face says you know. I just want to tell you that you are all right but your momma ain't." As Collete went back inside, finished with her sweeping, I could not decide if her words were supposed to be reassurance that nothing was wrong with me, or a warning that something may become wrong because my mother wasn't "right in the head."

Later that evening Collete asked if she could borrow my mother's Social Security card. My mother, always a little scared of Collete, gave it to her with little hesitation.

The next day I was playing at Big Carol's apartment with her 2-year-old son, Timothy. She lived across the hall from Collete, and I frequently spent time visiting her. I asked Big Carol, "Why would Collete want to borrow my mother's Social Security card?" Big Carol stopped cooking, turned to me, and said, "What do you mean?" I told Big Carol what Collete had said about my mother not being right in the head and my being OK and how she borrowed my mother's Social Security card. Big Carol laughed and said, "I suppose you are OK, but your momma should have never, ever, let nobody have her Social Security card."

Big Carol went to my mother, and later Collete, and made Collete give my mother back the card. As Collete went down the stairs, she said to me, "Child, you talk too much. This was no one's business but your mother and mine's. No one's business!"

I had Collete, in part, to thank for my beating. I understood what everyone meant when they said Collete was dangerous. She had used my mother's "not being right in the head" as a way to get revenge on me for telling Big Carol about her "business" with my mother. Collete's message was quite clear: "Don't fuck with me or I'll fuck you back." Her smug look paired with everyone's silence was more than I could take. As I made my exit, I hated my mother for needing and enjoying Collete's approval, for beating me, and for not understanding what Collete was getting out of this.

And here I was, at 8 years of age, standing, taking it from my stupid mother again, this time innocent of the crime for which I was accused. I said, "I called you, don't you remember? Or don't you want to remember? Are you enjoying hitting me?" This made her angrier. She remembered that I called; I saw it in her face. Perhaps she had forgotten, but she remembered now. Before, her "anger" was a staged thing, mocked up to match what she perceived as the necessary drama for the moment. Now she was really mad—mad that I knew the truth, mad that I had the nerve to accuse her out loud, and afraid. She had started this course of action and she could not withdraw from it, not after hitting me. She could not just go back out into the living room and say to Grandmother, "Oh yeah, now I remember, she did call."

So she proceeded to beat me with even more vigor and conviction. I was taking fists to the head, to the stomach, and to the sides. I did not try to get away, nor did I put much effort into trying to block her punches and slaps. I was on fire with a righteous fury. I knew I had called. I knew I was right and she was wrong, and I knew she was beating me for no reason. As she hit me, my face burned with the pressure of the blows and the tears. The burn in my face was merging with the burn of my fury. The beating became a kind of purification ritual. I started to "enjoy" the beating. The more she hit me the more guilty she became. The more guilty she was the more righteous I became. I was right, right, right, and that was all that mattered. The more she beat me, without my resistance, the more elevated I became as a being who was, once and for all, superior to her.

After about 10 minutes my grandmother entered the room and said, "Suzanne, stop it. I think she might be telling the truth. She's not acting like someone who's lying." This was a big deal because Grandmother felt that since I was Suzanne's child, she should not intervene in my mother's disciplining of me. If Grandmother had decided to get directly involved, this was major.

"Call Cheryl," I said. "You call her and I'll talk to her and her mother," Grandmother replied. I promptly got on the phone, and when Cheryl answered, I said, "My mother just beat me up for being late." My mother grabbed the phone, hung it up, and hit me again. "You shouldn't have told her that." My grandmother came into the hall where the phone was located and agreed with my mother, "You shouldn't have said that, give me the phone." Grandmother called and spoke for a while with Cheryl's mother, thanked her, hung up, and said, "Cheryl's mother said that Cheryl told her that Carol called here at 3:30, Suzanne. Are you sure you didn't forget?" My mother screeched, "Oh I don't know," threw her hands out at Grandmother as if to melodramatically brush her off, and stormed out of the room.

Not to be upstaged, I likewise flung myself onto the sofa and whined, "What is wrong with her? I was telling the truth and we all know it." My grandmother answered quietly, "She is mentally retarded. She isn't like other people. You have to make allowances for her." I quieted down and asked, "What's wrong with her?" My grandmother responded, "She has brain damage." She went on to explain that no one knows for sure how she became brain damaged. One possible cause was that Grandmother bled a great deal in the third month of the pregnancy. Another possibility was that my mother was delivered in under 45 minutes and that she may have suffered trauma from the speed of the delivery. Many things locked into place once I understood my mother was retarded. I had only one question. "Am I retarded too?" "No," Grandmother responded.

Suzanne loved to play dolls. The only problem was that she always insisted on playing dolls her way—nicey, nicey. I wanted Barbie to rob banks, get her period—anything but fashion shows and tea parties. Mother always insisted the dolls play "nice," so I often left and let Mom finish playing dolls by herself, only to return later to play out a good plane crash.

I believe my mother was once conned into posing for nude photos by a man we trusted, though I cannot be sure because I was not allowed to witness the actual event. He asked her if she would like to earn some money and she agreed. We went to his apartment while his wife was away, and he asked Mom to take off her clothes so that he could see if her body was good enough to photograph. Pointing at me, my mother said, "Not with her in the room." He promptly shoved me into a closet. I listened at the door while he gradually talked her out of her clothes. It sounded like he was snapping pictures. I will never know if there was film in the camera, or if this was just a ploy to get her naked. When she was dressed, they let me out of the closet. I was given orange candy and told not to tell anyone. He gave my mother $10 and as far as I know that is the only money she ever earned from her illustrious modeling career.

In the first grade I had an inner ear infection that caused me to be deaf for six weeks. Some neighbors brought me a get-well present, saw my mother taking my temperature, and finally insisted I go to the hospital. My mother and father did not know a 106-degree fever was dangerous. I was out of school during that time and had my homework brought to me by classmates. My mother loved to do my homework, so I let her. When I went back to school, the teacher took me aside, explained that *all* of the answers on my homework were wrong, and that she was afraid I had fallen so far behind that I would have difficulty catching up. I suggested that the real problem might be that I was sick while doing my homework. I begged for another chance to make it up. She let me take home a different set of dittos, which I filled out in secret and returned to the teacher. She acted surprised and relieved that I had shown so much improvement. I, on the other hand, was shocked that my mother had missed so many "easy" problems, and I did not know how to account for it.

Knowing my mother was retarded explained a great deal to me, but it also created new problems, new crises about exactly who she was and who I was. Sure, Grandmother was going to tell me I was OK, but she may have been telling me that just to make me feel better, the same way she kept retardation a secret from my mother. Maybe the whole world knew I was retarded too, kept it a secret from me, and laughed behind my back.

I am being forced to unravel an emotional knot in my gut to finish this. My heart is racing, my hand trembling, my limbs limp. I can feel my center dissipate, bleeding outward, as if entropy will catch me up in its flow and I will fail to be. I despise feeling like this—vulnerable, scared, a little out of control. Yet, when asked by readers to dig even deeper (fucking vampires, draining the emotional life out of me), I come up with a truth that leaves me hanging in midair with nowhere to stand, as surely as if the floor had been yanked out from under me. What could this devastating kernel of knowledge possibly be? I have just discovered, through the process of writing this, of seeing it all before me on paper, that I am ashamed to love my mother.

When we first went to live with my grandmother, my mother and I shared a bedroom with two twin beds. I went to bed each night several hours before my mother. Every night I stayed awake until she came to bed because I needed my mommy.

Let me draw in a sharp, husky breath, tremble, and whisper it longingly in your ear again: I needed my mommy—BAAAD.

I HATE this! I hate that fucking needy little girl. I hate it, hate it, hate it . . .

I had the best mom ever! She played with me just like a girlfriend: cards, dolls, jump rope, make believe. Yeah, sometimes it was a pain. She could pull rank and remind me that she was the mother. Then we had to do what she wanted.

One day at school, it was third grade, Pat Suez was caught stealing candy from my friend Jennie's cubbyhole. Before that, Pat was a friend and we used to walk home together with several other girls. When she tried to walk with us this time, we all told her to go away. We yelled, "Thief," and "Pig," and one of the girls even threw pebbles at her. We all laughed.

Pat put her hands on her hips and said, "Carol, your mom likes me and you're going to get in trouble for making fun of me." I laughed at her. She clearly didn't know my mom! A couple of the other girls looked worried. "Just wait, you'll see!" I said. I never doubted my mother for a second. She would take my side in any argument with any of them. "You just go and tell her, piggy," I jeered gleefully, now leading the pack making fun of her. "And tell her what a fat pig thief you are too, while you're at it."

Everyone joined in laughing except Pat, who walked ahead of us and met my mom at the corner. My mom walked up to me and said, "What's this all about?" I answered, "We don't like her any more." My mother instantly turned to Pat, thumbed her nose at her and blew her a raspberry. My friends howled with laughter.

Pat stood staring and then ran across the street. She yelled, "I'm telling my mother you did that, Mrs. Rambo!" My mother turned around, bent over, her rear facing Pat, and raised her skirt. Some of the girls were laughing so hard they were crying; others were rolling on the ground. It was too funny—someone's mom acting like that to a kid. Pat started to cry and Mom mooned her again. It was like having a pet do tricks for your friends. "See, my mom is always on my side. Don't forget it!" I said, playing it cool, as I walked off with her to the house. My friends talked about and relived the incident for a week. Pat found a different route home, and we never heard from her mom. My mom was the best ever. No one else's mom would have done that for them!

When Mother got money at birthday and Christmas time, she would treat us both to lunch at McDonald's. Standing in line, it became routine for her to ask, "Do you want one or two cheeseburgers?" "Two," I would respond, grinning. She would giggle and say, "I want two, too." She always purchased for each of us two cheeseburgers, fries, a coke, a shake, and a pie, if we wanted it. I loved her so much for doing that. It was our gesture of resistance against Grandmother and her boring food. She never let us pig out like this!

I betrayed my mother by growing up. Year after year we grew further apart until finally I abandoned her to the dolls, the coloring, and her make-believe world. She was not growing with me, and as time went by, she became an embarrassment and a liability.

That was a shallow explanation of what happened. I trusted her and she betrayed me! She represented herself to me as my mother, but she was not a normal person, much less a normal mother. The world played a bad joke on me for years until finally Grandmother had to let me in on it. Once I knew about her, I had to reject her. To keep on loving her like a mom was to keep on being fooled. I could no longer trust her, the world, nor myself. Nothing was as it was supposed to be. I still needed someone very badly but I could not count on my father, my grandmother, or my mentally retarded mother. I was alone.

As I write, I grieve the loss of my love for my mother. I must face the reality that I am unable to love her again in the intense, unbridled way I did as a child. But she carried me in her womb and would not abort me when Grandmother begged her to. And she conspired to save me from Frank and once even took a beating for me. But she also beat me, delivered me to Frank, and sexually abused me herself. She was strong and weak in the strangest ways. Yet she was my only stability growing up, the only thing that was with me consistently over the years. Don't I owe her something for that?

There is no answer, no final truth to this conundrum—only ambivalence. I feel as if I live in the margins, waiting for this feeling to settle into something else, to transform, or to transcend. But there is no resolution, at least not yet. Try as I may, I cannot work it all out. I cannot label everything neatly and explain it to you, the reader, wrapped up in a neat, bundled conclusion. I feel ambivalent, one moment protective of my mother, the next furious at her, and the next profoundly sad. I want to avoid her and control her life for her, all at the same time. Thus my ambivalence is a feeling between moments, between labels, between feelings. This feeling serves as a marker in my consciousness, which proclaims: "A codified feeling label should exist here but it does not— remember that and do something about it later."

When I am forced to deal with my mother, it is all I can do to contain myself from being angry at her. I remember loving her when I was a kid. But I am alienated from that now and have no clue how to forgive her and tap back into that feeling again. I'm not sure I want to. I mostly feel guilty that I can't stand her, and I try my best to do "things" for her, monetarily or otherwise, so that I do not have to spend time with her. Mostly, dealing with her is just too damn much work; it always leaves me exhausted.

When I first got pregnant, my mother commented, "It's sure been a long time." "A long time what?" I barked into the receiver with my usual impatience. "You know, a long time since you were little." A cold chill ran down my spine. "Yes, and . . ." I asked, obnoxiously, demanding she spell it out. "Well it's just been a long time since I had someone to, *you know*," she said. I did know. It was startling, grotesque, but I knew. My child represented her last chance to fully connect to someone again and perhaps her last chance to grow up. Her first childhood occurred with my uncle John who was 3 years her senior. She had a second childhood with my aunt Kathy who was 12 years her junior. Finally, she had a third childhood with me, 29 years her junior. With Kathy and me, there was a time when we were her intellectual equals, roughly between 5 and 8 years old. Later, all three of us grew up and left her behind. Her implication was that somehow she could start fresh with my baby and, perhaps this time, she would mature with him and catch the last train into adulthood.

I just reread that last passage and had to smile. If you had listened to my mother on the phone you probably would have heard nothing sinister, no *Twilight Zone* music, only an aging woman who wants the company of grandchildren. But her tone—if you had known her all these years—the voice of urgency, desperation, hunger, a junkie needing a fix. Then again, I've heard my girlfriends describe their mothers nagging them to have children. How will I ever know if I'm dealing with "normal" mother-daughter issues or those of a mentally retarded parent? Why must I?

References

Ellis, C. 1991. "Sociological Introspection and Emotional Experience." *Symbolic Interaction* 14: 23–50.

Ellis, C., and A. Bochner. 1992. "Telling and Performing Personal Stories: The Constraints of Choice in Abortion." In *Investigating Subjectivity: Research on Lived Experience*, edited by Carolyn Ellis and Michael Flaherty. (Newbury Park, CA: Sage): 79–101.

Feldman, M. A., F. Towns, J. Betal, L. Case, A. Rincover, and C. A. Rubino. 1986. "Parent Education Project II: Increasing Stimulating Interactions of Developmentally Handicapped Mothers." *Journal of Applied Behavior Analysis* 19: 23–37.

Finkelhor, D., and G. T. Hotaling. 1984. "Sex Abuse in the National Incidence Study of Child Abuse and Neglect: An Appraisal." *Child Abuse and Neglect* 18: 23–33.

Heighway, S. M., S. Kidd-Webster, and P. Snodgrass. 1988. "Supporting Parents with Mental Retardation." *Children Today* (November/December): 24–27.

Kantrowitz, B., P. King, and D. Witherspoon. 1986. "Help for Retarded Parents." *Newsweek* (June 23): 62 .

Klein, B. C. 1990. "Survival Dilemmas: Case Study of an Adult Child of a Schizophrenic Parent." *Clinical Social Work Journal* 18: 43–56.

Peterson, S. L., E. A. Robinson, and I. Littman. 1983. "Parent-Child Interaction Training for Parents with a History of Mental Retardation." *Applied Research in Mental Retardation* 4: 329–342.

Robinson, L. H. 1978. "Parental Attitudes of Mentally Retarded Young Mothers." *Child Psychiatry and Human Development* 8: 131–144.

Ronai, C. R. 1995. "Multiple Reflections of Child Sex Abuse: An Argument for a Layered Account." *Journal of Contemporary Ethnography* 23: 395–426.

Ronai, C. R. 1992. "A Night in the Life of a Dancer/Researcher: A Layered Account." In *Investigating Subjectivity: Research on Lived Experience*, edited by Carolyn Ellis and Michael Flaherty. (Newbury Park, CA: Sage): 102–124.

Stoneman, Z. 1989. "Comparison Groups in Research on Families with Mentally Retarded Members: A Methodological and Conceptual Review." *American Journal on Mental Retardation* 94: 195–215.

Tymchuk, A. J. 1992. "Predicting Adequacy of Parenting by People with Mental Retardation." *Child Abuse and Neglect* 16: 165–178.

Tymchuk, A. J. 1991. "Self-Concepts of Mothers Who Show Mental Retardation." *Psychological Reports* 68: 503–510.

Whitman, B. Y., B. Graves, and P. J. Accardo. 1989. "Training in Parenting Skills for Adults with Mental Retardation." *Social Work* (September) 431–434.

◆ ———————

Carol Rambo Ronai is an Assistant Professor in the Department of Sociology at the University of Memphis. As she gazes over a stack of manuscripts waiting to be edited for her forthcoming edited collection, *Everyday Sexism: Gender Oppression in the Late 20th Century* from Routledge Press with coeditors Barbara Zsembik and Joe Feagin, Carol finds herself grateful to have a healthy baby, a good relationship, and a terrific job.

I am grateful for the assistance of Rebecca Cross, David Karp, Tiffany Parish, and Jack Ronai in the preparation of this manuscript.

CHAPTER FOUR

Thrown Overboard
The Human Costs of
Health Care Rationing

Aliza Kolker

February 1, 1994

When I first enter the oncologist's office I tell myself that here the denial ends. Droopy-looking patients sit in the waiting room, some with turbans or in wheelchairs, one with an oxygen tank. Brochures on the rack: "Chemotherapy and You," "Myths of Nausea and Vomiting," "Eating Hints During Cancer Treatment," "What is Hospice?" It dawns on me that patients who are treated in this office are condemned. First they get very sick—it is not clear which is more devastating, the disease or the treatment—and then they very likely die, sooner rather than later. I have entered a narrow, dark tunnel of horrors I cannot even imagine. And there is no way back.

Today is my 46th birthday. Like most healthy people, I have always viewed the seriously ill as "the other" in the anthropological sense: someone different from myself in some fundamental way, someone to study or read about but not a person I am likely to become or one with whom I can identify. Always the social scientist, I tell myself that now I irrevocably have crossed the line into the "other" kingdom. But I will zigzag back and forth across this border for a long time. Acceptance of the "ill" identity is a slow process, made slower for those with breast cancer because there are usually no symptoms (or in my case, relatively minor ones). For much of the next year I will still be in denial.

Every year 182,000 women in the United States are diagnosed with breast cancer. Recently I became one of those statistics. I may also become one of the 46,000 who die from it each year (*NCI Fact Book* 1994).

Here I recount an unexpected battle in my personal, ongoing war against breast cancer—a battle that no one should have to fight, but one that has become increasingly common. This story is about my battle with the health insurance industry, which I lost.

As a medical sociologist, I have often criticized the American health care system for its tendency toward aggressive overtreatment. In my graduate course on medical sociology in the spring of 1994, I was using textbooks that stated, among other points, that for-profit corporations sell unnecessary diagnostic and therapeutic services. The textbooks argue that hospitals and physicians, motivated by open-ended insurance reimbursement and fear of malpractice lawsuits, overuse technologies—often on patients who cannot benefit from them—at huge costs to the health care system (Relman 1994, 1980; Zussman 1992). I emphasized the same point in my research (Kolker and Burke 1994, ch. 11). At the same time, however, I was to discover in my own life that this is not always true.

Managed care—the reorganization of the health care system to streamline services, cut costs, and increase profits for insurers—has caused cataclysmic changes that have largely gone unnoticed by those not in need of medical care. One consequence is that it is no longer overtreatment but undertreatment—or denial of care—that poses a grave danger to American patients. Myerson (1995, D1) points out that standards published by a little-known consulting firm, Milliman & Robertson, quietly have become the supreme arbiter used by insurance companies to deny care: "A health plan asks a new mother to leave the hospital one day after her baby is born. Or it refuses to cover cataract removal in more than one eye unless the patient is fairly young and needs both eyes for work. Or it presses a generalist, not a neurologist, to treat epileptic seizures." A physician forced to discharge hospital patients against his judgment is quoted as saying, "The trouble is that rather than becoming a guide, [the standards] have become a crucifix, a cross of gold" (Myerson 1995, D5).

Merton (1968, 253) defines goal displacement as the process by which "an instrumental value becomes a terminal value." The profit motive has always played an important role in the American health care system. But with managed care, it has become more prevalent and more legitimate—and more damaging to individual lives and well-being. And, as Hilzenrath (1995, A10) points out, "many of the revolution's strongest exponents—the leaders of the managed care industry—are profiting greatly from the cost cutting. They pay themselves, their employees, and their shareholders with money they squeeze out of the system."

This trend will probably get worse in the future. If, as some ethicists claim (Callahan 1987, 1992; Macklin 1985), health care in an environment of limited resources is a lifeboat, millions of Americans have been thrown overboard, and the numbers are growing. The poor and the uninsured, particularly women, children, and the elderly, who already suffer the most, will continue to suffer, but the rest of us will not be far behind.

First-Person Sociology
◆

Sociologists and anthropologists seldom write about themselves. We see our task as recording and analyzing the lives and worlds of our "subjects." Except for a brief methodology section, our autobiographies are supposed to stay invisible, our own voices mute. As Linden (1993, 139) points out, "On the whole, ethnographers have assumed that valid and reliable representations and interpretations, told from a 'native's point of view,' can be achieved only by effacing their own subjectivities." Ellis (1995, 308) questions the positivist tradition in sociology, which insists that "to be scholarly our work should be impersonal" and which calls for the "separation of subject and researcher." Behar (1991) laments that anthropologists seek rootedness and meaning in the stories of exotic "others" while distancing themselves from their own roots.

Two events in my life persuaded me to undertake, in midcareer, a difficult reorientation of my role as a researcher and of my style of writing. One was a presentation by Carolyn Ellis, who described her own journey away from traditional sociology and into autobiographical writing, "from science . . . to interpretation . . . from realist ethnography

. . . to storytelling . . . and evocation" (Ellis 1995, 304–318). Another was my own illness. I want to tell my story, informed by the tools and conceptual frameworks of sociology. Like anthropologist Barbara Myerhoff, producer of the film *In Her Own Time;* sociologist Barbara Rosenblum, author (with Sandra Butler) of the book *Cancer in Two Voices;* and sociologist Marianne Paget, author of the book *A Complex Sorrow,* all of whom died of cancer before they could complete their work, I may not have time for anything else.

Perhaps what I am doing is not revolutionary after all. In *The Sociological Imagination* (1959) C. Wright Mills placed sociology at the intersection of biography and history and claimed that only by combining the two, by translating "private troubles" into "public issues," can we make sense of our lives. In two decades of doing traditional sociology I focused on contemporary history—the social structure and forces of our time. Now I will concentrate on the other side of the equation: on understanding my own life in the context of these forces.

December 23, 1993
◆

For several weeks my right breast has been sore, hard, and swollen. I can no longer fit it into my brassiere cup. It is probably an infection, I tell myself. Years ago a gynecologist told me, "If it hurts it's not cancer." I cannot afford time out for illness now; I still have to get myself and the kids ready for a trip to Israel right after Christmas. Yet the pain finally forces me to see Dr. A., our family physician, between shopping trips to the mall. He tries unsuccessfully to aspirate the lump—now the size of the whole breast—and then sends me for a mammogram and an ultrasound. His face looks alarmed. The private offices are closed for the holiday, so I go to the emergency room to have the tests. I am not worried.

The tests prove inconclusive. "Can I go ahead with my trip?" I ask the attending physician, Dr. D. "Yes," he says. "Take this painkiller and the antibiotics with you. That should bring down the swelling. If it doesn't go away, we will schedule a biopsy when you come back. There is no rush. Nothing will change in a few weeks."

I dig up some old stretched-out brassieres that fit and pack the antibiotics and painkiller.

January 1994

◆

Snow and ice in New York delay our departure by many hours. But in Israel the sky is blue, the temperature is in the 60s, and because it is off-season the rates are low and there are no crowds. My relatives, as always, act as though I have never left. Although the swelling and the pain do not go away, I tell nobody about my troubles.

When we return home the public schools and medical offices are closed because of new snowstorms. I have another inconclusive mammogram. Dr. D., whom I first met in the emergency room and who is now my surgeon, insists that it looks no different from one taken three years ago. Yet he schedules me for a biopsy "just to be sure."

On Friday, between snowstorms, I have the biopsy. Dr. D. calls back on Saturday. "Bad news," he says. "It's cancer. Inflammatory breast cancer, the fastest moving and the most lethal type of breast tumor."

I have already suspected this news from the look of my breast and from my sister-in-law's experience. Incredibly, Debbie (a pseudonym) has the same rare form of breast cancer and has just emerged from a hellish series of treatments. We are not related by blood. How can lightning strike twice in the same family? Everything I know about probability and risk statistics tells me it's a hideous error.

Over the weekend, a pause: I am convinced it's a mistake. I tell friends but not my children or my mother. I teach my class on Monday night.

On Monday and Tuesday things move fast. I see Dr. B., the oncologist, then I visit another oncologist for a second opinion. I keep hoping that someone will tell me it's a mistake, a false positive, an ambiguous finding that just "needs to be watched." But they all confirm the bad news and add gruesome news of their own. I am informed that I have less than a one in two chance of being alive in five years.

Tomorrow I start chemotherapy. I expect to be very sick. I lie awake during the night, trying to stop the clock. But I am being pulled into a whirlpool and cannot stop.

February 3, 1994

◆

The first chemo goes OK. Powerful toxins are injected into my body intravenously. I am not nauseous, just a little queasy and flushed.

The kids are wonderful: "I know it will turn out OK," they say. "I will make you breakfast in bed" and "Let me give you a hug." My mother takes it bravely. "I know you are tough," she says, "and won't give in." My husband, as always calm and practical—doesn't he realize I may be dying?—says, "We need to see a lawyer about giving me power of attorney over your finances in case you are incapacitated. You also need to draw up an advanced directive." I freak out: "You are writing me off already!" I scream. To make me feel better, we decide to draw up advanced directives for both of us. This way it seems more of a reasonable precaution and less of an imminent death sentence.

Debbie, who has regaled me with horror stories about her therapy and especially about her bone marrow transplant, "the treatment from hell," now reassures me that none of this is really horrible. I am glad to hear this; the denier in me fears the treatments more than the disease.

I am supposed to have six to eight chemotherapy treatments, three weeks apart. After the first chemo I try to regain some control over my life. How much worse is it going to get? Nobody in the oncologist's office will tell me. Later, I learn that the effects of chemotherapy are cumulative: It definitely gets worse.

I dread every shampoo, every blow-drying: How many more shampoos am I going to have before my hair falls out? At night I try to escape from reality into blissful sleep. Sometimes it works. But I can't—must not—spend my days brooding over the cancer. There are obligations that must be met: my reduced teaching schedule, the kids' needs, bills to pay. It's better to keep busy anyway.

May, 1994

After almost five months of chemotherapy I have a mastectomy during the Memorial Day weekend. My body looks horribly deformed, but when I wear the temporary prosthesis (made of cotton stuffed in a satin pocket, safety-pinned into my brassiere) the outside appearance is normal. At first I can't lift my right arm beyond shoulder height, but little by little my shoulder muscles regain motion. When I sit in the driver's seat in my car, I can't open the right-side car door, an easy reach before. I will never have full use of my right arm.

Yet my recovery is fast. Five days after the operation—one day after coming home—my energy level is high and I feel bored, so my husband and I take a day trip to Harper's Ferry. My mother and brother come to visit and are surprised at how well I look and act. I have not seen my brother, who lives in California, in several years. It seems that my illness has finally shaken him out of a torpor induced by his own illness, chronic fatigue syndrome. He had to pay the full fare to come and see me since no super-saver fares were available. This fare is higher than I have ever paid out-of-pocket for a cross-country flight. I am touched.

During the first days after the surgery I am in a high that is fueled partly by having this behind me and partly by the surgeon's report that he could not see any cancer in the breast or the lymph nodes. Then the pathology report comes back: 10 lymph nodes (out of 13 removed) are positive. Again, the denial: How can the pathology report be so bad when the surgeon's demeanor is so reassuring? Maybe it's all a mistake. Maybe 10 years from now they will discover that our generation's obsession with breast cancer produced a lot of false positive diagnoses.

July, 1994

◆

After a relaxed Fourth of July holiday, a bad week. The veins in my arm have been ruined by the chemo and can't be used for intravenous lines anymore. I have a catheter surgically inserted into my chest so that I can receive chemotherapy and other drugs directly. The procedure is performed under general anesthesia. After many tries, the nurse can't find a usable vein for the anesthesia and summons the anesthesiologist. He succeeds only after producing a tiny baby needle.

Afterwards, my shoulder hurts. The next day I go to a breast prosthesis show at the American Cancer Society. There are 40 or 50 different prostheses on display. How is anyone supposed to choose? I can barely stay awake because of the pain and the lingering drowsiness from the anesthesia. At noon I go to the university for Edith's dissertation defense. I do not tell Edith about my condition; she has enough on her mind. But I tell the other faculty members in the room. Evelyn, the committee chair, asks, "Are you sure you want to go through with this?" Edith is one of my best students; I really want to see her through, so I insist on staying the course. Fortunately the defense goes smoothly.

At 3:30 I meet my husband at Intracare, an outpatient clinic. We receive instruction on taking care of the catheter. It's a bigger deal than I realized. The damn thing needs lots of care and feeding: The insertion point has to be cleaned every day and the dressing changed, the caps have to be changed once a week, and both tubes have to be flushed twice a day with Heparin, an anticlotting drug that looks like water. I remain calm and focused through the hour-long session; I actually learn how to do this. At the end of the session I think I can manage, though I still wish I could have a nurse do it. Just after I get dressed, the nurse brings in the Heparin-flushing equipment that she has forgotten about and starts telling me how to use it. At this point I lose it: I cry uncontrollably and can't absorb any more information. Though seemingly minor, having to learn this new procedure is the proverbial straw. I cry, "Enough already!"

The next day I go back to Intracare and another nurse watches me change the dressing and shows me the flushing business. I am finally in control of my emotions.

My body has been violated and mutilated, and the violations are escalating. First I lost my hair, then my eyebrows and body hair, then my breast. Now I have two plastic pipes about eight inches long hanging out of my chest. I am aware that this is just the beginning of the illness odyssey. It's amazing what a human being can tolerate.

I spend most of the weekend in bed, too tired from the chemo to do anything. What's next? I am in a holding pattern. I know that it's going to get worse before it gets better. I wish I could speed up the process—fast-forward the tape—and come out at the other end to resume my life.

Somehow, I do not really expect to die, so the enemy in my mind is the treatments, not the illness. I guess the denial of dying and the tendency not to think too much about it are part of a protective mechanism. It helps to make the unbearable bearable.

I try to decide whether I can write a sociological piece about my cancer. In preparation, I read literary and sociological illness accounts. Some of the sociological accounts seem dry, but Carolyn Ellis's recent book, *Final Negotiations,* and Stewart Alsop's now-dated book, *Stay of Execution,* are gripping. My question: What is the secret of their writing? How do you make your own story important and interesting for other people?

When you are battling a major disease or another crisis, you mobilize all your reserves to deal with the crisis; you have no reserve patience or goodwill for the little screwups. Today is another very frustrating day. First, I have to wait 25 minutes in the doctor's office. Then I find out that my blood counts are very low, which means that I will need growth factor shots to stimulate the generation of white cells. I also will need a transfusion of red blood cells. I go over to the pharmacy two buildings away to pick up the shots, which I have to administer to myself. There I am told to return to the oncologist's office because they forgot to draw one more blood sample. I get lost in the medical building where I have been many times. Feeling trapped and weak with rage, I start sobbing in the empty corridors. At home, I spend much of the day on the telephone, trying to untangle screwups with medical bills. Although all the mishaps are minor, several times I end up slamming down the telephone and screaming obscenities into the air. Fortunately there is no one at home to hear me.

There is no question that even when it doesn't make you very sick chemotherapy takes a toll. I hate feeling drained. I hate growth factor shots and blood transfusions. I hate having to spend so much of my life shuttling among medical offices. I feel that (1) there is no end to the demands being sprung up on me out of the blue, (2) nothing is ever resolved—I keep treading in place or going backward.

(Later that day) Clearly, I overreacted earlier because of my tense frame of mind. Fortunately my 11-year-old comes and gives me a wordless hug several times. Just the right medicine!

Rabbi K. died this morning. I am taking this very hard. He was my friend. Last year he bar-mitzvahed my son. At 66, he finally decided to retire and was looking forward to spending his remaining years with his children and grandchildren. Last month I ran into him in the hospital lobby, where he was visiting patients (he was a chaplain there). He told me about his forthcoming heart bypass surgery and how terrified he was. The surgery went OK but afterwards his kidneys failed and his white blood count shot up, indicating an infection. The source of the infection could not be pinpointed, so it couldn't be treated. He remained in intensive care, heavily sedated, for three weeks. His wife, children, and grandchildren kept a vigil in the hospital lobby. I have visited them there. This morning, when I cannot find them in the lobby, I call the synagogue office, and the receptionist tells me the rabbi has just died.

This is a shock and a blow. Like me, he was not ready to die. This death is different from those of my father and my father-in-law, both of whom died after long and debilitating illnesses. In a sense they had already been "dead" for years. Rabbi K. should not have died yet, whatever that means.

I am not religious, but I was looking forward to his visiting me in the hospital the next time I had to go in. Now I feel orphaned. I cry for him and for me. I am sure tomorrow at the memorial service I will cry again.

Another horror is unfolding. Dr. B., the oncologist, is recommending an autologous bone marrow transplant (ABMT). This treatment, until recently considered experimental, has been proven effective for advanced or metastatic breast cancer (see Chevallier et al. 1993). I anticipated that I would need it because Debbie went through this. What I did not anticipate—how could I?—was that my insurance carrier, Blue Cross/Blue Shield of Virginia, as well as my husband's carrier, BC/BS of the National Capital Area, would refuse to authorize it, claiming it is not a covered service. I am in shock.

When I am not battling the chemo's side effects or chauffeuring kids to day camp, I spend my whole time trying to get coverage for the ABMT. I write requests and appeals, make phone calls, visit my congresswoman's and my state senator's offices. All to no avail. No reason is ever given for the denial. A typical reply from BC/BS of Virginia states, "This hospital admission has been reviewed for medical necessity as required by your health care policy. Upon review, it was determined that the services requested are not covered under your health care policy." A tautology: It is not covered because it is not covered. The state Department of Personnel and Training, which oversees health benefits for state employees, confirms this. Aware that I may well die without the treatment, the bureaucrats add polite regrets: "We are very sorry that our contract excludes the desired services."

The real reason for denying coverage, it seems, is that they can get away with it. If they can't be sued successfully, why should they pay? This is horribly arbitrary. Insurance companies' coverage of this procedure is inconsistent, with approval granted to some patients and denied to others with the same medical characteristics (Peters and Rogers 1994). In 1994, insurers in all other states in the mid-Atlantic region and most states in the country pay for this procedure. After several lawsuits and extensive lobbying efforts, the Virginia legislature will make this coverage optional (with additional premiums) beginning next year, but it will be too late for me.

I am really disgusted. The medical procedure itself is horrible enough. Yet, the psychic energy that I was beginning to mobilize to prepare for the physical assault has to be diverted to fight for the insurance coverage. My blood count is close to normal, so at least this week my energy level is reasonably high. Fighting my battles when I am weak will be harder.

My husband and I see a lawyer about suing BC/BS for coverage. The issue hinges on what seems to be an inanity—whether I knew at the time I signed on with BC/BS that they did not cover ABMT for breast cancer and whether they "deliberately" hid it from me. The lawyer, battle weary, tells us there is no point in suing because the insurance benefits booklet states clearly that ABMT is not covered for this condition (although it is covered for other cancers like leukemia). It doesn't matter that I have been with BC/BS for 19 years and, never expecting to get breast cancer or to need an ABMT, did not think to look for this coverage. "You may go ahead and sue, but you will probably lose," the lawyer says.

Aware that what is happening to me is part of a broader social issue that I am struggling to comprehend, I go to the library to search for articles about health insurance. I find out that the debate about rationing health care has been going on for at least a decade. The controversy, fueled by rising medical costs, unwanted aggressive treatments, and concern over the plight of the uninsured, has heated up in recent months because of President Clinton's proposed health care reforms.

The term *rationing,* I find out, is frequently used as a scare tactic to warn that if reforms are (or are not) enacted, many Americans will be denied optimum health care. An article in The *New England Journal of Medicine* gives the following description:

> The specter of health care rationing—the deliberate withholding of potentially beneficial care—is usually invoked in health policy discussions as a dreaded consequence of either the containment of soaring medical expenditures or the expansion of health insurance coverage. The implication is that rationing is something that has not yet occurred, but might. The reality is that rationing occurs in some form in every country, including the United States . . . Implicit rationing can be carried out in a variety of ways: by budget, as when capitated health plans limit certain services; by price, when services such as cosmetic surgery are not covered by health insurance; by queue, when certain services are not immediately available; by hassle, when administrative barriers facing physicians and patients deter the delivery of services; by insurance coverage; and by subtle social factors (Schroeder 1994, 1089).

Rationing by insurance status and by ability to pay has always been a feature of the American health care system. Today the uninsured population numbers some 40 million Americans, or approximately one sixth of the population; the number is growing by 2 to 3 million every year. Many millions of others, insured only by Medicaid or Medicare, also are inadequately protected. Both those who favor health care reform and those who oppose it agree that in order to extend coverage to the uninsured, the extravagant benefits that the rest of us have come to expect must be curtailed (Callahan 1987, 1992; Mechanic 1985). However, managed care has ushered in an era of rationing for all—without the trade-offs of expanded or more equitable coverage. The only beneficiaries are the leaders and shareholders of the managed care industry (Marmor and Mashaw 1993).

One form of rationing is medical triage. First used in World War I field hospitals, *triage* refers to sorting the wounded into three categories: "those hurt so badly they would not survive even if they received medical attention; those who needed medical attention but would survive anyway if they did not get immediate treatment; and those whose survival depended on their receiving immediate treatment" (Macklin 1985, 612). With a critical shortage of medical personnel and equipment, only those who could benefit most from medical care—the third category—were attended to. Of course, true triage applies only in a supreme emergency. A modified, contemporary version would dictate that in an era of limited resources, those who can benefit most should be given highest priority, while unnecessary or futile treatments (such as those that merely prolong dying) should be curtailed.

Macklin (1985, 611) uses the metaphor of a lifeboat to dramatize the ethics of ultimate rationing: "The proverbial 'lifeboat ethic' story describes a situation in which some individuals must be selected to be thrown overboard lest everyone perish. On the assumption that it is better for some to be saved than for everyone to perish . . . the problem is to decide on the best scheme for dealing with this tragic situation."

Apparently I have been selected to be thrown overboard. Selected by what criteria, I wonder? All human life is worthy; I do not wish to imply that I deserve to live more than others. Yet it is inescapable (at least to me and my family) that here I am at midlife and midcareer, a mother of young children and a productive member of society. I have a life-threatening illness whose chances of cure are significantly improved by the recommended treatment, and I feel that I am being denied that treatment simply because the insurance companies can get away with it.

Meanwhile, health insurance carriers routinely pay millions of dollars to prolong the dying of patients, both young and old, who cannot be saved. One is Baby K, born with anencephaly in the same hospital where I am to receive treatment. Her deeply religious mother refuses permission to withdraw treatment. Baby K will remain technically alive for a year, her care financed by Kaiser Permanente. Another is newborn Ryan Nguyen, born in Spokane, Washington, whose doctors decided to stop life support when it became clear that he was massively damaged and would not survive infancy. His parents, too, refused permission to withdraw treatment. His care continues at a cost of $2,000 a day, covered by Medicaid (Kolata 1994). My case is, evidently, simpler: Two insurance companies simply decided not to authorize treatment. Unlike the parents of the two doomed infants, I do not have to give permission.

The bone marrow transplant network has worked out a strategy for private fund-raising appeals, which apparently are a commonly used last resort for women denied insurance. I am advised to start raising $100,000 from relatives, friends, and strangers. This is not bake-sale money. They advise me to ask everybody I know for contributions of at least $500; smaller amounts are not worth the effort. I refuse.

◆ ◆ ◆

Dr. B. suggests postponing the ABMT until January, after we switch insurance coverage during open enrollment month to Aetna, which covers this. Apparently if you change during open enrollment, preexisting conditions cannot be used against you. Meanwhile Dr. B. will keep me on chemotherapy to shrink the tumor. I am discouraged by having to wait four more months—six more treatments—progressively sicker from the chemo. It's like the fighting during the two world wars: It went on much longer than anybody had anticipated. You can't go home; you are in it for the duration, and it's hell.

We decide not to wait until January but to pay for the bone marrow transplant ourselves. My husband points out that since we have been living frugally and our house is paid up, our savings are enough to cover the cost. I am touched by his devotion. Of course, I would do this for him if the situation were reversed. I may still die anyway. I feel so impotent—medical coverage is something I have always taken for granted.

August, 1994

It's time to set up the bone marrow transplant. Without insurance, everything is a hassle. The hospital demands full payment in advance. After much bureaucratic haggling, they agree to give me a small discount. Some of the physicians involved agree to reduce their fees; others do not.

I meet Dr. B. at the bone marrow clinic. He explains that the procedure involves removing part of my bone marrow, the substance that produces blood cells. This is necessary because the subsequent chemotherapy is given in such high doses that it would kill bone marrow cells along with the cancer cells. My own bone marrow will then be reinfused into my bloodstream, where it will begin to replenish my blood cells. In the interim period of two to four weeks, I may experience opportunistic infections, hemorrhages, or organ failures. Since I will lack any infection-fighting white blood cells or clot-forming platelets, these complications may be fatal. Dr. B. gets me into a clinical trial of one of the new drugs that speeds up the regeneration of new white blood cells, so that part of the treatment will be free. Unfortunately it turns out that I will receive the placebo.

There is a 2% mortality rate from the procedure, down from 10–20% a few years ago. I am scared: it's a chill feeling in my lower abdomen. I also detest being away from my family during the beginning of school and the Jewish High Holidays, but any delay means more chemo, and I passionately want to get this over with. I guess I will have to make my peace with the chances of dying or of major complications.

Dr. B. says there won't be any complications, but his tone indicates more wishful thinking than conviction.

(A few months later Myra Sadker, 51, noted education professor at American University, and Betsy Lehman, 39, health columnist for the *Boston Globe,* die after a bone marrow transplant for breast cancer. Betsy Lehman's death is caused by an accidental overdose of a chemotherapy drug.)

My husband, supportive as he is, is not worried. To him it's all a logistical question—who will do the shopping and carpooling in my absence. Engineers!

AAAGH! I scream. BC/BS is denying coverage for the catheter insertion on the grounds that preauthorization had been denied. But preauthorization was denied for the bone marrow transplant, not for the line insertion. Now they claim that all treatments—including "chemo," whatever that means—will be denied unless the oncologist can convince them that there is a new treatment plan that excludes this procedure. In other words, once the B-word is mentioned and is entered in their files, even if I pay for it, they will deny every other treatment for my cancer. With a perhaps unfortunate choice of words, I tell the claims adjuster at BC/BS that basically my only option now is to drop dead. She takes it seriously and calls back to make sure I am not planning to commit suicide.

(I think they eventually paid. My insurance files from 1994 are three inches thick, however, and at the time of writing I cannot find the follow-up records about this item.)

Physically I am feeling fine now, with the chemo torture stopped. I am being "restored" for the bone marrow transplant. It's the second such temporary break I have had; the first was for the mastectomy. My appetite and strength come back, my hair starts growing, and then my body is poisoned again. This time, with the high-dose chemotherapy, it will be much worse. After this, no more chemo.

Charmaz (1991) points out that the illness experience may range from "intrusion" (bounded in time) to "immersion" (literally consuming all of one's existence). Often the first acute episode is experienced as an intrusion, only to be followed by remission, then recurrence, chronic debilitating illness, and dying. Subjectively, I still view this nightmare as an intrusion or interruption in my life, not the prologue to its end. More than anything else I want this to be over. I have no regrets about choosing to pay for the bone marrow transplant so the ordeal for me and my family won't be prolonged more than necessary.

With my strength restored, I become impatient to return to normal life, personally and professionally. Projects present themselves. Kim (my research assistant) and I are scheduled to present a paper at the American Sociological Association meeting in Los Angeles. I really want to go.

Although I feel better physically, I have to have frequent blood tests to keep track of my blood counts. The nurses try to draw blood from my catheter and fail, and in the end have to use one of my few surviving veins. This upsets me. What is the point of the expensive (and apparently unreimbursable), painful, pain-in-the-neck catheter?

We decide not to risk traveling to California in my fragile condition. No ASA convention this year.

To: Friends
From: Aliza Kolker <AKOLKER@GMU.EDU>
Date: September 28, 1994
Subject: Bone Marrow Transplant

I have finally returned home after four weeks at Fairfax Hospital, where I had a bone marrow transplant. First my bone marrow was harvested from my hip bone under general anesthesia and I had another catheter inserted in my chest—a total of five dangling lines to be used for chemo and other drugs. Only three turned out to be useful; the others are clogged for some reason. I received high-dose chemotherapy continuously over four days and nights, then a three-day pause, then my own bone marrow was reinfused. Then the long wait began for my bone marrow to start producing blood cells. During that period I contracted a potentially life-threatening fungal infection. Despite massive doses of intravenous antibiotics, the infection persisted because I had almost no white blood cells (the cells that fight infection). My temperature shot up to 105 degrees, my blood pressure was down to 60/40 (a normal reading is 120/80), and I shivered uncontrollably. Intravenous injections of Demerol controlled the shivering but not the other symptoms.

Finally my white blood cell count started to build up and I was able to fight off the infection. But the fight left me exhausted. It's hard for a healthy person to imagine this kind of physical exhaustion. For several days I slept almost around the clock; I could barely lift my head from the pillow. Even using the bedside commode was an ordeal. Verticality—just sitting or walking—seemed like an insurmountable challenge.

I found out that without insurance you receive less care in the hospital. I don't know whether that's a blessing or a curse. When I had passed the life-threatening stage I received fewer costly blood transfusions (at $1,500 per platelet transfusion) than I might have; the physicians decided to wait for my bone marrow to resume functioning by itself. I was not placed on intravenous feeding ($300 per day) until it was clear that I was becoming dangerously undernourished, a common side effect of high-dose chemotherapy. The physical therapist, who should have been nagging me to exercise, left me alone (much to my relief, since I was too weak to move). Even the air humidifier was removed from my room (saving $70 per day).

I owe a great debt to the nurses in the oncology unit. They are gentle and caring. I was also impressed by their intelligence and their technical knowledge. Two of the nurses, including the unit coordinator, were former students in my graduate courses. From professor to patient, it's a short trip.

Now that I am home, my life revolves around daily visits to the hospital for blood draws and transfusions. Yesterday I spent three and a half hours at the bone marrow clinic. These visits use up what little stamina I have.

My thanks to all those who called, visited, sent cards, or tried to call when my phone was turned off because I was too weak to talk. Thanks *especially* to those who donated blood for me (or who tried to). This is a true gift!

November, 1994
◆

After recovering from the bone marrow transplant I start radiation treatments. My hair, which fell out entirely during the transplant, is beginning to come back: I have a fuzz about one millimeter long.

I meet over a bagel and coffee with Nancy (a pseudonym), an attractive 50-year-old high school teacher with a young child. Nancy is facing a bone marrow transplant for recurrent breast cancer. Now it is my turn to reassure her that it is not so bad, as my sister-in-law has done for me. I feel good about giving her moral support. But at night I keep dreaming about recurrence. Just the spelled-out word (no visual images) bothers me all night.

Later, in the aftermath of her bone marrow transplant, Nancy's heart, lungs, and kidney malfunction and she suffers from a massive infection. While I am revising this paper, she spends a total of three weeks in intensive care, close to death. Her husband does not leave her bedside even though, doped up with Demerol, she does not recognize him. Fortunately her insurance covers her treatments.

December 21, 1994
◆

Today I have my last radiation treatment. Today the minor delays—waiting to be called in, waiting on the treatment table while the technologist consults someone—seem somehow worse than usual. Now that the end of treatment (and of the acute phase of my illness) is so close, I am more impatient. When it is over, I feel relief, as when paying the last installment of an oppressive debt or when turning in my grades at the end of the semester. The difference, of course, is that the course is not really over. In the end I may well flunk (to change the metaphor from teacher to student). I will never be cured and will always worry about a recurrence.

January, 1995
◆

Today in Dr. B.'s waiting room, where I have come for blood counts, patients start a conversation. One man has had a lung removed because of lung cancer and is now in chemotherapy. He can't return to his job as a commissioned salesman because he has enough breath to go out only for an hour a day. He is dependent on church and community charity. A woman says her breast cancer has metastasized in the bone, where she has an inoperable tumor. There is also a man in a business suit, ignoring the conversation and immersed in a newsletter. He is in a wheelchair. The legs of his pants are empty.

All of this brings home the reality of a metastasis, further bodily losses, and of course death. I walk out nauseous, my head reeling. I don't recover for many hours.

The illness will not let up. Just when I think it's over and start making plans—explore new research projects, start redecorating the house (long overdue), sign up for programs or courses—there are symptoms or treatments that must be attended to. Right now I have persistent headaches, so Dr. B. has scheduled an immediate MRI today, although it's almost dusk on a wintry Friday afternoon. It's like having your feet march in two different directions: One is pointed toward health and the things that go along with it, the other toward illness and its implications—tests, doctor visits, treatments. One foot is turned in the direction of normality and control; the other, lack of control. It's a confusing metaphor, but I can't think of a better one.

The MRI turns up nothing; sometimes a headache is just a headache. Later, BC/BS will deny reimbursement because someone had forgotten to get preauthorization for this. What do I do the next time I get a headache or another ache?

April, 1995

Debbie calls to tell me her CEA—a blood measure that indicates the presence of a tumor—has gone up. She is convinced her cancer has recurred. She refuses to go back for treatments. She says she does not want to suffer anymore and would rather have a quick but relatively painless death. She sounds as though death is a foregone conclusion. I tell her that she owes it to her young children not to give up.

Throughout the cancer I have slept soundly—for which I am thankful, because I feel that as long as I can sleep, I can cope—but tonight I can't sleep. I am paralyzed with fear: It is a cold hand gripping my heart; a thick cold fog between me and the world. Normally (to the extent that this new phase of my life—living with a horrible type of breast cancer—is normal) I manage to push the disease into a small black cloud in an otherwise normal existence; the cloud gets progressively smaller as memories of the acute phase fade. But now this is reversed. Normality is a small island of blue in an overwhelmingly black sky. Other people I know who have had a recurrence are still separate from me. But my sister-in-law and I are virtual sisters, the same person. That she pulled through the identical diagnosis and treatments was immensely helpful to me all along: I could see the proverbial light at the end of the tunnel. Now, if this is really happening to her (I am still hoping it's a false positive), then I know there is no hope for me either.

A week later, Debbie's elevated CEA count turns out to be a nonevent. Her physician finally tells her that CEA is an unreliable indicator; she will have another blood test later. I return to "normal." Life, not death, is again occupying center stage in my psyche. But why did the doctor who gave her the initial results have to scare the hell out of her—and me? It seems to me that doctors are excessively casual about making announcements that amount to a death sentence, yet turn out to be unsupported.

While I still don't know what the future will bring, today I am elated because I have passed a milestone on the road to recovery from this episode. I have my "debut" with my own hair. Although my hair is very short—really a flat crew cut—the message it (and caring for it) give me is, "this is normal."

Before venturing out in public, I have my hair trimmed and shaped by a hairdresser. She is unfamiliar with wigs; when I remove mine in her presence, she shrieks in horror. I tell her about the chemotherapy and say, "Make my hair presentable." Naturally the conversation turns to breast cancer. The hairdresser, a young woman with a Spanish accent, tells me that her aunt has been treated for breast cancer. Then she asks whether treatments are expensive, particularly if you don't have health insurance? She doesn't say, but obviously she is worried about herself—hairdressers don't have health insurance or other benefits. I decide not to give her a lecture about the political economy of health insurance. What good would it do?

June, 1995

Both BC/BS of Virginia and that of National Capital Area have started paying for bone marrow transplants for breast cancer, as a result of lawsuits and lobbying efforts. Maybe even my own appeals helped turn the tide. It seems, however, that I fell between the cracks.

The Consequences of Rationing

I have resumed teaching full time and taking care of my family. The illness that consumed my existence has been relegated to a disruption, an episode. The only lingering reminders are my missing breast, the terrifying fear of recurrence, and the bills.

Sociologically, my story illustrates the transformation of health care in America. In the new reality, which largely has gone unnoticed outside the health care system, the denial of coverage or of treatment may pose a much greater risk than does overtreatment (Eckholm 1994). I would like now to turn to the ramifications of that transformation for American society.

The toll that health care rationing takes in patients' lives and health has been amply documented in the medical literature (Ayanian et al. 1993; Braveman et al. 1994; Lewin and Sharfstein 1990). One of the areas most severely affected is mental health. Lewin and Sharfstein relate the case history of a severely malfunctioning borderline patient who should have been treated in a carefully structured long-term setting. Her insurance policy, however, mandated quick discharge. Unable to function on her own and without treatment, she needed repeated emergency hospitalizations. No progress with her treatments could be accomplished in such settings. The psychiatrists note in frustration (Lewin and Sharfstein 1990, 120–121):

> Treatment goals in the hospital are increasingly compromised with arbitrary and excessive managed care in which the case managers attempt to dictate on an almost daily basis the patient's course of treatment and treatment goals. Sometimes there is "the double message": if the patient is getting better, rapidly come up with a discharge plan; if the patient is not getting better, rapidly come up with a discharge plan since this is a "custodial case" . . . In the environment of great clinical and economic uncertainty in which we live, the catastrophically ill patient is likely to suffer.

Insurance gaps may spell not only medical but financial catastrophe for patients and their families. Covinsky (1994) studied more than 2,000 patients discharged from hospitals after treatment for major illness and found that nearly a third of the families lost most of their life savings and many lost their incomes as well. The most remarkable aspect of this finding is that 96% of the patients had some form of hospital insurance, yet 31% used up all or most of their life savings on the unreimbursed costs of home care and disability.

Defenders of the present American health care system argue that, for the insured majority, the United States provides more and faster access to advanced medical technology than do countries with universal health care coverage, and that the quality and timeliness of care would be eroded if our health care system were to broaden coverage (Iglehart 1984). In fact, the United States leads the world in the use of expensive treatments such as coronary-artery bypass procedures and kidney dialysis. However, many of these procedures are performed on patients who are already very old, terminally ill, or unlikely to lead a normal life outside the hospital. By contrast, other patients are frequently denied beneficial treatment because they are unable to pay for it, lack health insurance, or their insurance plan denies coverage.

Silberman et al. (1994) compare the availability and prompt use of allogeneic bone marrow transplants (that is, using a matching donor's marrow), a treatment of proven effectiveness for some types of leukemia, in 10 economically developed, democratic countries. They found that the United States ranks somewhere from middle to bottom in both availability and prompt usage of the technology, that is, the likelihood of patients being given the treatment at an early stage of the disease when it is most likely to save their lives. They conclude that the American health care system, with its emphasis on the patient's ability to pay and on independently practicing specialists, offers no advantages in access to high-technology treatments. On the contrary, these features of our system may cause potentially fatal denials or delays in treatment. Health care systems that feature universal coverage, global budgeting, or single-payer financing fare no worse, or even better, than does the American system.

Each of us must face the inescapable conclusion that because of rising costs, managed care is here to stay. Hence some form of health care rationing is unavoidable. If we accept the need for rationing care, ethicists argue, we must ensure that it is allocated in accordance with some criterion of justice. There is a broad consensus among ethicists and many health policy analysts that, at the minimum, a just system would provide universal access to basic health benefits (Abels and Rice 1990; Macklin 1985; Pawlson, Glover, and Murphy 1992). Further, a just system would require abolishing restrictions on enrollment and discrimination in coverage and in premiums. These goals could be accomplished by adopting a single-payer system.

At the other end of the ideological spectrum, some health economists and health care managers argue that a market system is the most appropriate model for health delivery. In a true market system, physicians would have financial incentives to cut costs, insurance companies would compete by offering attractive benefit packages at the lowest premiums, and savvy consumers would pick the most suitable insurance plan for themselves and their families. These analysts believe that such a system would result in rational decision making and in significant savings for individuals and society.

However, the ideal of rational choice regulated only by the free market is unrealistic. It is employers, not employees, who buy insurance contracts for their companies. Individuals' choices are usually limited to one managed-care provider and one HMO. Further, no healthy person can predict future health care needs. When illness strikes, the amount and quality of health care people will receive is subject to forces beyond their control. Despite media accounts of spectacular court settlements awarded to patients (or their survivors) for denial of coverage, carriers can protect themselves from litigation by plainly specifying any restrictions in their contracts. Which services are covered and which excluded varies among different insurance carriers and in different parts of the country.

The words *rationing* and *rationality* have the same root. Yet the transformation of the health care system has not been guided by the principles of equity or rationality advocated by ethicists and policymakers (Aaron and Schwartz 1990; Abels and Rice 1990; Macklin 1985; Pawlson, Glover, and Murhpy 1992). Instead, in the prevailing free-market environment, it has been driven by the dynamics of private enterprise, whose goal is cutting costs and maximizing profits. Medical care in the United States is rationed, first, by excluding many citizens from any medical insurance, and second, by the insurance companies' policies on premiums and reimbursement. Carriers determine which providers, procedures, and drugs will be reimbursed and at what rate. Whether these regulations conform with physicians' judgments or patients' needs is scarcely relevant except as a marketing tool.

Whatever the merits of the market system in promoting efficiency and rationality in other spheres, in health care this model is marked inevitably by arbitrariness, waste, and injustice. Persons with the same diagnosis are covered by some carriers but not by others, protected in some states but not in others. I was denied potentially lifesaving treatment because at the time I needed it both of my insurance companies did not cover this procedure and my state did not mandate it, unlike most other states.

I cannot control my illness. But I would like to use my experience to plead for a wider debate over what would constitute sane guidelines for American health policy.

References

Aaron, H. and W. B. Schwartz. 1990. "Rationing Health Care: The Choice Before Us." *Science* 247, (January 26): 418–422.

Abels, P. and S. Rice.1990. "Stop the World, I Want to Stay On: Rationing Health Care, First the Aged, and Then?" *Social Thought* 16, no. 1: 41–47.

Alsop, S. 1973. *Stay of Execution.* Philadelphia: J.B. Lippincott.

Ayanian, J., B. Kohler, T. Abe, and A. Epstein. 1993. "The Relation Between Health Insurance Coverage and Clinical Outcomes Among Women with Breast Cancer." *The New England Journal of Medicine* 329, no. 5, (July 29): 326–331.

Behar, R. 1991. "Death and Memory: From Santa Maria del Monte to Miami Beach." *Cultural Anthropology* 6, no. 3 (August):346–384.

Braveman, P. M. Schaaf, S. Egerter, T. Bennett, and W. Schecter. 1994. "Insurance-Related Differences in the Risk of Ruptured Appendix." *The New England Journal of Medicine* 331, no. 7 (August 18): 444–449.

Butler, S. and B. Rosenblum. 1991. *Cancer in Two Voices.* San Francisco: Spinsters Book Company.

Callahan, D. 1987. *Setting Limits: Medical Goals in an Aging Society.* New York: Simon & Schuster.

———. 1992. "Symbols, Rationality, and Justice: Rationing Health Care." *American Journal of Law and Medicine* 18, 1/2 (Spring/Summer): 1–13.

Charmaz, C. 1991. *Good Days, Bad Days: The Self in Chronic Illness and Time.* New Brunswick, NJ: Rutgers University Press.

Chevallier, B., H. Roche, J. P. Olivier, et al. 1993. "Inflammatory Breast Cancer." *American Journal of Clinical Oncology.* 16, no. 3: 223–228.

Conrad, P., and P. Brown. 1993. "Rationing Medical Care: A Sociological Reflection." *Research in the Sociology of Health Care* 10: 3–22.

Covinsky, K. E. 1994. "Impact of Serious Illness on Patients' Families." *The Journal of the American Medical Association* 272, no. 23 (December 21): 1839–1844.

Eckholm, E. 1994. "While Congress Remains Silent, Health Care Transforms Itself." *The New York Times* (December 18): 1, 34.

Ellis, C. 1995. *Final Negotiations: A Story of Love, Loss, and Chronic Illness.* Philadelphia: Temple University Press.

Hilzenrath, D.1995. "Costly Savings: Downside of the New Health Care." *The Washington Post* (August 7): A1, A10.

Iglehart, J. 1984. "Opinion Polls on Health Care." *The New England Journal of Medicine* 310: 1616–1620.

Kolata, G. 1994. "Battle Over a Baby's Future Raises Hard Ethical Issues." *The New York Times* (December 27): A1, A12.

Kolker, A., and B. M. Burke. 1994. *Prenatal Testing: A Sociological Perspective.* Westport, CT: Bergin and Garvey.

Lewin, R. and S. Sharfstein. 1990. "Managed Care and the Discharge Dilemma." *Psychiatry* 53, no. 2: 116–121.

Linden, R. R. 1993. *Making Stories, Making Selves: Feminist Reflections on the Holocaust.* Columbus: Ohio State University Press.

Macklin, R. 1985. "Are We in the Lifeboat Yet?" *Social Research* 52, no. 3 (Autumn): 607–623.

Mariner, W. 1984. "Diagnostic Related Groupings: Evading Social Responsibility?" *Law, Medicine and Health Care* 12, no. 6 (December): 243–244.

Marmor, T. R., and J. Mashaw. 1993. "Rhetoric and Reality." *Health Management Quarterly* (October-December): 406–409.

Mechanic, D. 1985. "Cost Containment and the Quality of Medical Care: Rationing Strategies in an Era of Constrained Resources." *Milbank Quarterly* 63, no. 3: 453–475.

Merton, R. K. 1968. *Social Theory and Social Structure.* New York: The Free Press.

Mills, C. W. 1959. *The Sociological Imagination.* New York: Oxford University Press.

Myerson, A. 1995. "Helping Health Insurers Say No." *The New York Times* (March 20): D1, D5.

NCI Fact Book. 1994. Bethesda, MD: National Cancer Institute.

Paget, M. A. 1993. *A Complex Sorrow: Reflections on Cancer and an Abbreviated Life.* Philadelphia: Temple University Press.

Pawlson, L. G., J. J. Glover, and D. J. Murphy. 1992. "An Overview of Allocation and Rationing: Implications for Geriatrics." *Journal of the American Geriatrics Society* 40, no. 6 (June): 628–634.

Peters, W., and M. Rogers. 1994. "Variation in Approval by Insurance Companies of Coverage for Autologous Bone Marrow Transplantation for Breast Cancer." *The New England Journal of Medicine* 330 (February 17): 473–477.

Relman, A. S. 1980. "The New Medical-Industrial Complex." *The New England Journal of Medicine* 303: 963–970. Reprinted in *Dominant Issues in Medical Sociology,* edited by H. D. Schwartz (New York: McGraw-Hill, 1994): 292–304.

———. 1994. "Medical Insurance and Health: What About Managed Care?" *The New England Journal of Medicine* 331, no. 7 (August 18): 471–472.

Rothman, D. 1992. "Rationing Life." *New York Review of Books* 39, no. 5 (March 5): 32–37.

Schroeder, S. 1994. "Rationing Medical Care—A Comparative Perspective." *The New England Journal of Medicine* 331, no. 16 (October 20): 1089–1091.

Silberman, G., et al. 1994. "Availability and Appropriateness of Allogeneic Bone Marrow Transplantation for Chronic Myeloid Leukemia in 10 Countries." *The New England Journal of Medicine* 331, no. 16 (October 20): 1063–1067.

Wikler, D. 1992. "Ethics and Rationing: 'Whether,' 'How,' or 'How Much?'" *Journal of the American Geriatric Society* 40, no. 4 (April): 398–403.

Zussman, R. 1992. *Intensive Care.* Chicago: University of Chicago Press.

◆ ───────

Aliza Kolker was born in Israel and moved to the United States with her family at age 13. Since receiving a Ph.D. in sociology from Columbia University in 1975, she has been a stick-in-the-mud, holding down a single teaching job and living in the same community. She has been teaching sociology at George Mason University in Virginia, where she is now a full professor. Her specialties include medical sociology, political sociology, and the sociology of aging. She is the author of four books, including most recently *Prenatal Testing* (with B. Meredith Burke, Greenwood Press, 1994). She is married and has two teenaged sons.

The Life Boat Is Fraught
Reflections on "Thrown Overboard"

R. Ruth Linden

The editors of this volume initially invited me to comment on "Thrown Overboard" as a "blind," anonymous reviewer because of my interest in sociologists' experimental writings and my research on the biopolitics of breast cancer. They may also have suspected that Professor Kolker's story would captivate me intellectually and emotionally, and they were right on the mark.

Because Aliza Kolker dares to bring her body into the text, her writing is bold and risky. Her narrative is a stunning exemplar of a new wave of embodied social science that displaces the familiar binaries of self/other, subject/object, literary/interpretive, narrative/analytic, healthy/ill, and private/public. There is much to be said about how the force of this account evokes the experiences of living with a rare form of advanced breast cancer and enduring a highly toxic, excruciatingly painful, and exorbitantly costly therapy.

In this commentary, however, my remarks will not focus on the illness narrative per se. Instead, I want to explore some of the origins and consequences of Dr. Kolker's articulated and unspoken assumptions about high-dose chemotherapy with autologous stem cell rescue (HDC/ASCR)—the procedures commonly referred to as bone marrow transplantation. This commentary, then, is part of an ongoing conversation, begun nearly a year ago, among the editors of this volume, Professor Kolker, and me; and it is also part of a wider conversation in the popular media and among breast cancer activists, clinicians, clinical researchers, and other actors in health policy and medical technology assessment arenas (Bone Marrow Transplant listserve; ECRI 1995; "From Health Net" 1996; Smith and Henderson 1995; Kelly and Koenig forthcoming; Larson 1996; Ruzek 1995b; Stewart 1992; Zones 1995).

In the summer of 1994, following Professor Kolker's mastectomy, her oncologist recommended that she undergo bone marrow transplantation. She states that "this treatment, until recently considered experimental, has been proved effective for advanced or metastatic breast cancer." The key terms in this sentence are *experimental, proved,* and *effective.* In the context of advanced breast cancer, meanings of these terms need to be examined carefully.

When I first read this description of ABMT, I wondered exactly how much Dr. Kolker had learned about this therapy—from talking with her physicians, from investigating the medical literature on her own, from her sister-in-law, or from other breast cancer survivors— before she decided to pursue her physicians' treatment recommendations. Interestingly, her narrative suggests that she hardly needed to be persuaded or convinced that this procedure might extend her life. Faced with a dismal prognosis, she seemed prepared to take her chances with what she believed was the best therapy that high-technology medicine could offer her.

For many women, the terror, uncertainty, and vulnerability of being diagnosed with breast cancer can pose massive obstacles to becoming mobilized as lay medical researchers and self-advocates. Typically, women with breast cancer may be afraid that if they ask too many questions or challenge the received medical wisdom, their physicians might refuse to treat them altogether. Such fears of being abandoned are by no means unfounded. Yet just as questioning or challenging medical authority has consequences, *not* questioning or challenging medical authority also has consequences. Medical authority, though, is not monolithic. Experts—in this case, medical oncologists—can and do disagree, as a matter of course, about which therapy is likely to be most effective for a particular patient.

My reading of several articles about bone marrow transplantation as a therapy for women with advanced breast cancer leads me to draw an entirely different set of conclusions from Dr. Kolker and her physicians. I do want to acknowledge, however, that optimistic opinions about ABMT may be found in the medical literature, and they are enthusiastically reported by the media.

Let me first identify my main sources of data: a 1995 review article by Smith and Henderson; and ECRI's executive briefing dated February 1995, based on a 200-page technology assessment report.[1] According to medical sociologist Jane Zones, ECRI, a nonprofit agency, is "a credible, well-reputed company that protects itself against conflict of interest so that it can make unbiased assessments of medical technologies" (Zones 1995, 1).

These articles suggest that ABMT is an experimental or investigative procedure. They also pose the complex questions of what shall count as *proof* in clinical practice, and how much proof is necessary or sufficient to support a claim that a new treatment actually confers benefit. Furthermore, these studies point toward the ambiguous and multiple meanings of the term *effective* in evaluating a patient's response to high-dose cytotoxic chemotherapy.

State-of-the-Art or Experimental/Investigational Therapy?

◆

What does it mean to say that ABMT is an experimental therapy for advanced breast cancer? Technically, any therapy that has not been thoroughly evaluated in a randomized clinical trial (RCT), in which it is compared with the current, best standard therapy or with a competitive therapy, is experimental (Zelen 1995, 10). While phase II studies have been conducted for a full decade (ECRI 1995, 8), randomized clinical trials, considered to be the gold standard of research design, have not been completed for ABMT in women with breast cancer.[2]

Widespread media attention has spawned high patient demand for bone marrow transplantation. This has meant that some phase III RCTs have had enormous difficulty accruing subjects. Clinical trials that compare ABMT to standard chemotherapy require that patients risk being randomized to the standard-dose chemotherapy arm of the trial (Smith and Henderson 1995, 1; Moss 1995, 58). Few women whose physicians recommend ABMT, who have other treatment options besides enrolling in an RCT, will be willing to take the risk of not getting their therapy of choice (Zones 1995, 9; Moss 1995, 58). Such hesitancy is certainly understandable.

Regardless, responsibility for the uncertainty surrounding the efficacy of bone marrow transplantation must be placed where it is due: on the for-profit health sector, which is positioned to exploit a patient market desperate for treatment. By playing off patients' "preconceived expectations regarding the effectiveness of this treatment based on anecdotal reports, the experience of family or friends, and the climate generated by popular media," ABMT has garnered massive revenues (Smith and Henderson 1995, 211).[3] The clinical research community, which has been slow to develop randomized trials with designs that are acceptable to women living with advanced breast cancer, must also be held accountable.

Three national, randomized trials investigating the efficacy of ABMT in women with breast cancer are currently in progress (ECRI 1995, 9). For instance, clinical researchers at the Philadelphia Bone Marrow Transplant Group and Duke University are studying the question of timing—whether women with metastatic disease who respond to conventional chemotherapy benefit more from early ABMT than later ABMT following a relapse. They also are comparing the benefits, for women who respond to conventional chemotherapy, of high-dose chemotherapy versus standard-dose maintenance chemotherapy given over a two-year period (Smith and Henderson 1995, 206). Until these and other questions are answered, ABMT will remain experimental for women with advanced breast cancer.

For women with Professor Kolker's diagnosis—inflammatory breast cancer, which accounts for 1–4% of all diagnosed breast cancers (Love, Lindsey 1990, 269)—outcome data are even more equivocal. In absolute terms, because fewer women with inflammatory breast cancer have participated in clinical research, how well they will do on high-dose chemotherapy cannot be reliably predicted. According to Smith and Henderson, "characteristics such as: patient age, menopausal status, prior chemotherapy received, or ER/PR [estrogen receptor/progesterone receptor-status]. . . can have a tremendous effect on prognosis, arguably greater than the treatment [ABMT] itself" (1995, 201). Other features of tumor biology as well as key gene abnormalities may be relevant to a woman's breast cancer prognosis (National Cancer Advisory Board 1994, B-16).[4] Separately and together, how these variables affect high-dose chemotherapy (not to mention standard-dose treatment) remains uncertain.

Politics of Proof
◆

Proving the efficacy of bone marrow transplantation has become highly contentious. The rapid diffusion of ABMT reflects the wider tendency of high-technology procedures and devices to move into clinical practice before they have been thoroughly evaluated (Kelly and Koenig forthcoming, 3). Yet even when studies demonstrate that a technology does *not* improve outcomes, extend life, or enhance quality of life, such findings may have only limited clinical impact.

Novel medical technologies are pushed into the marketplace by a complex weave of cultural, political, and economic forces that shape local practice patterns (Kelly and Koenig forthcoming, 3–6; Banta 1983; Greer 1988). Thus, whether a technology actually confers clinical benefits may only be incidental to its use and to physicians' beliefs about best practices. As Smith and Henderson note, "a recent survey of American physicians revealed that 80% believe women with metastatic disease should be treated with a bone marrow transplant despite inconclusive evidence that this approach is superior to standard chemotherapy" (1995, 201). Consumers, clinicians, and technology assessment analysts have all been slow to recognize that proof of clinical benefits does not in itself account for the adoption of a wide range of new technologies.

In clinical research, proof is established by providing reliable evidence of beneficial health outcomes. Yet data are a necessary but not sufficient condition for demonstrating benefit, because clinicians and clients interpret statistical findings in the context of their prevailing world views, professional commitments, prior experience, and deeply held beliefs and values. In the words of one medical oncologist commenting on the high frequency of breast cancer relapses in women who had undergone ABMT:

> . . . different people interpreted that in different ways. If you were a transplanter, you said, Well, we just haven't found the right drugs, or we haven't given them early enough, or we haven't selected our patients well enough. . . . And if you were a nontransplanter, you'd say, "We're wasting our money doing this, it's clearly not going to work" (Good et al. 1995, 148).

Which Outcomes Measure Therapeutic Efficacy?
◆

What shall count as an effective treatment for advanced or metastatic breast cancer? This is a practical question, one that the Food and Drug Administration must consider when it reviews a new drug for approval. The available outcomes data for bone marrow transplantation are based on meta-analyses of phase II ABMT trials, which have been compared with studies reporting on women who received standard-dose chemotherapy. Using meta-analysis, the results of many smaller studies have been combined and analyzed to obtain greater statistical power (ECRI 1995, 5; Bulpitt 1988, 93).

The ECRI technology assessment report evaluated all studies published through September 1994, and found that the published data for inflammatory breast cancer patients are insufficient to determine the efficacy of ABMT for this type of cancer (1995, 9). However, it did draw conclusions about outcomes for women with Stage IV (metastatic) breast cancer, which may be summarized as follows: Women who receive standard-dose chemotherapy are more likely to remain free of disease and survive longer than women who receive high-dose chemotherapy with ABMT (8–9).

While ABMT is associated with higher short-term response rates than conventional chemotherapy (as measured by tumor regression), this finding may reflect a serious sampling bias and is generally not sustained (ECRI 1995, 7; Zones 1995, 1). There is only a weak correlation between tumor response and life extension (Moss 1995, 66; Epstein 1993, 19), yet the FDA grants approval of cancer therapies based on data that demonstrate tumor response, among other factors. Thus, the higher correlation between objective response rates and high-dose chemotherapy is unrelated to the crucial outcomes of disease-free survival rates and overall survival time.

Smith and Henderson arrived at the same conclusions as the ECRI report. In their words, "when compared to trials of standard combination chemotherapy, . . . it might be concluded that HDC/ABMT shortens the survival of women with metastatic breast cancer" (1995, 212). These authors do not specifically mention outcomes for women with inflammatory breast cancer, but I presume that they would concur with ECRI's finding that the published data are insufficient to make any determinations.

I do not have breast cancer—not yet, as far as I know.[5] However, if I were diagnosed with advanced breast cancer, I cannot say whether or not I would choose to undergo aggressive cytotoxic chemotherapy. When people with life-threatening illnesses are faced with actual treatment decisions, they do not necessarily act as they would have predicted. With the increased proximity of dying (or the possibility of dying), other considerations that cannot be anticipated may come into play.

I would not want to judge another person's treatment decisions, but not only because I cannot know how I would respond under similar circumstances. Even for "standard of care" regimens that have been studied in rigorous, phase III clinical trials (decidedly *not* the situation with ABMT for advanced breast cancer), data are only and at best probabilistic. People with life-threatening illnesses often "defy" their prognoses by surviving in reasonably good health or living with disease progression for extended periods of time. Mysteriously, they confound their physicians' and outcomes researchers' expectations. Biostatistics can only tell part of the story.

In writing this commentary, my intention has been to present a complex and problematic picture—one that casts a shadow on high-dose chemotherapy and raises more questions than can possibly be answered. My view is that people with cancer, HIV, and other serious illnesses should, if they wish, have access to life-extending investigational therapies before "all the data are in" (whatever "*all* the data" might mean). As a rule, I also believe that managed-care companies and third-party payers ought to provide their clients with or reimburse the costs of such therapies. However, the extreme toxicity of high-dose chemotherapy, coupled with the absence of solid, scientific evidence of benefit for women with advanced breast cancer raises the question of whether, in the case of ABMT, this view is morally and scientifically sound. At this writing, I am uncertain about where I stand on this issue.

Professor Kolker's discussion of health care rationing suggests altogether different grounds for why Blue Cross/Blue Shield should have paid for her treatment. "Thrown Overboard" brings to life many abstract debates about health care reform and the failures of "unmanaged competition."[6] But her narrative does not tell a story about rationing, as the term is conventionally understood in bioethics and health policy arenas.

Professor Kolker uses the concept of rationing to link her situation with the plight of people who are medically uninsured or underinsured. Yet her analysis glosses over the specific structural and political conditions that are reflected in the uneven distribution of health services and treatment options. I must admit that I am unconvinced by her argument that she has been "thrown overboard," even as I am moved by her courage in making agonizing treatment decisions.

It will probably be many years before we have conclusive data about the outcomes of ABMT for different subgroups of women with advanced breast cancer. In the meantime, many treatment issues beg to be addressed. Such issues can be addressed locally, independent of the Clinton administration's failed efforts at health care reform.

While the jury deliberates on ABMT (to borrow Smith and Henderson's metaphor), women with advanced breast cancer should be aware that other experimental therapies, most of which are far less toxic than high-dose chemotherapy, are being studied in phase I, II, and III clinical trials. These third-, fourth-, and fifth-line, potentially life-extending treatments represent a new generation of biological therapies that are more specific than cytotoxic chemotherapy, which kills cancerous and healthy cells without distinction.

Several monoclonal antibodies to the HER2, antigen, an oncogene overexpressed in about 25% of women with breast cancer, are in different phases of investigation. Genentech's product has an expanded access protocol under which women who do not meet the phase III trials' inclusion criteria may still attempt to obtain access to the drug.

Expanded access to investigational drugs is one of many regulatory reforms initiated by AIDS treatment activists (Crimp and Rolston 1990). For many months, Genentech resisted negotiating with breast cancer activists about this issue. However, the efforts of a small group of women and men from the Breast Cancer Committee of ACT UP Golden Gate, which staged a demonstration with civil disobedience, eventually brought Genentech to the negotiating table (McGregor 1995; Evans 1995). A coalition of activists from ACT UP Golden Gate, Breast Cancer Action, and Project Inform is learning how to translate the enormously successful technologies of AIDS treatment activism into the breast cancer arena.

Another family of drugs, called *azoles,* inhibits synthesis of aromatase, the enzyme that interconverts androgens and estrogens produced in the body. For some postmenopausal women with metastatic disease, a new azole called Arimidex (generic name annstrozole), recently licensed by the FDA, may relieve common, debilitating symptoms such as bone pain, decrease tumor mass, or delay disease progression while not interfering with good quality of life for 6 to 18 months (see McGregor 1993; Zeneca Pharmaceuticals 1996). Still another promising therapy in phase II and III clinical trials is liposomal doxorubicin (trade name Adriamycin). Adriamycin, a highly toxic form of chemotherapy used to treat breast cancer, was developed more than 20 years ago. Liposomes are a novel mechanism for delivering cytotoxic drugs to specific organs while sparing the body the systemic burden of cytotoxic chemotherapy. This transport system may prove to be more effective as well as less toxic than standard-dose chemotherapy.

Women with breast cancer have an unprecedented opportunity to rewrite the dominant narrative about breast cancer with its privileging of the technologies of slash (surgery), burn (radiation therapy), and poison (cytotoxic chemotherapy). This oppositional narrative could, eventually, displace the cytotoxic chemotherapy paradigm, which has maintained a stronghold on clinical research and treatment for decades. It could substitute righteous anger for the relentless cheerfulness and quiet suffering that are expected of women with "the dread disease" (Patterson 1987).

Women with breast cancer could learn two crucial lessons from the astonishing history of HIV/AIDS treatment activism.[7] The first lesson is the importance of holding fast to the goal of extending the lives of women with advanced disease. This would mean: inaugurating a campaign to demand that pharmaceutical manufacturers provide expanded access to promising experimental drugs; insisting that continuation protocols are built into premarket studies, where appropriate;[8] and lobbying all relevant public and private institutions to ensure that research and development of innovative, noncytotoxic therapies are a top priority.

The second and perhaps more urgent lesson is not, technically speaking, a treatment issue. The affected community must educate itself on a broad range of scientific, clinical, and policy matters: epidemiology, endocrinology, tumor immunology and biology, molecular genetics, the science of clinical research design, the politics of scientific peer review, and federal drug regulatory policies. Just as AIDS treatment activists have done, women with breast cancer must develop their own effective media to disseminate cutting-edge treatment news. They must learn how to make news stories happen and then get those stories covered, on *their* terms, by mainstream electronic and print media. Once women with breast cancer and their political allies become at least as conversant as the official "experts" on these issues, then we will be able to argue a convincing case for saving our own lives.

Notes

1. The Emergency Care Research Institute, located in Plymouth Meeting, Pennsylvania, is known by its acronym, ECRI.
2. A phase II trial determines whether a drug, procedure, or device has efficacy. A phase III trial compares the therapy under investigation with the standard of care.
3. According to Moss, in 1994, over 1,000 women with breast cancer received ABMT outside of a clinical trial. If the cost of each procedure was $100,000, the total revenues for breast cancer patients alone exceeded $100,000,000.
4. Factors in tumor biology include: HER2 overexpression, S phase fraction, protein tyrosine, cathepsin D, cathepsin B, phosphatase, cyclin D, cyclin E, and heat shock proteins. Among key gene abnormalities are p53, c-myc, and ataxia-telangiectasia.
5. My phrasing echoes Patti Lather (Lather and Smithies 1995, xxix), who writes, "I am . . . not yet, to my knowledge, HIV positive."
6. The term was coined by Sheryl Ruzek (1995a).
7. The following two paragraphs are adapted from Linden (1995).
8. Continuation protocols enable clinical research subjects to stay on a drug once a trial is completed, but before it has been approved by the FDA.

References

Banta, D. H. 1983. "Social Science Research on Medical Technology: Utility and Limitations." *Social Science and Medicine* 17: 1363–1369.

Bulpitt, C. J. 1988. "Meta-analysis." *Lancet* (July 9): 93–94.

Crimp, D., with A. Rolston. 1990. *AIDS/Demographics*. Seattle: Bay Press.

ECRI. 1995. "High-dose Chemotherapy with Autologous Bone Marrow Transplantation and/or Blood Cell Transplantation for the Treatment of Metastatic Breast Cancer." *Health Technology Assessment Information Service Executive Briefings* (February): 1–12. (Available from ECRI at 5200 Butler Pike, Plymouth Meeting, PA 19462–1298.)

Epstein, S. E. 1993. Evaluation of the National Cancer Program and Proposed Reforms." *International Journal of Health Services* 23: 15–44.

Evans, N. 1995. "Prodded by Activists, Genentech Moves Toward Compassion." *Breast Cancer Action Newsletter* 32 (October): 4. (Available from BCA at 55 New Montgomery, Suite 624, San Francisco, CA 94105.)

"From Health Net: A Frank Discussion about Health Care and Transplants." 1996. *San Francisco Examiner* (January 26): A–26.

Good, M-J. D. V., et al. 1995. "Medicine on the Edge: Conversations with Oncologists." In *Technoscientific Imaginaries: Conversations, Profiles, and Memoirs,* edited by George Marcus. (Chicago: University of Chicago Press): 129–152.

Greer, A. L. 1988. "The State of the Art vs. the State of the Science: The Diffusion of New Medical Technologies into Practice." *International Journal of Technology Assessment in Health Care* 4: 5–26.

Kelly, S. E., and B. A. Koenig. Forthcoming. " 'Rescue' Technologies Following High-Dose Chemotherapy: How Social Context Shapes the Assessment of Innovative, Aggressive, and Life-Saving Medical Technologies." In *Getting Doctors to Listen: Ethics and Outcomes Data in Context,* edited by Philip Boyle. (Washington, DC: Georgetown University Press.)

Larson, E. 1996. "The Soul of an HMO." *Time* (January 22): 44–52.

Lather, P., and C. Smithies. 1995. *Troubling Angels: Women Living with HIV/AIDS.* Columbus: Greyden Press.

Linden, R. R. 1995. "Re-inventing Treatment Activism." *Breast Cancer Action Newsletter* 33 (December): 3–4. (Available from BCA at 55 New Montgomery, Suite 624, San Francisco, CA 94105.)

Love, S. M., with K. Lindsey. 1990. *Dr. Susan Love's Breast Book,* 2nd ed. Reading, MA: Addison-Wesley.

McGregor, M. 1993. "Waiting for Lentaron." *Breast Cancer Action Newsletter* 21 (December): 1. (Available from BCA at 55 New Montgomery, Suite 624, San Francisco, CA 94105.)

———. 1995. "Takin' It to the Streets." *Center News* (Spring): 4. (Newsletter of the Women's Cancer Resource Center. Available from WCRC at 3023 Shattuck Avenue, Berkeley, CA 94705.)

Moss, R. W. 1995. *Questioning Chemotherapy.* Brooklyn: Equinox Press.

National Cancer Advisory Board. 1994. *Cancer at a Crossroads: A Report to Congress for the Nation.* National Cancer Institute.

Patterson, J. T. 1987. *The Dread Disease.* Cambridge, MA: Harvard University Press.

Ruzek, S. B. 1995a. "Problems for the Future of Women's Health: Women's Interests in Health Reform." Paper presented at "Re/visioning Women,

Health and Healing: Feminist, Cultural and Technoscience Studies Perspectives." University of California, San Francisco, October 6–7.

————. 1995b. "Technology and Perceptions of Risk: Clinical, Scientific, and Consumer Perspectives in Breast Cancer Treatment." *Health Technology Assessment Information Service Executive Briefings* (January): 1–6.

Smith, G. A., and I. C. Henderson. 1995. "High-Dose Chemotherapy (HDC) with Autologous Bone Marrow Transplantation (ABMT) for the Treatment of Breast Cancer: The Jury is Still Out." *Important Advances in Oncology:* 201–214.

Stewart, S. K. 1992. *Bone Marrow Transplants: A Book of Basics for Patients.* Highland Park, IL: BMT Newsletter. Reprinted by NYSERNet, Inc. with permission of the *BMT Newsletter.* (Newsletter is available on the World-Wide Web at http: //cancer.med.upenn.edu or by writing to the *BMT Newsletter* at: 1985 Spruce Avenue, Highland Park, IL 60035.)

Zelen, M. 1993. "Theory and Practice of Clinical Trials." In *Cancer Medicine,* 3rd ed., edited by Holland, et al. (Philadelphia: Lea & Febiger): 340–360. Reprinted in syllabus for "Fourth Regional Symposium on the Design and Methods of Clinical Trials." 1995. Department of Epidemiology and Biostatistics and Department of Medicine, University of California, San Francisco (September 14–15): 9–29.

Zeneca Pharmaceuticals. 1996. Arimidex product information sheet. Zeneca Inc.: Wilmington, DE.

Zones, J. 1995. "What Is the Price of Hope?" *Breast Cancer Action Newsletter* 33 (December): 1, 8–9. (Available from BCA at 55 New Montgomery, Suite 624, San Francisco, CA 94105.)

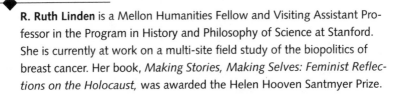

R. Ruth Linden is a Mellon Humanities Fellow and Visiting Assistant Professor in the Program in History and Philosophy of Science at Stanford. She is currently at work on a multi-site field study of the biopolitics of breast cancer. Her book, *Making Stories, Making Selves: Feminist Reflections on the Holocaust,* was awarded the Helen Hooven Santmyer Prize.

I would like to thank Marilyn McGregor and Susan E. Kelly for their insightful comments on earlier drafts. A fellowship from the Andrew W. Mellon Foundation through Stanford supported this writing. This chapter is dedicated to Irv Zola, *zikhrono livrakhah,* may his memory be blessed.

CHAPTER FIVE

Collecting Ourselves at the End of the Century

Mark Neumann

You never seem to find what you're looking for at the Dusty Memories thrift store on the corner of Nebraska and New Orleans Avenues in Tampa. Like a dimly lit attic, the shop is a collection of old chairs, end tables, lamps, records, books, mirrors, plates, candleholders, and ceramic nicknacks. All of them bear some trace of a stranger's life—scratches, tears, fingerprints. I wandered the narrow trails through the merchandise one afternoon, pondering items that curiously called out to me. I went in to buy a bookshelf for a house I'd just rented. Instead, I walked out with a glass Niagara Falls souvenir ashtray, a slightly scratched recording of Curtis Mayfield's 1972 soundtrack for *Super Fly*, and a tattered copy of *The Secret Museum of Mankind*.

We find and lose and find ourselves through the objects and images we gather around us. In different ways, the thrift store and *The Secret Museum of Mankind* remind us of a desire to possess the world through collecting (Clifford 1988), and how collections may change, lose value, or fall apart over time. The thrift store is a potential museum as well as a salesroom. Its exhibits reflect how people once arranged their lives and presented images to themselves and others. And it's a place where old possessions may take on a new life as they fall into another's hands. *The Secret Museum of Mankind*, produced by a little-known New York publisher (Manhattan House) in the mid-1930s, lists no authors, photographers, page numbers, or dates. But it contains more than a thousand photographs depicting primitives, exotics, and peasants who once stood in the popular American imagination as representatives for Western typologies of culture. Today, these images linger as a comic and tragic testimony to a way of seeing cultures that has unraveled over the past 30 years. Whether we laugh at the racial and ethnic stereotypes of an antiquated imperialist eye, or soberly confirm a politically corrected vision of cultural diversity, the views gleaned in *The Secret Museum* make us self-conscious about how we see, who we look at and why, and how we collect ourselves through the stories and images that often come to *possess us*. Flipping through its pages, I notice a conspicuous absence of people from the modern Western world. It is that world where the text originally found its home, a world of the observers who gazed into its pages of others and elsewhere, looking for their own reflection.

The numerous critiques of ethnography have taught us to read culture differently and to see the dimensions of representational politics with a hopeful urging toward alternative and democratized forms of writing (Clifford and Marcus 1986; Marcus and Fischer 1986; Clifford 1988; Rosaldo 1989). This is a familiar road, but one I want to travel in this essay to collect some different snapshots of the "crisis of representation" ethnographers have been ruminating over. While ethnographic writing has tried to describe the transitory nature of cultural life in diverse societies, its own transformations carry another purpose. The road is marked by a discourse seeking a sense of location and stability in modern life that emerges out of a desire to find one's place in a broken world.

Here, I want to revisit briefly the rupture in authoritative models of ethnographic interpretation by focusing on how the shifting gaze of cultural observation continually retells a story about the dialectics of self and culture, and how writers historically have looked in different directions to search for the meaning of each. In many ways, I tell the story of the dialectics of self and culture as a textualized set of inverted relationships. In the first section, I characterize how cultural observers embraced an *ethnographic impulse* that looks outward, at worlds beyond their own, as a means of marking the social coordinates of a self. In the second section, I describe how writers have been moved by an *autobiographical impulse* that gazes inward for a story of self, but ultimately retrieves a vantage point for interpreting culture. Finally, I discuss how these two impulses have converged for some ethnographers and critics in the idea of *autoethnography*. As a term of textual analysis and as an orientation to textual production, *autoethnography* renames a familiar story of divided selves longing for a sense of place and stability in the fragments and discontinuities of modernity. Writing and reading such stories has long been a means of collecting ourselves, of seeking order and meaning in a world that often conspires against continuity, and of actively confronting the vague empty spaces of modern life, as Marshall Berman (1982, 6) says, to "make ourselves at home in a constantly changing world."

The Ethnographic Impulse: Looking Outward and the Desire for Place and Identity

◆

The Secret Museum of Mankind offers its own dusty memories of a curious anthropological eye that at one time saw the world with authority and clarity. Faces from around the globe stare back at me from the pages caught by the fractioned seconds of a camera shutter. From a caption below the image of a topless Sudanese teenager we learn that since "childhood she has been taught to respect the flag of France." A Laotian teenager, hands on hips, looks defiantly into the camera. "Like most of her people she is inclined to be lazy and fond of gossip, but she is devoted to music and flowers," we are told. In the middle of *The Secret Museum*, eight Andamanese islanders stand with bows and spears. "Once an independent and formidable race, the Andamanese are now a sickly people," reads the caption. "Contact with civilization has proved disastrous to the aborigines, introducing diseases which have decimated them." Appearing near the end of the book, I find one of a few photographs of Europeans. A distinguished Austrian farmer wearing a tie and overcoat smokes a pipe. "Europe's Biggest Brain Capacity," says the caption. "This well-to-do farmer of Northern Tirol represents the fine highlander stock, which has been found to possess the largest average brain capacity of all races yet closely studied by men of science. He wears the Tirolean hat." Such captions reveal the seeds of a story often rehearsed since anthropology found itself conducting its own reflexive political, ethical, and representational inventory.

Although I wouldn't say the images and captions from *The Secret Museum* compose an ethnography, the book implicitly suggests a succinct index of the major rhetorical and representational issues ethnographic writing has been struggling with since the now familiar critiques of the mid-1980s (Clifford and Marcus 1986; Marcus and Fischer 1986). It is difficult *not* to read these photographs and captions as occasions of textual power, histories of colonialism, race and gender politics, "salvage" anthropology, or Eurocentric superiority. Maybe the only real secret of the images in *The Secret Museum* is, as Marianna Torgovnick (1990, 9) suggests, "the primitive can be—has been, will be(?)—whatever Euro-Americans want it to be." And the recent critical readings of ethnographies certainly have erased much of the silence surrounding that secret.

Whereas ethnographic descriptions once carried home images of the primitive who lay waiting outside the civilized world, critics now tend to consider how representations of the exotic and the primitive have been a way of characterizing and mediating the experience of modernity. Constituting exotic and primitive cultures in ethnographic writing firmly embedded cultural difference, the Other, in an oppositional and imaginary realm of discourse that marked the contours of Western life. Primitive societies served as a baseline for representing modern progress, notes Michel de Certeau (1988, 120), and "the relation between the civilized and the savage [became] a relation inherent with modern societies" in which privileged forces and values become a means of "categorizing all others." The oppositions of civilized and primitive, familiar and exotic, and self and other have been in a dialectical textual tension since the mid-sixteenth century. Since that time, the Other, a symbol of elsewhere, of exoticism, has been a mediating vehicle that continually provided an inverse image of home, place, self, and power. As ethnography textually "captured" the exotic and primitive, it mediated a vision of the familiar and the self through the controlling values and motives of Western cultural life.

Fueled by the politics and moral imperatives of an increasingly mobilized Western world, ethnography textually offered a reconciliation between the foreign world of exotic life and a rapidly modernizing society captured in the swinging moods of progress and nostalgia. Between them sat field-workers and ethnographers composing texts that often searched for unities in the midst of experiential difference. The conventions of early ethnographic writing point to the divided experiences of field-workers pulled between objective ideals of scientific authority and acknowledgment of their own subjectivity, ambiguity, and emotion (Pratt 1986, 32). "Anthropological fieldwork has been represented as both a scientific 'laboratory' and a personal 'rite of passage'," notes Clifford (1986, 109). "The two metaphors capture the disciplines' impossible attempt to fuse objective and subjective practices." As a form of institutional and scientific investigation, ethnographic reports privileged the "neutral" voice of the writer over the authority of subjective and personal experience. Yet, elements of fascination, adventure, romance, and desire leak through, suggesting how ethnographic discourse functions as location for addressing issues of identity, place, and uncertainty in modern life.

Although ethnographic narratives carry the controlling motives and values of Western culture, Torgovnick (1990, 245) suggests there is also a "rhetoric of desire, ultimately more interesting, which implicates 'us' in the 'them' we try to conceive as Other." This implicit sense of desire opens up ethnography as an imaginative discursive space expressing ambivalence and uneasiness toward modern experience. Ethnography has long been a site for "handling, by displacement, the series of dislocations that we call modernity and postmodernity—handling it by studying places where, supposedly, it does not exist and yet does exist," says Torgovnick. "In the fears and hopes we express for them, the primitives, we air fears and hopes for ourselves—caught on a rollercoaster of change that we like to believe can be stopped, safely, at will" (245). The primitive, she argues, reappears in ethnography, literature, and art as a symbol mediating suppressed sexual desires, justifications for colonialism, the loss of an idyllic relationship with the natural world, and the alienating dimensions of existential "homelessness" in modern life. The primitive functions as an alternative discursive space, a site of difference, imagination and fantasy, where the worlds of others are constructed in terms that affirm the place and identity of the observer's world.

Even before twentieth-century anthropologists filed reports about the Pacific Islands or Africa, urban observers had been employing "the primitive" as an interpretive model for mediating cultural differences and marking the boundaries of home and civilized life. In the nineteenth century, upper-class social reformers set out into the social worlds beneath them and returned with tales of the urban poor. In 1861, Henry Mayhew's *London Labour and the London Poor* noted the lifestyle differences between the "wandering" poor and the "civilized tribes" of which he was a member. In contrast to the civilized, he described the urban nomad by his "repugnance to regular and continuous labour," "passion for stupefying herbs and roots, and, when possible, for intoxicating fermented liquors," "love of libidinous dances," "the looseness of his notion to property," and "by the absence of chastity among his women" (Mayhew [1861] 1967, 2). Nearly 40 years later, George Sims viewed his *How the Poor Live* (1899) as a "book of travel" into the slums of nineteenth-century London. "In these pages," he wrote, "I propose to record the result of a journey into a region which lies at our own doors—into a dark continent that is within easy walking distance of the General Post Office" (Keating 1976, 65). For bourgeois observers such as Sims and Mayhew, the world of the poor offered a place to not only exercise male privileges of class mobility, but classify their "own antithesis" (Stallybrass and White 1986, 128) and legitimate their excursions with a reformist agenda.

A century later, the differential image of an "exotic" remained alive in reports of urban life. As geographical distances between the civilized and uncivilized collapsed upon themselves in an increasingly fragmented and institutionally pluralized sphere of the city, ethnographic writing textually affirmed class, economic, political, and moral distances of a highly differentiated world. For example, in sociological studies dealing with social deviance produced in the 1950s and 1960s, the idea of the primitive and exotic seemed recast in debates over social deviance. As social observers and critics made forays into the worlds of musicians, narcotics users, beatniks, pool hall hustlers, and mental wards, they refracted an image of a society seemingly at odds with any consensual notion of a status quo. The textual figure of the social "deviant" marked the distances between "outsiders" and a relativized locus of social normalcy. Like writers of the previous century, sociologists embraced different sides of a reformist agenda. Their studies often approached issues of social deviance and difference with intentions of breaking down rigid social labels. At the same time, their texts located political, ideological, and social allegiances to culturally dominant and subordinate groups. As sociologists looked outward on the social landscapes of deviance, their reports traced the coordinates of their own sense of place and identity. In other words, the world of others—in this case, people labeled as deviant—offered a site for marking the social locations of observers.

Harold Finestone (1964) draws from interviews conducted between 1951 and 1953 to develop a composite profile of young, male, African American drug users in Chicago. He describes this "social type" as a "creature of contrasts . . . turn[ing] up for interviews in uniformly ragged and dirty condition. And yet he talked with an air of superiority derived from his identification with an elite group, the society of 'cats' " (282). Finestone's article, ultimately aimed toward social reform through educational opportunity, attempts to create a portrait describing the world of the "cat"—his attire, idiom, views of society, and how he sees himself. "The most difficult puzzle for him to solve was the 'square,' the honest man. On one hand the 'square' was the hard-working plodder who lived by routine and who took honesty and the other virtues at their face value," reports Finestone. "On the other hand the cat harbored a sneaking suspicion that some squares were smarter than he, because they could enjoy all the forbidden pleasures which were his stock in trade and maintain a reputation for respectability in the bargain" (283).

The young drug user describes himself as a cat, and Finestone expands on the idiom to create a larger scenario of life in the "asphalt jungle." He refers to the drug user as a "species" and "creature," terms that help develop a narrative of predatory life in the city where the honest working man is the prey of the cunning criminal. This difference is furthered as the author describes the cat's ongoing quest for the "kick"—any activity that intensifies experience and distinguishes it from the routines and boredom of everyday life. "Sex in any of its conventional expressions is not a 'kick' since this would not serve to distinguish the cat from the 'square,' " notes Finestone, "but orgies of sexual behavior and a dabbling in the various perversions and byways of sex pass muster as 'kicks' " (284).

The drug user's view of the square and his quest for kicks becomes a point for the author's moral commentary. The drug user attacks "the value our society places upon planning for the future and the responsibility of the individual for such planning," notes Finestone. "Planning always requires some subordination and disciplining of present behavior in the interest of future rewards" (288). Although the cat lives at a distance from the good life, proper social reforms offer a means to change. "Insofar as the social type of the cat represents a reaction to a feeling of exclusion from the access to the means toward the goals of our society," he writes, "all measures such as improved educational opportunities which put these means within his grasp will hasten the extinction of this social type" (297).

I am reminded of Mutual of Omaha's television program *Wild Kingdom* as I read Finestone's article. His ethnographic journey into the urban jungle is underwritten by grants from the National Institute of Mental Health and the Public Health Service. It is also backed by a sense of moral obligation that could potentially bring the drug user closer to the comfort and value of a middle-class lifestyle. The cat is a stray, but a proper education may transform him into a house cat. Finestone's interpretation of the black urban cat is an image of an Other who affirms the centrality of middle-class values. This is much like John Berger's (1980, 12) description of the relationship between domestic pets and their owners: "The pet *completes* him, offering responses to aspects of his character which would otherwise remain unconfirmed."

In the same decade that Finestone was interviewing Chicago addicts, Howard Becker (1963) was similarly studying deviance as a means of criticizing the social construction of deviant categories and labels. Becker's intentions for studying deviant groups and liberating them from the judgments established by social categories and rule-making "moral entrepreneurs" is fueled by a liberal politics. Becker is an advocate of moral choice and individual freedom. His work relativizes the boundaries between "outsiders" by showing how interaction in social groups is a means of symbolically interpreting their own status. They depict themselves as "insiders" at odds with outside definitions of their lifestyle. For example, in a study of dance musicians, Becker provides interview transcripts that identify musicians' active attempts to preserve social distances and distinctive identities. Like Finestone's drug user, Becker's musicians often identified themselves as members of a privileged social group set apart from the confines of a social mainstream.

"Musicians live an exotic life, . . . it's like a jungle, except that their jungle is a hot, crowded bus. You live that kind of life long enough, you just get to be completely different," says one of Becker's subjects. "Being a musician was great, I'll never regret it. I'll understand things that squares never will" (86). Here, it is the subject who employs metaphors of exoticism and the jungle. Becker immediately follows this quote by noting that an "extreme of this view is the belief that only musicians are sensitive and unconventional enough to be able to give real sexual satisfaction to a woman" (86). This is an interesting textual juxtaposition of ideas as the musician's rather general appreciation of his difference from the square is quickly carried by Becker toward an aura of heightened sensitivity, unconventionality, and sexual prowess.

My point is not to criticize Becker or Finestone as duplicitous academic observers or reluctant members of differentiated status groups. Instead, their works suggest to me how ethnographic observers and writers have looked across social and cultural differences, across boundaries, into the worlds of others as a means of laying claim to their own. As they collected reports about socially differentiated and demonized groups from the borders of mainstream conventionality, civility, and moral judgment, they inherently located themselves in a textual landscape where dominant notions of consensus had begun to erode.

These are only two isolated examples of ethnographic texts. However, they express symbolically intact social borders beginning to shift, break down, and create new questions about individual freedom. As a scientific and literary practice intending to probe primitive and strange worlds, early ethnography gave an institutional legitimacy for looking into those other worlds and the lives one found there. While the differentiations of urban life have long offered locations for an incessant reimagining of "exotic" life, the distance between the familiar and the exotic has since become problematic as ethnographic observers continually turned inward to study their own world. The categories of distance and difference that once fueled the ethnographic tale no longer seem to work. Becker's work on deviance is an early instance of how such categories were eventually dismantled. If those categories are at all present today, they seem to take an inverted form: contemplating the familiar with the hope of making it exotic.

Looking for the strange in the familiar is a problem I can appreciate. In my ethnographic research on popular travel (Neumann 1994, 1992a, 1992b), for instance, I see little of the exotic in the groups of tourists who amble out of buses at every observation point to photograph the Grand Canyon. In fact, they are like me, practicing a vernacular ethnography, observers looking for experience and meaning away from home, trying to make a constructed tourist landscape of nature stand still for a moment. We are both of the same world with motives not so different from each other. But at the same time, I find myself fascinated with people who do represent a lifestyle that resembles some vague notion of the exotic I have held on to. Often, I am drawn to them for their differences from me. When people ask me about my studies of tourism at the Grand Canyon, I usually say little about the average tourist who stands on the rim. Instead, I tend to draw from a stock of stories about unusual characters whom I've met while doing my research: Jake, a Navajo who stands by the roadside near the canyon and charges tourists to photograph him; Sam, a biker from Texas who drove his Harley up to observation points at the Grand Canyon and photographed the faces of tourists who gawked at him; or Lucas, a 63-year-old hitchhiker I picked up in the California desert who insisted on taking me to see the intersection where James Dean was killed.

To some extent these people represent what is attractive about otherness; they signal a world more mysterious than my own. They occupy a place in my stories so I can imagine myself as part of their world. I look to them, I suppose, because they offer a temporary connection to experience that seems to exist apart from the social reserve and conventionality of what so often seems like a mass tourist world. In the end, they serve only to remind me that I'm a visitor, an observer who has sought to live at a distance from a center I can't precisely identify, yet I'm unwilling to commit to a life on the margins where the rules at least seem clear. I find something of my own stance toward them in the voice of Sal Paradise, Kerouac's narrator in *On the Road*, who recalls wandering through a section of Denver "wishing I were a Negro, feeling that the best the white world had offered was not enough ecstasy for me, not enough life, joy, kicks, darkness, music, not enough night . . . I wished I were a Denver Mexican, or even a poor overworked Jap, anything but what I was so drearily, a 'white man' disillusioned" (Kerouac 1957, 148). The black ghetto world mediates an absence for Sal characterized as a larger quest for mystery. Yet, it isn't a mystery that asks him to bring back an explanation of the world; rather it's a mystery because he goes into a world looking to "solve" something of himself. The world of the other calls out to Sal with signs that set him on a search just as the footprint on the beach sent Crusoe searching for that other who might make him whole. It is in Sal's voice that I hear echoes leading all the way back to Henry Mayhew and George Sims wandering the streets of London at the turn of the century. And I hear that voice as my own when I realize how I'm hoping something interesting, unplanned, or mysterious will happen, that I'll find a good story while I'm taking field notes at the Grand Canyon.

Perhaps the ethnographic imagination so often sought the exotic because it promised a connection with a mystery—a world of adventure, physicality, sexuality, difference—that could not be found in the world of one's home. The promise, however, could not be kept because the ethnographic voice typically refashioned the mystery into a quest for control and order, a problem that could be explained and solved. Such an orthodox approach, however, keeps us from acknowledging that we are born into a mystery and that our search is a struggle to understand the puzzles of our own "nativeness."

I believe this is one of the difficulties that accompanies writing ethnographies of contemporary life. The once stable distinctions between foreign and familiar that located "the field," as well as the place where one returned to write, have collapsed and dissolved. Now we find ourselves walking on the ruins of a world once imagined by anthropology, turning over the rubble, still trying to find an exotic. In many ways, ethnography is a genre of writing that relies on that mysterious other who exists "out there." And this tension only becomes confounded when we acknowledge how much "out there" looks a lot like "in here."

The crisis of representation that is framing so many debates in contemporary discourse *about* ethnography testifies to an eroding of traditional models for interpreting cultural experience. A modern world incessantly reorganized by travel and mobility has undermined the firm and authoritative vantage points of observation, interpretation, and representation of ethnographic writing (Clifford 1988, 1992). Once stable distinctions between self and other are now occasions for critically examining representational politics. Epistemological critiques of objectivist social science leave cracks in the foundations of participant-observation methods. Ethnographers are left to describe a modern culture of "transient urban and suburban settings," suggests Clifford in which "the prevailing narratives of Western identity are contested," and quests for authentic traditions seem nostalgic and sentimental aesthetic exercises (Clifford 1988, 4–7). Conventional notions of the "field" for conducting field work have become obscured by an incessant remaking of modern cultural geographies, and marginalized groups, once the subject of Western observation, are beginning to write for themselves. "Nowadays nobody attempts to approach the 'other' without first taking a body-dip in psychoanalysis and French poststructuralist theory," quips Dick Hebdige (1993, 187), suggesting the move toward literary criticism that so much writing about ethnography has taken. A growing interest in autobiographical writing among ethnographers is, perhaps, an appropriate response to such circumstances. When consensus is shattered by the divergent interests of various groups vying for representation, it is the voice carrying the particular and concrete dimensions of individual experience that may offer a point of orientation.

The Autobiographical Impulse: Looking Inward for a View of Culture
◆

In the preceding section, I discussed how the ethnographic impulse toward an outside world implicitly expresses a desire for location and identity by looking away from the self and outward into modern life. In this section, I examine how an autobiographical impulse shifts the observer's gaze inward toward a self as a site for interpreting cultural experience.

Leo Braudy (1982, 485) reminds us that in "times of cultural crisis, the interpretation of modern culture frequently presents itself as a species of storytelling," often featuring a first-person or autobiographical voice as a point of narrative coherence among the shifting markers and events of contemporary life. "Once again we seem to be in similar straits, with kindred interests in the individual processing of cultural data and in the personal witness of events, with kindred uncertainties about the relation between personal and social identity, spiritual integrity, and public fame," observes Braudy (487), noting a simultaneous sense of urgency for a common view of culture and uncertainty over the authority to determine consensus. "Yet there is an urge to coherence, which such mediators never satisfy, a seeking of the story that will tie all this together or at least allow us to trace a calmer path through the many stories spun out every day" (487). The study of contemporary culture, says Braudy, should emphasize "the way in which culture *moves* rather than the way in which it is systematizable and patternable in any static way." Rather than conceive of culture as a group of related images, he says it is a "search for images and [the] stories that hold them together" (484). As we move through culture, culture moves through us, and in this mobilized configuration, the individual story leaves traces of at least one path through a shifting, transforming, and disappearing cultural landscape.

Autobiographical accounts draw a relationship between experience and language, and the individual and culture. Autobiography should be read for its anthropological value rather than its position in the genres of literature, argues Janet Gunn (1982). An anthropologically motivated reading of autobiography calls attention to how individuals act as "vehicles of meaning." The act of reading—one's own experience and the experience of someone else—constitutes an autobiographical "situation," a place and time where the dimensions of experience are made meaningful along a variety of narrative lines. The autobiographical moment gives individuals a "presence" in the deep levels of experience. It calls forth the individual from the depths of experience and displays a self. Autobiography is produced out of a juncture between the known and the unknown, that which has been lived and the ambiguity of experience not yet made meaningful. As an interpretive activity, autobiography is a moment when a self risks display in the cultural dimensions of time, space, and language. The real question of autobiography is *not* "Who am I?," says Gunn; instead it is a question of "*where do I belong?* . . . the question of the self's identity becomes a question of the self's location in a world" (23). Equating the autobiographical *situation* with questions of belonging and location focuses attention on texts beyond the conventional scope of an autobiographical genre. As individual voices appear in a variety of texts, they offer a point of coherence that allows a view of a mobilized culture as experienced by a self that is constructed in narrative.

Pico Iyer (1988) suggests the anthropological value of an autobiographical voice in *Video Night in Kathmandu: And Other Reports from the Not-So-Far East*. His book is not a conventional autobiography, but an account of traveling through contemporary Asia. Iyer's experiences of transitoriness, instability, and identity find orientation as a narrative self journeys through a landscape where the signs marking cultural and historical borders have become unreliable. Traveling through Bali, Tibet, Nepal, Thailand, Hong Kong, China, India, and Japan, Iyer describes the hybrid forms of cultural life that merge the West and the East. In India he finds a film industry paralleling Hollywood in the 1950s. In China he finds hordes of people swarming to see *Rambo*. In Japan, he finds a wholesale importation of everything that is American.

Iyer has spent much of his life moving between diverse cultural locations. "For more than a decade while I was growing up, I spent eight months a year at boarding school in England and four months at home in California—in an Indian household," he writes." As a British subject, an American resident, and an Indian citizen, I quickly became accustomed to cross-cultural anomalies and the mixed feeling of exile. Nowhere was home and everywhere" (24). Home, self, and other are transient terms that become concrete when they are given structure and meaning through a narrative. Iyer's travel account offers moments of such coherence and provides a perspective revealing the dimensions of different selves experienced over time. "Rather than showing how one personality acts on different places, I have sought to show how different places act on one personality," he says of his travels through Asia. "Places to some extent remake us, recast us in their own images, and the selves they awaken may tell us as much about them as about ourselves" (26).

As different selves are awakened through travel so, too, do they disappear. Near the end of his account, Iyer describes returning home to the United States only to realize he had left the experience of "feeling at home" on the other side of the International Dateline. "It was only when I returned home that I felt homesick—not just for the gentleness and grace that I had found in many parts of Asia, but also, and more deeply, for the gentler self it had found in me," he writes. Back in New York, Iyer describes his efforts to keep alive the spirit of his travels in Asia:

> I took long walks by the river at dawn and listened in the darkening afternoons to the unearthly strains of the gamelan. I read deeply in the Zen poets by the light of a single candle and I fasted and burned incense when the moon was full. I joined local groups of Tibetans in their seasonal festivities, and I haunted Thai cafes on the East Coast and West. Mostly, though, I spent my hours flipping through photographs and reading old diaries, trying to revisit, in memory and imagination, the places and friends I had known (363).

Moving through the cultural, temporal, and geographical discontinuities of contemporary Asia, Iyer's narrative suggests an interior dialectic of place and self. While a firm cultural and geographical sense of "home" continually evades him, Iyer yearns to recover the intense feelings of belonging he ironically finds through travel. His story expresses the interior experience of nostalgia by sorting through the diaries, photographs, and letters he collected along the way. These fragments of memory find coherence in Iyer's narrative. His Asian travel accounts are an occasion when deep questions of self continually reappear to him. While acknowledging that "home" is always elsewhere, Iyer yearns to overcome the distances, discontinuities, and difficulties of finding firm cultural moorings.

Iyer's story is a site where the stability of a narrating self offers temporary lodging for transient experience. "We grasp our lives in a *narrative*," notes Charles Taylor (1989, 47), arguing "that making sense of one's life as a story is . . . not an optional extra; that our lives exist also in this space of questions, which only a coherent narrative can answer. In order to have a sense of who we are, we have to have a notion of how we have become, and of where we are going." Life has to be lived as a story, for it is in the story that orientations, meanings, and questions of identity are reinvented and sorted through (Crites 1971, 1986).

Like Iyer's, Richard Rodriguez's autobiography, *Hunger of Memory: The Education of Richard Rodriguez* (1982), probes uncertainties about the meaning of home in a narrative search through internalized conflicts of identity. Rather than arrive at a firm destination, his story characterizes the contours of a modern cultural landscape where he confronts questions of self and belonging. Born of immigrant laborers, Rodriguez knew no more than 50 words in English when he began his education in the parochial schools of Sacramento. It was the start of an education that ultimately led him to the quiet reading rooms of the British Museum to write a doctoral dissertation on Renaissance literature. At face value, his story could easily have been a tale of success, achievement, and upward mobility. Instead, Rodriguez tells of the loss and confusion brought on as his education separates him from his family and Mexican heritage. "I grew to hate the pages of my dissertation on genre and Renaissance literature. (In my mind I heard relatives laughing as they tried to make sense of its title.)," he recalls. "One day I heard some Spanish academics whispering back and forth to each other, and their sounds seemed ghostly voices recalling my life. Yearning became preoccupation then" (71).

Rodriguez eventually returns to his parents' home but finds he cannot truly return. He looks across the space separating himself and his parents only to realize the profound ways that his education has come between them. "My need to think so much and so abstractly about my parents and our relationship was in itself an indication of my long education," he says. "My father and mother did not pass their time thinking about the cultural meanings of their experience. It was I who

described their daily lives with airy ideas." Yet, he notes that although
his education changed their relationship in ways that he could not
foresee, it provided him with a means of understanding their
differences. "If, because of my schooling, I had grown culturally separated from my parents," he writes, "my education finally had given me
ways of speaking and caring about that fact" (72).

Rodriguez's autobiography gazes inward to express an experience
of cultural mobility and transformation that has left his identity a
bundle of questions. He does not solve the inner conflicts of a divided
self, but characterizes a world that gives rise to questions of belonging,
family, heritage, class, and place. While Rodriguez interprets the ambiguities of his own cultural experience, at times his narrative becomes an
occasion for a broader cultural criticism. For instance, he describes his
own spiritual quest in the face of religious reform in the Catholic
Church, racial politics, class mobility, affirmative action policies, and
the consequences they held for his professional identity. In other words,
his autobiography becomes an opportunity to analyze culture critically
from the levels of concrete, individual experience. The inward gaze
becomes a means of constructing an image of self who has crossed and
lived between borders. His story is a way of dropping anchor to station
himself in the pull of competing cultural currents, a collecting of self
from the hyphen that separates and connects the term (and experience
of) "Mexican-American."

My discussion of the ethnographic and autobiographical impulses in
these texts is an attempt to retrieve questions about the representational
dialectics of self and culture, and the directions different writers have
looked to answer them. My concern with each of these directions—outward and inward—is not focused on issues of methodological critique
or obligation. Rather it is centered on textual responses to a modern
condition which Georg Lukacs (1920) aptly summarized in the concept
of "transcendental homelessness"—a deeply nostalgic quality he saw in
modern novels. It is a quality of yearning for past idealizations of integral communities in the face of individualism, searching for sacred life
in the face of increasing secularizing forces, and desire for immanence
and continuity in the midst of fragmentation (Lukacs [1920] 1971; Torgovnick 1990, 188 and 281). In different ways, all of these writers

identify, affirm, and negotiate borders and distances separating themselves and others from centers of community, power, history, tradition, and a sense of place. Each speaks to an anthropology of modern experience in which cultural boundaries perpetually disintegrate and become renewed. Although ethnographies traditionally have looked outward toward constructing worlds of the primitive, poor, or deviant; between their lines—sometimes only as a phantom tracing—we often may read a language of desire and control, stories of those who seek grounding and affirmation for their own world. Ethnographic voices speak a story of a self looking for a point of orientation in the representational constructions of others. Conversely, autobiographies have traditionally been a genre in which a writer looks inward and, as George Gusdorf (1980, 48) says, "wrestles with his shadow, certain only of never laying hold of it." Reading autobiography with an anthropological eye, however, can allow us to follow a writer's singular path through a diversified culture as he or she constructs a story of a self.

(Re)Collecting Ourselves Near the End of the Road
◆

The "crisis of representation" declared by Clifford and Marcus and Fischer in 1986, and embraced by countless others since, created a clearing for an "experimental moment in the human sciences" that fostered numerous critical readings of ethnographies and autobiographies and designs for new ethnographic writing strategies. In this section, I focus on the *idea* of autoethnography as a particular response to issues of modern representation. While the term autoethnography suggests a meeting place for the inward and outward gazes of cultural observation, it carries different meanings and purposes among critics and researchers.

Mary Louise Pratt's (1991) conception of autoethnography, for example, recognizes a difference between the *auto* and *ethno* orientations of writing as part of a dialogic enterprise in the politics of representation. "If ethnographic texts are those in which European metropolitan subjects represent to themselves their others (usually their conquered others), autoethnographic texts are representations that the so-defined others construct *in response to* or in dialogue with those texts," says Pratt (35). "Such texts often constitute a marginalized group's point of entry into the dominant circuits of print culture."

Pratt illustrates this idea by describing a 1,200-page letter written in 1613 by Felipe Guaman Poma de Ayala in Cuzco, Peru and addressed to King Philip III of Spain. Although King Philip never received the letter, it was accidentally discovered 300 years later by a Peruvianist scholar conducting research in Copenhagen's Danish Royal Archive. Guaman Poma's letter, Pratt says, is the product of an indigenous Andean who, 40 years after the fall of the Inca empire, learned to write while working under Spanish colonialists. Written in awkward Spanish and Quechua, much of the letter is a critique of the abuses and exploitation leveled by Spanish colonialists. It offers a "revisionist account of the Spanish conquest, which, [Guaman Poma] argues, should have been a peaceful encounter of equals with the potential for benefiting both" (Pratt 1991, 35). Apart from the enormous length of the letter, Pratt says its significance comes from realizing the Inca empire had no writing system. "Guaman Poma constructs his text by appropriating and adapting pieces of the representational repertoire of the invaders," she says. "He does not simply imitate or reproduce it; he selects and adapts it along Andean lines to express (bilingually, mind you) Andean interests and aspirations" (36). In other words, the letter was not only a moment of entry into a world of textual production, it was simultaneously a moment of critiquing the conquering world that had dramatically changed Inca life.

For Pratt, the letter exemplifies how autoethnographic texts consciously confront dominant forms of representation and power in an attempt to reclaim—through a self-conscious, individual, political response—representational spaces that marginalize individuals and others. Pratt uses Guaman Poma's letter to give definition to an idea of autoethnography as a political gesture in a larger textual economy of representation. The 300-year-old letter represents an "art of the contact zone," argues Pratt (34), a social space "where cultures meet, clash, and grapple with each other, often in contexts of highly asymmetrical relations of power, such as colonialism, slavery, or their aftermaths as they are lived out in many parts of the world today." Pratt employs autoethnography as a critical term that identifies a way of reading heterogenous texts produced in the often conflicted convergences of cultures and languages. One value of authoethnographic texts is that they democratize the representational sphere of culture by locating the particular experiences of individuals in a tension with dominant expressions of discursive power.

While Guaman Poma's letter never found its way to the King of Spain, Jamaica Kincaid's *A Small Place* (1988) is a more recent work that carries a similar objective. Kincaid's brief memoir also reads like a letter, but one sent to tourists who have colonized her world with their fantasies of paradise. It offers a contemporary illustration of what Pratt describes as an "autoethnographic text." *A Small Place* provides a personal and historical account of what it feels like to live in Antigua, an island whose economy and identity is largely centered in tourism. Kincaid's memoir responds to dominant cultural narratives that often shadow the experiences of those who live under them. For instance, Kincaid describes the native-tourist relationship from the native's point of view.

> That the native does not like the tourist is not hard to explain. For every native of every place is a potential tourist, and every tourist is a native of somewhere. Every native everywhere lives a life of overwhelming and crushing banality and boredom and desperation and depression, and every deed, good and bad, is an attempt to forget this. Every native would like to find a way out, every native would like a rest, every native would like a tour. But some natives—most natives in the world—cannot go anywhere. They are too poor. They are too poor to go anywhere. They are too poor to escape the reality of their lives; and they are too poor to live properly in the place where they live, which is the very place you, the tourist, want to go—so when the natives see you, the tourist, they envy you, they envy your ability to leave your own banality and boredom, they envy your ability to turn their own banality and boredom into a source of pleasure for yourself (18–19).

The economic and cultural forces of tourism may fashion the islanders of Antigua in the exotic images of tropical paradise, but Kincaid's voice shouts back a reminder about the dim realities of boredom, desperation, and economic disparity that underlie the everyday realities of both visitor and native. With outrage and anger, her voice shatters the image of the native as a quiet, complacent servant of the tourist; a relationship evolving historically out of British colonialism. By inverting a traditional ethnographic relationship between the familiar and the exotic, she cracks the fantasy mirror of Antigua that is fostered in tourist brochures and packaged vacations, a place, she says, visitors come looking for their own reflection: "Still standing, looking out the window, you see yourself lying on the beach, enjoying the amazing sun. . . . You see yourself eating some delicious, locally grown food," she says to the tourist/reader perched in an Antiguan resort hotel. "You see yourself, you see yourself. . . . You must not wonder what exactly happened to the contents of your lavatory when you flushed it" (13).

Although she writes from the position of an oppressed Antiguan, Kincaid belongs to more than one world. She is a native of Antigua and a recipient of a literary award from the American Academy and Institute of Arts and Letters. Writing *A Small Place* was supported by a grant from the Guggenheim Foundation. She has published in the *New Yorker*. Clearly, she has traveled and crossed many borders. In her book, however, Kincaid constructs her Antiguan identity as a response to the representations that precede her. In different ways, other authors have employed the autobiographical voice as a means of speaking out or talking back to fill a silent void and claim a self. "Moving from silence into speech is for the oppressed, the colonized, the exploited, and those who stand and struggle side by side, a gesture of defiance that heals, that makes new life and growth possible," argues bell hooks (1989, 9). "It is that act of speech, of 'talking back,' that is no mere gesture of empty words, that is the expression of moving from object to subject—the liberated voice."

As a term of textual *analysis*, autoethnography reminds us that ethnography—like other forms of cultural representation—matters deeply in the lives of others who find themselves portrayed in texts not of their own making. I am not the first to point out the grim inheritance claimed by those whose worlds and experiences have been constrained rather than broadened by ethnographic writing. As Pratt describes it, autoethnography historically originates as a discourse from the margins and identifies the material, political, and transformative dimensions of representational politics. Autoethnography is a form of critique and resistance that can be found in diverse literatures such as ethnic autobiography, fiction, memoir, and texts that identify zones of contact, conquest, and the contested meanings of self and culture that accompanies the exercise of representational authority. Guaman Poma's seventeenth-century bilingual letter merely suggests how quests for self-representation have appeared for centuries in the wake of modern mobility, colonialism, religious missions, or tourism that have reconfigured societies, geographies, and culture.

Historically, the experience of modernity has been a "maelstrom" of "perpetual disintegration and renewal, of struggle and contradiction, of ambiguity and anguish," argues Marshall Berman (1982, 15–16). "People who find themselves in the midst of this maelstrom are apt to feel that they are the first ones, maybe the only ones, to be going through it. . . . In fact, however, great and ever-increasing numbers of people have been going through it for close to five hundred years." Although neither Guaman Poma's letter nor Kincaid's memoir was written as an autoethnography, the term autoethnography points to an experience these texts share with Iyer's travelogue and Rodriguez's autobiography: a desire to find one's self in a world broken and transformed by the progressive and political ideologies of another's modernist vision.

While Pratt views autoethnographic texts as products of a contact zone, others have used the term autoethnography to describe a methodological approach to the problems of contemporary cultural interpretation (e.g., Fiske 1990; Denzin and Lincoln 1994, 101). For some ethnographers, autoethnography appears as a methodology for exploring the borders of subjective and cultural experience. John Fiske's description of autoethnography, for example, envisions a systematic method of introspection with an aim toward critiquing the practices of everyday life. "What autoethnography may be able to do," argues Fiske (1990, 90), "is to open up the realm of the interior and the personal, and to articulate that which, in the practices of everyday life, lies below any conscious articulation." He uses an autoethnographic approach critically to interpret the furniture, books, posters, the placement of the television, and the programs on his TV screen that furnish his living room. His interpretive reading of the space is a point for reflecting on questions of individual taste, status, and class. "I wanted to explore, in a specific instance, the idea of a symbolic environment that is constructed by a social agent out of the socially available resources, and that equally constructs that agent as a social member and marks his (in this case) position in the social space" (89). In this sense, autoethnography is an attempt to interpret the public and private dimensions of cultural experience and seek a critical distance and perspective on each.

Ethnographers trained in what now seem like obsolete notions of objective social science methods may find the idea of autoethnography a methodological approach for examining personal experience in a world in which the lines between fact and fiction often seem confusing, unclear, or unreliable. In this way, autoethnography becomes, among social scientists, part of a larger rediscovery of long-standing literary genres. For example, Laurel Richardson's (1994) renewed appreciation for the techniques of fiction, drama, poetry, and autobiography suggests a desire for self-expression in interpretive communities where academic conventions have constrained rather than enabled the representation of subjective experience.[1] For centuries, these literary genres have explored various dimensions of subjectivity and cultural experience. The reappearance of autobiographies, poetry, plays, and novels as "experimental" and "innovative" forms of writing among social scientists perhaps says more about a past methodological provincialism than it does about identifying a particularly new approach to understanding cultural life. Yet, behind this effort to reclaim familiar literary genres is a desire to cultivate creativity and a literary aesthetic in the fallow fields of traditional social science.

Current motivations to write autoethnography may seem an appropriate response to the crisis of cultural representation if only because it replays a familiar set of questions people have faced for centuries. Although somewhat paradoxical in name, autoethnography is a term and idea that renames the dialectics of self and culture that ethnography and autobiography have, in the different ways I've discussed, also addressed. In this way, autoethnography stands as a current attempt to, quite literally, *come to terms* with sustaining questions of self and culture. Like ethnography and autobiography, it is a discursive activity that finds its bearings, practice, and value as a response to the ambiguities of a particular cultural and historical context. Historically, ethnography and autobiography are among a variety of literary genres that remind us how cultural crisis is an endemic quality of modernity. Yet, we don't need to review the past five centuries to see how others have confronted and interpreted the ambiguities of modern life, or the "postmodern moment" in which we now look for home.

In the two decades before critics characterized a "crisis of representation" in anthropology, writers from other quarters were responding to a cultural crisis over conventionalized models for interpreting contemporary life. By the end of the 1960s the New Journalism had "revitalized reporting as a form of storytelling while giving shape to many of the cultural changes occurring," observes David Eason (1984, 52). "The New Journalism took its energy from the shifting relationship between the individual and the society, which located the process of creating meaning in diverse subcultures, and chronicled the symbolic quest for significance in a fragmenting society." In the reports of the New Journalists, Eason identifies two approaches for interpreting cultural experience that anticipate later representational concerns in ethnographic writing. "Ethnographic realism," he notes, was a response to cultural fragmentation by re-creating consensus textually in the account. "The realism of the text constitutes the subculture as an object of display, and the reporter and reader, whose values are assumed and not explored, are cojoined in the act of observing," argues Eason (52). A second approach of the New Journalism Eason calls "cultural phenomenology" attempts to describe "what it feels like to live in a world in which there is no consensus about a frame of reference to explain 'what it all means'. Instead of arguing that 'This is reality,' the reports focus on the experiential contradictions that call consensual versions of reality into question" (52). I mention these two approaches, because Eason's distinctions between "ethnographic realism" and "cultural phenomenology" capture a dilemma similar to the issues ethnographers are currently debating, and because New Journalism may offer some useful models for those writers considering alternatives to ethnographic writing.

For some ethnographers who make a home in the university, the New Journalists may hardly seem like appropriate teachers. As John Van Maanen (1988, 134–136) points out, the lack of citations to previous works on the same topic, the topical nature of the accounts, and the innovative representational techniques of literary journalism may be "somewhat worrisome to ethnographers." Although New Journalism is not a singular antidote for writing through a crisis of representation, it offers examples of cultural observation and criticism that seem consistent with the goals of those seeking new forms of ethnographic expression and self-expression. While new journalists often study everyday life and culture in ways that resemble participant-observation, they also tend to preserve the subjectivity of the observer. Like many social scientists invigorated by fiction and drama, literary journalists are also interested in telling a "good story," playing with language, metaphors, deep characterization, and mixing literary genres. As with any good novel, short story, play, or poem, the value of their reports is found in their lines, and they offer appropriate examples for those who are interested in mixing and blurring genres, and writing "messy," indeterminate texts.

However, ethnographers and New Journalists share more than an effort to examine segments of cultural life critically. They also share a similar confrontation with authoritative conventions that have typically been aimed toward consensual views of accuracy, truth, and objectivist notions of cultural reality. Neither those who aspire to the traditional conventions of objectivity nor those who become absorbed by post-modern sanctions for subjectivity can claim the authority of repre-senting a unified and integrated vision of cultural life. But what New Journalism models, and the current debates in ethnography mirror, is a renewed appreciation for constructing reports about the concrete details and confusing practices of historically specific conditions in which people live out their days. Standing beside those who theoreti-cally fascinate over the extreme themes of postmodernism, or look for the contours of contemporary cultural life in entertainment industry fic-tions projected in movie theaters and on television screens, the tradi-tions of ethnography—for better or worse—ask us to pay attention to a world beyond the routines of our own and to seek them out. Undoubt-edly, a small army of critics continually show us the significance of examining the pervasive texts of popular culture. However, beyond our roles as consumers and audience members, we spin out other fictions that sustain us collectively and divide us from each other. We experi-ence our lives in ways that are not always collected and contained in the stories that circulate through the mass media. At a time when informa-tional technologies promise us we may never have to leave home, ethnography insists we keep in touch in another way.

Indeed, claiming an allegiance to one literary genre or some hybrid of genres as a point of methodological orientation might offer some direction in one's attempts to make sense of contemporary culture. In the end, however, approaching the border of the next century may be most useful as a moment for acknowledging the reappearing questions and puzzles of self and culture that perpetually return to us in modern life. Looking at some of the ethnographic and autobiographical impulses different writers have followed in this century and the last, I'm inclined to believe similar questions of self, place, or power will surely carry into the next. Thinking that entering a new century will mark a turning point is, perhaps, a hopeful and progressive fiction we have learned to indulge. But ethnographers and autobiographers continually remind us is that borders are always with us and *within* us. Their accounts show how we mark and cross those lines, carrying back artifacts and stories to collect ourselves as we seek to understand the dialectics of self and culture. I'm hard pressed to think otherwise as I crush my cigarette into Niagara Falls, put *The Secret Museum of Mankind* on the bookshelf, and hear Curtis Mayfield's vinyl voice print, ". . . the only game you know is do or die," spinning out of the groove into the rooms of another rented house.

Notes

1. Richardson (1994) suggests writers create "evocative" and "experimental" texts that "deploy literary devices to re-create lived experience and evoke emotional response." The extent that texts *re-create* lived experience is a matter of debate and beyond the scope of this essay. However, for an excellent comparison to Richardson's notion of the "evocative" text, see Stephen A. Tyler's (1986) earlier description of ethnographic "evocation."

References

Becker, H. S. 1963. *Outsiders: Studies in the Sociology of Deviance*. New York: The Free Press.

Berger, J. 1980. *About Looking*. New York: Pantheon.

Berman, M. 1982. *All That Is Solid Melts into Air: The Experience of Modernity*. New York: Penguin.

Braudy, L. 1982. "Popular Culture and Personal Time." *The Yale Review* 71: 481–498.

Clifford, J. 1986. "On Ethnographic Allegory." In *Writing Culture: The Poetics and Politics of Ethnography*, edited by J. Clifford and G.E. Marcus. (Berkeley: University of California Press): 98–121.

———. 1988. *The Predicament of Culture: Twentieth Century Ethnography, Literature, and Art*. Cambridge, MA: Harvard University Press.

———. 1992. "Traveling Cultures." In *Cultural Studies*, edited by L. Grossberg, C. Nelson, and P. Treichler. (New York: Routledge): 96–116.

———, and G.E. Marcus, eds. 1986. *Writing Culture: The Poetics and Politics of Ethnography*. Berkeley: University of California Press.

Crites, S. 1971. "The Narrative Quality of Experience." *Journal of the American Academy of Religion* 39: 291–311.

———. 1986. "Storytime: Recollecting the Past and Projecting the Future." In *Narrative Psychology: The Storied Nature of Human Conduct*, edited by T. R. Sarbin. (New York: Praeger): 152–173.

de Certeau, M. 1988. *The Writing of History*, translated by T. Conley. New York: Columbia University Press.

Denzin, N. K. and Y. S. Lincoln, eds. 1994. *Handbook of Qualitative Research*. Thousand Oaks, CA: Sage.

Eason, D. L. 1984. "The New Journalism and the Image-World: Two Modes of Organizing Experience." *Critical Studies in Mass Communication*. Vol 1, no. 1: 51–65.

Finestone, H. 1964. "Cats, Kicks, and Color." In *The Other Side: Perspectives on Deviance*, edited by H. S. Becker. (New York: The Free Press): 281–297.

Fiske, J. 1990. "Ethnosemiotics: Some Personal and Theoretical Reflections." *Cultural Studies* 4: 85–99.

Gunn. J. V. 1982. *Autobiography: Toward a Poetics of Experience*. Philadelphia: University of Pennsylvania Press.

Gusdorf, G. [1956]1980. "Conditions and Limits of Autobiography." In *Autobiography: Essays Theoretical and Critical*, edited by J. Olney. (Princeton: Princeton University Press): 28–48.

Hebdige, D. 1993. "Redeeming Witness: In the Tracks of the Homeless Vehicle Project." *Cultural Studies*. Vol. 7, no. 2: 173–223.

hooks, b. 1989. *Talking Back: Thinking Feminist, Thinking Black*. Boston: South End Press.

Iyer, P. 1988. *Video Night in Kathmandu: And Other Reports from the Not-So-Far East*. New York: Vintage.

Keating, P., ed. 1976. *Into Unknown England, 1866–1913*. Manchester: Manchester University Press.

Kerouac, J. 1957. *On the Road*. New York: Viking.

Kincaid, J. 1988. *A Small Place*. New York: Penguin.

Lukacs, G. [1920]1971. *The Theory of the Novel*,translated by A. Bostock. Cambridge, MA: MIT Press.

Lutz, C. A., and J. L. Collins. 1993. *Reading National Geographic*. Chicago: University of Chicago Press.

Marcus, G. E. and M. M. J. Fischer. 1986. *Anthropology as Cultural Critique: An Experimental Moment in the Human Sciences*. Chicago: University of Chicago Press.

Mayhew, H. [1861]1967. *London Labour and the London Poor: Volume I*. London: Frank Cass.

Neumann, Mark. 1992a. "The Traveling Eye: Photography, Tourism and Ethnography." *Visual Sociology* 2: 22–38.

———. 1992b. "The Trail Through Experience: Finding Self in the Recollection of Travel." In *Investigating Subjectivity: Research on Lived Experience*, edited by C. Ellis and M. Flaherty. (Newbury Park, CA: Sage): 176–201.

————. 1994. "The Commercial Canyon: Culturally Constructing the 'Other' in the Theatre of the West." In *Discovered Country: Tourism in the American West—A Critical Reader*, edited by S. Norris. (Albuquerque, NM: Stone Ladder): 198–209.

Pratt, M. L. 1986. "Fieldwork in Common Places." In *Writing Culture: The Poetics and Politics of Ethnography*, edited by J. Clifford and G. E. Marcus. (Berkeley: University of California Press): 27–50.

————. 1991. "Arts of the Contact Zone." *Profession 91* 91: 33–40.

Richardson, L. 1994. "Writing: A Method of Inquiry." In *The Handbook of Qualitative Research*, edited by N. K. Denzin and Y. S. Lincoln. (Thousand Oaks, CA: Sage): 516–529.

Rodriguez, R. 1982. *Hunger of Memory: The Education of Richard Rodriguez*. New York: Bantam.

Rosaldo, R. 1989. *Culture and Truth: The Remaking of Social Analysis*. Boston: Beacon Press.

Stallybrass, P., and A. White. 1986. *The Politics and Poetics of Transgression*. Ithaca, NY: Cornell University Press.

Taylor, C. 1989. *Sources of the Self: The Making of Modern Identity*. Cambridge, MA: Harvard University Press.

Torgovnick, M. 1990. *Gone Primitive: Savage Intellects, Modern Lives*. Chicago: University of Chicago Press.

Tyler, S. A. 1986. "Post-Modern Ethnography: From Document of the Occult to Occult Document." In *Writing Culture: The Poetics and Politics of Ethnography*, edited by J. Clifford and G. E. Marcus. (Berkeley: University of California Press): 122–140.

Van Maanen, J. 1988. *Tales of the Field: On Writing Ethnography*. Chicago: University of Chicago Press.

◆

Mark Neumann is an Assistant Professor in the Department of Communication at the University of South Florida in Tampa. His research and teaching interests include cultural studies, popular culture, tourism, and ethnography. He has published articles on leisure travel, casino gambling, and documentary photography. Currently, he is completing a book about tourism at the Grand Canyon.

PART ◆ TWO

Sociopoetics

SIX

Reconstructing
Apsaras from Memory
Six Thoughts

Judith Hamera

i

The intersections of form and frailty are haunted places. They are not places amenable to saying, but to unsaying; not to commensurability, but to the incommensurable. These intersections are charming and gentle and terrible places, as precise and as elegant and as cruel as miracles. The solace of good form organizes and warms our frailties; the persistence of our damage empties out form and wears it away. The intersections of form and frailty are haunted places.

ii

In Cambodian cosmology, Apsaras are celestial female dancers who guard the heavens, serve as intermediaries between the sacred and the secular through their dances, and epitomize the beauty of Khmer culture. Apsaras are pure potential, asymptotic not actual, gloves waiting for hands.

iii

The Sam family arrived in Los Angeles from Cambodia, via a Thai refugee camp, in 1981 or 1982. Family patriarch Ben Sam had been trained in classical dance at the National Conservatory in Phnom Penh as an adolescent. His wife Maya had studied briefly at the conservatory and, after barely escaping the Khmer Rouge autohomeogenocide, made her way to the camp where she continued her training under the tutelage of fellow dancers. Ben and Maya married in the camp; their three children, son Sovanty (15), and daughters Sothya (13) and Devi (12), were also dancers, studying under their parents.

I met the family through Sovanty when he and other extended family members were selling handmade Cambodian puppets at a performance of the Classical Dance Company of Cambodia in Los Angeles in 1990. The Sam children suggested that, as I was interested in classical dance, I should meet their parents who "danced *real* Cambodian dance in Cambodia and in [refugee] camp." For approximately two and a half years, we navigated treacherous intersections of form and frailty; our relationship ended abruptly when, after an earthquake, after the donut shop in which they were partners was vandalized and Devi frightened by a shooting near her school, the Sams left the city for northern California.

iv

The intersections of form and frailty are haunted places, and the stories which live here carve out as much silence as sound and sense as not-sense from the particulars. Indeed, the drive for brutal sense seems at odds with such stories; imagine instead, that reason and necessity are etched onto damaged and articulate bodies by and through performances which, in turn, resolve into ghostlier intersections and quieter and more precarious choreography. The Sams and I relied on incommensurable choreographies to orient our steps.

v

Maya: I hear them sometimes.
JH: Hear who?
Maya: I hear my teachers who did not get out.
I hear them sometimes in the day . . . I
don't see, just hear. I am afraid but they
tell me the steps. . . I listen to them tell
me the steps, then I do.

His first imaginary performances were innocent enough: air guitar
at parties. They were energetic, social. They had a context. They
made sense. From there, he moved to imaginary sax recitals, but
these too had a context of a sort, though smaller.

> Devi: I know these monsters and monkeys
> [figures from the Khmer repertory]
> aren't real, but I feel like I know them
> because we see them all the time. I
> think my mom and especially my
> dad . . . I think they think they're real.
> I think they wish they were. Sometimes
> it's like they live here.

From here to imaginary sonatas, piano mostly, but sonatas are a
little more solitary and so he began to recede a bit, as though he
was moving—slowly—toward the horizon of an imaginary landscape.

> Sovanty: A lot of people used to come over to play
> [Khmer music]. Some were pretty old
> and it sounded funny, but my dad would
> get mad—I don't know why. They don't
> come any more, but he goes out, I guess.

The sonatas still had titles. I would have to guess the names of his
concertos, then of the symphonies. He was conducting here, and
because conductors are odd and still more solitary, I would watch
at even greater remove.

> Maya: Not I hate it here, understand? Not I
> hate it. Here is not my country. Not my
> home. But the dance can make home,
> understand? Maybe more home after so
> many die. They [Cambodian exiles in
> the community] say, "Go back [to Cam-
> bodia] and fix," but I think maybe no.
> Too many die, maybe. Maybe just
> dance and fix here. That's all.

Here's my refrain:
What's wrong?
Okay?

The imaginary operas came next. He sang all the roles and conducted as well—Wagner mostly, I guessed. He was so far away now that he looked very small. I thought, perspective always confused me.

> Maya: I dance to keep music in my [ears] and keep talk out.

What's wrong?
   Okay?
   Please?

> Maya: It's hard to say, but no one talked. What to talk about? Why this one [killed], this one, this one and not you? Talk about who sees the worst? Whose more family die? I tell you—no one talked. Me? I don't think . . . I dance.

Then came the imaginary portraits: pages of blankness over every flat surface. Then the pages themselves disappeared and the imaginary photos began.

> Ben: I am so tired some day . . . Why I fight with my children, no tv, no out with friends, no this loud music. Why so hard to teach this dance? It live to come here, die to be here? Sometime I think yes. Then I am very tired. Hard to think. Hard to teach.

Click, he'd say, turning to me. Smile. Click.

What's wrong?
And I pushed. I pushed through the hard world
and the gone world, through word webs, through
the flat sounds and smells and more sounds and the
footfalls,
pushed toward bright and brutal and alien sense,
and was alone then, and blinking.
And I thought,
this is why duets are hard, and this is why
memory sleeps in clear and hollow and scary places,

and this is why there is so much soundless motion
and motion and motion and motion in good form.
But now I think they must have been startled
by the crackling of my voice
in the midst of all that luminous and terrible quiet.

vi

The intersections of form and frailty are haunted places. The solace of good form organizes and warms our frailties; the persistence of our damage empties out form and wears it away. The intersections of form and frailty are haunted places and duets there are beautiful and horrible, so vivid and so austere.

Notes

This essay alludes to texts, performances, and poems by Michael Meyers, Charles Wright, Wallace Stevens, Michel deCerteau, and Walter Benjamin. The words spoken by the Sam family are direct transcriptions of tapes or field notes.

◆————

Judith Hamera is the Chair of the Department of Communication Studies at California State University, Los Angeles and holds a joint appointment in the Department of Theatre Arts and Dance.

CHAPTER SEVEN

Kaleidoscope
The Same and Different
Deborah A. Austin

One of the most important qualities endemic to the development of close friendship and love is the capacity to "celebrate the other" (Sampson 1993). As writers from Mead (1934) to Bakhtin (1981, 1986) have emphasized, the essence of who we are, what we think, and how we talk is contingent largely on the others we celebrate. The celebration of others through dialogue bends back upon us reflexively, sustaining, altering, or transforming our comprehension of ourselves and our social world.

Annie Ngana and I are doctoral students. Annie studies anthropology while my field is communication. Born and reared in Zaire, Annie is interested in indigenous educational systems because, as she puts it, "the people are educated, but if they don't go on to college to become some kind of professional, the education does them no good." Her dissertation develops a pragmatic educational model that will provide her people with knowledge and skills to enhance their lives. I am an African American from North Carolina. My research focuses on communication in close relationships, particularly African American families. My dissertation examines the relationships and families of African American men and women seen through the lens of the Million Man March.

Annie and I conversed with each other frequently: in class weekly, at a symposium on indigenous knowledge, at meals in both her house and mine, and with mutual friends. My goal was to create a story based on our interaction that invites the reader into our lives, into the complex ways we attended to each other. As our conversations evolved, I discovered that my own eyes, personality, history, judgments, body, and sensibilities were integral parts of our interaction (Meyerhoff 1978, 30). It was important, therefore, to use a form of expression that would allow me to show these aspects of our experience being negotiated. Because getting to know Annie as "other" involved at least two subjectivities (mine and hers), I found it necessary to take into account that what at first appeared to be an immediately accessible account of a life or episode became a site of interpretive tension (Gluck and Patai 1991, 2).

Searching for an appropriate form in which to share our story, I joined Laurel Richardson (1992) in breaching qualitative writing norms by constructing my experiences with Annie as a narrative poem. I used our spoken words as well as the thoughts, memories, and judgments that flashed through my mind during and after our interactions. As Annie and I talked, I was mesmerized by the musicality of her voice, which sounded like the hush of many waters. As she strained to explain certain things to me in English, she created fascinating metaphors. I wanted to capture this musicality and linguistic struggle, as well as the circularity that characterized our conversations. Often, as one thing reminded us of another, we moved to examine that thought, coming back to the "original" at a later time. Sometimes we never returned. As I pondered this interaction, I realized that poetry helped me express the tension, lyricism, and circularity of our interaction. Through poetic representation, I celebrate Annie Ngana and the unique relationship we developed through dialogue and conversation in the context of interactive research interviews.

Kaleidoscope
◆

Africans are the same
wherever we are, she says to me
   matter-of-factly
I look at her and smile
And ask
   like a good researcher should
   How so?
I can't explain, she says
    with that voice that sounds

like the rush of many rivers
It is the way we all are
The way we move
The way we think
I look at her again
and see her smile
with full lips closed over pearly white teeth
We do look alike
high cheekbones under taut brown skin
cheekbones that my family
claimed
were a sign that we had Indian blood
in the days when nobody
wanted to be African
But I am the daughter of slaves
as some Africans
so quickly remind us
Still, she says
as she looks at the pictures
of me
pasted all over my kitchen refrigerator
while I cook barbecued chicken, collard greens,
macaroni and cheese
butternut squash, homemade biscuits, and ice tea
the kind of dinner
my grandmother would make
I hope she does not consider me vain
And I tell her that
the pictures
story part of my life
in a purple silk dress
sitting in the grass
at Boston's Arnold Arboretum
smiling at Loretta
who says that anyone
can take good pictures
of someone they love
You look like
A true African woman

I wish I looked like that, she exclaims
I am surprised and honored
   How can an African woman
   Say that I look more African
   than she?
But I know that identity
   at least some parts of it
is intentionally constructed
   and I intentionally wear
   this short curly hair
Because
   my former secretary
   a Chilean Indian
   told me
      you could pass for any South American Indian
      except for that hair
   So I wear that hair
   as a sign of my Africanity
   But I am not African
   in the same way as she
I look at her
      reared in the city
        in an African country   colonized by Belgium
      college educated in France
         she is not
         the poverty-stricken
         preliterate
         native villager
         we see on *National Geographic*
Oh yes, she says
   There is something in the way you move
   In the way you reach out to people
   That is very African

Annie seems genuinely excited
about having dinner
at my house
She wants to know   about me
   As much as I want to know
         about her

I see her watching me
   As though she has some theory
      some perception
         she wants to test
And as we talk I discover
   that she needs a friend
     a girl friend
  she needs womantalk
      and I hope
     that she does not
        become too attached
          (Nia, a mutual friend
            says
           Annie needs a tittie Mama)
I listen
as she tells me
that she needs help
with her English
help to speak more beautifully
   like her fiancé
   the Gabonese attorney
     educated in Paris
       where they met
       where she received her undergraduate education
       where he learned, she says
       to speak English so beautifully
ahhhh the way she says
   beautifully
     caressing it
I think she is thinking
   of more than his English
   as she caresses   *beautifully*
But then
she caresses all her words
   as though she experiences life
     differently than I
   as though people and life
     ought to make beautiful

passionate love
She continues
　　to talk about
　　　him
she smiles
　　and tells me
that she misses him
　　I hear the longing
　　in her voice
　　　　I know that longing
　　　　I know that longing
　　　　　all too well
We become sisters
　　who long for men
　　　who are far away
But I feel selfish
　　what is 500 miles
　　compared to 5000?
I did not want
　　she says
To get involved with him
　　It is not good
　　　to be so far away
But he persuaded me
　　　　　　It's the lawyer in him, I interrupt
laughingly
He persuaded me
　　　that I
would become the object
　　of gossip
　　without him
At home, she says
when you are my age
　　　and you are not married　　not involved with a man
the people ask
　　What's wrong with her?
　　Is she like other women?
　　Does she have her period?
Why in the world, I ask

would they ask about your period?
They think, she says
Maybe the woman
    cannot have children
    and that is why
    she doesn't marry
        Children are so important
        in my country, she says
And he persuaded me
She looks at me
  and smiles
I decide that I am not ready
  to tell her
  that I don't want children
  I am not ready
    to incur her disapproval
      if that is how
      she reacts
Children are important, she says again
  But they must come
    at the right time
There was a time
  when people told my mother
    that I was pregnant, she says
I was at boarding school
  vomiting all over the place
  I went to the hospital
    and they were taking so long
    to see me
    I left
    and went to class
Some women in the neighborhood
  told my mother
    Annie is pregnant
    and she wouldn't even stay
    at the hospital
My mother gave my sister money
  to get me   and bring me home
  My father was crying

ohhhh my baby
will not be able to go to school
My brother said
   Things happen   and there is nothing
we can do
about it
But my mother just looked
   she looked with the eyes
     of the mother

               Annie looked at me
               intently
               knowingly
               like her mother
               must have looked at her
Annie is okay, her mother said
   She is just sick
She told my father
   You go tell those women
   they better stop talking
   about my daughter
And my mother put me in her bed
   and cried and fretted
   until I got well
Mothers know, she says
When I give my body
   My mother will know
How will she know? I ask
   fascinated by this
     mother's intuition
She will just know, Annie replies
When I was at school
   a friend used to come
   and   jump and play   with me
One day my mother said
   she is pregnant
How do you know? I asked her
   She said, I just know
And two, three months later
   The girl wants to kill herself

she is pregnant
Mothers know
    she says
        with unshakable assurance
And I think about
        how un   academic   that sounds
    from a woman who has studied
                    in
                Zaire
                France
                Gabon
                Ghana
                America
What must it be like
    to find
    "I just know"
    an absolutely acceptable response

I wonder
    what we are missing
    because we must have
    all the hows, whys, and wherefores

While I think
    and romanticize this experience
she says
    I cannot live
    like the other women
        I will not have a man
        who will take
            another   wife
    You suffer so
    when he takes
    another wife
But you must
have   a man
It can be so hard
    without a man
When my father died

my mother stayed, she says
Stayed single? I ask
Yes, she says
    so that we could be
    around my father's brothers
       sometimes the widow
       marries one of the brothers
    but Mommy stayed single
What if she had married
someone else? I ask
Ohhh   that usually   does not work Deborah   she exclaims
    the children will say
       he is not my father
    the man will say
       they are not my children
    maybe they send the children
    to their poppy, toto
             that means little uncle
    but they need a man, she says
       as if her assertion cannot be refuted
    there is something missing   when there is no man, she says
What's missing? I ask
Annie looks puzzled
    as if she has never
    been asked such a question
In our country she says
    you know when the father is home
    the children   the wife   even the dogs
         are quiet
    when he is away
    everyone is running around
       jumping   screaming   laughing   shouting
Like at my house
    when we heard Poppy
    come up
    in the car
    we quieted down
       got everything in order
the mother can't do that

only the father has the authority
   to get things in order
the children need the father
   to develop discipline
   to teach them to respond to authority
It is hard without a man, she says again
            That's one way we are not alike, I think
            African American mothers
            keep things   in order
What about love? I ask
He loves, she says
But it is different than here
   a man and his wife are not affectionate   in public
      that belongs at home
   husbands and wives   do not touch each other
                   in front of the children
     that belongs in private
When I tell my students this
They ask me
   how do they know they love each other?
   They know, I say
   You will have to
     go over there and see

I return to her assessment
that she cannot live
like the other women
I think/I ask
   if you were at home
   would you feel
     like this?
Oh yes, she says

We
             especially the educated women
   say what we feel
     We know
     that some of the stories   we love
     are not true

Like
    only men can eat eggs
        or
    children are not allowed
    to eat
    certain parts   of the chicken
(Oh yes, I say)
When resources are scarce
  the privileged people
  get the best
Yes, Deborah
  we know
  but sometimes
  we let them think
  we don't know

We talk more about Matt
  who is what she looks for
    an educated man
    from the village
  In the village, she says
  when you marry
  the whole village
  is involved in the wedding
    when you marry
    you marry the whole family
      if you divorce
      you have to deal
      with the whole family
I long for the village, she says
  When I was in Gabon
  I was amazed at the
  knowledge of the villagers
    all their water
    came from the brook
      you washed your clothes
      and your body
      and took care of your business   downstream

you got drinking water
                                    upstream
    you could be killed   for doing the wrong thing
        in the upstream water
    without our technological knowledge, she says
    they know what to do
I long for the village
the provinces in France were like that
    the people lived simple communal lives
    they know so much

Annie stops cooking dinner
    to show me Matt's photograph
        I smile at how handsome he is
            like the African American men
            I know
            on Wall Street
                tailored suit
                neatly trimmed short hair
                trouser legs
                    hitting their shoes
                    just where *GQ* says
                    they should
This time
    she tells me
    how much she loves him
I don't want her
    to stop talking
    so I don't ask
    if this story
        is different than the other
She tells me
    the first time I saw him
    I said in French to my friend
                        and she blushes and laughs as she tells me
    Pas mal, not bad
        I suffered so, she says
        because he was in my heart
        and when we finally started

seeing each other
I told him
    that I had him in my heart
    from the very first time
    I saw him
he laughed, she says
and told me
    I know
    you were in my heart too
But my mind, he said
    was on finishing my degree
    going home to Gabon
    paying back the government
    and deciding what to do
      about a falling apart marriage
He is divorced, she says
My parents know that
    but they don't know
    he has children
      I won't tell them
      because he is in my heart
      and they won't like it
Families don't always   like our choices   I say
My family
    did not like the fact
    that my friend is
      18 years older
        than I
She looks at me   wide-eyed
    and lets out that exclamation
    I have come to love
      Ahhhhhh Deborah, she asks
      why do you love
      an old man?
I laugh at her
    That's what
    my family asked
Until he won their hearts
        Then I admit

I was concerned too
at first
about his age
what if he dies and leaves me?
what would I do?
Then I chastised myself
What stupid thoughts
remember 10-year-old Penny
and your best friend when you both   were 17?
I love him
because he is kind
I say
She moves away from her stove
and looks intently at me
He supports and affirms me
When I am discouraged I cry to him
When I am happy I laugh with him
When I am angry I yell at him
He is my playmate
He makes me laugh
My biggest problem, I say
was that he had children
and I did not want to be
the wicked stepmother
But he never allowed
his children
to come between us
once they discovered
that he loved me
they seemed to accept   it
She moves closer
He is in your heart, Deborah
he is in your heart
why are you here?
How could he stand
to let you go?
We talk often, I say
and because I am so aural
I am okay   as long as

I can hear   his voice
I am proud of my explanation
   but Annie goes on
   as though she is not really
      in the room
      with me
         I know a girl
         that an old man loved
         she wouldn't marry him
            but he said
            I will wait
               until she is ready
They did get married
and   she exclaimed
   her pitch higher
   than I have ever heard
he even cooks for her
Cooking is special
in my country
we say food
creates solidarity
   and it is woman's work
   to make sure
   that we serve fresh fruits and vegetables
            to our guests
      that we have fried corn and beer
         before the rest of the meal
            It would be bad, she says
            to let a guest   sit down
            and not offer food   and drink   immediately
               that is why, she says
               we had to stop
               at the store
                  the fruits and vegetables
                  had to be fresh
She smiles at me
While I continue to look at
   the photograph of Matt
She takes a peek

and
returns to her stove
with that look   I get
   when I am thinking about
   him in my heart
   when I am thinking about love
And I wonder
   if she entered this relationship
      because of community pressure
         or because
   he was
                  in her heart
I chastise myself
   for thinking in
      either/or terms
         but
   she told me the stories
   on different occasions
      why not at the same time?
maybe she had to get comfortable with me
maybe there are things
   like having a man in your heart
that you don't talk about
until you are ready
   She would not talk about
   the siblings who died
But she talked about her father
in response to my story
   about how I promised my mother
      on her deathbed
   that I would keep her children together
   and make sure
   we all
   got through college
Annie wanted to know more
And I told her
how strange   that experience was
         I was living in New York
         and traveled home with a cousin

who had not been to North Carolina
in over ten years
my Mom talked with me on Saturday
on Monday she was gone
Your mother was calling you, Annie says
We say   that when
people are dying
they either   call you
or push you away
if they think   you will cry
Your mother called you
she said
like my father called me
Annie seemed very pleased
with her analysis
I have come to recognize the twinkle in her eyes
the furrow in her brow
the levity in her voice
as a sign of her pleasure
Your mother was calling you
because she had something
to tell you
When my dad died, she says
I was at boarding school
and I had a dream
that I went home
and there was the box
with a dead person in it
in the front yard
I asked someone
in the crowd
Who is it?
They said it was one   of my parents.
I asked
Is it my mother?
They said
It is not your mother
The next day
I went home

and told my mother
about my dream
They told me
to go back to school
  but for three weeks
  I had these dreams
I went home again
  to find my father
  very sick
  I stayed and cried for him
  Then   one day
  he told me   to fix him some food
  When I came back
  he was dead
He called me, she says
  in my dream
    just like your mother
    called you

Annie
looked at me
and smiled

Return of/to the Body

My first meeting with Annie was over dinner at my apartment. The experience was a largely sensual one: preparing the meal made me feel close to my grandmother and the other "cooking ladies" in my community. The menu was the same as the Sunday dinner my grandmother prepared during my childhood and throughout my young adult life. I created a little tune while I worked, using the words from Gloria Hull's (1991, 113–114) "The Taste of Mother Love," a poem about the warmth and comfort provided by our mothers' food. I reminisced about my grandmother's kitchen, about how I was trying to replicate her style, only to find that "My food just won't taste like hers." Annie's delight in the meal, coupled with memories of the warmth and comfort of my childhood food experiences, made our dinner no less than sensual. Dwight Conquergood (1991, 180) reminds us that although participant-observation privileges the body as a site of knowing since the "doing" of ethnography entails speaking, listening, and acting together, ethnographers and other qualitative researchers often fail to acknowledge the bodily nature of fieldwork. Similarly, anthropologist Michael Jackson (1989) advocates indicating the bodily nature of fieldwork in our ethnographic discourse (18).

The sensuality of our "kitchen" experiences was magnified as Annie helped me to understand her culture's belief that food creates solidarity. Although I never had experienced food in this way, our conversation reminded me that we did use food to express emotion, whether anger, concern, or joy. I remember stories of food used as a weapon. One of our family friends assuaged her anger by throwing hot grits and maple syrup on an unfaithful husband. Likewise, we used food to show concern for neighbors. One of the worst transgressions we could commit was the failure to bring food to the home of the bereaved. Because the bereaved were obliged to focus on grieving, it was our responsibility to facilitate the process by assuring that the family never had to be concerned about meals. This display of concern ultimately brought joy to the grieving family as well as those involved in the preparation of the meals.

I also recalled that much of our food was not purchased at grocery stores. Mint for the tea grew around the front porch. Apples for the pies grew in a mini-orchard at the east end of the yard. Figs for preserves grew in the backyard at the edge of the vegetable garden where the children's early spring was spent digging holes and dropping seeds into black North Carolina earth. Chickens ran around in wire coops adjoining the garden space. In those memories, I began to understand that food was a unifying factor in our community. We experienced a solidarity that encompassed the relationship between people and the soil, the sun, the rain, and the animals, all working together to sustain human life.

I Am Because We Are

Although I felt competent to grasp the concept of "food as solidarity," there was a great deal about Annie's life I did not initially believe I could understand. She stands in a precarious place, reared in a country formerly colonized by Belgium, and college educated in France, Ghana, Gabon, and the United States. She lives on a cusp between the burgeoning urbanization of her native Zaire and a personal longing for the village that has never really been her home. She, like many others, does not fit our accepted notions of African women as *National Geographic* beasts of burden or as free and equal as African men (Aidoo 1992, 322).

African women today number more than 200 million, some as professional as Annie—doctors, lawyers, judges, professors, university lecturers—fewer in "rarified" professions such as creative writing, publishing, engineering, architecture, and management. Most African women, however, are farmers, responsible for growing and cultivating the food that feeds and brings extra money into their families (Aidoo 1992, 323). As various countries advocate independence, women leaders assert that independence will not be possible until women believe they will have the best their nations can offer. Annie's struggle with what is best for her reflects African women's changing roles in the midst of continuing gender oppression. While violating her society's mandates, asserting that she will never marry a man who takes another wife, she also succumbs to them, believing that any normal woman must marry and have children. Despite their increased professionalization, Annie and many other women believe that marriage is the most important single event in a woman's life. All forms of personal fulfillment and success are defined ultimately in terms of marriage and motherhood. Research on market women traders and "outside wives" (Karanja 1987, 247–261) indicates that it is difficult for these woman even to define marriage without children. A frequent response to the question, "What does marriage mean to you?" was, "Marriage means living with a man and having children" (249).

Although Annie never described in detail the polygyny that she so vehemently despised, Obbo (1987, 264) contends that the women who become second or outside wives in East Africa tend to be lower-income women who believe their support comes out of the family budget without the knowledge of the wife. Thus, economic situations influence dominant ideologies governing sexuality and fertility, ideologies defended by most men and tacitly accepted by most women (Obbo 1987, 264). Whether or not most women observe or disregard current laws and traditions against polygyny often depends on the level of economic need or desperation. The highly educated wives of men who take second or outside wives tend to turn blind eyes and deaf ears, while perpetuating the mythical division between good and bad women. Unfortunately, their ignorance or refusal to accept the economic reality of "uneven distribution of resources and power between men and women" (Obbo 1987, 266) obfuscates the fact that all women, both the privileged and not, are constantly attempting to transcend this economic condition. Annie's concern, then, is not qualitatively different from that of other women whose relationship goals are vastly influenced by their economic needs.

What I labeled as the tension between societal adherence and resistance in Annie's discourse might also be interpreted from the perspective of social interactions patterned after the presumed existence of natural rhythms in indigenous African communities. Mbiti (1969) notes that traditional African community is based on the synergetic functioning of the "I" and the "We." Thus, the community survives on the rhythm, "I am, because we are; and since we are, therefore, I am" (141). Neither the "I" nor the "We" have any meaning apart from what happens to the entire community. This functioning, he asserts, is revealed in their attitude toward marriage:

> For African people, marriage is the focus of existence. It is the point where all members of a given community meet: the departed, the living and those yet to be born. All the dimensions of time meet there, and the whole drama of history is repeated, renewed, and revitalized. . . . Therefore, marriage is a duty, a requirement from the corporate society, and the rhythm of life in which everyone must participate. Otherwise, he (sic) is a rebel and a lawbreaker, he is not only abnormal but "underhuman." Failure to get married under normal circumstances means that the person concerned has rejected society and society rejects him (sic) in turn (174).

Annie's continued assertions that she and her community had the ability to "just know" things is foreign to many Americans. Mbiti (1969) insists, however, that it proceeds naturally from traditional Africans' perceptions of a "spiritual universe," the concept of a dynamic, hierarchical unity between the spiritual and material aspects of life. There is a unity among God, humans, and nature, with God serving as the head of the hierarchy (Parrinder 1954, 20–28). There is no room for a clearcut separation of spirit and matter as opposites. The dichotomy between religion-superstition-revelation and logic-science-rationality (Shweder 1991, 2) is unknown in indigenous African societies. Their religious ontology constitutes a unity in which one mode of existence presupposes all others. "Just knowing" by spiritual or psychical discernment is no different from knowing by the evaluation of external data.

"Africans Are the Same"
◆

Although Annie believes that "Africans are the same wherever we are,"
I perceive that she and I are both different and similar. Some of our
greatest differences are attributable to our upbringing. I was reared in
semirural, southern, African American communities, while Annie was
reared in the urban centers of Zaire, Gabon, Ghana, France, and the
United States. Some of our similarities are attributable to our deliberate
identification with our African ancestry. Believing ourselves "culturally
challenged," we study indigenous African cultures and emulate the
more positive patterns of behavior. Yet, my time with Annie helped me
realize that I was not reared devoid of African culture. My "old folks"
knew and conveyed a great deal more about their African ancestry than
even they understood. My time with Annie took me back to them.

Aunt Sue has a head full of stories.
Aunt Sue has a whole heart full of stories.
Summer nights on the front porch
Aunt Sue cuddles a brown-faced child to her bosom
And tells [her] stories.

Black slaves
Working in the hot sun,
And black slaves
Walking in the dewy night,
And black slaves
Singing sorrow songs on the banks of a mighty river
Mingle themselves softly
In the flow of old Aunt Sue's voice,
Mingle themselves softly
In the dark shadows that cross and recross
Aunt Sue's stories.

And the dark-faced child, listening,
Knows Aunt Sue's stories are real stories.
[She] knows that Aunt Sue never got her stories
Out of any book at all,
But they came
Right out of her own life.

The dark-faced child is quiet
Of a summer night
Listening to Aunt Sue's stories.
(Hughes [1921] 1994, 23–24)

References

Aidoo, A. A. 1992. "The African Woman Today." *Dissent* 39: 319–325.

Bakhtin, M. M. 1981. "Discourse in the Novel." In *The Dialogic Imagination: Four Essays by M. M. Bakhtin,* edited by M. Holquist, translated by C. Emerson and M. Holquist. (Austin: University of Texas Press): 259–422.

———. 1986. "The Problem of Speech Genres." In *M. M. Bakhtin: Speech Genres and Other Late Essays,* edited by C. Emerson and M. Holquist, translated by V. W. McGee. (Austin: University of Texas Press): 60–102.

Conquergood, D. 1991. "Rethinking Ethnography: Towards a Critical Cultural Politics." *Communication Monographs* 58: 179–194.

Gluck, S. B. and D. Patai. 1991. "Introduction." In *Women's Words: The Feminist Practice of Oral History,* edited by S. B. Gluck and D. Patai. (New York: Routledge): 1–5.

Hughes, L. [1921] 1994. "Aunt Sue's Stories." In *The Collected Poems of Langston Hughes,* edited by A. Rampersad and D. Roessel. (New York: Alfred A. Knopf): 23–24.

Hull, G. T. 1991. "The Taste of Mother Love." In *Double Stitch: Black Women Write About Mothers and Daughters,* edited by P. Bell-Scott, B. Guy-Sheftail, J. J. Royster, J. Sims-Wood, M. DeCosta-Willis, and L. Fultz. (Boston: Beacon Press): 113–114.

Jackson, M. 1989. *Paths Toward a Clearing: Radical Empiricism and Ethnographic Inquiry.* Bloomington: Indiana University Press.

Karanja, W. W. 1987. "'Outside Wives' and 'Inside Wives' in Nigeria: A Study of Changing Perceptions of Marriage." In *Transformations of African Marriage,* edited by D. Parkin and D. Nyamwaya. (Manchester, UK: Manchester University Press): 247–261.

Mbiti, J. S. 1969. *African Religions and Philosophies.* New York: Doubleday.

Mead, G. H. 1934. *Mind, Self, and Society from the Standpoint of a Social Behaviorist.* Chicago: University of Chicago Press.

Myerhoff, B. 1978. *Number Our Days.* New York: Dutton.

Obbo, C. 1987. "The Old and the New in East African Elite Marriages." In *Transformations of African Marriage,* edited by D. Parkin and D. Nyamwaya. (Manchester, UK: Manchester University Press): 263–280.

Parrinder, E. G. 1954. *African Traditional Religion.* London: Hutchinson House.

Richardson, L. 1992. "The Consequences of Poetic Representation: Writing the Other, Rewriting the Self." In *Investigating Subjectivity: Research on Lived Experience,* edited by C. Ellis and M. G. Flaherty. (Newbury Park, CA: Sage): 125–137.

Sampson, E. E. 1993. *Celebrating the Other: A Dialogic Account of Human Nature.* Boulder: Westview Press.

Shweder, R. A. 1991. *Thinking Through Cultures: Expeditions in Cultural Psychology.* Cambridge, MA: Harvard University Press.

◆────────────

Deborah A. Austin

She became
who she is
   being right in the
              middle
   of things

   that's how she came to know the world
        (a little differently than some others
        . . . so she learned their way too)
Yet
she still believes
that being right in the middle of things
   talking   listening   doing   watching   asking
is how one comes to understand
   contradictions   contingencies   multiple realities
the stuff of everyday life

This is how she studies
and represents
        close relationships and family
           gender, ethnicity, spirituality
those things that interest her most

CHAPTER EIGHT

Speech Lessons

Laurel Richardson

"Perform for the visitors, Laurel." "A child should be seen and not heard." These contradictory messages from my father found resolution through my taking on a theatrical role, speaking through a character, being quietly whoever it was I thought I was when I was only "seen." Once I slyly retorted, "Children should be obscene and not hurt," but I said it softly, nonsatirically, and I don't think Father heard me, for he would not have let my impudence pass unpunished.

When I was barely seven and thought I might be Miss America when I grew up, I chose acting as my talent. I borrowed a large brown book from the Uptown Chicago Library, titled something like "Fifty Monologues Guaranteed to Win Contests." I don't remember one of them now, but back then I'd curl up in my bed with my dog, Happy, and memorize them. Following the "helpful" directions for emoting, staging, and costuming, I'd practice in front of Happy and my full-length mirror. Each Friday at school we had "show-and-tell" our class-mates, and I'd "tell" a monologue; some weeks, my teacher sent me to perform in other classrooms, even my older brother's classroom. Each weekend at home we had "show-and-tell" the visitors—mostly relatives, sometimes Father's law or political associates—and I'd "tell" a mono-logue. It was an easy kind of symbiosis, I realize now. The adults (teacher, parents) could take credit for my performance, while I raked in applause and, as a byproduct, diminished my brother's value. In good weeks, my performances would diminish him at home and at school.

Then something happened to my unscripted speech. Teachers and relatives complained they couldn't understand me. I talked too fast. At breakneck speed, I delighted in saying my name—"Laurel Gloria Cookie-Face Talking-Machine Richardson BOING!"—which, except for the *Laurel* and *Richardson* were definitely not my given names. As I write this now, I hear my cousins, aunts, and uncles at Olivet Camp on Geneva Lake, where we vacationed each summer, teasing me, embarrassing me, calling me "talking-machine." Telling me effectively to shut up. I have just had an "A-ha!": I think my seven-year-old's solution to being told she talked too much was to talk faster, to say what she wanted to say in less time, and to evaluate that effort positively—to name herself Talking-Machine. I marvel at "her" resourcefulness.

But my parents didn't see my fast speech as compensatory. Experts told them the problem was that my brain moved more quickly than my tongue. The solution was to send me to elocution lessons the year I turned seven. I don't know if elocution lessons were supposed to speed up my tongue or slow down my brain, but every Saturday morning for a couple of years, I'd board the Michigan Avenue bus by myself and get off at the Goodman Theater-Art Institute of Chicago. After my lessons I'd immerse my whole being in the Thorne miniature rooms housed in the Art Institute's basement, free in those days to children. It was a relief to be where I could be quiet, but where I could imagine that if I did talk my speed would be just right for the tiny rooms; I imagined that small spaces required quick speech, that somehow these were universal laws of time and space.

In the Goodman Theater, "Madame," dressed in burgundy and smelling like lavender, taught "her young ladies" how to warm up and soften their voices, when to project, when to demur, and how to sit, stand, and move in ladylike fashions. "A well-mannered woman never shakes a man's hand." "A well-mannered man never offers a woman a handshake, but cradles hers in his. Do not spend time with ill-mannered men." "Hold both your white gloves in your hand, palm up." "Feel the back of the chair with your leg before sitting." "Cross your legs at the ankles." "Walk toe-heel, toe-heel." "Speak when being spoken to." "Smile pretty."

We also practiced increasingly difficult tongue twisters—ironically, the faster the better. We trilled *r*s enunciated *ng*s, tongue-tipped *t*s, and denasilized *a*s, suppressing any hints of "Sheekawge-eze." Before long, Madame advanced me to acting classes. She cast me in what I considered even then to be awful, predictably silly children's plays; never as the ingenue, because I was brown-haired, and brown-eyed, as well. But I liked being directed onstage, being told where and how to say my lines. What I liked least was I made no friends there, and no one I knew except my mother ever came to a performance. And, I had to share applause with the others and exit, leaving the ingenue stage-center for her ovation.

I'm not sure if the elocution and acting lessons succeeded in slowing down my brain or speeding up my tongue, but they did teach me how to manage my "problem." I learned to treat my thoughts as a script I was writing and could scan and edit, while speaking that which I had already scanned and edited. If anything, my brain was working even faster—writing, editing, scanning, reading, evaluating, taking in how others were responding, giving my tongue less to do. I learned how to cut back what I might say, to limit my speech, to rarely repeat myself, to synthesize, and to take up very little of other people's time with my spoken words. I still have these skills. I can make a point, orally, in a few seconds that might take others several minutes. I can "read" people; students sometimes think I'm "psychic." And, I'm easy about relinquishing the floor. These are skills honed since I was seven, I realize as I write this, that are useful to me as an ethnographer, but oh, how great the cost—censoring, monitoring, limiting the young self that might have been spoken into being, not because what she might have said was wrong or cruel, but because it was "too fast" and "too much."

When I was in my 30s, I participated in a bioenergetic group in which we were to go from birth to adolescence in our minds and bodies in about 40 minutes. When the leader called time, the other participants were driving cars and dancing the twist while I was nine months old, barely walking and talking. There was so much, I felt, to see and assimilate; life was multifaceted, complex, and constantly refracting upon itself. The way to communicate this complexity and therefore of communicating *who I was in this world* would be to do it fast and detailed, telling who I was through my relationship to this "booming, buzzing" reality, before it changed again. Sometimes, nowadays, I meet a child who talks lots and fast. I speak at the child's tempo, support the breath points, and despite our rapid-fire talk—or maybe because of it—I feel a deep sense of connectedness, and peace.

But performing was not the only way to communicate: There was writing. One day in fourth grade, probably after one of my "monologues," or maybe after my excitement with an etymological lesson with which we always started the day, my teacher, Miss West, invited me to sit in the student chair next to her desk, a sacrosanct space that one

entered only by invitation. She said that children's plays were hackneyed—that was her word—and suggested I write some plays, myself.
Since I would have done anything to please her, I got my best friend,
Gloria Fenner, to turn historical events into dramas with me. Miss West
exotically blue-penciled the scripts. Bending history somewhat, we
wrote in lots of girls' parts. Sometimes, I cast myself in the lead. All of
this probably sounds like a hackneyed "inspiring teacher story," but my
fourth-grade teacher, supporting herself for the while through teaching,
"my Miss West" was soon to become a famous novelist. Although I read
her novels as an adult, I have only recently realized that the frizzly red-
haired, thin author and my frizzly red-haired, Wheat-Thin eating
teacher were one and the same: Jessamyn West. I had lucked out.

Writing plays with friends—never alone—became a major side-
line activity for me through high school. In fifth grade, Suzy Verb and I
operated a Saturday morning preschool in Suzy's dining room. We
charged 50 cents per child, per morning—including snacks and sup-
plies. We never lacked for "students." We directed them in plays we
wrote, and then published the plays in our "Gazette" (sold separately to
students' parents); our reviews of our plays were always magnanimous.

My eighth-grade girls' club, "Just Us Girls"—innocently
acronymed JUGS on our pristine white sailor hats—was moved by the
plight of a poor sick girl featured one day in the *Chicago Tribune*. We
decided to raise money for her through staging a drama—well, melodrama—about her life, sickness, and near death. I think I played the
girl, but I am hazy about that. We sold advertising space on the playbill
to neighborhood stores and relatives and performed, with lights, cos-
tumes, and curtain, to a full house in my basement. We raised $40. A
Tribune photographer took our pictures, in our regulation pyramid
pose, wearing our JUGS hats. That picture, our names, and a human
interest story about us appeared in the Sunday *Tribune*. I got a special
mention in "Kup's Column." Probably all of this publicity happened,
although I hadn't realized it then, because of my father's downtown connections.

Alpha Girls was the "best" sorority at Senn High School, where I
went. Its members were school "leaders" like majorettes, homecoming
queens, and cheerleaders. It was also the only sorority that accepted
both Jews and Gentiles. At a time when high school social life was totally
organized around sororities and fraternities, Alpha was the only sorority
I could join. My older brother, a basketball jock, and thereby a school

leader, was a member of Alpha Boys. Although unprecedented, I was pledged to Alpha my freshman year as a "legacy."

Pledge duties included supplying gum and cigarettes, fetching meal trays, carrying books, washing gym clothes, kissing feet (left one first) and writing a skit about the "actives." Obviously, the skit could not offend any actives and would have to honor the hierarchy established among them. Offensive pledges were called "bad pledge," given demerits, and, if bad enough, dropped from the pledge class. For the first time, I had to think about the consequences of my writing. As chief scriptwriter, I decided the skit would not razz any of the actives, and that the amount of time spent on a particular active would be commensurate with my perception of their ranking in the sorority. Now, I might call my considerations the politics of poetics, or the ethics of writing. The skit was a success, and for the next two years—until I left Senn, early off to college—I was the chief skit writer for Alpha Girls' parties with Alpha Boys. I wrote a lot of double entendres.

With the exception of adapting, with my college roommate, Thurber's "The Thirteen Clocks" for children's theater, I stopped writing plays after high school. Thinking about it now, I see that playwrighting had been a vehicle for my "becoming a woman," for practicing skills expected of a woman slated to marry a professional man and mother his children. The activity was always on the sidelines, never mainstreamed, always something to do after fulfilling my duties and obligations. I wrote with friends, bonding, practicing the arts of compromise necessary to a future, say, Junior League member. We gently manipulated the guys through double entendres; we could be simultaneously inviting and innocent. We worked with "deserving" children, teaching them, literally and metaphorically, "how to act." We produced plays as charity events, young Lady Bountifuls, transmutating, like alchemists, our base fun into golden nobility. We even got press coverage.

Something more happened to me in high school, though. Madame's and Father's speech lessons took on a new dimension. Becoming a woman, my voice grew ever softer, "becoming in a woman." I remember speeding up my talk. Did I think that if I spoke softly, fast would be OK? Was I trying to retrieve the sense of self I had previously censored, integrating "her" into the woman I was becoming? By my sophomore year in high school, people routinely asked me to speak louder; they said they couldn't hear or understand me. "How true," I must have thought, "how painfully true."

The next year, a loud college roommate told me she thought I spoke softly as a control mechanism, making people shut up and strain to hear me. Perhaps she was right; perhaps I had found an "offstage" way to be both feminine and command attention. But, mostly I think I had grown shy; I had come to doubt the value of my way of perceiving, organizing, and "wording the world." As an early entrant in the University of Chicago's College, I had plenty of proof of my shortcomings by way of comparison to the truly gifted students around me.

By the time I was in graduate school in sociology, I was speaking quietly—and quickly—in seminars, except when seriously ticked off by the sexism of my peers. ("A female can't understand X [Weber, Marx, social structure, etc.]," a male student would say to me whenever I was besting him in an argument.) My Ph.D. advisor's job-placement letter, I learned much later, said I would be a poor teacher because I spoke too softly. He had never seen me teach. He didn't "understand me"; he didn't understand that for me the classroom is a theater, a place to play the role of "professor," to project, to move an audience of students. He didn't know I had theater skills.

But I did have theater skills—reading, performing, and improvising. These I had sharpened at University Theater (U. T.), a student and community activity at the University of Chicago, when I was an undergraduate in the 1950s. I spent much more time with U.T. than I did with my schoolwork. The year my mother had my dog, Happy, put to sleep and I didn't cry about it, I won a "UTEY" for best acting performance by a female. The *Maroon's* theater critic singled out my performance in "The Member of the Wedding" for two paragraphs of accolades. But I didn't "roll over" for him, and my name never again appeared in his column.

Our director staged "Lord Byron's Love Letter," a one-act play, in the round. Theater-in-the-round was an innovative and risky way to block drama, then, because it was unfamiliar and brought audiences closer to the action. I played Ariadne, the soft-spoken, unmarried daughter of an aging New Orleans woman, a shopkeeper. From offstage the mother's loud, piercing voice controls Ariadne's actions onstage. The pair's livelihood comes from showing a love letter from Lord Byron to tourists; the pair's emotional life comes from telling about the mother's and Lord Byron's romance, from their initial meeting on the steps of the Acropolis to his love letter. Telling the story, the mother's voice fades, gives way to Ariadne's; sometimes, they speak in unison, emotionally as one. As the drama unfolds, the audience believes that Ariadne is Lord Byron's illegitimate child. But the brash couple to whom they are telling the story shatters the myths of Ariadne's life: the letter, they say, is a forgery; Ariadne is not Lord Byron's daughter. At the dramatic apex, the couple refuses to pay Ariadne for viewing the "fake" letter. Raising her voice and expressing for the first time in the drama her own emotional life, not her mother's, Ariadne flings her arms, wails, and screams at them, "Canaille! Canaille." (Think "swine," the director said.) A dramatic pause, and then the denouement—the mother comes on stage, silent, a broken woman.

Opening night, the audience was quiet at the end of the play and then broke into wild applause and a standing ovation. My parents came to the second night's performance, sitting a few rows back. Before the denouement, immediately following my intense dramatic moment, Mother stood up, opened her purse, and said out loud through her tears, "Here honey, I'll give you the money." She didn't understand why her action mortified me or how it destroyed the drama's resolution. In consolation, I decided I was a really great actress to trick my own mother that way. Later, I thought I wasn't so good, or Mother wouldn't have confused me with the character. Now, I think she was incapable of making a distinction between her daughter and Ariadne—between reality and theater.

I was a good actress, but not as good as some of the others, especially the community people who brought in Viola Spolin's improvisational techniques. Now, I'm going to name drop. My theater troupe included Mike Nichols, Elaine May, Barbara Harris, Ed Asner, Alex Hassilev, and Sevren Darden. I was part—a minor part, to be sure—of a fledgling "Second City." Called the Compass Players, we did improvisations on a makeshift stage at the 55th Street tavern, The Compass.

But, I didn't have what they had. I wasn't determined, driven, the way some of them were. Acting was not going to be my life. A brief fellowship at Actor's Studio in San Francisco after college convinced me I lacked the motivation. I also didn't like how I "became" a character, how the character slipped into my daily life. I didn't like how being tall severely limited my parts. And, something else was different: I didn't like the applause. I had grown highly critical of my own performances—they didn't meet my own expectations. So, when audiences generously clapped for me, I felt only contempt for them. But if the applause was merely polite, I was furious. "Pearls before swine—Canaille!" I thought. I was becoming a moody, demanding prima donna, and I didn't like "her" at all.

Like other adults who had talents or hobbies as a child, I put theater behind me. How could I fit hours of rehearsal, method acting, "personality changes," or scriptwriting into an adult life of scholarship and parenting? But, how could I completely suppress the "theater" in me? As I write this, I realize that the ease with which I took to sociology and the way I fell in love with it—sociology felt absolutely natural and true to me—might have had something to do with my theater experiences of playing roles, acting in context, seeing from multiple points of view, and knowing that all of the above are constructed, interrelated, and changing. Perhaps sociology for me is one big "displacement;" a place where I thought I could undo and redo.

That said, I find myself smiling. How delicious to think of my career in sociology, at least in part, as a restitutive journey, a reclamation of the self, a complex, life-affirming, application of "speech lessons."

I use acting skills in teaching, adjusting style to context. Giving conference papers, I mark my text as a script (accents, skip, pause), rehearse it, and check out the "feel" of the room and the "stage" setup. For a 14-city national book tour (1985–86 for *The New Other Woman*), I videotaped improvisational role-plays with "coaches" playing nasty talk-show hosts; I practiced spontaneity; and I enrolled in modeling school to learn good television postures, demeanors, makeup, and clothing. My desires were to spread sociological gospel, sell books, and perform well—flawlessly, seemingly effortlessly. My professional acting ego, my child ego, and my academic ego were all on tour. I doubt if academics without "speech lessons" would have gone to the same lengths that I had, or have such absurd expectations.

Preparing for the book tour in 1985, I realize now, sent me back into "real" theater, not its surrogate academic "theater of the absurd." After that tour, I experienced a "crisis of representation." Resolution of that crisis came through writing *performance texts*—dramas, narrative poems, responsive readings. I found new "best" academic friends, and the excitement of co-constructing with them new "fields of play." The possibilities for the fields of sociology now seem vast, uncharted, unbounded. This summer I even made a tentative first step back into real theater.

About this next thing I may be wrong. Sometimes we don't see ourselves as others see us. But, this is what I think is true of my life-in-theater and beyond. The more I "became" a character, the better my performance and the greater my loss of Self. Fear and anger about what was happening to me, I displaced into contempt for audiences. The danger for me was letting a role take me over, letting a part in someone else's drama suppress my own Self. So, I've not been willing to play the demeaning stock university parts for women—pet, victim, good mother, bad mother, tag-along, mistress. Nor have I been willing to play border guard, disciplinary police officer, roll-overer, science fetishist. These were not the parts I tried out for, not the ones I came to academia to play. My contempt for audiences has not transferred to students—who I view as co-creators of the performance called education—but to the "male gaze" of colleagues and administrators, of either sex. I have thus not been completely successful in department politics. But, in retrospect, I can't say I'm sorry; I can't say I'd do it any differently—speak more softly or speak more slowly.

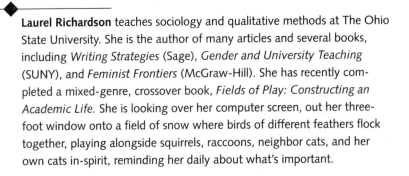

Laurel Richardson teaches sociology and qualitative methods at The Ohio State University. She is the author of many articles and several books, including *Writing Strategies* (Sage), *Gender and University Teaching* (SUNY), and *Feminist Frontiers* (McGraw-Hill). She has recently completed a mixed-genre, crossover book, *Fields of Play: Constructing an Academic Life*. She is looking over her computer screen, out her three-foot window onto a field of snow where birds of different feathers flock together, playing alongside squirrels, raccoons, neighbor cats, and her own cats in-spirit, reminding her daily about what's important.

CHAPTER NINE

Maternal Connections

Carolyn Ellis

With one hand, she holds tightly to the support bar along the wall of the bathroom. I take her other hand gently in mine, wash each finger, noting the smoothness of her skin, the beauty of her long, slender fingers. "My fingernails," she says, "they're dirty." Without speaking, I run my index nail, covered with a washcloth, under each of her nails, systematically snapping out the dirt as I go. It's a good sign that she cares. Until now, she hasn't been that concerned even about urinating in bed.

When I push hard on the soap dispenser, small globs of thick, pink, liquid soap, smelling of perfumed bleach, drop onto the translucent washcloth. I load the white cloth with many squirts, hoping to wash away the lingering smell of feces, urine, perspiration, bile bags, plastic tubes, stale hair oils, and hospital odors.

She extends her arm and I slowly wash from wrist to shoulder, observing the intrusion of the spreading black bruises marking needle points. Her washed hand holds onto my wrist for support now as I unclasp her other hand from the railing. I repeat the process on that side.

"I'm going again," she says, sucking in slowly through open lips and closed teeth, eyebrows raised as though she is asking my permission and apologizing at the same time. I'm glad she is sitting on the toilet. It'll be less of a mess than before.

"That's okay," I respond, "maybe this will be the last time. Hopefully the laxative has run its course."

I hold her hand and touch her shoulder gently as she lets it all go. Then, "I'm sorry about last night," she says. "It seemed like it was every hour. You shouldn't have to do that."

"I didn't mind," I say, remembering my reflex gag reaction the first time her bowels exploded in the night. Only my determination that she not know how much the smell—that rotten, chemical odor—bothered

240

me kept me from adding my regurgitation to the brown liquid I poured into the toilet on her behalf. "I'm glad I was here for you."

"Yeah, the nurses don't come right away," she says. "Even with you here, some ended up on the bed, didn't it?"

"Yes, but now we know better how to do it, get the bedpan under you sooner. It helps when you raise your hips."

"If anybody told me I'd have to be doing this . . ."

". . . you used to do it for me," I interrupt. We laugh like two good friends sharing a memory.

Being careful of the tubes and IVs, I unsnap and remove her soiled gown. She tries to help. I cover the front of her body with a towel, to protect her from cold. "It feels good when you wash my back," she says, and I continue rubbing. When she shivers, I run the washcloth under hot water. I wonder about washing the rest of her body.

Around front, I wash her belly, noting the faded scars of my younger brother's cesarean birth—and shudder at the reminder that he is now dead—and I look closely at the new scars of the gall bladder surgery. Her stomach is puffy, but almost flat now, not rounded as before. The extra skin hangs loosely. Then her legs. Although her skin is dry and flaky, I admire her thin, almost bony, yet still shapely, legs. Our bodies have the same form, I note. Long, slender, and graceful limbs, fatty layers on top of the hips and belly, and a short and thick waist.

I move to her breasts, still large and pendulous. Now they hang to her waist and, as her shoulders curve forward, they rest on her belly, like mine, only lower.

I take one tenderly in my hand, lift it gently from her belly to wash it, noting the rash underneath. "Would you like cream on that?"

"Oh, yes, it's real sore." She holds her breast while I rub in the cream.

Feeling no particular emotion, I observe from a distance. Her body is my body, my body in 36 years. So this is what it will look and be like. I see.

I hand her the soaped washcloth. "Can you wash your butt," I ask, "and between your legs?"

"I think so," she replies, taking the washcloth, holding onto the support bar to balance one side of herself a few inches above the seat. My pubic hair also will be thin and gray, I think, as I notice hers. Then I walk away, to give her the illusion of privacy.

"Are you ready to get back in bed now?" I ask.

"Yes, I'm worn out."

I extend both arms. The bile bag pinned to her gown threatens to become entangled in our embrace. "Put it around my neck," she cleverly suggests. "It'll be my necklace." I smile, appreciating her humor, which bonds us and makes it easier to refer to the bag. But what a breakdown in boundaries—her bile is on the outside of her body for everyone to see, more personally revealing than the butt that sticks out of the back of her gown!!

I hold my arms out straight again. When she grabs on, she and I pull her to a standing position. When she winces in pain, I embrace her around her middle, steadying her for the long journey back to bed, eight feet away. The tubes extending from her chest and abdomen, the bile bag necklace—all are properly positioned. She shuffles her feet in baby steps, all the while holding onto my outstretched arms. She looks into my eyes as I walk backwards, to pick up my cues, when to move forward, when to turn. We are intimately connected. We are totally trusting.

Taking care of her feels natural, as though she is my child. The love and concern flowing between us feels like my mom and I are falling in love. The emotionality continues during the four days and nights I stay with her in the hospital. My life is devoted temporarily to her well-being. She knows it and is grateful. I am grateful for the experience. I do not mind that she is dependent on me. I am engrossed by our feeling, by the seemingly mundane but, for the moment, only questions that matter. Are you dizzy? In pain? Comfortable? Do you want to be pulled up in bed? Can't you eat one more bite? Do you need to pee? Have gas? Want water? Prefer to sleep now? As I help with these events, I do not question their meanings, as I so often do about most things in my life.

While my mom sleeps, I take my daily walk down the hall to peer at the newborn babies. On the other side of the glass partition, there are three—one boy covered in blue and two girls in pink. I wince at the institutional marking of gender roles and then shrug. I strain to read the identification cards, to have a story about each one: birthday, weight, length, parents' names—not much to go on.

A man stares intently at one of the girls. Knowing the answer, I ask anyway, "Are you the father?" He nods yes and beams. "She has jaundice," he says, "a mild case." I feel his bond to her even through the glass pane. I recognize the connection from the feelings I have for my mother. He leaves and another young man, in his early 20s, arrives. Ignoring the young son pulling on his pants leg for attention, this man stands off to the side, to peer through the glass into an inner room almost out of view. Out of the corner of my eye, I watch and imagine his story. His new baby must be in there, perhaps he is worried about it, like I am worried about my mother. If he could just get a glimpse, or better yet, do something, he would feel better.

I continue watching, fantasizing that one of the babies is mine, and try to generate what the feeling would be. What would it be like to take the baby home? To bond? The dependence? Experiencing unconditional love for my mother makes me, for the moment, crave to feel it toward and from a child as well. Do I just want someone who will wash me when I'm 79? What if something is wrong with the baby? What about my career? Travel plans? Yet how can I omit this meaning-giving experience from my life?

When I return, my mom is having her vitals read by a nurse who "usually works in the nursery," my mom announces. "How old is the oldest mother you have had?" I ask nonchalantly, hoping my question is not too transparent.

"Forty-two," the nurse answers.

I must look disappointed, because she adds quickly, "But I have only worked there for 18 months, I'm sure there have been some older. Yes, I'm sure."

I'd be almost 44 before my first child could be born, I think, turning back to my mother.

◆————————

Carolyn Ellis (Professor of Communication and Sociology, University of South Florida) lives in Tampa with her soul mate, Arthur Bochner, and their four dogs, who seduce her into "dog reality" several times each day. She is the author of *Final Negotiations: A Story of Love, Loss, and Chronic Illness* (Temple) and coeditor of *Investigating Subjectivity: Research on Lived Experience* (Sage). In her work on narrative, subjectivity, and illness, she seeks to write evocative texts that remind readers of the complexity of their social worlds. Writing autoethnographic texts has intensified her life experience; she hopes they also contribute to the lives of readers.

CHAPTER TEN

An Ethnographic Act
The Construction of Consensual Theatre

Jim Mienczakowski

Act I Scene i: A Beach Party at Night

◆

A teenage girl, Maria, lit by a solitary spotlight, stands center stage. She has a half-full bottle of bourbon in her hand. Dressed in a cotton lumberjack shirt and jeans she turns to one side and raises the bottle to her lips. She freezes in that position and upstage the cyclorama is suddenly littered with several slide images that show the same girl in the same stance, drinking from a variety of bottles of brand-name alcoholic beverages. These slides are cross-faded to depict several different women echoing Maria's drinking posture. Gradually the slides change to show Maria in other "street drinking" situations. Eventually the cyclorama becomes illuminated with a bright collage of slide projections depicting nightclubs, bars, and parties. Music starts. A heavy, thumping rock melody.

Maria begins to dance, a slow rhythmic movement in time to the beat. She is dancing for herself and is oblivious to everything around her. Her bottle now is empty and she throws it to the ground.

A male figure, Jason, moves across stage toward her and attempts to dance with her. He is uncoordinated, lurching and almost comic in his movements. He offers her a fresh bottle. She takes it, but as she does so he slides behind her and starts to kiss her neck. At first she resists but, then concentrating on drinking, ignores him while he tries to pull open her shirt and unbuckle her jeans belt. Maria pushes Jason away and drinks heavily from the bottle but he becomes aggressive. She struggles

*more forcefully and he slaps her. She hits him back and he then knocks
her to the floor. For a moment he stares at her, menacingly, giving the
audience the impression that he is going to carry his abuse further. She
starts to vomit over herself and he snatches the bottle back and staggers
off. [Exit Jason, stage left.]*

And so begins *Busting: The Challenge of the Drought Spirit* (Mienczakowski and Morgan 1993), an ethnographically derived play graphically detailing the experiences of persons undergoing detoxication processes. This opening sequence is not an example of an authorial intervention representative of the sort of incident assumed as typical of alcohol-affected behavior but is the enactment of an informant's description of self. The majority of *Busting* is derived from verbatim ethnographic account work that has repeatedly been confirmed by informants as truthful in its representation of their behaviors. The scripting process involved several layers of informant participation and confirmation, as did both the rehearsals and eventual performances of the play. This paper describes the methodological issues involved in constructing *ethnodrama* and discusses the theory and heritage of this ethnographic alternative.

Foundation Work
◆

Busting and its predecessor, *Syncing Out Loud*, an ethnographically based play concerning experiences of schizophrenic illness, were born out of a desire to meld theatre and ethnography into a reflexive, reflective teaching tool. Both of the above plays were constructed after prolonged, intensive research phases and involved student nurses, health professionals, health consumers, trainee actors, and caregivers in their writing and performance. The pilot project, *Syncing Out Loud*, performed by nursing students and actors in a residential psychiatric setting to health informants and health professionals, followed a well-established heritage of psychotherapeutic nursing strategies intended to impact both nursing students and health consumers (Cox 1989; Price 1992). Cox (1989) describes the use of professional actors who assume the role of patients in order for medical students to practice nursing interventions.

Watkins (1990, 47–48) takes the role-playing use of actors further in enacting critical incidents from actual nurse-patient histories so that trainees can explore the emotional experience of patient/family and health professional relationships. The *Busting* and *Syncing Out Loud* projects extend that relationship by seeking dramatized firsthand informant interpretations of life experiences to be presented to audiences by nursing students (and others) and reinterpreted to informant groups via "forum performances" (Boal 1985). This is done in order for the informants to be able to reflect on the actor's interpretation and representation of self (Turner 1986; Conquergood 1988, 1991) and for the health community, in general, to realize how particular social and mental health issues are experienced.

The third facet of the *ethnodrama process,* as it has become known, is to provide an educational and health promotional element for student work. Health education messages, derived from the experiences and agendas of health professionals on the team, are included in the script. These inclusions are worked into the writing in such a way that they also pass repeated informant consensus tests and are considered valid, appropriate, and true. As well as playing in hospital and psychiatric settings to health informants, the plays are performed to public audiences and audiences of students. Each performance is followed by an electronically recorded forum of audience and cast, which provides further data for the study's base. As the entire process depends on notions of communicative consensus (Habermas 1984), elements of the script and performance that are seen as inaccurate, disenfranchising, or disadvantageous to health informants in the audiences are always open to amendment. Therefore, the script is never finished and always subject to revision after every forum performance.

Setting and Method
◆

Commencing in the late months of 1991 with *Syncing Out Loud*, these research projects began with an intensive period of participant observation within health settings. Informants then engaged in open-ended interviews (Denzin 1970, 1989), which were recorded over a period of four months. Research was conducted by ethnographers, nursing lecturers, student nurses, and health professionals working in the field.

Syncing Out Loud involved observation and informal interviewing within a secure state government psychiatric setting as well as with members of a day care center. The aim of the pilot project was to create experience of psychosis for an audience and to act as an agent for better community and nursing understanding of mental health problems. As research protocols and human decency made observing and recording known informants during actual episodes of schizophrenic psychosis an untenable prospect, clinical accounts of schizophrenic illness, recorded in an overseas teaching hospital, were supplied to the research team. This was essential in order to guide understanding of the scope of this health phenomenon and to maintain informants' anonymity.

Busting involved research in an urban drug and alcohol detoxication unit that specialized in residential periods of detoxing for casual admissions. Clients within the unit were drawn from the local population of street people as well as from the waged inner-city population. Services within this unit were free to detoxees, and the unit concentrated on accommodating and supporting women from the local street and red-light communities. Many of these women were considered by the health care community to be disadvantaged or otherwise not catered to by the existing male-oriented support groups within the area. A full detoxing and counseling program would, ideally, last 10 days, but most detoxees discharged themselves after completing only the clinical stages of alcohol and substance withdrawal. In the case of *Busting,* the intention was to research, explain, and inform audiences of the health issues surrounding alcohol abuse by giving informant explanations of the experience of acute alcohol withdrawal. During intensive periods of observation and interviewing, student/professional researchers were paired with staff already working in the detox unit in order to lessen their impact on the setting (Hammersley 1992; Atkinson 1992). In all cases, the gender signification of informants and researchers was, where possible, given consideration (Warren 1988).

Data gathered during the research phase were returned to informant groups for comment and amendment. Typically, the discussion of informant accounts and transcripts was conducted by nursing clinicians on site as part of routine counseling sessions. A "conditional matrix" (Strauss and Corbin 1990), or in our case a conditional "plot" matrix, was then formed in conjunction with a phenomenological reduction of themes (van Maanen 1984; Giorgi 1985) in order to explicate informants' essential health and professional experiences and to reduce the themes and events to a manageable level (Silverman 1994). The reduction of themes, or *essentialising,* was performed in group settings by the researchers, key health consumer and health professional informants, and by the project writers. The essential elements were then returned for amendment, adjustment, and comment to groups of health informants in residential settings (Rolfe, Mienczakowski, and Morgan 1995). In order to maintain coherence, I now discuss the ethnodrama process in more detail, relating it to the major *Busting* project, which refined the processes of the earlier pilot phase.

Scripting
◆

Scripting sessions in *Busting* entailed an adherence to and preference for verbatim account work as opposed to fictionalized account work. This preference was that of the informants who, greatly experienced in the disclosure counseling techniques of Alcoholics Anonymous, were adept at and accustomed to listening to and telling their stories. Several informants expressed strong opinions that unnecessary literary and plot fabrication would render the performance merely "a fiction" instead of being "a truth." The counterargument of fictional account work appearing true, and in many cases appearing more true than verbatim account work (Atkinson 1990), was dismissed by informants who felt that the project had credence only if the audience tacitly understood that the play's authority rested on its factual research status and could not be dismissed as authorial invention.

Where necessary, to link plot, subplot, and narrative, fictional inclusions were inserted into the *Busting* script. Such inclusions were fictitious in the sense that they were amalgamations of separate elements of informant data and were not direct verbatim transcriptions of single interviews. Most often they included scenarios constructed by informants as typical of interactions with clients or health professionals within the domain under study. Fictional links were always based on informant accounts or anecdotes and were considered plausible by informants (Mienczakowski 1994, 1995). When no such consensus was achieved, scenes were deleted from the text.

In relation to the notion of fictionalized account work appearing more real than faithful account work, the opening sequence of the play was considered by several informants not to go far enough. Some suggested that their own experiences of similar situations led them to believe that the scene would, most probably, end with more violence. However, the fictionalization of Maria and Jason's opening scene to include a greater degree of physical assault contradicted both the emancipatory nature of the project and the integrity of the ethnographic venture.[1] Moreover, although dramatic emphasis might have been served by fictionalizing a greater degree of violation as being a typical outcome, the factual representation of the incident seemingly depicted a moment of self-discovery and choice. Through consensus, the informants moved away from a typified or stereotypical fictionalization of the outcome to a representation of the actual events related by the informant. As informants controlled the determination of the report process, they wished not to depict a stereotypical representation of self but an empowering and accurate representation that revealed them to be rational and choice aware.

The informant (known as Jason in the play) is a central figure in the narrative and to fictionalize a grievous violation merely to satisfy the poesis of plot would not have been an act of empowerment. The play does not attempt absolute mimesis but seeks to combine mimesis with polyphonic "communicative praxis" (Fabian 1983, 71–72) and therefore relies on negotiating and constructing informant meanings and privileging informant voices rather than condoning authorial interpretations of meanings.

Here Jason's own verbatim transcription of self is given as part of the play's health education message to young audiences. Jason speaks directly to the audience and communicates, in his own words, his predictions for his own life and his warnings to others.

Jason: G'day, my name is Jason and I'm an alcoholic. I'm 21 and I've been through detox in Kakuri, Cairns, and a couple of Salvo places, and now here. Sometimes I think that it's all too late for me now. I did a stretch in jail up North but I couldn't dry out there. You can get drugs in some prisons easier than on the street so I couldn't really get it together. I don't really want to talk to people unless I've had a drink and I'm sorry about me shakes today. But we all know about withdrawals here so I expect you'll understand if I don't make much sense.

I am nobody to give advice—I can't show youse how to be but I have something to say: I want to make something of my life, but I just can't seem to make it. I've been drinking that much, I can't get up for work. You just get lazy. All I want to do is just get drunk. I think that it's all too late for me now. I feel it is you know, yeah. I should have taken me chances. I tried to get into the navy but they wouldn't accept me, you know. I got a job in a gold mine, but I turned that down an' all. I'd like to say . . . I mean this for kids who are only getting pissed for fun now, I want to say to them, I can't help youse out, you know, I can't show you how to be. Just don't end up like someone like me, you know. 'Cos I just like getting drunk, like partying, having a good time, but I tend to go overboard; don't know when to stop. I'd like to say that, you know, keep going in this kind of life and you've signed your own death certificate. *(Tears are welling in his eyes.)*

. . . If you don't bust you've made it. Yeah, that's it. That's what it's about—you've made it: the big win. Just don't bust. *(He is crying so much that Chrissie helps him from the stage. Mark takes the lectern. Long pause.) Busting Act II Scene i. (AA Youth Disclosure Meeting.)*

Jason demonstrates the potential of the ethnodrama process to give voice to the health concerns of disenfranchised, or subordinate (Fraser 1990), health consumers in their own words. This "voicing," to audiences of health professionals, caregivers, and others, is essentially reflexive in nature as it informs those officially responsible (Apple 1993) for determining health provision of their consumers' needs and experiences. Nor does the process singularly utilize informant monologue as a means of conveying narrative. Much of the script reflects participant observation, informant anecdotes, informant role-playing of scenarios and the blending of verbatim transcription within such scenarios.

The following passage from *Busting* (Act II, Scene ii) was taken from a nurse's account of informing a detoxee that his liver was malfunctioning seriously. In this particular scene other characters, besides the nursing informants, have been added but the dialogue remains largely unaltered. Glen's humor and dignity in discovering what he knows only too well to be a life-threatening degeneration of his liver, serves several purposes within the script. It opens an agenda for dialogue and acts informatively in clarifying the long-term health implications of abusive drinking while also dealing with nurse-patient relationships and the role of the nurse within such circumstances (Cox 1989; Watkins 1990; Jennings 1992). Perhaps more importantly, it shows the health client's humor, dignity, and acceptance in the face of adversity. Glen, by his own reckoning, had endured over 40 visits to detox centers and was under no illusion as to what the test results meant. Far from using levity to lessen the impact of what is being said, the humor poignantly brings home the full implication to the audience of what is happening to Glen.

Glen: Is my wife after me? She'll have guessed where I am by now. Has she phoned for me?

Lisa: No Glen. It isn't about your wife. It's about your test results.

Glen: I know. Me liver isn't in such good shape is it? I was warned last time. But I'm not going to bust again.

Lisa: I hate having to say this Glen, but your liver is in pretty bad shape.

Glen: Getting bigger is it?

Lisa: I'm sorry, Glen. We can't treat you here.

Glen: (*Whispering*) Shot is it? Me liver? (*Pause*) How long then? You know? . . . before it packs up?

Lisa: I don't know—but they'll do some more tests at the R.C.H. They're much better equipped . . . there.

Glen: (*Still whispering*) I reckon I knew it was coming, but. Been warned enough. Seen this happen plenty—had to be my turn sooner or later. (*Pause*) Don't want to depress me mates before I go, though. Don't tell them will you Lisa? (*Pause*) I knew when they pulled me into the R.S.L. (*Returned Servicemen's League*) that night that this could be me last bender. Don't tell them, but. It's pointless scaring them and all. Most of us boys have been going through detox a dozen times a year since school. I don't have a single mate who hasn't busted. Me Dad went the same way. Scotch drinker he was. Bottle a day man. Cremated last year—took three days to put the fire out. *(Laughs with Lisa)* Will you let my wife know where I am, if she asks, that is?

Lisa: *(Squeezes his hand)* Of course I will, Glen. It might not be that bad after all.

Rehearsals
◆

All rehearsals for this type of performance offer potential for the research data to be further informed and updated. Although the *Busting* script had been read and validated by informants in (clinical/residential) group settings, it was still essential for informants to confirm that the physical and semiotic representation of their ethnographic realities were authentic and cogent. To that end informants were invited to participate in the rehearsal process to guide actors. In return, actors undertook periods of immersion within the clinical setting. All rehearsals involved health representatives, particularly nursing staff, and the stage setting of the play was constructed so that nursing and health informant behaviors, routines, and so forth, could be portrayed accurately. Besides informing actors of the perceived veracity and worth of their scripted dialogue, their physical representations of health and nursing behaviors within the setting were also subjected to close scrutiny and consensual change.

Character work was approached through Stanislavskian (Stanislavski 1936, 1986) observational methodology and amended via Bakhtinian (Bakhtin 1984, 1986) dialogical interactions that negotiated meanings (understandings) among actors, the director, writers, and informants. In the final phase of rehearsals the script was performed to audiences entirely composed of health consumers and caregivers, and the ensuing forum audience interactions were also recorded and used to update the performances.

In the case of *Syncing Out Loud,* the clients of a psychiatric day care center (not otherwise used in the research) were bused to a special showing and participated in the forum validation, alteration, and reconstruction of the actors' portrayals of schizophrenic illness. Similarly, the play was subsequently performed in a residential psychiatric setting that had contributed data to the study. This process was undertaken before the play opened to general audiences. Thus the "informed performances" were repeatedly amended and validated before opening to general and school audiences. In the case of *Busting*, validation performances involved the health professionals and health consumers of two detox units besides the one in which the research took place. The play was eventually performed to an invited audience of health care community members including informants, educators, administrators and caregivers, as well as to students (high school and university) on two different academic campuses.

Performances and Target Audiences

The goal of the project's funding bodies was to create community understanding and awareness of issues surrounding mental illness and alcohol and drug issues. The theatrical spaces designated for performances to school and university audiences were concomitantly used as health education arenas by community and government health agencies. In the case of *Syncing Out Loud,* literature relating to psychiatric support agencies was made available to all audience members. Counselors and psychiatric nurses were present throughout each performance and during both the intermission and forum sessions. In *Busting,* free drinks followed by penalty free alcohol impairment breath tests were provided for audience volunteers by community police during the play's intermission. Again, social services and AA counselors were present at each showing, as were other health support agencies. Packages of health education support materials were supplied to participating schools, and full copies of the scripts/project report, funded by community health agencies, were made available to audience members. (The script versions of the performances have subsequently been included as teaching materials for nurse education students in three different university nursing departments and as course material for undergraduate degree courses in the performing arts.)

Each performance involved an element of forum interaction between the audience and actors. These took place either in the auditorium immediately after the play had ended, or in the foyer bar area shortly after the performance's conclusion. These interactions were recorded on audiotape and added to the project's data. Forum sessions were supplemented with audience questionnaires and surveys aimed at assessing the performance's impact and shortcomings. Performance venues were carefully chosen to guarantee that the plays reached their specific target audiences. By researching within institutional settings and performing the pieces within or close to those settings, the projects guaranteed that audiences would include health professionals, health consumers, caregivers, and care agencies. Representatives from major government health agencies and from other teaching institutions were also invited to special forum presentations, and wide media coverage further ensured public and professional interest. As the cast consisted of large numbers of nursing and theater students, peer-group support for the productions was never in doubt. Similarly, schools were invited free to performances to encourage high school student attendance. The final validating (invited) audience for *Busting*, for example, consisted of over 400 persons, including GPs, human resource officers from large multinational corporations, psychiatric nurses, students, health consumers, psychiatrists, government agency representatives, academics, health area managers, health administrators, informants and their families, police representatives, and interested others.

Heritage

Although the ethnodrama process addresses several methodological concerns about how limited forms of emancipation may be practically achieved (in constrained and specific circumstances), it does not do so without acknowledging or benefiting from the ethnographic heritage of Victor Turner and Derek Paget (1987). In acknowledging that some elements of the amalgamation and exploration of performance values and ethnography have already been undertaken by Turner (1986), Mulkay (1985), Conquergood (1991), and more recently, Richardson and Lockridge (1991), and Richardson (1993, 1994), it must be further noted that the exploration is only just beginning. Turner (1986) most clearly calls for a revision of ethnographic practice that will include the performance of ethnography as a means of investigating channels of reception and human understanding. As part of this investigation, the ethnodrama process specifically attempts to travel a nexus among the traditional values of textual, academic, presentation, and performance. It is a position that Conquergood (1991, 190) describes as "deeply subversive and threatening to the text bound culture of the academy." The threat lies within the challenge made to the revered status of textual presentations by the notion that performed ethnography provides more accessible and clearer explanations than are achievable by words alone. By blurring the boundaries (Geertz 1988) between not only the marginal sites of conventional ethnography and their counterparts in urban environments, but also between the allegorical nature of all ethnographic texts (Clifford 1986) and the perceived factual status of the written report process, the public performance of ethnography deacademizes and popularizes the report process. Furthermore, it returns the ownership, and therefore the power, of the report to its informants as opposed to possessing it on behalf of the academy.

The ethnodrama text, derived from polysemic informant narrative, adheres to strict research protocols and established research methodologies in order to present its arguments through performance. Nonetheless, part of its argument, conversely, lies in the authority of its textual construction as an alternative form of research report. Performance of the research enhances and interprets the report to audiences, and challenges the status of textual report processes, but in no way is seen as alone replacing the written research report. Nor, advises Conquergood (1991), would this be a wholly desirable development for ethnographic practice, as performance alone would be prone to ephemeral inconsistencies and necessitates instant, and potentially superficial, interpretation. Hence, the ethnodrama report is both the current version of the script and its performance, which are legitimated by seeking audiences and authentication outside the academy and by being continually open to revision. It is the construction of the report as a public voice (Agger 1991) medium that speaks in the words of informants and is constructed upon the agenda of informant concerns that is most significant in the ethnodrama process. Here the ethnographer's influence on the report process is continually negotiated, reduced, directed, and interpreted into performance, and consensualised until, ideally, it is no longer heard within the work.

Theoretical Basis

The critical theory base motivating the emancipatory intentions of these projects hinges on a theoretical amalgamation of communicative consensus (Habermas 1971, 1984, 1987) ameliorated by Alberoni's (1984) vision of "the nascent state." Within this conception, emancipation is seen as the origin of a nascent moment in which insight and critical reflection lead individuals into a state of achieved or latent objectivity. Such objectivity and insight potentially act to change both the individual and group experience of oppression. Alberoni (1984) rejects Marxian Enlightenment and critical theory as part of a political project that is motivated by a desire to mobilize masses "in the name of their interests, their resentment, and their desire for revenge" (1984, 229). Such a project, he proposes, will perpetually construct new enemies against which to move. In return, he redefines the search for truth and enlightenment as the individual discovery of a form of self-consciousness "which appears at a certain point as consciousness of one's own historicity" and allows the individual to acritically degrade his or her understanding of the past into prehistory. This is simply because within the nascent state "all of history is the history of errors; it is one-sided and incomplete and, to use the Marxist term, is prehistory" (64).

In the area of health care consumption, oppression is not alone politically defined but shares synergies with its historicised public perception:[2] Nor can emancipation be guaranteed from the constraints of physical illnesses which are individually experienced but collectively defined. In respect to the ethnodrama process, individuals are offered (potential) emancipatory opportunities via voicing their unique agendas of concern to those who are responsible for constructing the terms, conditions, and material provision (Apple 1993) of their daily health care. Moreover, the process of publicly voicing informant experiences and concerns is in itself an empowering and emancipatory action, as the informants involved in the ethnodrama process are generally disenfranchised through both their experience of illness and through the institutional and public (historicised) disposition toward their medical conditions.

The reduction of the authorial role in favor of a multivoiced, validated narrative constructed from the agenda and experiences of real health informants is an important hermeneutic adjunct to this performance methodology. As Ricoeur (1981) and Gadamer (1989) propose that an objective determination of any author's works, even by the author him- or herself, is an impossibility (as readers are conditioned, prejudiced, and ultimately victims of their historical existences), the removal of the ethnographer as author also is the removal of another layer of historicisation and cultural prejudice between the informants and their audiences. The event of performing ethnographic narratives to informed and general audiences in forum settings is a process of creativity, not reproduction, in which the audience participates as much as the informants in putting together and negotiating shared meaning and local understanding (Bakhtin 1984; Habermas 1987) of an aesthetic experience. That is, through performance and language, communicatively negotiated consensus may reflexively deliver something "other than itself" or even effect some "significant, nonlinguistic, material emancipation" (Gallagher 1992, 11).

Fabian (1990, 87) argues that "in ethnographies that pretend to give naked texts or data, nakedness is but another costume." He maintains that, as an anthropologist using ethnography, he "fashions and forms his material" but is different from a writer of fiction in that "he needs to justify his presentations as contributions to a body of knowledge." In Fabian's work the public performance is constructed, debated, and scripted (as a cultural interpretation of folkloric stories) by a vibrant community of actors, with the ethnographer acting as "claimant" upon the script. To the contrary, the "nakedness" of the verbatim nature of the ethnodrama text offers no authorial mask or cloak to its intentions and is openly challenging and critical in its informant narratives. In effect, it wishes no costume and pretends to be no more than it is—informant agendas and concerns performed to educated and general audiences in a theater format. It simply intends to be a public and emancipatory voice for its informants and lays no claim to being constructed as "art" or "literature." Nonetheless, it too needs to justify its worth by adhering to methodological protocols which sanctify the text's contribution to knowledge while maintaining validity in the opinions of its participants.

Emancipation through Vraisemblance
◆

In constructing authenticated accounts of informant experiences, the ethnodrama process relies on a specific determination of Todorov's (1968) notion of *vraisemblance* as being something more than just the creation of "plausible accounts" of informants' lives (Atkinson 1990). The difference is, perhaps, best expressed as a subtle semantic shift between the more commonly held term *verisimilitude* and Todorov's use of *vraisemblance* as a construction of truth. Whereas verisimilitude may be said to depict a similarity with a given truth, vraisemblance reflects a notion of probability or likelihood. Consequently, as the ethnodrama methodology seeks to depict only that which is "given as truth" or authenticated as "probably true" by informants, it uses vraisemblance to describe its scripted content and messages as being "of" or "from truths" rather than "similar to truths."

Victor Turner's (1986) appeal for ethnographers to make and not fake, that is, to discount mimesis in favour of poesis in order to utilize the ethnographer's potential as a coperformer within the ethnography, rests on a valid understanding that the expression of ethnographic discourse does not entirely rely upon limited literary constructions or verbal representations. In sum, the performance of ethnographic texts opens complex (interpretive) channels of meanings which utilize performance codes that do not privilege written words over other mediums for conveying meaning. The premise behind ethnodrama is that for ethnography to act as an emancipatory tool it must first gain credibility, via vraisemblance, in the eyes of its informants who are seeking emancipation. In so doing, it does not equate mimesis with a simple form of fakery or simulation that masks the ethnographers' influence, as is identified by Turner (1986, 126–129) and Fabian (1990), but seeks to be a construction of truths and may well be both mimesis and poesis. However, if, in order to be perceived as real, ethnodrama needs to speak in the words of its informants, be determined and controlled by its informants, and remain in the codes of language interpretable by its informants, then its form will necessarily be closer to mimesis than poesis. If, on the other hand, an ethnography only is concerned with explanation and does not seek informant emancipation (within the terms and agenda of informant needs as expressed by the informants themselves), then it can move beyond the language given by participants and become an expression in those channels and codes favored by the ethnographer. This would be in no way a less worthy form of ethnography but simply a different one.

When Laurel Richardson (1994, 10) claims that conventional adherence to accepted textual practices is little more than "subversive repetition of science practices" and that correspondingly, an "ideal typic" portrait of informants may be culled from a variety of textual sources rather than from one verbatim source, she is not advocating the reduction of the authorial role of the ethnographer but a reduction in the status of informant transcription. The ethnodrama process similarly forms "ideal-typic" character constructions, but not without the direct authority of repeated informant consensus. Again, it is the intention behind ethnography that is different. The ethnodrama process seeks to remove the voice of the ethnographer from the text as opposed to inscribing it within the text. Richardson (1994, 10) uses the "inner life of the writer" to reduce the emotional distance (Ellis 1991) between the writer and the informants; but for the emancipatory potential of ethnodrama to be realized, it is desirable that health informants alone are given voice and understand, exactly, what is said. This entails a notion of constructing a public voiced (Agger 1991), polyphonic narrative which is understood by informants to say what they want it to say.

The emancipatory potential of the ethnodrama process relates directly to the public performances of verbatim and authenticated transcription and to the validated construction of scenarios linking fictional inclusions. In the sense that Alberoni's (1984) perception of "the nascent state" is one in which emancipation is limited to individuated self-discovery, the process of informants arriving at consensual and conscientizing insights that lead to emancipation is also limited to an understanding of potential (individuated) emancipation(s) rather than mass public upheaval. The ethnographic presentation of health informants in the circumstances of their health and social oppression to themselves, other health care consumers, caregivers, health agencies, and educators is the beginning of a consensus-seeking dialogue along Habermas's (1984) road to communicative consensus and social change.

Although the ethnodrama process is not claimed to bring about emancipation cathartically, it retains the potential to effect instrumental change through the insights it gives to audiences and informants alike. For example, in the forum sessions for *Busting*, a senior corporate human resources officer for a large multinational corporation (specifically invited to the performance) expressed a newfound sympathy and understanding for dealing with issues of alcohol abuse in the workplace. Her intention at the end of the forum session was to review her dealings with alcohol-affected employees and to introduce drug and alcohol awareness education sessions into the workplace. Several months after the performance she had instigated changes in the company's employee health awareness program and was seeking further funding to assist in counseling programs for alcohol-affected employees. In particular, informants expressed views that they, at last, felt as if they had been listened to and at times had gained insight from the way they were portrayed and from discussing the performances with other members of the health care community. Without doubt, the greatest amount of insight, and therefore potential emancipation, was gained by nursing students working on the projects, many of whom expressed a profound change in their understanding of persons involved in these health issues.

Conclusion
◆

Although pursuing a form of mimesis within a framework Geertz (1988) describes as the theater of language (in which the enchantment of verbal construction vies with the authenticity of the text), the ethnodrama process clearly does not legitimate an absolute, slavish adherence to textual realism. Rather, it seeks explanation and expression in a public and deacademized form that opens its meanings to its informants as well as to the academy. In this way it does not fit the conventional notions of report writing (Cherryholmes 1993), but is consistent with the negotiative and consensual processes on which Habermasian emancipatory action is founded. Similarly, as Habermas (1984) guarantees that there will only be participants on the journey toward enlightenment, the ethnodrama process also cannot guarantee enlightenment or emancipation as a direct outcome of its processes. Nor can ethnodrama authoritatively establish that the insights it gives will be beneficial to those who receive them. However, by offering insights, it moves participants toward potential (individuated) emancipation and therefore gives rise to opportunities for informants to be heard whereas previously they were silent.

Notes

1. The informant account on which the incident was based did not include further violation and was, for the informant concerned, representative of a moment of realization and (negative) recognition of self. The attempts of nursing and health informants (in scripting and rehearsal sessions) to direct and shape the plot to fit their own notions of telling a good story became known as the "Spielberg Syndrome", and were usually easily identified and contained through dialogic interactions and group consensus.
2. This pertains to the anecdotal evidence used to support such notions as the moon's cycles influencing mental disorders. Luce (1971) highlights the ten-

dency of seventeenth- and eighteenth-century physicians to report, as fact, regular monthly cycles in case studies of epilepsy and other lunacies and the continuation of psychiatric staff and police to associate aberrant behaviors with the cycles of the moon (Rich 1993). Rich's own research, involving detailed study of 178 acute admissions to a psychiatric ward over six months, failed to record any correlation or truth in the dominantly held unofficial association. The logic remains, however, that if animal biology is affected by the moon's cycles, so too must be human biology.

References

Agger, B. 1991. Theorising the Decline of Discourse or the Decline of Theoretical Discourse? In *Critical Theory Now,* edited by P. Wexler. (New York & London: Falmer Press): Chapter 5.

Alberoni, F. 1984. *Movement and Institution*. Translated by P. Arden Delmoro. New York: Columbia University Press.

Apple, M. 1993. *Official Knowledge: Democratic Education in a Conservative Age*. New York: Routledge.

Atkinson, P. 1990. *The Ethnographic Imagination: Textual Constructions of Reality*. London: Routledge.

———. 1992. *Understanding Ethnographic Texts*. Newbury Park, CA: Sage.

Bakhtin, M. 1984. *Problems of Dostoevsky's Poetics*, edited and translated by Caryl Emerson. (Minneapolis: University of Minnesota Press.)

———. 1986. *Speech Genres and Other Late Essays*. Translated by Vern W. McGee. Austin: University of Texas Press.

Boal, A. 1985[1979]. *Theater of the Oppressed*. Translated by C. A. McBride and M. L. McBride. New York: Theater Communications Group.

Cherryholmes, C. H. 1993. "Reading Research." *Journal of Curriculum Studies* 25: 1–32.

Clifford, J. 1986. "On Ethnographic Allegory." In *Writing Culture: The Poetics and Politics of Ethnography,* edited by J. Clifford and G. E. Marcus. (Berkeley: University of California Press): 98–121.

Conquergood, D. 1988. "Health Theatre in a Hmong Refugee Camp: Performance, Communication and Culture." *TDR - The Drama Review - A Journal of Performance Studies* 32, no. 3: 174–208.

———. 1991. "Rethinking Ethnography: Towards a Critical Cultural Politics." *Communication Monographs* 58 (June): 179–194.

Cox, H. 1989. "Drama in the Arts Lab." *Australian Nurses Journal* 19, no. 1: 14–15.

Denzin, N. 1970. *The Research Action in Sociology.* London: Butterworth.

———. 1989. *Interpretive Interactionism.* Newbury Park, CA: Sage.

Ellis, C. 1991. "Sociological Introspection and Emotional Experience." *Symbolic Interaction* 14: 23–50.

Fabian, J. 1983. *Time and the Other: How Anthropology Makes Its Object.* New York: Columbia University Press.

———. 1990. *Power and Performance: Ethnographical Explorations Through Proverbial Wisdom and Theater in Shaba, Zaire.* Wisconsin: University of Wisconsin Press.

Fraser, N. 1990. Rethinking the Public Sphere: A Contribution to the Critique of Actually Existing Democracy. *Social Text* 25/26, 56–80.

Gadamer, H-G. 1989. *Truth & Method.* 2nd rev. ed. Translated by J. Weinsheimer and D. G. Marshall. New York: Crossroad Press.

Gallagher, S. 1992. *Hermeneutics and Education.* Albany: State University of New York Press.

Geertz, C. 1988. *Works & Lives: The Anthropologist as Author.* Cambridge, UK: Polity.

Giorgi, A. 1985. Phenomenology and Psychological Research. Pittsburgh, PA: Duquesne University Press.

Habermas, J. 1971. *Knowledge and Human Interest.* Translated by T. McCarthy. London: Heineman.

———. 1984. *The Theory of Communicative Action.* Translated by J. Shapiro. Boston: Beacon Press.

———. 1987. *Philosophical Discourse of Modernity: Twelve Lectures.* Translated by Frederick Lawrence. Boston: Beacon Press.

Hammersley, M. 1992. *What's Wrong with Ethnography?* London: Routledge.

Jennings, S. 1992. *Dramatherapy in Families, Groups and Individuals: Waiting in the Wings.* London: Kingsley.

Luce, G. 1971. *Biological Rhythms in Human and Animal Physiology.* New York: Dover.

Mienczakowski, J. 1992[1994]. *Syncing Out Loud: A Journey into Illness.* Brisbane: Griffith University Reprographics.

———. 1994. "Theatrical and Theoretical Experimentation in Ethnography & Dramatic Form." *ND DRAMA, Journal of National Drama, U.K.* 2/2: 16–23.

———. 1995. "Reading and Writing Research: Ethnographic Theatre." *ND DRAMA, Journal of National Drama, U.K.* 3/3: 8–12.

Mienczakowski, J., and S. Morgan. 1993. *Busting: The Challenge of the Drought Spirit.* Brisbane: Griffith University Reprographics.

Mulkay, M. J. 1985. *The Word and the World: Explorations in the Form of Sociological Analysis.* London: Allen & Unwin.

Paget, D. 1987. "Verbatim Theater: Oral History and Documentary Techniques." *New Theater Quarterly* 12: 317–336.

Price, N. 1992. Theatre for Health. *The Queensland Nurse* (Oct.).

Rich, D. 1993. "Lunacy—A Valid Concept?" *The Australian Journal of Mental Health Nursing,* 2, no. 6: 251–256.

Richardson, L. 1993. Poetics, Dramatics, and Transgressive Validity: The Case of the Skipped Line. *The Sociological Quarterly* 35: 695–710.

———. 1994. Nine Poems. Marriage and the Family. *The Journal of Contemporary Ethnography* 23: 3–13.

Richardson, L., and E. Lockridge. 1991. "The Sea Monster: An Ethnographic Drama." *Symbolic Interaction* 14: 335–340.

Ricoeur, P. 1981. *Hermeneutics and the Human Sciences.* Translated by J. B. Thompson. Cambridge, MA: Cambridge University Press.

Rolfe, A., J. Mienczakowski, and S. Morgan. 1995. A Dramatic Experience in Mental Health Nursing Education. *Nurse Education Today, UK* 15, no. 3: 224–227.

Silverman, D. 1994. *Interpreting Qualitative Data: Methods for Analysing Talk, Text and Interaction.* London: Sage.

Stanislavski, C. 1936. *An Actor Prepares.* Translated by E. R. Hapgood. New York: Theater Arts Books .

———. 1983. *Creating a Role.* Translated by E. R. Hapgood. London: Eyre Methuen.

Strauss, A., and J. Corbin. 1990. *Basics of Qualitative Research.* New York: Sage Publications.

Todorov, T. 1968. "Introduction, Le Vraisemblable." *Communications* 11: 1–4.

Turner, V. 1986. *The Anthropology of Performance.* New York: Performing Arts Journal Publications.

van Maanen, M. 1984. *Doing Phenomenological Research and Writing. Monograph 7.* Alberta: Faculty of Education Publication Services, University of Alberta.

Warren, A. 1988. *Gender Issues in Field Research.* Qualitative Research Methods, Series No. 9. Newbury Park, CA: Sage.

Watkins, P. 1990. "All the World's a Stage." *Nursing Times* 86, no. 21: 47–48.

Jim Mienczakowski trained at The Central School of Speech & Drama and King's College, London, and after working in theater and television moved on to teaching, gaining experience in England, the West Indies, and Australia. For several years his theater and academic research work were parts of separate worlds, seldom overlapping. Happily, this is no longer so and his current work merges theater, ethnography, and reflexive educational practices in order to create a form of consensual, public voice, performance ethnography. Dr. Mienczakowski is Deputy Dean (Research) of the Faculty of Education & The Arts, Griffith University.

PART THREE

Reflexive
Ethnography

CHAPTER ELEVEN

Devil, Not-Quite-White, Rootless Cosmopolitan

Tsuris in Latin America, the Bronx, and the USSR[1]

Marc Edelman

In Mexican Easter Week pageants, the red-painted men who represent devils are called *judíos*. Anti-Semitism in rural Mexico is so well known that my Jewish colleagues who travel there never identify themselves as Jews.

—Judith Elkin Laikin (1992, 7)

They call him "the Jew Man" because he's a Jew Man. All the stores around here used to belong to either whites or Jews.

—Freddy (South Bronx, 1983)

An antipatriotic group of followers of bourgeois aestheticism has arisen. . . . These critics have lost their sense of responsibility to the people and transmit rootless cosmopolitanism of the most disgusting kind, hostile to the Soviet citizen. . . . We must be resolute in putting an end once and for all to liberal acceptance of all these aestheticist good-for-nothings, devoid of the healthy feeling of love for their motherland and for their people, who have nothing in their souls but malignancy and exaggerated self-conceit.

—*Pravda* ("A Certain Antipatriotic Group of Theatre Critics" 1949)

Bygone *tsuris* [troubles] are good to relate.

—Yiddish folk saying (Rosten 1970, 416)

Virginia Domínguez (1993) observes that Jewishness, like homosexuality, is often "closeted" and, where it remains stigmatized, "must always be managed." Anthropologists, she suggests, have a "professional problem with Jewishness" that they have handled by "subjecting only non-European-origin Jews to ethnographic analysis, and by ghettoizing anthropological work on Jews or Jewishness as either Judaic Studies (with an emphasis on ritual and community) or folklore (with an emphasis on lost worlds, dying customs, and studied nostalgia)" (623).

This chapter examines a different, neglected dimension of "the epistemology of the Jewish closet." Jews have been well represented in professional anthropology, and the vast majority of Jewish anthropologists have done research among non-Jews. Yet despite anthropology's reflexive turn and a growing reflexive ethnographic literature on Jews by Jews (Boyarin 1991; Kugelmass 1986; Myerhoff 1978), few Jewish anthropologists have discussed how their Jewishness enters into their fieldwork among non-Jews. Do Jewish anthropologists feel that they have to "manage" their Jewishness, especially in historically anti-Semitic contexts? What are their strategies of presentation of self, of disclosure and concealment, of confrontation and silence? How does Jewishness shape perceptions of and relations with research subjects, and when does it influence what ethnographers fail to see and hear? What do these questions mean for the ethnographer's identity and inner life, for the production of social scientific knowledge, and for anthropology's relation to antiracist politics? Although this work can provide only a partial examination of these issues, it underscores the importance of *posing* the questions, of interrogating ourselves—and the texts we have written— about some very striking "not-saids" (to borrow an apt expression from Foucault [1972, 25]).

This essay's epigraphs depict images of Jews that I encountered in Latin America, New York, and the USSR. My approach is necessarily exploratory and autobiographical, since knowledge about how other anthropologists "manage" Jewishness during fieldwork depends on a process of relating that has begun only recently. Reflecting on how these images surfaced during research has required me to reconsider my own processes of sanitizing ethnographic experience and, more broadly, the parallel inattention to fieldwork experiences with anti-Semitism and racism that characterizes anthropology as a whole. Disclosing our experiences rather than "privatizing" them forces us as Jewish anthropologists to confront our strategies of physical, emotional, and professional survival, as well as a sinister side of the societies in which we work that is too often ignored in our training and written accounts. Since non-Jewish anthropologists, who also encounter bigotry in the field, have yet to reveal much about how they manage such incidents (or whether they believe these require managing),[2] the problems raised resonate beyond the borders of exclusively Jewish concerns.

The ways we experience anti-Semitism and other bigotry in the field cannot be neatly separated from our identities or written work. And the identities any one of us brings to the field cannot, of course, always be neatly subsumed under an overarching rubric of ethnographer or scholar. Encounters with anti-Semitism in fieldwork embody a collision between our informants' histories and our own, and test both our ability and our desire to practice lofty principles of relativism (once again popular, albeit in refurbished form, after falling out of fashion during the 1940s struggle against Nazism), and our commitments to truth, human equality, respect, and democratic politics. These sensibilities may conflict with our professional identities. Despite the pretense that ethnographers are always on the job, many, when off duty, see things through lenses other than those closest to their professional selves (cf. Boyarin 1988, 71).

The vulnerability that many Jews feel, and that conditions the psyches of other diaspora peoples, may become especially acute in the field. The ethnographer is ultimately alone (or nearly so) among people who at times seem very different and who may manifest anti-Semitic biases. In thinking about my own reactions to the special vulnerability of Jewish ethnographers, I have found it useful to distinguish between research situations that were primarily ethnographic (fieldwork in Latin America or the Bronx) and those that were not (archival work in Latin America or the USSR). Nonethnographic research involves less dependence on a broad range of people and permits a less self-conscious and in some ways more genuine presentation of self. My most intense confrontations with anti-Semites during research have involved individuals who were not key to my work. Obviously more of these "unimportant" individuals were around when I was in the archives or walking down city streets than when I was in a small community or neighborhood where my access to information and possibly my physical survival depended on not being a stranger.

Built into ethnographic work is a powerful wish and a profes-
sional-methodological need to be accepted in the milieu of our research.
Yet Jewish ethnographers have an intrinsic quality—Jewishness—that
in historically anti-Semitic areas may, if known, generate antipathy in
informants. This may lead us to not reveal our ethnicity. In contrast to
the stereotype of Jews as overly sensitive to ethnic slights, this strategy
of concealment may produce self-delusion and an inability to acknowledge expressions of anti-Semitism or to grasp the degree to which anti-
Jewish assumptions are integrated into the most basic social and
linguistic categories. It also may lead to rationalizing informants' prejudices and our own lack of candor.

As Jews, our existence owes a lot to the grit and determination of
many generations, to great historical forces such as the allied victory in
World War II, and—at the individual level—to a large measure of accident. Our family histories are suffused with stories of a parent or grandparent who moved while others stayed put, who boarded some
forgotten steamer instead of the ill-fated *Saint Louis*, who left the Pale of
Settlement for America rather than go elsewhere in Europe.[3] These
details of personal history have sensitized Jews to the ultimate arbitrariness of cultural difference and make the collective memory of the
pogroms and the Holocaust vivid, immediate, and threatening; they also
determined whether we (or someone like us) grew up speaking English,
Spanish, Hebrew, or Russian and whether we ended up in New York,
Buenos Aires, Tel Aviv, or Moscow, with all of the potentials and
tragedies that each option eventually entailed. The ways we integrate
these immediate histories are highly particular, making the Jewish identity we bring to the field different for each Jewish ethnographer.

One Identity

I grew up in a secular, left-leaning family that paid little attention to
Jewish tradition. Very early, however, I learned that Jews had suffered
greatly and unjustly and that the best thing one could do in one's life
was to work for justice. My father, who fought in the U.S. Army against
the Nazis, told war stories to my brother and me at bedtime. At an early
age, we heard how he had been in newly liberated slave-labor camps
and of his sorrow at not being able to communicate with the emaciated

victims, who often realized he was Jewish and approached him speaking Yiddish. The H on his dog tags signified that he would have been given Hebrew rites if killed in combat. It would also, he said, have meant almost certain death if he fell into Nazi hands, since the Germans sometimes denied POW status to captured Jewish GIs and sent them to labor or death camps.

Our one concession to Jewish tradition was Passover, which we celebrated with relatives who could read enough Hebrew to get through the ceremony. I never learned any, however, in part because my father, when asking me if I wanted a bar mitzvah, remarked only somewhat tongue-in-cheek that attending an Orthodox cheder to prepare for his bar mitzvah had been the worst experience of his life. I never went to synagogue, but I did develop a thoroughly secular sense of Jewishness that was linked to reading fiction and history, to several years of living on New York's historically Jewish Lower East Side, and to an appreciation of the central role that Jews had played in progressive politics. I also loved the way my grandmother and her friends would sprinkle English conversation with wry Yiddish proverbs and impossible-to-gloss terms for particular human-types and then turn to me and chuckle, "Well Marc, do you know what *that* means?" My grandmother, who came to the United States at the turn of the century as a young girl, returned to Poland in the early 1950s to see what she could find out about the relatives who had never left. The town where she was born had disappeared. It wasn't on the maps anymore. The people there had left no trace.

My introduction to the idea of Jewish blood guilt came at age 7 on the tree-lined street in Greenwich Village where I had moved not long before. I was outside, making friends with a neighbor from down the block who attended a local parochial school. After talking together for some time, my newfound friend asked me my religion. "Jewish," I said without thinking much about it. Immediately he spat out, "You dirty Jew, the Jews killed Christ." To say Judaism was my religion wasn't quite accurate since my parents were inveterate atheists and I knew next to nothing about Jewish tradition. Still, I recognized that Kevin had done something deeply offensive, and I jumped on top of him and pounded his head on the sidewalk until his mother ran out of their building and dragged me off him.

Kevin did more to educate me about the idiocy of racism than any of the numerous civil rights activists and leftists I knew as a child.

Perhaps because I had banged his head on the concrete too hard or perhaps because he was somewhat dull to begin with, he never seemed to remember who I was after that or even that I lived on his block. But he did appear to suffer from a perpetual, disturbing uncertainty about my ethnicity. Over the next several years, he and "his" boys jumped me dozens of times in different playgrounds and parks, sometimes because I was a "kike" and other times because I was a "wop," "spic," or "greaseball." I came to disdain what I saw as their moronic hatred of everyone who had olive skin and curly hair (including their Italian American fellow Catholics, with whom I also had my share of tussles) and took pride in being able to outrun them backwards, thumbing my nose or giving them the finger.

I mention these boyhood skirmishes both because they shaped my own sense of Jewishness and because they made me aware at an early age that the Catholic Church was propagating an intensely negative view of Jews. The Irish and Italian American kids who were my neighbors lived in dread of the sisters who would rap their knuckles for the slightest infraction of parochial school rules. In between fistfights, chases, and insults, I had enough conversations with them to know that the sisters taught them that we Jews today in the United States were responsible for killing Jesus in Palestine almost 2,000 years ago.[4] I tried to reason with them about this, but with little success. I pointed out, for example, that Jesus was Jewish, which they didn't believe. Years later I encountered the same teachings in a setting where there were no Jews at all and where nobody seemed to imagine that I, as a human being, could be Jewish.

Rural Mexico

◆

My first anthropological fieldwork was on agricultural technology and social change in rural Mexico. I had arrived in the Sierra Norte de Puebla through a chain of contacts that led from academics and agronomists in Mexico City to a regional development program to Víctor and Rosa, a mestizo couple who rented me a tiny room. During my first days in the largely indigenous village, I spent a lot of time walking in the beautiful green mountains with don Víctor as he made his rounds as a folk medical practitioner. His practice consisted of using a suspicious-looking needle to inject substantial doses of antibiotics and vitamins into grateful patients, most of whom probably would have been better off taking aspirin for their fevers and aches and pains. I soon stopped going around with him, though, since I felt I was verging on a serious ethical breach by lending him the legitimacy that came with my lighter-skinned, foreign, educated presence.

One of my first conversations with don Víctor concerned the Protestant missionaries. He was vague about when they had come, but he was quite clear about how the villagers had responded. They surrounded the heretics with drawn machetes and escorted them several kilometers to the highway, telling them that in this community the people were good Catholics ("Apostolic and Roman") and that they had better start walking away, toward the district capital. At the time, I registered this account of religious intolerance as just one more of the myriad parochialisms that I was encountering in the course of everyday conversations—things like the widespread incredulity when I remarked one day that to the north of the United States there was another country just as large. While village men had long migrated to the nearby lowlands, only one had ever gone to the United States. When I finally had the chance to speak with him near the end of my research, it turned out he had been working in Tijuana.

The villagers' horizons were in many ways very limited. Once I took out a map, and as a small crowd gathered around, I pointed out Mexico, the United States, Canada, and Argentina. It became clear that many had never seen a map before and that most were not at all accustomed to the kind of abstract reasoning required to understand one. This type of exoticism, while touchingly reminiscent of my favorite magical realist novels, became a barrier to greater shared subjectivity. How could I expect people who hadn't believed in the existence of Canada, who thought Tijuana was in the United States, and who had run the Protestants out of town, to understand Jewish history or to accept me as a Jew? I also sensed that as a newly arrived foreigner, a Jew, and a neophyte in anthropology, I had little cultural capital with which to challenge nearly 500 years of Catholic indoctrination.

I had fewer discussions with doña Rosa, who was less accessible, given the conventions governing male-female interaction in traditional rural Mexico. The chats we did have usually occurred when she served Víctor and me our food. Religion was her favorite topic. Once I mentioned that in my country there were Catholics, Protestants, and Jews. "Even Jews?" Rosa asked in disbelief. The hatred and revulsion etched

on her face when she said *"judíos"* brought back memories of the
parochial school kids in Greenwich Village accusing me of killing Jesus.
This, and the pictures of saints, virgins, and Jesus that covered an entire
wall, convinced me that I should keep the subject of my ancestry to
myself.

A few days later, don Víctor and I were eating our midday tortillas
and doña Rosa was standing in the kitchen door. My host began interrogating me, following up an earlier conversation about religion. While
I remembered this interchange clearly many years later, only when I
went back to my diary in preparing this essay did it occur to me that a
peculiarity of Spanish grammar had made it possible for me almost will-
fully not to hear what he and Rosa had been saying. In American
Spanish, the second- and third-person plural forms are conjugated the
same way and pronouns are often left out, to be inferred (hopefully)
from the context. Even though I was quite fluent in Spanish, this ambiguity allowed me to hear something other than what was being said.

	The Conversation	What They Meant	What I Heard
don V	¿Verdad que hay muchas religiones allá?	Is it true that there are many religions there [in your country]?	
ME	Sí, hay varias religiones.	Yes, there are several religions.	
doña R	Pero ¿qué religión tiene el señor?	But what is the man's [my] religion?	

Before I could tell the truth or lie, don Víctor responded for me. His
wife had, after all, been addressing him, not me.

	The Conversation	What They Meant	What I Heard
don V	La católica.	The Catholic religion.	
doña R	Pos, está bien entonces.	Well, that's good then.	
don V	Allá creen en el cristo, ¿verdad?	There [in your country] you all believe in Christ, right?	There [in your country] they believe in Christ, right?
ME	Sí, por supuesto.	Yes, of course.	

don V	Y ¿creen en la virgin o sólo en el cristo?	And do you all believe in the virgin or just in Christ?	And do they believe in the virgin or just in Christ?
ME	En los dos.	In both.	
don V	Está bien entonces.	Very well then.	

Don Víctor then told me for the umpteenth time that the virgin in the church was 450 years old and that Cortés himself had brought her to their village.

Although I had failed to contradict Víctor when he responded to Rosa's question about my religion, I did have the sense of having adequately answered their queries about what people believed in the United States. Not what *I* believed, but what *people* believed, since that had been the question as I understood it. I never told don Víctor that I wasn't Catholic, and since I seemed to be a decent human being, he apparently assumed that I was. In much of Latin America, *cristiano* and *human being* are virtual synonyms.

Perhaps don Víctor suspected I wasn't Catholic and wanted to prevent me from giving Rosa the wrong answer, in which case they might have had to march me out to the highway, as they had with the Protestants, also losing the rent from my tiny room. The doubts they may have had, however, were allayed a few weeks later when my girlfriend arrived from the United States. An Argentine Jew, whom I prematurely but confidently presented as my wife (we married two years later), she had even less acquaintance with Jewish tradition than I and considerably less patience for talk about virgins and saints. Nevertheless, when we went to a nearby market town (thinking, of course, that we were alone and anonymous) and attended a colorful Sunday mass, somebody from the village spied us and reported to Víctor and Rosa. This surveillance, which we found out about some time later, convinced them not only that we were Catholics, but that we were *good* Catholics. I remember thinking that if Víctor knew I wasn't Catholic—or, worse, that I was Jewish—my research project would have collapsed. Whether these catastrophic fears were justified, I can't say. At the time I was content with the thought that I wasn't studying religion anyway, and I recorded these observations not in typed field notes but in a journal that I kept for personal impressions and thoughts.

Costa Rica
◆

In contrast to Mexico, Costa Rica, where I worked on my dissertation, did not at first seem racist or anti-Semitic. A Jewish Costa Rican and fellow graduate student had warned me about anti-Semitism there, but he also said that I would be perceived first as a foreigner and this would be much more salient than my identity as a Jew, which he correctly predicted would generally pass unnoticed.

Most Jews in Costa Rica had come from a few small Polish communities in the late 1920s and 1930s. At first they worked as peddlers, but in a few decades many had become wealthy industrialists, whose children carried on family businesses or entered liberal professions. Not surprisingly, given their origin, the Jews came to be called *polacos* or Poles. This conflation of country as origin with ethnicity and religion gave rise to some odd syllogisms. In 1978, for instance, when Karol Wojtyla was elected Pope John Paul II, a leading newspaper, *La Prensa Libre,* ran a picture caption that declared him "the first non-Christian pontiff in 455 years" ("Ciudad del Vaticano," October 17, 1978).

Another kind of *polaco*, closer to my fieldwork, also illustrated the blurred boundaries of the category and the confusing nature of its referents. In 1981–82, when I was doing research on rural class relations, Costa Rica experienced its worst economic crisis since the 1930s. Many of my conversations were about economic difficulties. Campesinos grumbled about having to pay off a pair of pants or a shirt with "*polaco* payments" (*cuotas de polaco*). I took this to be a kind of mild anti-Semitism, which irritated me, but I also understood *their* irritation at having to buy overpriced shoddy goods on credit. The problem was that I didn't see any *polacos* around. Occasionally I would see other peddlers, but never any *polacos*. Once when someone complained about *polaco* payments, I asked and was told that the "real" *polacos* showed up on Saturday afternoons—payday—at the big farms. I wondered if by now the real *polacos* weren't too prosperous to be pushing polyester at farm gates in the hot northwestern lowlands. And *polacos* working on Saturday?

Later I realized that I had a particular image of a *polaco* that was preventing me from seeing what was going on. In 1972, on a trip through South America, I had taken a freighter to the Galápagos Islands. The ship, the source of provisions for the five inhabited islands, held vast quantities of beer, some cattle and goats, a human cargo of six international backpackers like myself, several dozen island residents, a crew of tough Ecuadorian sailors, and a handful of what today might be referred to in Latin America as *microentrepreneurs*. Among the latter was an elderly clothes peddler whom I immediately recognized as a *landsman*. How? He looked as if he had stepped out of a Roman Vishniac photograph: short, bearded, a little stooped, with large hollow eyes. He was in the thread trade and everyone called him don Simón. In the two weeks of travel from Guayaquil to the islands and back, don Simón told me that he had been born in Bessarabia and had escaped to South America in the 1930s. When we reached the islands, he spread out his bundles of cheap clothes at each place the ship anchored, dickering, gossiping, and joking with the locals, who seemed to know him well. Don Simón became my image of the Jewish peddler in Latin America, but I never saw anyone like him in Costa Rica.

Years later, and after much time in Costa Rica, it hit me that *polacos* weren't Jews any more in rural Costa Rica. In the cities, and among the well educated, *polacos* were still Jews, but in the countryside the term had come to refer simply to peddlers, all of whom were non-Jewish. At first, this realization made me feel relieved. The peasants muttering about *polaco* payments weren't anti-Semitic after all, since the peddlers weren't Jewish. Then, of course, I realized that the provenance of the peddlers might not make much difference. Anti-*polaco* remarks could reflect simple, economically based indignation at the non-Jewish peddlers' stiff credit terms, or they could be a variety of "disembodied" anti-Semitism or anti-Semitism without Jews. The more I heard about *polacos*, the more uncertain I felt about the possibility of sorting out the two options. The referents attached to *polaco*, with the exception of Pope John Paul II, were invariably negative and hopelessly mixed up with one another.[5] To make matters worse, almost any comment about *polaco* payments could be construed as anti-Semitic, but once challenged could plausibly be considered "just an expression."

The most intense anti-Semitism I encountered in Costa Rica was not in the field, but from a university-educated political activist. One day, while walking near the university, I ran into a friend, who invited me for coffee. We sat down in a café and shortly thereafter were joined by an acquaintance of my friend, who turned out to be a militant of the Juventud Vanguardista, the Costa Rican Communist Party youth group. At some point the *vanguardista* launched into an impassioned attack on Jews, declaring that they were all rich and reactionary and that they were interested only in money. His invective was not limited to the Costa Rican *polacos*, but extended to Jews in all times and places. I was taken aback by the vehemence of the onslaught. My friend, who knew I was Jewish, looked at me, rolled his eyes up in disgust and remained silent.

I started off on the unsuspecting *vanguardista* by rebuking him for his pathetic ignorance of the historic role of Jews in progressive and working-class movements in Europe and the United States, something of which I—as a Jew—was genuinely proud. His "fraternal party" in my country was, I said, largely Jewish. When he seemed satisfactorily ashamed of himself, I marched him down the block to the Communists' bookstore and treated him to the Spanish translation of Michael Gold's *Jews Without Money* (1930), which I had noticed there a few days earlier. I remembered Gold's book, which I had read years before in English, as a maudlin account of life on New York's Lower East Side at the turn of the century, one of the better, less didactic examples of 1930s "proletarian literature." I was aware that humiliating my interlocutor with a lecture on progressive Jewry had the potential for feeding the stereotype of Jews as overly intellectual, overly sensitive to slights, or overly aggressive. Buying him Gold's book would, I hoped, put a Party imprimatur on my argument and convince him that I wasn't simply manifesting the innate cunning of the Jew. I also was aware that purchasing a book for him was ostentatiously generous, considering the insults to which I had been subjected. I think I wanted not only to disabuse him of his misconceptions regarding Jews as rich and reactionary, but also to show him that at least one Jew didn't mind parting with a few *colones* to buy an adversary a souvenir of their quarrel.

I later realized that the rage and contempt with which I reacted to this young anti-Semite had roots beyond the attack itself. I had been in Costa Rica two years and was increasingly disturbed at the subtle but pervasive racism. For example, a black chemist who ran for rector of the university became the butt of racist jokes. Many in the university disliked him for his conservative views, but his skin color clearly didn't help. A black lawyer friend told me that he always wore a suit and tie so that store clerks and taxi drivers wouldn't treat him "like dirt." Fans in the soccer stadium chanted "*indios, indios*"—a pejorative term—as the visiting Guatemalan team ran onto the field. People in the northwest complained of how "white" Costa Ricans referred to them as "*cholos*" (a derogatory word for mestizos or mulattoes) or "gift Nicaraguans" (*nicas regalados*), even as they themselves expressed virulent prejudices against the Chinese who ran many local stores and restaurants. And the contra war in Nicaragua was just beginning, fueling historic disdain for violent Nica "savages."

In 1991, back in northwestern Costa Rica, I unexpectedly ran across an intriguing storytelling tradition about a large landowner who had died in the 1940s and who was believed to have made a pact with the devil in return for land, money, and women (Edelman 1994). The first anecdotes I heard stressed the landlord's economic traditionalism and generosity as compared with other figures in the regional elite who more clearly epitomized a modernizing agrarian capitalism. This led me to question the key dichotomies in Michael Taussig's fascinating book, *The Devil and Commodity Fetishism in South America* (1980). Whenever I encountered a delay with my main project on peasant movements, I sought more stories from elderly informants. One afternoon I was sitting in a shady backyard, joking and trading stories with a garrulous octogenarian. Don Chepe was telling about the greed of merchants he had known, including a particularly evil one who had inherited seven hardworking little black devils from the landowner about whom I had been gathering information. "That man was the most Jewish of all," he said, "the stingiest."

This was the only time the equation devil-merchant-Jew had come up (cf. Nugent 1996). I quite liked don Chepe and I'm very certain he liked me as well. I challenged him gently. "Why do you call him that, Jewish? I've known many stingy Christians too."

"*Sí, es cierto*," don Chepe responded. "*Hay muchos cristianos tacaños también.*" ("Yes, it's true. There are many stingy Christians too.")

I felt I had received satisfactory acknowledgment of my viewpoint. But I later realized that I may not have "heard" the conversation well, because of a lexical ambiguity in Latin American Spanish, the use of *cristiano* as a synonym for *human being*. When I commented that there were stingy Christians and don Chepe agreed, he could have been recognizing that some *human beings* were stingy. He may well have understood our interchange in *both* his and my terms. The identity of *cristiano* with *human being* is an unquestioned part of many Latin Americans' worldview.[6] Writing on Ecuador, Ronald Stutzman (1981, 82) describes this equation in terms that, with minor dialectal variations, could apply to the rest of the continent:

Cristiano is the preferred form of reference to self. *Cristiano* is the word for human being. . . . It designates people as opposed to animals and, by extension, human beings who behave themselves properly rather than as beasts: *¡Qué bestia, no sea mal criado!* Behaving properly includes correct use of the language: *¡Hábleme en cristiano, pues!* 'Speak Spanish,' that is, 'Stop your babbling.' . . . A proper *cristiano* prefaces all serious claims about future states of affairs with a 'God willing.' *'Si Dios me da vida y salud . . .* 'If God grants life and health . . .'

Another benign context in which my ethnicity came up in Central America had to do with the logo of Yale University, where I taught from 1987 to 1994. Yale's emblem contains the motto *Lux et Veritas* surrounding a book with the Hebrew inscription *Urim V'Thummim* (light and perfection). Several times people commented on the logo on my business card and asked me if Yale were a Jewish university. This logical but erroneous supposition never failed to amuse me, given the ignominious history of institutionalized anti-Semitism in the Ivy League, especially at Yale, where anti-Jewish incidents occasionally still occur.[7] Several times I took the comments about Yale's seal as an opportunity to reveal my ethnicity. But despite my explanations that Hebrew, like Latin, was a language of classical learning and therefore appropriate for a university symbol, it was hard for Central Americans to comprehend that a non-Jewish university had a "shield" with Hebrew letters. It only confused matters more that this Jewish professor worked there yet also claimed the place had a history of anti-Semitism. I never found a satisfactory way of explaining this. Candor made my responses appear incoherent to those reared in a different culture, where certain kinds of prejudices seem timeless and immutable.

The South Bronx
◆

I spent 1983 writing up my first Costa Rica research and doing fieldwork on juvenile delinquency as part of a Fordham University team in the South Bronx. After the beautiful green mountains and rolling savannas of Costa Rica, the burned-out buildings, rubble-filled lots, numbers joints, and clandestine auto-chop shops around Fox Street and

Longwood Avenue were profoundly depressing. In retrospect, however, this was not a bad time to be in the South Bronx—after the gang warfare and the arson wave of the 1970s and before crack hit in the late 1980s. My qualifications for the Fordham position, apart from academic credentials and a certain recklessness exacerbated by economic necessity, were that I spoke Spanish, could play basketball, and had experience working with tough kids.

I had some contacts in the community through a youth program, but mostly I was on my own, charged with exploring the environment, activities, and inner lives of the young Puerto Ricans who were the subject of study. On my first day out alone, I turned a corner on Simpson Street and found several cops peering into garbage cans and under parked cars. The scene appeared research relevant, and I politely asked one of the officers what they were looking for. "If we fuckin' find it, you'll fuckin' hear about it." In a flash, I realized that cops here didn't see me as a white, middle-class, educated citizen, as they might in midtown Manhattan. I was wearing jeans and an old army coat and still had two years of Central American sun on my face.

My more sophisticated informants realized I was Jewish from the beginning, when I jotted down for them my phone number and full name. In a few cases we talked extensively, honestly, and empathically about interethnic relations. Several had known Jewish teachers who had made a positive difference in their lives. I never heard even a hint of anti-Semitism from them, although I occasionally heard others use "Jew" as a verb that meant "to cheat" (much as another racist term—"to gyp"— is used unself-consciously by a broader spectrum of Americans). Many people seemed to know each other only by first names or nicknames, and most simply assumed, like the abusive cop on Simpson Street, that I was Latino. Elderly Puerto Rican women remarked on how I spoke Spanish "more politely" than their grandchildren and delighted at my occasional use of quaint Central American expressions. Younger people heard me speaking Spanish with their grandmothers and categorized me as some kind of Hispanic, obviously not Puerto Rican or Dominican but perhaps a South American like the unlicensed Colombian dentists who filled cavities for five dollars apiece in an unmarked second-floor office. ("We don' like to speak Spanish with you," one boy told me, " 'cause you speak it more correct than we do.") I doubt that anyone spent much time pondering my ethnicity. For most, it was inconceivable that a Jew would be hanging around in the ghetto, inviting teenagers for hamburgers and Cuban sandwiches, or playing pickup basketball games on courts painted with graffiti and littered with broken glass.

In my first week in the Bronx, however, I also met "the Jew Man." I had returned from Central America wearing cheap Salvadoran sneakers that gave me blisters when I played basketball, and I had asked several young people about where to buy some Adidas high-tops. They all referred me to 'the Jew Man,' a store on Southern Boulevard just above Westchester Avenue that had the best selection and the lowest prices and that didn't charge sales tax. I asked one young friend why the place was known as "the Jew Man." "They call him 'the Jew Man' because he's a Jew Man. All the stores around here used to belong to either whites or Jews." When I asked if he really meant that Jews weren't white, he bristled at what he considered my second dumb question. "Jews lived *here, in the ghetto,* man. Whites never lived here."[8]

Rose Dry Goods Store—"the Jew Man" famous in much of the South Bronx—belonged to an elderly Jewish couple assisted by their 40ish son and several black and Hispanic teenagers. I never found out why they, of all the Jews who had once been in the area, had chosen to stay (see Kugelmass 1986). When I went to buy my shoes, the employee who helped me only let me try on one sneaker at a time—store policy to prevent the fleet-of-foot from dashing out the door with the merchandise. I noticed that quite a bit of good-humored bargaining went on between proprietors and customers. I tried unsuccessfully and half in jest to get in on this with what I thought was a novel angle, telling the woman at the counter that I was a *landsman* and should get a discount. She said something in Yiddish that I didn't understand and began to laugh uproariously. Then she started to speak in Yiddish to her husband and son. The only word I caught was *landsman* and they too began to chuckle. The only three Jews left in this part of the South Bronx didn't believe I was Jewish either.[9]

Despite the South Bronx's "Fort Apache" image and the less than upright activities of many of my informants, I rarely felt physically threatened. The few occasions when I did, however, suggest to me that my sense of safety derived in part from downplaying my ethnicity and from others' perceptions—based on my complexion, knowledge of Spanish, Adidas, and army coat—that I fitted in. I did nothing to disabuse people of their notion that I belonged, and I think that at least once it kept me from serious harm. On one occasion, while standing with some Puerto Rican acquaintances in front of a small grocery store, an aggressive panhandler named Richie hit me up for a quarter and then locked me into a conversation. I didn't tell him about why I was there, but the discussion nonetheless turned rapidly to crime. He turned out to be a psychotic Vietnam veteran who within minutes was showing me massive scars on his back from the machine-gun fire that nearly killed him during a covert operation in Laos. ("Only niggers was chosen for that mission, with black parachutes, so the slopes couldn't see us.") Richie bragged about the "hundreds of Viet Cong" he had killed, the murders he had committed in Washington to avenge his father, who had been thrown from a window by dope dealers, and various other violent encounters. "I've seen so much blood, I see blood in my footprints when I walk," he told me. His manner alternated suddenly and unpredictably between extreme hostility and a friendly intimacy, and I was distressed that I couldn't extricate myself from the situation. Whenever he paused in his violent monologue, I made a point of saying something in Spanish to the store owner in the doorway or the other people leaning on parked cars. They responded by laughing about my predicament but warned me to be careful, that this guy was dangerously crazy. Even though the encounter did not explicitly have an ethnic dimension, I pointedly tried to make it look as if I had ethnic allies. I was trying to make him, the lone black, feel outnumbered by the Hispanics and, of course, to conceal my own ethnic aloneness.

Unable to shake loose of Richie, we entered the bodega and I treated him to a can of malt liquor in an effort to mollify his aggressive behavior. I noticed that he carefully watched in which pocket I put my money. He then said he had something to show me in a nearby empty lot. I asked what it was, and he responded, "If you tell people that Richie robbed you, they say you crazy, because he don't do that kind of thing. He don't even carry a knife or nothing." I told him that I couldn't go to the lot, that I had to stick around because I was waiting for someone. "Well, what I wanted to teach you is death blows." As he said this, he came over and stood with his fist next to my chest. I told him as nonchalantly as I could, "I don't need to learn that shit." He said, "You never know when you might need it, and I'm showing it to you because you're my friend." I bluffed, "Nah, I don't need to learn that shit because I know it already."

Then his manner became more consistently friendly. "You alright, you nice, man. You got a nice manner 'bout you. You remind me of my friend Peewee." Peewee, it turned out, was dead. I managed to escape

Richie when a friend came by and I directed him, in Spanish, to act as if we had an appointment for which we were late. This was my closest brush with danger in the South Bronx. I had the distinct feeling that I had saved myself by making someone believe that I was something I wasn't. In most cases I felt no need to misrepresent myself this way actively, but I came to think that in this violent milieu the capacity to blend in was an important part of survival.

The USSR
◆

In Latin America, for most people my salient identity was "foreigner" or "gringo," and in the Bronx most assumed I was Hispanic. In both settings, my Jewishness was usually unnoticed or unimportant. In the Soviet Union, in contrast, my Jewishness was of concern to a variety of people from the minute I arrived. Flying into Moscow on an icy night in 1986, I was greeted at the airport by a driver and an engineering student who worked as an exchange program functionary. He spoke excellent English and was the proud owner of a Jacqueline Susanne novel and some U.S. engineering magazines. As we sped along deserted dark Moscow boulevards past rows of housing projects and huge red banners hailing the upcoming XXVII CPSU Congress, we chatted about Soviet films, from Eisenstein classics to Derzu Uzala. At some point, the middle-aged actor who was moonlighting as our chauffeur started to talk to me in Russian about jazz. Oscar Peterson and Count Basie were his favorites, and he had never heard of the Modern Jazz Quartet. He asked me if I knew of this pianist Vladimir Horowitz who was supposed to give a concert in April or May. I was doing better as a conversationalist with American music, even in Russian, than I had been doing with Soviet film. The driver and I hit it off well. When we got to the hotel he helped carry my luggage inside.

When we were alone in a corner of the hotel lobby, the driver, whose surname was Sheiman, told me he was Jewish and asked me if I was too. Yes, I said, and he then asked if I spoke Hebrew or Yiddish and where my grandparents were from. I told him—Minsk, Berdichev, Poland—and he seemed genuinely pleased. I was too. I didn't know if the conversation had been simply with Sheiman or if he was going to report on me to state security, indicating that I claimed not to know

Hebrew or more than a few words of Yiddish. I didn't care. The talk had seemed perfectly natural and innocuous.[10]

The three-day train ride from Moscow to Tashkent was my real introduction to the fractured mosaic of Soviet ethnicity. I shared a compartment with an elderly Uzbek who was folkloric in the extreme. "Are there birds in America?" he asked in all seriousness. "Is there a moon in America?" "Does it look the same as our moon in the Soviet Union?" "Do you have a car?" "Is it a Moskvich or a Chaika?" When the two 30ish Russian women who also shared our compartment stepped out into the corridor, he switched to the familiar second-person form, began to make obscene hand gestures, and cackled that I should marry one of them, that it didn't matter if I was married already. When I stepped into the corridor to escape his incessant badgering, one of the women, both of whom turned out to be school administrators in Kuybyshev, asked me something in Russian that I didn't catch. I told her I didn't understand and she laughingly accused me of joking. Then her expression became serious as it dawned on her that I really was a foreigner. "At first I thought you were one of our nationalities," she said. "Perhaps an Azeri, or an Afghan."

I ignored the remark about Afghans being one of "our nationalities" and, back in our cramped compartment, started a long and initially quite enjoyable discussion with the Russian women. It was the first of a kind of dialogue of which I had many in the USSR and that I came to categorize as *u nas i u vas* (in our country and in your country). We passed around photos and chatted about our families, about education and politics, about whether it was true that there are cafés in America where blacks can't go. At some point, one of the women asked me if in my country there were many Jews. I said no, that in some of the larger cities—New York, Chicago, Los Angeles—there were quite a few, but in the country as a whole not many. Her face lost its easy relaxed smile. "They are traitorous [*predatel'skye*] people," she declared with great conviction and sudden seriousness. "They have no love of the motherland [*rodina*]. I saw on television the ones who were paid to leave and thought they would live sweetly, that life here was bad and that there [in the west] it was better. But they came back."

I felt anger and disillusionment that this person with whom I had shared several hours of enjoyable conversation and with whom I was stuck at least until Kuybyshev had turned out to be ingenuous at best or viciously anti-Semitic at worst. Since she had already revealed herself to be a good Communist, suitably outraged though hardly well informed about racism in the United States, I decided to hoist her by her own petard. "You know," I said, trying to act unruffled, "I'm really surprised to hear you talk about Jews like this, because it sounds like the same kind of thing they say about blacks in South Africa, talking about a whole group of people as if they are all one way. I'm really disappointed, because I thought that racism was illegal in the Soviet Union."

"How can you say that?" she demanded indignantly. "We're not talking about racism, we're talking about the Jews' essence [*osobennost'*]. You know what I'm saying is true. The Jews are also a very cunning [*khitrye*] people, and I have many Jewish friends."

I observed that in my country we thought that you could tell racists because they often claim to have friends of the group they hate. She pronounced this illogical. The "cunning" remark was, I sensed, directed at me. After all, I had confounded her, even with my lousy Russian, and since I wasn't an Azeri or one of the "nationalities," perhaps I was of some other despicable but canny ethnic group. The old Uzbek on the top bunk started to mutter about how Hitler had exchanged Jews for money. We lapsed into a long silence that lasted until the train reached Kuybyshev. The Uzbek was going all the way to Tashkent, but fortunately other passengers replaced the two school administrators. Months later a refusenik friend whom I hadn't told about this incident commented to me, "What I can't stand about this country is the anti-Semitism at the level of the people [*narod*]. It always happens when I take trains. I don't look Jewish, and I'm always hearing about the Jews this, the Jews that . . ."

Tashkent State University had no Latin America specialists and only three books and one journal on Latin America in its library. There wasn't much I could do there to advance my research on Soviet scholars' views of Central America other than begin the process of obtaining permission to return to Moscow. The history faculty entrusted me to Kamil, a chain-smoking, very Russified professor of Uzbek "nationality" who spoke excellent English, and to a gaggle of young Komsomols, mostly Russians and Uzbeks, with a sprinkling of Tadjiks and Kirghiz. My handlers' job seemed to be to keep me entertained, taking me to museums and plays, to make sure that I didn't form unpleasant impressions of Tashkent or the USSR, and perhaps to keep track of my movements.

The Komsomols' leader was Vasily, a tall, strapping Russian who rode herd over the Uzbek Komsomols and blustered continuously about the virtues of everything Soviet. At first I saw him as a sanctimonious blowhard, but eventually we became friends, when he took me into his confidence and revealed that he thought people who didn't work ought to be fired, that he wanted to know more about the early history of the CPSU than was revealed in the doctored photographs and documents of the local Lenin Museum, and that one of his main desires was to visit the Hotel Uzbekistan's hard currency bar.

One day Vasily and I were walking through the Alaiskii Bazar, one of Tashkent's magnificent outdoor markets. He was bragging about the great variety of fruit and other food and telling me that "here we have everything." At some point he grew pensive and asked me a question that had apparently been on his mind for some time. "*Kakoi v'i natsional'nosti?*" (What's your nationality?)

I sensed what he was getting at, but I didn't want to make it easy for him. "*Ia amerikanets,*" I answered, pretending to understand the word in its non-Soviet sense.

"*Net. Kakoi v'i natsional'nosti?*" (No, what's your nationality?)

"*Ia amerikanets.*"

I reminded him that he had seen my U.S. passport a few days before, when we had examined each other's documents. Frustrated, Vasily tried another word, *proiskhozhdenie*, roughly "origin," "extraction," or "provenance." I decided to bust his chops just a little more.

"*Ia nachilsia v N'yu Yorke*" (I was born in New York), I answered as cheerily as I could.

Vasily let out an exasperated groan and then he nailed me. "*Edel'man eto evreiskaia familiia, da?*" (Edelman, that's a Jewish surname, isn't it?)

"Of course," I said. "What did you think it was?"

Then something happened that was unprecedented in the two weeks or so I had been hanging out with Vasily. He became absolutely quiet and lost in thought. We walked for two blocks to the History Faculty and he didn't say a word.

After this exchange, various conversational slips demonstrated that my handlers must have discussed their Jewish problem, namely me, at some length. The next day several of us were in an ice cream bar, the kind of place where healthy, nonalcoholic young people socialized in the mid-1980s USSR. We were in the midst of a heated argument about Afghanistan when one of my escorts, a charming Russian woman who had taken me on a tour of Tashkent's beautiful parks and metro, piped up with a peculiar non sequitur. "Marc, you know that Boris Pasternak was not an anti-Semite; they say that about *Doctor Zhivago*, but it's not true."

I was dumbfounded by the sudden thematic shift from superpower intervention to suspect literature, but I tried to roll with the punches. I asked if she had read *Doctor Zhivago* and if we could get it in the library so that we could check. My questions were, I realize now, entirely rhetorical, but motivated not so much by wanting to win an argument as by simple aggravation combined with a desire to gain some understanding of how my Komsomol friends really thought and felt. By needling them I was also hoping to learn how they dealt with the dilemma of being individuals in a society that required such narrow conformity.

A couple of days later a more disturbing Freudian slip revealed the darker side of what was behind the questions about my "nationality." I was walking with Kamil, my history professor guide, through downtown Tashkent. He spoke the idiomatic, virtually unaccented English that Soviet language schools were so good at imparting even without trips abroad or native speakers for teachers. A swarthy woman in a ragged dress, with dirt smudges on her face, was seated on the sidewalk, nursing a baby with one hand and pointing with the other to a box that contained a few coins. Unlike the few other beggars I had encountered in Tashkent, there was nothing furtive or apologetic about her request for money. Kamil almost spat at her, he was so angry. I sensed that much of his indignation had to do with my seeing a beggar on his watch. Turning to me, he declared, "The dirty Jews, all they're interested in is money, they'll do anything for money."

I felt my blood beginning to boil, but I tried to maintain my equilibrium. "Huh? How'd you know she was Jewish?" I asked. I was thinking that she didn't "look" Jewish at all, but there was some possibility that she could be a Bukharskiy (Central Asian) Jew. Kamil responded something along the lines of "I can always tell, they're all the same."

I ventured that the woman didn't look Jewish to me, but that here everything was different. The next day Kamil came to me very perturbed and told me he had "used the wrong word in English, I meant gypsy, not Jew, and I'm afraid I might have upset you." I thought this was a peculiar error for someone with such an impressive command of English; it was hard to avoid the conclusion that the Jew-for-gypsy slip had revealed some intense, irrational hatred. I kept this to myself and said instead that such remarks were upsetting even when they didn't refer to my own ethnic group. Kamil then tried to soothe my bruised feelings by explaining that all gypsies really were thieves and beggars.

In the USSR I saw touching cases of people of different "nationalities" eating, working, playing, and dancing together. But very frequently I also heard remarks that indicated that racism was very deeply rooted. A member of the Central Committee of the Uzbekistan Communist Party, who years before had been mugged by black teenagers while visiting Washington, bragged about how he had obstructed the "center's" (i.e., Moscow's) campaign to free Angela Davis in the entire Uzbek Republic because he hated blacks. My Russian dormitory mates muttered about the "nationalism" of the Uzbeks, and the elderly Russian woman who guarded the door was constantly asking if most people in America were white like her or black (*cherniy*) like me. Uzbek and Afghan friends made sure that I knew of their dislike for Russian "big brotherism," a term that referred not to Orwell's *1984* but to the propaganda that held that the Russian Republic and people were the "big brother" of the other nationalities (including the Afghans, who some joked then were about to become the "16th republic of the USSR"). Even the multicolored Cubans whom I hung out with in Tashkent detested the Uzbeks, especially the Uzbek women's prim-and-proper manner and the whiny, minor-key love songs that blared forth from dormitory windows early weekend mornings. The pervasive prejudice was shared by many Jewish refuseniks I met in Moscow, some of whom told offensive jokes about what African student "cannibals" at Patrice Lumumba University ate in the cafeteria. Some refuseniks also articulated a sociobiological, anti-ethnic-Russian theory of the degeneration of Soviet society, arguing that Stalin had killed off so much of the intelligentsia that those left to run things were *zverovidnyie*, of such inferior genetic stuff that they "looked like wild animals."

I didn't go to the USSR out of romanticism, though my grandfather Abraham nearly did. He was from near Minsk but came to the United States as a boy, 12 years before the 1917 revolution. In the old country he had been relatively assimilated, from a family of tenant farmers, a status usually forbidden to Jews, who spoke Russian as well as Yiddish at home. Shortly before his untimely death in the early 1930s, he had wanted to return to the land of his birth to build socialism. Older relatives recall hearing him argue into the night with his brother-in-law Boris, an anarchist, who insisted that the regime was killing anarchists and even Bolsheviks and would kill him too if he were foolish enough to go back.

My relatives' memories of my grandfather came back to me in a powerful rush of feeling in Moscow, where I met grandchildren of 1930s American Jewish Communists who in the 1980s were embittered refuseniks. Their families—after enduring decades of on-again, off-again anti-Semitism and abiding the repression of Stalinism and the absurdities and boredom of the "era of stagnation"—had, as one acquaintance put it, "faded from red, to pink, to white." Jewish exchange scholars and refuseniks shared a disquieting, inchoate sense that our radically different fates had been decided not by grand historical forces but by the tiniest of historical accidents: a grandparent's dogmatism or utopian ideals, one individual's travel itinerary (or the lack of one) decades or even a century before. "Papa was an idiot," my Muscovite friend Zhura stated matter-of-factly, in a tone that conveyed melancholy, resignation, anger, and bittersweet refusenik irony. "They were four brothers in Warsaw. Three of them went to America and became wealthy men. Papa left Poland too, but he came here to build socialism."

Unlike Tashkent, where I had little contact outside "official" society, in Moscow I worked in libraries and met with colleagues by day and came to know an unofficial, largely Jewish world by night and on weekends. Some of my contacts were relatives of my Russian teachers in the States, some were friends of other friends, and most had lost their jobs when they applied to emigrate. What they had in common were harrowing stories of institutionalized and unofficial discrimination, bureaucratic capriciousness, KGB repression, and endless waits for the promised exit visas. Despite their naive idealization of everything Western and their absolute unwillingness to acknowledge any positive aspects of their own society, I came to appreciate their warmth, good humor, and stamina in the face of overwhelming adversity. As I flew out of Moscow, two weeks after the explosion at Chernobyl, I was consumed by guilt and rage that these fine scientists, musicians, and filmmakers were still oppressed as Jews and as people, that they were not able to simply fly away from their oppressors, as I was doing.

Closing Remarks
◆

Stereotypes of Jews are hard to confront in part because the same images often contain anti-Semitic and "philo-Semitic" elements. Jews have lots of money. They are intelligent and powerful. They are sensitive. Esteem, admiration, envy, and hatred accompany each stereotype. The same formula may serve all four emotions, and a single display of prejudice may shift contradictorily between positive and negative expressions. Typically those convinced of the veracity of these images believe that there are more Jews than there really are. The Soviet anti-Semites I met invariably believed, for example, that there were many more than just a few million Jews each in the USSR, the United States, and Israel.

Anti-Semitism can change into philo-Semitism (or vice versa) as fast as you can say "Einstein." This difficulty in confronting anti-Semitism is compounded by a Catch-22 inherent in the stereotypes. If we challenge anti-Semitism intellectually (in order not to seem too excitable) and best the anti-Semite in rational argument, we end up substantiating the notion that Jews are very intelligent (philo-Semitic version) or cunning (anti-Semitic version).

Recently the "overly sensitive" stereotype has received some apparent confirmation in Arthur Hertzberg's (1993) analysis of survey data that suggest Jews in various countries perceive more anti-Semitism than is expressed by non-Jews. Survey research may not be the best tool for eliciting officially condemned yet deeply held biases. But what is striking to me in reflecting on ethnographic encounters with anti-Semitism is not so much my oversensitivity as *my almost willful obtuseness in not recognizing anti-Jewish prejudice or in putting a benign gloss on it.* To some extent, this failure to notice bigotry stemmed from the ways anti-Semitic assumptions are woven into basic social and linguistic categories, especially in Latin America. But my failure to fully grasp this stemmed as well from three largely unconscious impulses: the desire to fit in and be accepted that is a key part of anthropological fieldwork; anxiety that to be identified as a Jew could ruin my research; and a wish to have informants reciprocate my positive feelings toward them. I heard the most galling expressions of anti-Semitism in settings close to my research but only peripherally related to it. Then, I generally felt few inhibitions about confronting anti-Semites. In my role as researcher, however, I heard fewer such expressions and was less confrontational.

This inability to fully "hear" anti-Semitism involves a managing of emotion that is ultimately a managing of the researcher's Jewishness. The Jewish ethnographer experiences the informant's anti-Semitic remark as an aggression, which provokes anger and aggressive impulses. To express this, however, would disrupt research. Anthropologists' representations of their subjects have certainly involved troubling processes of "othering" and "exoticization." Yet researcher-subject interactions *in the field* necessarily involve efforts to transcend that sense of otherness. So the anthropologist responds by denying the other's aggression and his or her own, repressing anger and managing ethnicity in the interest of continued communication.

More common than overt anti-Semitism, however, is the assumption that the Jewish anthropologist is Christian. How could this not be the case—in Latin America at least—when to be human is to be *cristiano*? This too has to be managed. I am reminded of walking by a church with two Central American male acquaintances who joke about going in and "getting rid of some of our sins." They take for granted that the joke includes all of us, but I have to ask myself each time something similar occurs whether the situation merits revealing that I am not *cristiano*. It is one thing to destroy a moment of levity with such a bombshell and yet another to deal internally with what is on some level a false presentation of self, an "act" or a "routine" (Goffman 1959, 17). To remain silent is a tacit affirmation of others' assumptions of one's Christianity, a disavowal of one's Jewishness. This can be distressing because it implies collusion with those holding negative images of Jews, as well as a denial of the history—catastrophic and a focus of nostalgia at the same time—that is now fundamental to many Jews' identities.

How have encounters with anti-Semitism affected my selection of research problems? Like many secular Jewish American anthropologists who have worked among non-Jews, I long thought that my Jewishness was irrelevant to my choice of research topics. Yet, like many of these colleagues, I studiously skirted the "anthropology of religion." Was this an effort to avoid uncomfortable encounters with prejudice or with the issue of whether to reveal my ethnicity? Perhaps so. But I am also a descendant of one branch of that great schism between religious and revolutionary millenarians in turn-of-the-century Eastern European Judaism. I grew up steeped in the militantly secular, purportedly universalistic values of those who saw (or had seen) socialism as salvation on earth, for Jews and others. Experience and historical events have made me more tolerant and rather less millenarian. But political-economic (and not religious or even narrowly ideological) research has always engaged me, sometimes passionately—a disposition rooted in this inheritance from proudly Jewish, but antireligious forebears.

It may be this same legacy that produces in me a certain skepticism about calls for making *reflexivity* central to ethnography. Reflexivity, as Loïc Wacquant remarks, is a "label . . . vague to the point of near vacuity" (Bourdieu and Wacquant 1992, 36). He nonetheless suggests ways in which a "bending back" of science upon itself might contribute to a critical yet empirically grounded understanding of society: by examining "the social and intellectual unconscious embedded in analytic tools and operations"; by analyzing the researcher's insertion in an "academic field . . . [and the] possible intellectual positions offered to him or her at a given moment"; and by buttressing "the epistemological security" of the social sciences, rather than trying to undermine it as often occurs "with phenomenological, textual, and other 'postmodern' forms of reflexivity" (36–39). It is in this spirit that I have indulged the impulse to focus inward, to probe the experiences described in this essay (which, in modernist fashion, I confess to having recorded in personal diaries rather than field notes).

Many self-referential accounts of field research, rather than viewing the ethnographer's role primarily in relation to specific research problems, consider privileging the "authorial voice" as a paramount value in and of itself (e.g., Behar 1993, ch. 17; Jackson 1989). Despite the autobiographical focus of this essay, I resist believing that an "author saturated" (Geertz 1988, 97) approach can or should be a primary goal of social scientific research. Is this the product of too much time in crisis-ridden Central America, where more pressing problems cry out for investigation, or of adherence to the remaining strands of my radical, universalist roots? Very likely both. However, it also needs to be stressed, in the face of claims that reflexivity is somehow a novel idea, that concern about positioning the researcher is hardly new and is not an invention or a monopoly of postmodernist writers. Numerous earlier scholars analyzed how both research and writing grow out of preexisting dispositions and how they involve decisions about what is relevant and what is irrelevant. But the many pre-postmodernists who examined the problems of "values," "objectivity," or "engaged" research steadfastly eschewed the currently popular "meta-skepticism" in favor of a reflexivity that saw the "social construction of reality" not only in history, culture, and daily life, but as an unavoidable and necessary accompaniment to the process of social scientific investigation itself (Berger and Luckmann 1966; Lynd 1939, ch. 5; Mills 1959, ch. 4; Murphy 1971, ch. 3; Myrdal 1969, ch. 11; Novick 1988; Sartre 1963; Scholte 1972).

"Managing" Jewishness has never been a constant preoccupation in the field, but I have found increasing ease in facing the issue when it has surfaced. This exercise in reflexivity, as I describe above, has led me to pay greater attention to expressions of bigotry. I have also ceased to feel that catastrophic consequences might ensue from confronting anti-Semitism in the field. For one thing, postdissertation projects have less riding on them than dissertation research. In early middle age, with greater career stability and personal security, there is less to be lost professionally by challenging those infrequent but disturbing manifestations of anti-Semitism.[11] And, of course, refusing to participate in a Goffman-esque "routine" of self-denial, "owning" rather than "managing" one's intrinsic qualities of identity, generates a sense of personal consistency. This can have positive effects in the field that compensate for informants' shock at the extent of one's "otherness."

The experiences described here, in addition to provoking attention to inner processes, also have brought home to me the historically contingent and still incomplete inclusion of Jews in the "white" category in late twentieth-century North America (Sacks 1994). Michael Lerner (1992, 123) has decried how some "multiculturalist" anti-Semites "view Jews as 'white' and as part of the . . . imperialist elite oppressing Third World nations." Jonathan Boyarin, more broadly, laments the "suppression"—under similar pretexts—of Jewish voices within cultural studies (1992, xix, 83). While I share these concerns, I think the whiteness question has another, more mundane dimension that has to do with the neglected issue of how ethnographers represent themselves *ethnically* in the field. If social scientists increasingly view ethnicity as a political phenomenon of groups in contact rather than as primordial characteristics, a lone representative of a particular group involved in research in a foreign land (or distant neighborhood) is out of context and may have an ambiguous and perhaps manipulable identity. Adding to this ambiguity, of course, is the beautiful phenotypic variability of Jews themselves. We have brown, olive, and pale white skin. Many of us, including myself, can be mistaken for a variety of Mediterranean, Middle Eastern, or Central Asian types.

How Jewish ethnographers deal with anti-Semitism in the field is ultimately related to two questions about which we know very little. How do ethnographers *in general* react to anti-Semitism in the field? How do ethnographers, Jewish or Gentile, react to racism against other groups in the field? Obviously, many anthropologists study ethnic relations, and to challenge informants' racism or to engage in antiracist polemics may interfere with their research. But most of us are not engaged in studies that require neutrality in the face of bigotry. The recognition that ethnographic interactions are "dialogic" or fraught with power asymmetries hasn't advanced us very far in understanding these questions. We have few accounts of researchers contesting racist or anti-Semitic "local knowledge," even though our opinions sometimes carry great weight with our native interlocutors. Anthropology, at least since Boas, has an admirable record of challenging racist pseudoscience in scholarly and public discourse. But as regards the anti-Semitism, racism, and national chauvinism that we encounter in the field, few anthropologists appear to have reflected seriously on where their responsibilities as human beings leave off and their responsibilities as scholars begin, or on the problematical lack of consistency between these two allegiances.

Notes

1. I presented an earlier version of this essay at a 1993 American Anthropological Association session titled "Twice Strangers: Jewish Field Workers in the Christian West." For encouragement and critical observations, I am grateful to David Gilmore, the session organizer, and to Philippe Bourgois, Harold and Judith Edelman, Michael Herzfeld, David Kertzer, Débora Munczek, Benjamin Orlove, Joel Wallman, and this volume's editors.
2. Nash, in a study of representations of Judas in Mesoamerican holy week festivities, describes how Mayan celebrants revile him as the "'killer of Christ'" and "'the leader of the Jews.'" . . . Under cover of the role of Christians outraged by the killing of Christ, the Indians were acting out their own hatred

of Ladinos [non-Indians]" (1994, 49). The idiom for this, however, is anti-Semitism, a conclusion Nash never states directly. The otherwise compelling article provides no insight into her reactions to "the spectators' raucous cries of 'the Jews!'" (47) or to the virulent anti-Semitism of priests and saint's cult officials (cf. Nugent 1996). This grassroots anti-Semitism reflected the Good Friday liturgy, when Catholics intoned, "Let us pray for the perfidious Jews." Pope John XXIII removed the word *perfidious* in 1959 (Lynch 1992, 158).

3. In 1939, over 900 Jews fled Germany for Cuba on the *Saint Louis*. Cuban officials demanded enormous bribes and refused to honor their visas. The Roosevelt administration ignored the passengers' and captain's pleas that they be permitted to disembark in the United States. Other western hemisphere nations also refused them entry. Coast Guard patrols near Florida made sure that none jumped ship. Most of the passengers perished in the Holocaust (Berenbaum 1993, 58).

4. Only in 1965, at the Second Vatican Council, did the Catholic Church state that the Jews of today and of Jesus's time should not be burdened with blood guilt. Even then, the Church did not engage in any systematic education of its laity that would have counterbalanced its centuries of anti-Semitic indoctrination (Lerner 1992, 16).

5. In the following tabloid crime story, headlined "Polaco Shoots 'Tarzan,'" the perpetrator—presumably non-Jewish—possesses a dangerous anonymity and propensity to violence, taking victims among even those with superhuman strength, who can then only be saved by "miracles."

> Guillermo Zúñiga Marín, known as "Tarzan," was filled with lead in front of the evangelical church of Dulce Nombre de Coronado: one bullet in the back, and four others in the right lumbar region, according to Judicial Police sources. The event occurred with lightning speed. According to witnesses, it was a man who sells clothes on credit (*polaco*) who fired nearly the entire cylinder of a .22-caliber revolver during what some consider to have been an assault by "Tarzan." A police spokesperson said that the author of the shots is not fully identified, because his name is not known in the barrio of El Carmen de Dulce Nombre, where he frequently came to sell clothes door to door. The wounded man was interned in Calderón Guardia Hospital, where he underwent an operation to extract the five slugs; although his condition is weak, it appears that he is out of danger, which is considered a true miracle (*"Polaco baleó a 'Tarzan'"* 1994).

6. Parallel to this identification of *cristianos* with human beings, traditional Spanish descriptions of non-Christians and *conversos* commonly employed comparisons with despised animals, such as wolves, dogs, and snakes (Beinart 1992, 112–113).

7. The episode best known to anthropologists was the 1931 denial of membership in the Graduate Club—"the center of faculty social life"—to Edward Sapir, who had just left Chicago for a prestigious Sterling Professorship at Yale (Oren 1985, 132). One strain of Yale oral tradition even linked Sapir's death eight years later to "nasty anti-Semitic treatment" (Bashkow 1991, 173). On a more recent incident, see Schwartz (1989).

8. During World War II, "anti-Semitism and anti-European racism lost respectability," producing "a more inclusive version of whiteness" (Sacks 1994, 87; cf. Boyarin 1992, 86, 101). Urban renewal and suburbanization, made possible by subsidized FHA and VA mortgages, as well as the end of anti-Semitic university admission quotas, buoyed Jews' rise to middle-class (and "white") status. Those poor, elderly Jews who stayed in the South Bronx remained partly outside the white category because they had not benefited personally from these forces.

    In the Soviet Union, as I discuss later in the chapter, barriers to mobility also kept Jews outside the white category and close to the "dark" or "black" (*cherniy*) category reserved for non-Slavic (and usually non-Christian) "nationalities." This is part of a European tradition of representing Jews as blacks that Gilman terms "the synthesis of two projections of Otherness within the same code" (1986, 8).

9. Later it occurred to me that they might have believed I was a Jew, but were just not impressed with my incompetent Jewishness. At the time, however, I was immersed in the Hispanic South Bronx and so accustomed to being taken for Latino that I assumed that they, like everyone else, had failed to recognize me as a Jew.

10. Eventually it became harder to accept such encounters at face value. Once on the Moscow metro, a man sat down next to me and started to read *Sovietish Heimland*, the Yiddish newspaper published in the Birobidjian "Jewish" Autonomous Region in Siberia. Moscow Jews later told me that it would be crazy to read a Yiddish paper on the metro, and this man was surely a KGB provocateur.

11. Di Leonardo's work on Italian Americans suggests another key dimension. "Gender has a fundamental influence on the way in which individuals perceive and respond to ethnic discrimination . . . Women seemed to feel freer to express indignation than men, even when the incidents described were less serious . . . The framing/feeling rules associated with gender here

coincided with those associated with discrimination. Only men gave responses centered on taking ethnic slurs as jokes, and working on their emotions to do so; [in] the prevalent gender ideology . . . to admit vulnerability is weak, womanish" (1984, 166).

References

"A Certain Antipatriotic Group of Theater Critics." 1949. *Pravda* (Jan. 28). In *Anti-Semitism in the Soviet Union*, edited by T. Freedman. (New York: B'nai B'rith, 1984): 518–522.

Bashkow, I. 1991. "The Dynamics of Rapport in a Colonial Situation: David Schneider's Fieldwork on the Islands of Yap." In *Colonial Situations: Essays on the Contextualization of Ethnographic Knowledge*, edited by G.W. Stocking, Jr. (Madison: University of Wisconsin Press): 170–242.

Behar, R. 1993. *Translated Woman: Crossing the Border with Esperanza's Story.* Boston: Beacon Press.

Beinart, H. 1992. "The Conversos and their Fate." In *Spain and the Jews: The Sephardi Experience 1492 and After*, edited by E. Kedourie. (London: Thames and Hudson): 92–122.

Berenbaum, M. 1993. *The World Must Know: The History of the Holocaust as Told in the United States Holocaust Memorial Museum.* Boston: Little, Brown.

Berger, P., and T. Luckmann. 1966. *The Social Construction of Reality.* Garden City, NY: Doubleday.

Bourdieu, P., and L. J. D. Wacquant. 1992. *An Invitation to a Reflexive Sociology.* Chicago: University of Chicago Press.

Boyarin, J. 1988. "Waiting for a Jew: Marginal Redemption at the Eighth Street Shul." In *Between Two Worlds: Ethnographic Essays on American Jewry*, edited by J. Kugelmass. (Ithaca: Cornell University Press): 52–76.

———. 1991. *Polish Jews in Paris: The Ethnography of Memory.* Bloomington: Indiana University Press.

———. 1992. *Storm from Paradise: The Politics of Jewish Memory.* Minneapolis: University of Minnesota Press.

di Leonardo, M. 1984. *The Varieties of Ethnic Experience: Kinship, Class, and Gender among California Italian-Americans.* Ithaca: Cornell University Press.

Domínguez, V. R. 1993. "Questioning Jews." *American Ethnologist* 20: 618–624.

Edelman, M. 1994. "Landlords and the Devil: Class, Ethnic, and Gender Dimensions of Central American Peasant Narratives." *Cultural Anthropology* 9: 58–93.

Elkin Laiken, J. 1992. "Quincentenary: Colonial Legacy of Anti-Semitism." *Report on the Americas* 25 (Feb.): 4–7.

Foucault, M. 1972. *The Archeology of Knowledge*. New York: Pantheon.

Geertz, C. 1988. *Works and Lives: The Anthropologist as Author*. Stanford: Stanford University Press.

Gilman, S. L. 1986. *Jewish Self-Hatred: Anti-Semitism and the Hidden Language of the Jews*. Baltimore: Johns Hopkins University Press.

Goffman, E. 1959. *The Presentation of Self in Everyday Life*. Garden City, NY: Doubleday Anchor.

Gold, M. 1930. *Jews Without Money*. New York: Horace Liveright.

Hertzberg, A. 1993. "Is Anti-Semitism Dying Out?" *New York Review of Books* 40 (June 24): 51–57.

Jackson, M. 1989. *Paths Toward a Clearing: Radical Empiricism and Ethnographic Inquiry*. Bloomington: Indiana University Press.

Kugelmass, J. 1986. *The Miracle of Intervale Avenue: The Story of a Jewish Congregation in the South Bronx*. New York: Schocken Books.

Lerner, M. 1992. *The Socialism of Fools: Anti-Semitism on the Left*. Oakland: Tikkun.

Lynch, J. 1992. "Spain After the Expulsion." In *Spain and the Jews: The Sephardi Experience 1492 and After*, edited by E. Kedourie. (London: Thames and Hudson): 140–161.

Lynd, R. S. 1939. *Knowledge for What? The Place of Social Science in American Culture*. Princeton: Princeton University Press.

Mills, C. W. 1959. *The Sociological Imagination*. New York: Oxford University Press.

Murphy, R. F. 1971. *The Dialectics of Social Life*. New York: Basic Books.

Myerhoff, B. 1978. *Number Our Days*. New York: Simon & Schuster.

Myrdal, G. 1969. *Objectivity in Social Research*. New York: Pantheon.

Nash, J. 1994. "Judas Transformed." *Natural History* 103 (Mar.): 46–53.

Novick, P. 1988. *That Noble Dream: The Objectivity Question and the American Historical Profession*. Cambridge: Cambridge University Press.

Nugent, D. 1996. "From Devil Pacts to Drug Deals: Commerce, Unnatural Accumulation and Moral Community in 'Modern' Peru." *American Ethnologist* 23: 258–290.

Oren, D. A. 1985. *Joining the Club: A History of Jews and Yale*. New Haven: Yale University Press.

"Polaco baleó a 'Tarzan.'" 1994. *Diario Extra* (Costa Rica) (April 25): 25.

Rosten, L. 1970. *The Joys of Yiddish*. New York: Pocket Books.

Sacks, K. B. 1994. "How Did Jews Become White Folks?" In *Race*, edited by S. Gregory and R. Sanjek. (New Brunswick: Rutgers University Press): 78–102.

Sartre, J.-P. 1963. *The Problem of Method*. London: Methuen.

Scholte, B. 1972. "Toward a Reflexive and Critical Anthropology." In *Reinventing Anthropology*, edited by D. Hymes. (New York: Vintage Books): 430–457.

Schwartz, S. 1989. "The Boy Who Cried Anti-Semitism." *Urim v'Tumim* 4: 12–13.

Stutzman, R. 1981. "*El Mestizaje*: An All-Inclusive Ideology of Exclusion." In *Cultural Transformations and Ethnicity in Modern Ecuador*, edited by N. E. Whitten. (Urbana: University of Illinois Press): 45–94.

Taussig, M. 1980. *The Devil and Commodity Fetishism in South America*. Chapel Hill: University of North Carolina Press.

◆————————

Marc Edelman is Associate Professor of Anthropology at Hunter College and the Graduate Center of the City University of New York. He is an editor of *The Costa Rica Reader* (New York: Grove Weidenfeld, 1989) and *Amérique Centrale* (Paris: Les Temps Modernes, 1989) and the author of *Siete décadas de relaciones soviético-latinoamericanas* (Mexico: Centro Latinoamericano de Estudios Estratégicos, 1987) and *The Logic of the Latifundio: The Large Estates of Northwestern Costa Rica since the Late Nineteenth Century* (Stanford University Press, 1992). He is currently involved in research on transnational peasant organizations in Central America.

CHAPTER TWELVE

"She Changes Everything She Touches"
Ethnographic Journeys of Self-Discovery[1]

Tanice G. Foltz
Wendy Griffin

This paper is a reflexive account of our fieldwork experiences with a coven of Dianic Witches, a feminist religious group that professes to be an agent of empowerment and change. In this account we examine ourselves as legitimate subjects of study, revealing how we were influenced through feminist ritual and magic and how those changes affected who we have become. Although many sociologists of religion have felt the pull of "conversion" and have been moved by their fieldwork experiences (see Brown 1985, 1991; Forrest 1986; Jules-Rosette 1975), this paper is the first to address the transformative process of doing fieldwork in the context of feminist ritual. We inject our voices into the experimental movement in ethnography that seeks to heal the artificial separation of subject and object, modulate the "authorial voice," and acknowledge our subjective involvement in the creation of social knowledge.

Our Reflexive Voices

◆

The encounter with ethnographic others is a therapeutic quest for meaning, a search for identity that can be considered a form of healing in the broadest sense . . . it includes the process of ethnographic writing as well (Danforth 1989, 300).

Postmodern ethnographers reject the concept of "objective truth" and remind us that writing ethnography is cultural construction, not cultural reporting. Thus ethnographic writing is "always a construction of the self as well as of the other" (Stacey 1991, 115). Since all knowledge is socially constructed, the researcher, as the instrument of data collection and interpretation, plays a central role in creating this knowledge. That is why Stanley and Wise (1983) emphasize the importance of researcher "vulnerability," of beginning with our experiences as people in a particular situation.

This vulnerability has the potential for unexpected consequences. While it is clear that field researchers will affect the members of the setting through their interaction over time, it is not immediately as obvious that researchers themselves often are changed by the research process. Some field-workers report self-transformation through the research experience, while, for others, this may be experienced as a "journey" of self-discovery.[2] Reinharz (1992, 194) claims: "Many feminist researchers report being profoundly changed by what they learn about themselves. Changes may involve completely reconceptualizing a phenomenon and completely revising one's worldview." Thorne goes even farther and argues that:

> What I have come to see . . . is that there is a deep logic to this way of writing, that these personal experiences were neither confessional, minor preliminaries, nor mere "how it was done" appendages to the main study, but were closely tied to and even generative of the study and its substantive findings (in Krieger 1991, 250).

Informed by Reinharz's (1983) experiential analysis and Marcus and Cushman's (1982) exploration of ethnographies as texts, interpretive sociologists have connected with the growing movement of experimental ethnography. This "experimental moment" (Marcus and Fischer 1986) values the narrative (Maines 1993; Richardson 1990, 1994), uses researcher experiences as primary data (Ellis 1991), and studies lived experience through investigating subjectivity (Denzin 1991; Denzin and Lincoln 1994; Ellis and Flaherty 1992). Speaking to the representation of "partial truths" (Clifford 1986), experimental ethnographers are self-consciously including their subjective involvement in the creation of texts (Ellis 1995; Linden 1993). Counting ourselves as part of this movement, we start from our situated experience as women and field researchers, and make our direct experience of the world and the research process the foundation for our knowledge as social scientists.

While writing this paper we found ourselves resisting the rhetoric of authority, authenticity, objectivity, and a "disinterested" perspective—all characteristic of traditional ethnographic writing (see Clifford 1983). Similar to Krieger (1991, 162), we decided that our resistance reflected our struggle with "alienated habits of research," that encourage an artificial separation of the researcher and the researched. As a result, we have attempted to modulate our academic "authorial voices" so that our ethnographic journeys of self-discovery can be "heard." In the following pages we invite the reader along as we reveal our stories of self-transformation through immersion into the world of feminist Witchcraft and magic.

Our Identities Prior to the Research

♦

In order to show the changes we underwent, we need to reveal a bit about who we were before we began our study and how the research came about. Entree was gained through a particularly bright student of Wendy's, who stood up in class and announced she was a "Dianic priestess and feminist Witch." She invited everyone to a ritual her coven was organizing. Initially, neither of us was interested, but for slightly different reasons.

Wendy:

I had been a lecturer in women's studies and sociology for three years and a long-time feminist activist at the local and state level. The only contact I had with feminist Witchcraft was in the late 1970s at a NOW conference, when a scruffy-looking woman entered a restaurant, sat down on the floor next to the cash register, and began to chant loudly. I had no idea what was happening and frankly found it silly. In the early 1970s, however, I had been briefly involved with a group that experimented with parapsychology, so this made me somewhat curious about my student's group, but not enough to go to the ritual alone.

Tanice:

Although I held feminist values, I was not an activist. Wendy and I shared an office at school and she invited me to the ritual with her. My immediate response was "no thanks." It sounded too weird. Through previous research on an alternative healing group, I had experienced various forms of ritual and altered states of consciousness, and I had great respect for the mind-altering techniques I had learned (see Foltz 1987, 1994). I did not want to "play with fire" in a group about which I knew nothing. Finally, our curiosity overcame our reservations and we decided to accept the invitation.

Spring Equinox Ritual: Our Initial Reactions
◆

Tanice:

In spite of my decision to attend, I was more than a little frightened about what to expect, and I was extremely anxious while driving there. Not only was I fearful of Witches, but the idea of radical, feminist separatists scared me. When we arrived, a huge red-headed woman greeted us, and I was even frightened of her size. Although it's embarrassing now, I categorized the nearly 30 women who participated as "lesbian" and experienced a homophobic reaction that I couldn't shake. This reaction surprised me, especially since I've had gay male friends. I was extremely uncomfortable and, when the ritual began, I was absolutely terrified by a woman called Raging Dove who yelled her intention to create separate communities for "women loving women." In spite of this, I found the chanting and guided visualizations, as well as the themes of the ritual—honoring the coming Springtime and the connection between mother and daughter—all deeply moving. I began to believe this could be a fascinating research setting.

Wendy:

Coming from a family of straight, lesbian, and gay members, and having spent many years around feminist activists, I was comfortable with women of a different sexual orientation. Aletheia, my student who greeted us at the door, played hostess and introduced us to everyone. I found the ritual strange and kind of fun, but not particularly moving. During the "feast" after the ritual, I got involved in a passionate discussion with Raging Dove about radical feminist separatism, with which I was familiar as an intellectual exercise but not as a deeply held personal belief and lived experience. I found myself being lectured to about feminist principles, a very unusual and uncomfortable experience for me. I struggled to balance the roles of feminist, polite guest, and the role I then thought appropriate for a professor in a student's home, with its attendant hierarchical shadings. On reflection, I'm not sure I succeeded at any of these roles. When Tanice wanted to leave, I was ready.

We later discussed the prospect of doing research with the group. Tanice was certain there was something important going on in the setting. I wasn't that sure. I was afraid they were kooks, and to be honest, I didn't want to do research on anything that I thought could discredit the women's movement. In addition, I was on the job market and had to consider how this research setting would look to the academic world.[3] I wish I could say that my decision to do this research was due to increased consciousness, but in the end it was because I needed a research topic, the Witches were there and welcoming, and Aletheia was no longer my student. I contacted the coven and we gained permission to do participant-observation. As part of the "research bargain" we agreed to actively participate in the group's activities to our level of comfort. Our presence at the Summer Solstice ritual marked the beginning of our journeys of self-transformation.

Methods

◆

Our team research in the coven spanned Spring Equinox 1988 through Summer Solstice 1989. We used a triangulation of qualitative methods, engaging in participant-observation, taking field notes, conducting interviews, and gathering information on Witchcraft from books, newsletters, and magazines.

Although we initially took "peripheral membership researcher roles" (Adler and Adler 1987, 36), which allowed us to maintain a certain distance between us and them, the Witches socialized us whenever we met. While we always arrived for ritual at the time requested, coven members arrived according to "pagan standard time," meaning whenever they got there. During these pre-ritual sessions, often spanning several hours, we learned a great deal about ceremony and ritual and gained considerable understanding of coven dynamics. We attended ritual planning sessions and eight major rituals (Sabbats), most of which took place in the home of Priestesses Aletheia and Spiderwoman, as well as weekend retreats in the mountains, a wedding, and a funeral.

Upon entering the setting, our initial research question was, "What is going on here, and how is it feminist or political?" Later on, however, our focus turned to examining how Dianic Witchcraft, or feminist Wicca, functions as a religion, and to explore coven dynamics and the use of ritual (see Lozano and Foltz 1990).[4] Our interview questions centered on life histories, involvement in Dianic Witchcraft and coven activities, and the magical training each had undergone.

Some time after publishing our original paper, we began to discuss how we had changed since beginning the study. This led us to reexamine our old field notes for the purpose of turning the lens on ourselves. We treated our field notes as continuous histories (Marcus and Cushman 1982), and in those pages of notes we found subtexts that addressed issues of identity and change.

Worldview

For these feminist Witches, the personal and spiritual are viewed as political. A major goal of the "Craft" is to eliminate the patriarchal "mindframe" and to replace it with feminist consciousness and actions that lead to women's liberation from oppression (Spretnak 1982) and eventually to eliminate all oppression. The Craft's emphasis is on personal experience and growth, and awakening the "power within," or the immanent Goddess (Starhawk 1988). The "Goddess," which is symbolized as an autonomous female divinity, is also a metaphor for the earth, the Great Mother, and the interconnection between every living thing. Feminist Witches experience the Goddess through ritual and meditative techniques, which they sometimes refer to as "magic." Noted Witch and author Starhawk defines magic as "the art of changing consciousness at will . . . the psychology/technology of immanence" (1988, 13).

Summer Solstice (6/24/88)

◆

Tanice:

When we arrived for the Summer Solstice ritual I felt more relaxed, more comfortable, and less intimidated than the first time there. Aletheia was the only one home, and she showed me how to "anoint" my candle by selecting and rubbing special oils on it which were designed to bring something to me or to chase it away. She further explained the process of "empowering yourself and your requests" by carving Witches' *runes*—ancient alphabetical symbols—on my candles.

The ritual that night focused on transforming gender identities into those of our own making. At one point, Spiderwoman dropped a match into a small cauldron on the altar, and it poofed into flame. We were instructed to "sacrifice the unproductive," symbolized by paper poppets. As we threw these into the fire, the Witches called out their sacrifices: "wanting to be liked by everyone," "being a nice girl," "thinking I can always help," and so on. Aletheia, dressed in an animal headdress and carrying a bow, then invoked the Goddess Diana and aimed an imaginary arrow upward. She spoke her magical intention, "to not be afraid of being wild," and we followed her example: "to write," "to be an artist," "to teach revolution!" The "magic" focused on creating strong self-images and goals and was clearly different from any I had ever heard of before.[5] Hearing the women's vulnerabilities and affirmations helped to demystify Witchcraft, and I became aware that, beyond the term "Witch" and beyond what I perceived to be their lesbian identification, we as women had much in common. I was impressed by their ritual focus on giving up taken-for-granted gender identities, which are at the heart of women's oppression.

Lammas (7/31/88)

◆

Tanice:

The Lammas ritual celebrates the first fruits of the harvest. Spiderwoman began the ritual with a prayerlike chant focusing on the need for rain (we were having a drought) and the necessity of nourishing our personal projects, ourselves, and the earth. While she relayed this message, she transformed before my eyes, and I later attempted to record it:

> Spiderwoman is so poetic with her words and her style. Her face changes from normal life-space into the ritual space; her mouth curves downward like an upside-down happy face . . . It looks very serious. She sways gently from side to side, slightly turning with her shoulders. She makes an impact on her listeners, her words are carefully chosen. Her words hit deep places. I recognize her words . . . they ring true.

During the ritual we sang songs for healing and chanted the sound "Ma." The group started the Ma chant in a very low pitch, and eventually it spiraled upward and around the circle, as each person continued the sound after taking a breath. I was awestruck by the effect of the chant, punctuated by one woman's hauntingly beautiful voice. I felt transported into an altered state:

> There was a great deal of chanting tonight, the chanting most definitely put me in an altered state of consciousness. The sound was all-encompassing . . . it seemed to clear out the cobwebs in my head. . . . The sounds that came from this group are phenomenal . . . Most people do not experience this kind of release, power, strength, togetherness. It had an incredible effect. I was drawn totally into it, totally participating, not self-reflecting, as now.

Afterward, a knife was passed around and each woman cut away a hair, symbolizing something nonproductive to be pruned from our lives. We called out, "procrastination," "wasting time" and moved to more macro issues of "pollution" and "AIDS," while placing our hair in the burning cauldron. As we sprinkled water on a bowl of earth on the altar, we made commitments to ourselves, the women's community, and the planet. I listened to the others' pledges and thought seriously about my commitment. When my turn came, I vowed to begin recycling newspapers and aluminum cans.

Near the end of the ritual, someone started "libations"—toasts of gratitude to the Goddess. Although many were personal, several concerned Wendy and me. We were told they felt comfortable with "our new sisters Tanice and Wendy"; one woman thanked us for asking questions that made her think, another said she appreciated our presence. At one point, Wendy said, "Sociology isn't the only reason I'm here" and held up the chalice of wine. Someone prompted me, and I took the chalice and thanked the group for allowing us to be with them. Full of a warm tingly feeling, I put my hand on my heart and said, "Sure this is a great research setting, but it's what's being experienced in here that counts." Spiderwoman smilingly replied, "We know." I felt very alive and connected to the women in the group.

The end result of this ritual was that we were both energized by our experience, and we began to feel a growing sense of spiritual community with these women. This moment marked a significant step in our changing feelings about them and apparently in their feelings toward us. We felt not only comfortable with but also a part of the group. They must have realized that, as they took full advantage of the situation and redefined our research membership roles at the next ritual event.

Full Moon in the Mountains (8/26–28/88)

The coven annually sponsors a mountain campout retreat. Advertised in feminist and occult bookstores, it is open to all interested women. In a sense, this is the coven's time to recruit potential coven members and converts to feminist Witchcraft.[6] We looked forward to having the opportunity to "hang out" with the Witches for several days and expected to be thoroughly socialized into their philosophy, practices, and worldview through the scheduled workshops. We had counted on taking copious field notes of our observations and conducting several in-depth interviews. We did not expect, however, to be placed in roles that would limit our goals as researchers, but this is exactly what happened.

The Witches effectively redefined our researcher membership roles from peripheral involvement to much more active ones by placing us in positions of responsibility, such as cooking for the group, moving equipment, and helping organize workshops and rituals. Although we were flattered by this expression of inclusion and acceptance, these duties were draining and they took up all our time. Attempting to keep up with their expectations, their tight schedule, and the rigors of primitive camping wore us out by the second day. It did not occur to us until much later that we had been manipulated into what felt like a greater commitment to the group. At the time, though exhausting and frustrating, it simply felt like we were helping out our friends. At one point, some women from another coven asked who we were, and the Witches introduced us as "being with" them, which somehow seemed protective, even possessive and flattering, to us. Perhaps we were being primed to become unofficial apprentices without our being aware of it. What is clear is that spending an extended period of time with the women, and being encouraged to take on extensive responsibilities for the coven's activities, helped to forge our changing researcher roles.

Tanice:

During some downtime we were talking with Spiderwoman and Aletheia and I noticed a huge lavender brassiere hanging from their tent post. Being the naive field researcher, I asked if the bra had a meaning. Without missing a beat, Aletheia told me it was the lesbian flag. Although I was incredulous, I was learning about lesbian and Witch culture and took her explanation at face value. I later used this information in a lecture on Dianic Witchcraft, and after class, a lesbian student told me that the women were pulling my leg. I felt really ridiculous and confronted the Witches at the next ritual. They laughed uproariously and said they were just playing. I decided to take this as a sign of growing affection and afterward checked things out with others before considering any explanation as "truth."

Autumn Equinox (9/24/88)

◆

Tanice:

The Autumn Equinox marked a turning point for me in the evolution of my feelings toward the coven. My fiancé was facing a crisis where we both worked. Because the situation was supposed to be confidential, I couldn't talk about it with my work friends. In effect I was silenced. So when Wendy and I arrived at the next ritual and Aletheia hugged me hello, I found myself uncontrollably bursting into tears. For some reason, I felt completely safe with her; I knew I could cry freely here. She did not ask questions, but just held me, breathing deeply, ritualistically, soothingly. This was the same "huge" woman I had been so frightened of just six months before.

I asked for special protection, and the others wanted to know what was going on. Without giving details, I broadly sketched the problem. They immediately set to providing spells. One suggested pouring "sand or sugar over a machine, to stop the wheels that are in motion from going farther." Others chimed in with talk that seemed more prank-like than magic. Spiderwoman suggested the "tree of life" meditation to create protection, and to "put mirrors on the outside" of it so whatever was sent to me would "bounce back" to the sender. The mirror imagery resonated with a meditative exercise I had learned from a Hawaiian Kahuna in my earlier fieldwork. In depicting my excruciating situation, I found the group to provide a "safe place" where I could express my silenced pain. As a result, revealing my vulnerability was an important step in my changing researcher role.

Wendy:

Shortly after this discussion, we were told we had to "take care of business" before ritual. This turned out to be a surprise celebration of my birthday. The Witches gave me cards inscribed with flowing original verse, plus oils for anointing myself and my candles. Other presents included a sterling silver pentacle and sterling and garnet spider earrings. I had no idea that the coven knew or cared about my birthday, and I was very touched by the sentiments. My field notes reveal my surprise:

> They ask me if I know the myth of Arachne and I say yes. I am *extremely* moved. It is clear I have been accepted on a much deeper level than I expected. I wonder what and who they see when they look at me.

When they presented me with the pentacle, one of the priestesses made the comment "out of the broom closet and into the sky!"— suggesting they believed that I was becoming "one of them."

Tanice:

Before ritual, Spiderwoman invited us to a "dark moon" planning session for Hallowmas the following month. This act signified our status as potential recruits, since Hallowmas is October 31, the Witches'

New Year, and is a very important ritual traditionally closed to non-members. Just as Wendy and I were reflecting on the invitation, we were asked by another coven member to come into the other room and "cleanse and purify" everyone and the ritual space—not an insignificant role. Wendy's field notes acknowledge our apprentice-like status:

> Spiderwoman gives me burning sage in a censer and tells me to cleanse people. Tanice is given water. I know that means I am to wave the smoke at them from head to toe, as I saw it done at the Full Moon ritual. Training is largely done by imitation, as explicit instructions don't seem to be given often. I have the feeling that we are considered apprentices of some sort—they tell us what to do and we do it . . . Tanice and I sprinkle and smoke (ceremoniously cleanse) them.

At the Witches' suggestion, we applied "flying ointment" to our pulse points, to facilitate altered states and bonding during ritual. Wendy records: "I find myself increasingly reluctant to record data the more I enjoy the women . . . must use more self-discipline!"

Neither of us attended to the specific activities during the equinox ritual as much as to our obviously changing status. The evening marked a definite shift in our acceptance of the Witches as well as in their revealed acceptance of us. Our willingness to try the flying ointment was a sign of our growing feelings of trust and comfort with them. We had taken on more active researcher membership roles and knew we were becoming more deeply involved with the group.

Dark of the Moon (10/9/88)
◆

Tanice:

During the first planning session we attended, we found ritual planning to be considerably less exciting than ritual participation. The consensus-based decision-making process was tedious and boring, I was feeling sick to my stomach, and we both were ready to leave long before the three-hour session ended. Just as we thought we were going to be released from this task, the group decided that it was still early and there was plenty of time for ritual. So we all moved into the living room.

Spiderwoman asked everyone to sit around a small round altar and focus on "women's tears, shed and unshed" and the pain we have experienced because we are women. This event marked one of the most excruciating processes I had ever faced in a field research situation. Spiderwoman shed her tears "for women who are raped," and she gently sprinkled saltwater from a small bowl onto the altar. As the bowl went around, the stories quietly and tearfully emerged, one by one: being beaten by a father, abused by an alcoholic husband, raped at knifepoint in bed, gang-raped, being threatened with a gun for being a lesbian. For nearly two hours, the stories poured out. They were sickening and nearly unbearable to hear. Except for the sound of weeping heard around the circle, the room was silent.

Then Spiderwoman attempted to redirect the pain into "righteous anger and rage" with the words, "I am an angry woman because . . . ," and each woman repeated the statement, filling in the blanks: " . . . because children are abused . . . women are raped . . . men pollute the earth . . ." The volume increased as we attempted to replace our sadness with righteous anger until Spiderwoman redirected us into a different visualization.

For me, the outstanding part of this ritual was the raw exposure to the hurt and pain each woman had experienced. Sitting in a circle of women and hearing each one voice her pain and abuses radically transformed my feminism and served as a consciousness-raising experience. I had an immediate visceral understanding of the violence committed against women worldwide in the name of patriarchy. I was incensed at these injustices, and at the same time I felt an incredible sense of spiritual community and bonding with all women. I knew that women had to help each other develop their own power, and I definitely felt empowered by this experience and said so. Wendy's field notes record this event:

> At some point, when things got a little lighter, Tanice said
> something about how we draw power from each other as women,
> and I suddenly turned to her and said, "Tanice, you're a Witch!"
> Everyone laughed. Tanice seemed very shocked. Spiderwoman said,
> "Are you just figuring that out?" Not sure exactly why I said that but
> was totally convinced of its validity. .

Although not comfortable with being called a "Witch," I left the meeting with a heightened consciousness of the connection between patriarchal institutions and the perpetuation and tolerance of violence against women. This was what feminists call a "click" experience. I embraced the group's political analysis of sexism, and I grasped on a deeper level the meaning of the feminist maxim "the personal is political." This experience marked the culmination of milestones on my journey: I had shifted away from my initial fear of the Witches, I was moved by my shared experience and deep sense of bonding with them, and I was quickly developing a feminist spiritual and political consciousness.

We found that as researchers we were engaging in "role making." By participating more fully in coven activities and acquiring the Witches' "first order perspective," we began "to penetrate beyond a rational to an irrational, emotional, and deep understanding" of the Witches' world (Adler and Adler 1987, 60).

Hallowmas (10/31/88)
◆

Hallowmas is a particularly significant religious holiday for feminist Witches, and participation in the closed ritual is as close to mandatory as the coven gets. It is used to mark the "dark time of the year when the veil between the worlds is thin," when the Witches remember and "call in" to ritual their "beloved dead." It is also a time to honor the women who were burned and hanged as Witches during the Renaissance, a period the Witches call "the Burning Times." This is especially important to them because they believe that approximately 9 million women died in this "women's holocaust."[7]

Wendy:

I was a bit ambivalent about the evening initially. My daughter had died eight years before, and the idea of inviting the "beloved dead" to join us was disturbing. I didn't know how I would handle it and voiced my concerns and the reasons for them. At the same time, I felt very privileged to have been invited and expected high drama and a real sense of what the Witches held sacred, which, incidentally, failed to materialize. Overall, the ritual seemed somewhat artificial, and I felt the group tended to lose focus and lack energy. Nevertheless, one incident during ritual was significant to me.

Early in the ritual, one Witch spoke dramatically about the time of year and its meaning. Draped in black veils, she waved her *athame*—traditionally a black-handled ceremonial knife—as we formed a line in front of her. My notes describe what occurred.

> Aletheia steps forward and Nete points her athame at her heart and challenges her right to enter this space. When Nete demands to know who attempts to enter, Aletheia recites all her Craft names. Nete tells her that it is better to fall upon the point of her blade than to enter in falseness, and then asks her how she enters. "In perfect love and perfect trust," is Aletheia's reply. She is embraced and allowed to pass. Nete becomes the veil through which we all must pass into the darkness, and each of us is challenged in turn. At one point, no one moves forward. It feels really awkward, so I step forward. It feels strange to go before coven members and apprentices.

I'm unsure what prompted me to do this, but suspect it had something to do with my sense of the dramatic and a need to keep the action moving. My move was greeted with warm approval by the coven members, as though I were an apprentice who had literally met an important challenge.

The Funeral (11/25/88)

In late November, when Tanice was out of town, Aletheia's father died. Wendy was contacted and told it was important to the bereaved woman that she be there (see Lozano and Foltz 1990).

Wendy:

I found that I was expected to play a part in the funeral put on by the coven, in part because I had learned many of the songs and chants that would be used, unlike most of the people who had come to pay their respects to the deceased. In addition, I found my presence was a comfort to Aletheia and signified my changing research role, as she introduced me to the family as the "coven auxiliary." During the funeral, I finally came to understand "at a gut level" that this was religious. Even though the Witches refer to their beliefs as a religion and the U.S. government recognizes it as one, I had never viewed the group or the experiences as religious.[8] Yet at the funeral, I saw how this belief system functioned to create meaning through the use of Goddess/Witch symbolism. In addition, there were elements in the ceremony that I found extremely moving. My field notes refer to religious symbols that:

> were so universal that they spoke to me. I find this religion or
> ethical belief system increasingly attractive. I like the evergreen, not
> that I believe in reincarnation. But I do believe we are all connected
> . . . each one of us, every redwood, every dolphin, every lizard
> sunning itself on every rock was born from the explosion of a star,
> and we all dance together on stellar winds.

It was one of the most meaningful last rites I have attended. It literally moved me to tears, and I had never even met the deceased! Although I knew the "personal was political," the funeral rites revealed to me that the spiritual could also be political. The Witches' beliefs were creating a new identity and source of strength for women. Through expressing their relationship with the sacred, they attempted to articulate the way to live and die in and of this world.

Yule (12/17/88)
◆

The Witches celebrated Yule and the Winter Solstice as one and the same. Part of the ritual consisted of making pledges "to the earth." This was done while softly singing, "The Earth is our Mother," as we hung homemade ornaments on a miniature fir tree standing near the altar. Each decoration represented a pledge. For example, the red top of a spray can symbolized the promise not to use aerosol cans. The ornaments were hung on the tree with great seriousness, and each pledge was met with the group's response and affirmation, "Blessed be!"

Wendy:

I had thought carefully about what I was willing to commit to do. Although four months earlier, when Tanice took her vow to recycle, the issue hadn't seemed important to me, it did now. I cut out a Neolithic-shaped female form or Goddess from a newspaper article on pollution, and as I tied it on the tree, I made my pledge to recycle newspapers. In the year that followed, I found myself taking my commitment as a "sacred oath," which, of course, it was intended to be. Initially, I was surprised at how seriously I took it, but as I grew to know the Witches' understanding of the interrelationship of all things, I became even more conscientious. Today, six years later, I am recycling everything that my city is willing to accept.

Candlemas (2/1/89)

◆

Wendy:

Candlemas is the ritual when coven oaths are renewed, apprentices are initiated, and Witches are made priestesses. Several days before the Candlemas ritual, Tanice phoned to say the Witches had informed her they wanted to do the ritual in three parts. The first part would involve only the initiated priestesses while the rest of us waited upstairs. Then the apprentices would be called down, and finally Tanice and I would be invited downstairs to "do something," and the ritual would be over. I was disappointed that we were so restricted and decided not to attend at all. Later that day, I received a call from Aletheia, who was very upset at my decision. Aletheia confirmed my suspicion that the last part was being made up for us. I told her that I respected the fact the Candlemas was closed to nonmembers and appreciated the coven's attempt to include us, but that it felt somewhat artificial, and I thought it best not to attend. My notes from this telephone call record her response:

> It's like you want to be with us because that is your work, not because you like us.

Gulp! I *did* like her! And I respected and appreciated the coven's desire to limit full participation to its members. But if I was going to drive an hour just to get there, I wanted to do research, not do something "inauthentic" made up for us.

Although I knew the telephone call was data, somehow it didn't occur to me that going there under those circumstances would also provide good data. I also failed to realize that the Witches frequently made things up. That is the nature of innovative ritual. As we spoke, it became clear that Aletheia's view of my role had changed dramatically.

She mentioned several times that the coven would be very upset when they hear we're not coming. I asked her if they would be angry and she replied no, they will miss us. She said, "Any time you come and ask to be apprenticed, the coven would accept . . . but you haven't asked. That's why your participation at Candlemas is so limited."

In an apparent contradiction, she said I was like a coven sister. It was a long, exhausting conversation, and I hung up still annoyed.[9]

Spring Equinox (3/18/89)
◆

Wendy:

The Spring Equinox celebration was unique for me. For the first time, one year after meeting the coven, I gave myself permission to "let go" during ritual and attempt to feel what the Witches were feeling. That in itself marked how my own perception of the women, of feminist Witch-craft, and even of myself had changed from the preceding year. When the flying ointment was passed around, I joined everyone in putting some on my wrists and genitals. The "trance tea," a blend of herbs supposed to facilitate altered states, was so bitter, I limited myself to one swallow. At the beginning of the ritual, when we usually "drew up energy" with chanting, Spiderwoman mentioned that there was a lot of energy in the room. We began a Ma chant and my notes reveal what I felt.

> The energy was incredible! I tried the visualization techniques from Starhawk's book, the tree of life as a path for energy through my body, and I began to feel this cone of energy rising in the air above the group and swirling . . . Tremendous energy. It was almost as though I could feel/see it whipping around the circle in yellow lines. I haven't had this experience before. But I haven't tried the techniques deliberately either.

It is clear that by this time I shared the vocabulary and the images to articulate my experience in the Witches' language. In addition, whether my experience can be explained by "interpretive drift,"[10] trance tea, or, as the Witches would have it, Witches' "sight," I had clearly stepped into a more active researcher role. The experience was exciting, even a little bit disturbing, and it certainly didn't seem "silly" any longer.

Tanice:

Although the evening was not nearly as exciting for me as Wendy, I had clearly become very comfortable with the women—so comfortable that I accepted their invitation to stay the night—something I never would have considered a year before. I wanted to interview two women who were hard to contact, and as the coven members typically spent the night after ritual, this opportunity seemed ideal. I had a great interview with Raging Dove, and afterward I slept soundly—no trepidation!—on a sofa bed, with other women curled up in chairs and on another sofa near me. I no longer saw them as kooks or as wild women who might attack me, but as women who had complex lives and families, who were seriously pursuing knowledge to become priestesses in their chosen fields of study—philosophy, ritual, acupuncture, herbal remedies. Over the course of the year I had gained the utmost respect for these women, which clearly shaped my reporting as a researcher.

Beltane (5/1/89)
◆

Beltane, like Hallowmas, is another ritual usually closed to outsiders that was opened to the two of us. It is a celebration of the "maiden coming into flower," of Spring, and self and sensuality. There had been considerable teasing about the sexual nature of Beltane, especially by the Witches who were lesbians, and we had some concerns about participating. Spiderwoman dealt with these with her usual insight and consideration, telephoning to say that anything that would happen would "be done in perfect love and perfect trust. No one's boundaries will be violated." Thus reassured, we decided to attend.

The ritual included considerable playfulness. At one point, after adorning ourselves with flowers, we stripped and got into the jacuzzi, which they referred to as "the bubbling cauldron of rebirth and regeneration." Eight women got into a tub designed for four and began to play "spin the goddess," with each of us taking a turn curled into a ball in the center and the rest of us spinning her around and laughing/cackling loudly. When the hot water began to relax us, Spiderwoman called us into the house for a ritual massage. Beginning with the crone, the eldest, and ending with the nymph, the youngest, each woman lay on a large towel while the others all massaged her simultaneously. As this was being done, one woman dipped her fingers in honey and fed the blessed one, inviting her to "taste the sweetness of the Goddess." Later another dipped huge strawberries in powdered sugar for her. All the while we massaged her with warm oils and sang songs telling her that she was a beautiful woman, she was loved, she was wonderful. One Witch with long black hair brushed it over the body of the woman being "ministered" to. Every part of the body, except the obvious erogenous zones, was thoroughly massaged.

Wendy:

My field notes show my reactions.

> I felt extremely alive and beautiful . . . *I really liked all this* . . . What I really want to stress is how safe it felt. Sensuality is a very important part of life, at least of my life, and certainly in Wicca. "All acts of pleasure are my ritual," says the Goddess. This was an evening of sensual experience without ever crossing into sexuality or violating any of my boundaries . . . the honey and strawberries, the music, the hot tub, the massage with oil, the incense, the songs and laughter, the "hair job" . . . it was a very safe and sensual and wonderful place to be.

Our willingness to participate that evening was an indication of how much we and our perceptions had changed during the course of our research. Our level of trust was so high at this point that we literally put ourselves into the Witches' hands.

Tanice:

I had been somewhat anxious about Beltane because of its sensual, bordering on sexual, emphasis. However, as I joined in the activities, my fears disappeared. In their place I felt a sense of wonderment that people could be so nurturing, caring, and sensual, yet not sexual, with each other. It was indeed a unique experience for me as a heterosexual woman. I felt captivated and refreshed by my experience, and Wendy and I talked about the ritual all the way home.

As we grew more comfortable with the Witches and their ritual practices, we became more comfortable with their worldview. Even though we gained an insider's understanding of feminist Wicca we did not become "complete member researchers." This would have required us to become apprentices and to join their coven. We did not choose to make that commitment of time and energy. I knew I would be leaving California soon, and Wendy was already thinking about her next research project. Nevertheless, it eventually became clear that the coven saw us as one of them. At our final ritual in June 1989, Spiderwoman confided that the coven was very disappointed we had not asked to apprentice and were now leaving. She said the women felt as if they were "losing two coven members in one year."

Discussion
◆

After publishing our findings (Lozano and Foltz 1990), each of us went on to do further research in the field of feminist spirituality—Tanice with separatist Witches in the Midwest and Wendy with a large California Goddess Circle that includes men in ritual. We discussed how our experience had affected us, and agreed we should write about it. But when it came to the actual writing, the self-revealing aspects of our experiences seemed to make us, as junior faculty, far too vulnerable. We were concerned that the unconventional subject matter and the methods we used might negatively affect our tenure cases. We were studying Witches, who often are mistakenly confused with Satanists, and some of these Witches were lesbians. Our methods didn't have the safety of a large quantitative study; we sensually celebrated Beltane, "shed tears" as we shared personal pain, and ritually and genuinely bonded with our "subjects." Nevertheless, as we conversed over the five years that intervened between then and now, it became clear that those research experiences helped to shape the women and the academics we are today. By silencing our own voices, we were missing an important source of data. We felt our research would be incomplete without commenting on the changes we experienced in our "inner landscapes."

Wendy:

On an academic level, understanding the power of religion to shape social relations has led me to refocus my research from gender and family to gender and religion, an area I previously dismissed. The power of religion as a social institution that shapes our realities is a subject I now emphasize in my women's studies classes. Thus, this field experience has affected both the content of what I teach and what I now research.

For almost two decades I played an active part in the political feminist community. On reflection, I realize this largely consisted of coming together with other women to work on a specific project or issue. Many of us experienced burnout during the Reagan years, giving out more energy than we were getting back. When I began this research, I was dutifully doing grassroots activism evenings and weekends, and teaching feminism during the day. It was clear to me that, except for the teaching, the joy was gone.

It began coming back with my participation in the Witches' rituals. An atheist since my early teens, I had never felt the need for a spiritual community. But on various occasions in my life, I had experienced what the Witches call *immanence* or the *Goddess*—that particular state of consciousness Spretnak (1991, 102) calls "grace" and describes as occurring when the membrane between the inner and outer worlds dissolves and one experiences "luminous moments of connectedness." The Witches gave me a framework through which to understand and a language to articulate that part of me which didn't seem to fit in and which I had been reluctant to examine. I learned that this was spiritual, that I was spiritual. So, although I still don't believe in a divinity, I have experienced Her.

There was a sense of "naturalness of fit" about some of my research experiences. These experiences brought back long summers in Wisconsin at my mother's camp for girls, where we would put on plays among the silver birch trees and have Sunday twilight meditations by the lake. I rediscovered the energy and creativity generated by women in "women's space" and so have a much better understanding and appreciation of separatist feminists and separate space.

My encounter with feminist Witches and the larger Goddess Movement was like coming home.[11] I have available to me a spiritual community that is feminist and energizing, one that values the things I value, including play and intuition. I admit that I am not always comfortable with the intuition generated nor with the essentialism bordering on simplistic biological reductionism that I continue to discover among Wiccans. As a sociologist, I cannot accept the concept of "the divine feminine." Nevertheless, the rethinking of the connections among mind, body, and spirit fascinate me. I presently drum in a women's drum circle; it is my form of meditation and "body-prayer" (Spretnak 1991).

This research has forced me to rethink my own personal relationship to the planet. The fact that DDT in our rivers can be linked directly to breast cancer among women is an image that moves me powerfully. It is an easy step to saying we are on the verge of committing matricide.

And finally, I feel that this research journey has been a healing one, one of movement toward integration of the selves into the Self. This is a difficult task indeed in a world that encourages fragmentation of the female self.

Tanice:

This research endeavor has involved a great deal of growth and movement for me both professionally and personally. On a professional level, my encounter with feminist spirituality has created a sense of continuity in my research agenda. My previous fieldwork gave me the academic and perceptual tools to understand the connections and resonance between the alternative healing group and feminist Wicca, where high drama, a sense of play, and performative ritual permeated each setting. The Witches, however, provided something that was unique, a religious setting where the female principle is viewed as divine.

Doing fieldwork in such a setting has created a shift in my life. I have moved from thinking that Witchcraft was something weird and scary, to understanding it as an agent of women's empowerment and change. Politically, I have moved toward a more radical feminism through my consciousness-raising experiences with this group. As a result, I bring attention in all my classes to issues of women's oppression and violence against women, I teach women's studies courses whenever I can and perceive myself to be a feminist researcher. I have become more active in my university and in my community on women's issues. My academic interests lie in the interplay of religion and women's health, with a focus on women's spirituality, healing the self, and recovery from addictions.

On many levels (emotionally, politically, socially, and professionally), I have moved into an understanding that the personal is indeed political. My environmental consciousness has been reawakened by this contact, and for six years now I too have been recycling "religiously." Finally, I have moved from earlier biases, which included homophobia and heterosexist beauty standards, to appreciating women regardless of sexual orientation or body shape and size. At the root of this movement is the feeling of sisterhood and spiritual connectedness that I acquired through rituals with the Witches. I now understand that spiritual separatism provides a safe place for women to discover their voices, which is an important step in the process of women's healing. Feminist ritual continues to provide a sense of deep communion and spirited playfulness in my life today.

Conclusion
◆

The experiences that facilitated our individual journeys are similar to those observed by Christ (1982). The legitimation of women's power and authority came through the sacred history of goddesses and the view of Witches as healers (Eller 1993). Our bodies were affirmed and respected, our sensuality celebrated in a safe context. Female will was affirmed during ritual as we did "self work" and made commitments to each other, the women's community, and the planet. The celebration of women's bonding was an ongoing feature. For contributing to our respective journeys, and for their generosity of spirit, we wish to thank the Witches who guided our first steps on this path.

We believe that the power of ritual had much to do with these changes in our inner landscapes. Turner (1967) saw ritual as a passage where genuine transformations of character and social relationships may occur. In the rituals created by this small group of Witches, words and symbols provided new meaning, empowerment, and the restoration of balance and harmony that McGuire (1983, 1987) refers to as healing. Mythical stories were told, guided visualizations were given, and chant and dance led us into the sacred reality that was being constructed.

Ritual consciousness is embodied, tactic knowledge (Grimes 1992). Through these forms of "body-prayer," we believe we experienced the transformative effects of ritual. We achieved the "flow state" Csikszentmihalyi describes (1975) in which "all sense of individual self vanishes." We had moments when we felt "in a time out of time, connected to 'the way things really are'" (Neitz and Spickard 1990, 24). The Witches taught us to call this experience of flow and connection *immanence*.

This theme of connection is important. Participation in other kinds of rituals (whether religious, tactic, or self-healing) have not had the same effect. Both of us have gone to traditional church services, dances, and had some counseling. We were not transformed. Jacobs (1990) says that women who are alienated from parts of themselves and from patriarchal culture experience a reintegration of self and community through women's rituals. We ask, in a patriarchal culture in which male and female are dichotomized and women are discouraged from being whole, what woman could *not* be alienated from some part of herself?

We believe the unique power of feminist Witchcraft lies in (1) the transformative potential of its innovative rituals, (2) the tactic experience of immanence through body-prayer, (3) the promise of integration of self and mind with the female body, (4) integration of the self with a spiritual community, and (5) its vision of a truly humane, peaceful, and ecologically sane world.

We are not suggesting that feminist Witchcraft is the only or even the best way to reach these goals, only that it is a way. It is clear to us that, as researchers participating in feminist rituals, we created the women we became. As our inner landscapes changed, they colored the way we view ourselves, our research, and the world.

Notes

1. The title borrows from a Goddess chant by Starhawk, Witch and noted author. It goes: "She changes everything She touches, and everything She touches changes."
2. Interestingly, this is the same language used by women travel writers, according to Mary Moris (Ms., May/June 1992, 69). She concluded that, unlike male travel writers, for women, "There is a dialogue between what is happening within and without."
3. I wasn't sure if this small group of women was really worth studying or the subject matter important enough to help my career. I now find it interesting that it never occurred to me that research on other alternative religions, all of which include men, might not be worthy of study. Obviously, I had internalized some gender bias, a particularly ironic and embarrassing experience for someone teaching women's studies.
4. Wendy Griffin was previously known as Wendy G. Lozano.

5. Prior to this encounter, my minimal knowledge about Witchcraft came from the media, a highly unreliable and misleading source. For example, the 1994 Encarta CD-ROM encyclopedia definition of Witchcraft reflects the views of the Inquisition. This type of distortion is reinforced daily by television evangelists who rail against Satanists and Witches as if they were the same.

6. Although the coven and most Wiccans would deny that they proselytize, sponsoring an "open" women's retreat filled with workshops on Witchcraft can be viewed as proselytization.

7. Although the women we studied did not know the origin of this number and accepted it as fact, it was an estimate made by Matilda Joselyn Gage in the late nineteenth century. Contemporary feminist historian Anne Llewellyn Barstow (1994) estimates that closer to 100,000 people were executed, and 85% were women.

8. Being raised a "Christmas and Easter Protestant," I never thought about the role of religion in providing meaning or community. To me, the word *religion* meant going to church and being bored listening to men preach about a divine father who might forgive me for something if I prayed hard enough, which I rarely tried to do, even as a child.

9. With today's understanding, I realize how unappreciative I was. Ritual is an act in which metaphors are used to capture meaning. The Witches had created something that was intended to evoke an alternative reality, provide meaning for us, and possibly redefine our relationship to them. Candlemas is the time of oath-taking, after all. But I didn't understand this at the time. I know I felt I was being manipulated into attending. Perhaps that helps explain my strong resistance.

10. Luhrmann (1989) describes this as the slow shift in interpretation experienced by a newcomer to a particular activity as she learns to perceive and ascribe meaning to new patterns.

11. I later discovered this was a phrase coined by Margot Adler (1986) to describe what women felt when they got involved in feminist Wicca. Several women I have talked with in the larger Goddess Movement resonate with this phrase as well.

References

Adler, M. 1986. *Drawing Down the Moon*. Beacon Press: Boston
Adler, P. A., and P. Adler. 1987. *Membership Roles in Field Research*. Qualitative Research Methods Series, Vol. 6, Newbury Park, CA: Sage.

Anderson, K., and D. C. Jack. 1991. "Learning to Listen: Interview Techniques and Analysis." In *Women's Words,* edited by S. Berger Gluck and D. Patai. (New York: Routledge): 11–27.

Barstow, A. Llewellyn. 1994. *Witchcraze: A New History of the European Witch Hunts.* San Francisco: Pandora.

Brown, K. McCarthy. 1985. "On Feminist Methodology." *Journal of Feminist Studies in Religion* 1: 76–79.

———. 1991. *Mama Lola: A Voudou Priestess in Brooklyn.* Berkeley: University of California Press.

Christ, C. 1982. "Why Women Need the Goddess." In *The Politics of Women's Spirituality,* edited by C. Spretnak. (Garden City, NY: Anchor Books): 71–86.

Clifford, J. 1983. "On Ethnographic Authority." *Representations* 1, no. 2: 118–146.

———. 1986. "Introduction: Partial Truths." In *Writing Culture,* edited by J. Clifford and G. Marcus. (Berkeley: University of California Press): 1–26.

Csikszentmihalyi, M. 1975. "Play and Intrinsic Rewards." *Journal of Humanistic Psychology* 15: 41–63.

Danforth, L. M. 1989. *Firewalking and Religious Healing.* Princeton: Princeton University Press.

Denzin, N. K. 1991. "Representing Lived Experiences in Ethnographic Texts." In *Studies in Symbolic Interactionism,* Vol. 12, edited by N. K. Denzin. (Greenwich, CT: JAI Press): 59–70.

Denzin, N. K., and Y. S. Lincoln, eds. 1994. *Handbook of Qualitative Research.* Thousand Oaks: Sage.

Eller, C. 1993. *Living in the Lap of the Goddess: The Feminist Spirituality Movement in America.* New York: Crossroad.

Ellis, C. 1991. "Emotional Sociology." In *Studies in Symbolic Interaction,* edited by N. Denzin. (Greenwich, CT: JAI Press): 123–145.

———. 1995. *Final Negotiations: A Story of Love, Loss, and Chronic Illness.* Philadelphia: Temple University Press.

Ellis, C., and M. Flaherty, eds. 1992. *Investigating Subjectivity: Research on Lived Experience.* Newbury Park: Sage.

Foltz, T. G. 1987. "The Social Construction of Reality in a Para-Religious Healing Group." *Social Compass, International Review of Sociology of Religion,* special issue on Religion and Health, 34, no. 4: 397–413.

———. 1994. *Kahuna Healer: Learning to See with Ki.* New York: Garland Publishing.

Forrest, B. 1986. "Apprentice Participation: Methodology and the Study of Subjective Reality." *Urban Life* 14: 431–453.

Geertz, C. 1988. *Works and Lives: The Anthropologist as Author.* Stanford: Stanford University Press.

Grimes, R. 1992. "Reinventing Ritual." *Soundings* 75, no. 1 (Spring): 21–41.

Jacobs, J. 1990. "Women-Centered Healing Rites: A Study of Alienation and Reintegration." In *In Gods we Trust.* 2nd ed., edited by T. Robbins and D. Anthony. (New Brunswick, NJ: Transaction): 373–383.

Jules-Rosette, B. 1975. *African Apostles.* Ithaca, NY: Cornell University Press.

Krieger, S. 1991. *Social Science and the Self: Personal Essays on an Art Form.* New Brunswick: Rutgers University Press.

Linden, R. 1993. *Making Stories, Making Selves: Feminist Reflections on the Holocaust.* Columbus: Ohio State University Press.

Lozano, W. G., and T. G. Foltz. 1990. "Into the Darkness: An Ethnographic Study of Witchcraft and Death." *Qualitative Sociology,* 13, no. 3 (Fall): 211–224.

Luhrmann, T. M. 1989. *Persuasions of the Witch's Craft.* Cambridge, MA: Harvard University Press.

Maines, D. 1993. "Narrative's Moment and Sociology's Phenomena: Toward a Narrative Sociology." *Sociological Quarterly* 34: 17–38.

Marcus, G. E., and D. Cushman. 1982. "Ethnographies as Texts." *Annual Review of Anthropology,* 11: 25–69.

Marcus, G. E., and M. Fischer. 1986. *Anthropology as Cultural Critique: An Experimental Moment in the Human Sciences.* Chicago: University of Chicago Press.

McGuire, M. 1983. "Words of Power: Personal Empowerment and Healing." *Culture, Medicine and Psychiatry* 7: 221–240.

———. 1987. "Ritual, Symbolism and Healing." *Social Compass* 34, no. 4: 365–379.

Neitz, M. J., and J. Spickard. 1990. "Steps toward a Sociology of Religious Experience." *Sociological Analysis* 51, no. 1: 15–33.

Reinharz, S. 1983. "Experiential Analysis." In *Theories of Women's Studies,* edited by G. Bowles and R. D. Klein. (Boston: Routledge & Kegan Paul.)

———. 1992. *Feminist Methods in Social Research.* New York: Oxford University Press.

Richardson, L. 1990. "Narrative and Sociology." *Journal of Contemporary Ethnography* 19: 116–135.

———. 1994. "Writing as a Method of Inquiry." In *Handbook of Qualitative Research,* edited by N. K. Denzin and Y. Lincoln. (Thousand Oaks: Sage): 516–529.

Spretnak, C, ed. 1982. *The Politics of Women's Spirituality.* Garden City, NY: Anchor Press.

————. 1991. *States of Grace: The Recovery of Meaning in the Postmodern Age.* San Franciso: Harper.

Stacey, J. 1991. "Can there be a Feminist Ethnography?" In *Women's Words,* edited by S. Berger Gluck and D. Patai. (New York: Routledge): 111–121.

Stanley, L. and S. Wise. 1983. "Back into the Personal." In *Theories of Women's Studies,* edited by G. Bowles and R. Duelli Klein. (London: Routledge and Kegan Paul): 192–209.

Starhawk. 1988. *Dreaming the Dark.* 2nd ed. Boston: Beacon Press.

Turner, V. 1967. *Forest of Symbols.* Ithaca, NY: Cornell University Press.

◆————

Tanice G. Foltz earned her Doctorate from U.C. San Diego in 1985, with an emphasis on Deviance, the New Religions, and Qualitative Methods. She taught at California State University L.A. for four years, published several articles, and married. After relocating, she took a position at Indiana University Northwest, divorced, and wrote her first book. As an Associate Professor, she teaches Sociology and Women's Studies courses, coordinates the Sociology Internship program, and is currently writing a book on feminist spirituality and healing. Tanice is a dancer, swimmer, and yoga enthusiast who enjoys hiking and gardening.

◆————

As a returning student and single mother, **Wendy Griffin** first attended community college and then U.C. Irvine, where she graduated Magna Cum Laude and received a Ph.D. in the interdisciplinary social sciences, with an emphasis in the Sociology of Sex and Gender. She is currently an Associate Professor of Women's Studies at California State University at Long Beach. In addition, she is a community activist, published novelist, koi keeper, and drummer. She is currently working on a book on feminist witchcraft which explores the use of women's bodies as sacred text.

Authors' Note: We would like to thank the referees who reviewed our paper in its earlier stages, and thanks to Arthur Bochner, Carolyn Ellis, Sherna Berger Gluck, and Rosanna Hertz for their comments and suggestions.

CHAPTER THIRTEEN

Silent Voices
A Subversive Reading of Child Sexual Abuse
Karen V. Fox

Prevention, intervention, and treatment of child sexual abuse requires understanding the perspectives of child victims, survivors, and offenders. Unfortunately, child sexual abuse researchers usually do not study the lived experiences of abuse from these perspectives, and when they do, only one perspective usually is included, making it difficult to understand the complexity of the relationships between offenders and children. Gilgun and Connor (1989), for example, conducted extensive life history interviews with 14 male offenders. Although some perpetrators expressed feelings of love toward children, Gilgun and Connor concluded that the offenders' comments reflected objectification of the children they abused. The children were not, however, "necessarily objects to the perpetrators outside of the content of the sexual acts" (1989, 251). By summarizing only offenders' views of the abuse experience, the researchers failed to probe the conflicting nature of the subject/object binary of the sex act.

Using a layered account, Ronai (1995) introduced an alternative to standard research procedures in the study of child sex abuse. In her approach she shifts back and forth between a narrative account of her abuse experiences and a theoretical analysis of abuse. The tension created by the layered method reflects the gap that often exists between the lived experiences of survivors and the codification of those experiences by researchers. Ronai challenges the authority of the researcher by juxtaposing graphic experiences of abuse with a distant voice of authority and thereby resists "force-feeding the reader a particular understanding of the world masquerading as *the* [emphasis in original text] understanding of the world" (396). By giving the reader introspective access to her experience of abuse, Ronai encourages readers to "project more of themselves into it and take more away from it" (396). Her approach shows the dynamic complexities of abuse by juxtaposing several accounts of abuse experiences, by giving the reader access to moments when the victim recalls expressing agency during the abuse act, and by suggesting that survivors can be proactive in defining their self-identities.

In this study, I include my story as a survivor and researcher of child sexual abuse with the story of another survivor and her offender. I blend these stories into a narrative account that challenges a dominant, realist reading of abuse by providing space for marginal experiences to be expressed. A subversive reading of the account gives a more complicated view of how agency and sexuality may be experienced by the offender and the child. This approach moves away from a dichotomous frame that superimposes a cultural view of abuse. The usual assumption that only the adult has agency hinders our investigation of how different types of interaction function in the abuse act. In particular, the perspective of the child victim, her sexuality, and her agency are lost in most child sexual abuse research.

The Case Study

The account that follows is written in an unorthodox manner to capture the experiences of a survivor (Sherry)[1] and her offender (Ben) as well as my subjectivity as a survivor and researcher of child sexual abuse. The text is displayed in three columns representing our three voices. By following the text, the reader moves among the voices in a weaving pattern so that a single perspective is not privileged. This three-column narrative style draws the reader into divergent perspectives of abuse.

The account is based on interviews, participant-observation, and phone conversations with Ben, a convicted sex offender, over a six-month period, including my attendance at one of his group therapy sessions. Ben was arrested for abusing his 12-year-old step-granddaughter, Mary, on two occasions. He also admitted to abusing Sherry, his stepdaughter, when she was a child. In an interview, Sherry contributed her perspective on Ben's abuse toward her and her niece Mary, her ongoing familial relationship with Ben, and the process of dealing with the public attention resulting from Ben's arrest. Contact with Sherry was limited after this because she found reading the field notes of our session a painful reminder of her abuse, and she felt incapable of discussing her experiences further.

I used an unstructured, informal interview style, asking open-ended questions to encourage Ben and Sherry to feel comfortable about discussing this sensitive topic. In Ben's case, our contact extended from private conversations about the abuse to having dinner with his wife and discussing other life experiences, such as retirement. Initially, I asked informants to describe their abuse experiences and later asked follow-up questions for elaboration on specific issues. For example, I asked Ben to tell me about the 16 years during which he claimed not to have engaged in sexual contact with children, whether or not he had sexual desire for children throughout that time, and how he now felt after being arrested and receiving therapy. I also asked Sherry to explain the feelings of love toward Ben that she expressed.

I took notes during the interviews and after participant-observation and gave them to each interviewee for review. Ben commented on field notes that contained not only the substance of our sessions but also my reactions to his abuse experiences. I wanted Ben and Sherry to read the entire three-person account and give me their feedback. This was not possible, however, because Sherry did not want Ben to read her interview notes, and she did not want to comment on his notes. I subsequently took excerpts from the field notes that focused on the experiences of Ben, Sherry, and me, as well as parts I recalled from my own abuse story. These excerpts are juxtaposed in columns to show the range of emotions and interconnections among the three of us.

Although the words presented in this text are Sherry's and Ben's, I chose how to present them. At first I attempted to get their stories "right," but then I realized that we are always in the process of revising ourselves (Bochner 1994; Crites 1971; Ellis 1995; Linden 1993). The telling of my own abuse story has changed over time until now I question whether I ever had the story "right." Rightness is "situated in relation to the present in which it is re-collected" (Crites 1986, 158) and is based on my current understanding of the "flashbacks, after-images, dream sequences, faces merging into one another, masks dropping, and new masks being put on" (Denzin 1992, 27) that I experience as I move through my life. There is not just one version of abuse, but there are many stories that are "differently contoured and nuanced" (Richardson 1994, 521). In the end, I was less concerned with "rightness" and more interested in the "practical value" (Bochner 1994, 23) of how the account contributes to current understandings and prevention of abuse.

Parts of the account are graphic in nature, and I am concerned that readers may view this as pornographic. But exposing these graphic stories may open up the "unexpected, shadow places" (Richardson 1992, 131) that can stimulate discussions about what is going on behind the closed doors of child sexual abuse. The silent voices in abuse research have an opportunity to speak in the three-person account and challenge us to go beyond seeing the issue exclusively in terms of offender/victim dichotomies.

A Three-Person Account

◆

Ben - Sex Offender

I was watching TV in the living room, and the bathroom was around the corner. I had the TV turned up loud the way I like it. I heard Mary screaming, "Poppop, Poppop." I thought maybe something had happened, that she was hurt or something. She was screaming so loud. So I went to the door. It was closed. And I didn't go in. I yelled, "What's the matter?" She told me to come in, and I did. There she was in the tub filled with bubbles. She was in it up to her neck. She said, "Look." I asked her where she

Ben - Sex Offender (cont.)
got the bubbles, and she said
she got into my wife's stuff. Well
I saw her there. And I had felt
things towards her before. I
justtook advantage of the situation. I went over to the tub and
bent down and fondled her
breasts. She sunk deeper into
the tub. Then I put my hand in
between her thighs, and she
clamped them shut and said,
"No!" So I left.

Sherry - Victim
She was 13. It's not the same
impact on a 13-year old as a
younger child. You're out of the
"I love you unconditionally"
stage. And he wasn't her parent.
He was a step-grandfather.
More damage is done when it is
the parents doing it.

Ben - Sex Offender
Later, she would still sit on my
lap and hug me. She was
starving for affection.

Karen - Researcher
I had that starving for affection
when I was a child. I had that
affection for my abuser. One
day, he took me to the bathroom with the other children in
my Sunday school class. He
wiped me and stayed too long.
It felt good. I liked this man. I
was only 5.

Ben - Sex Offender
I admitted to molesting Mark
and Sherry. I didn't want to
admit to abusing Mary when I

Ben - Sex Offender (cont.)
was arrested, for legal reasons.
You know, the sentence might
have been worse.

> **Karen - Researcher**
> (I wonder, did he pay enough
> for what he did?)

Ben - Sex Offender
I plea-bargained. One thousand
hours of community service, 5
years probation.

> > **Sherry - Victim**
> > He paid some fines. And he lost
> > the right to vote. And he had to
> > go to counseling.

> **Karen - Researcher**
> (Why did he get off?) (He tells
> me later about a man in his
> therapy group. This man was
> having sex with his 17-year-old
> girlfriend. He was 21. The girl's
> mother got him arrested. He
> served two years in prison. He
> was black.)

> > **Sherry - Victim**
> > The punishment fit the crime.

> **Karen - Researcher**
> (What?!)

Ben - Sex Offender
The only reason the case did
not go to court was because
Sherry decided not to testify
against me.

> **Karen - Researcher**
> (What's wrong with this
> woman!?)

> > **Sherry - Victim**
> > I didn't testify against him
> > because of the statute of
> > limitations. They would have

Sherry - Victim (cont.)
ripped me up one side and
down the other for the details
of my abuse. What was the
sense? I could have been put
through that, and the judge
could have thrown it out. Mary
didn't want to testify either.
Both of us were embarrassed.

Ben - Sex Offender
I love her, you know. You see
we really had a good relationship. And I think this is the
reason she couldn't testify
against me.

Karen - Researcher
(How can they have a good
relationship. I feel sick.)

Ben - Sex Offender
The district attorney wanted to
take the case to court, but
Sherry threatened to give testimony that would find her not
credible.

You know, I love her. And
she loves me.

Karen - Researcher
My mother told me that this
man who abused me loved children, "especially you four girls,"
my mother said (my sisters and
me). "Why, he always had one
of you on his lap," my mother
said. Yeah, I just bet he did.

Sherry - Victim
The prosecuting attorney didn't
think my testimony would be
considered. I think he would
have gotten a lighter sentence if
we had gone to a jury trial. The

Sherry - Victim (cont.)
prosecuting attorney and I sat down and discussed it. Ben got the maximum sentence for that crime. Remember he was only arrested for molesting Mary, not me. He did it to her two times.

Ben - Sex Offender
I know what I did was wrong. I hurt her. But more than that, I hurt many more people. I didn't realize that at the time, when I was doing it. Then one day I was at a counselor's office in a hospital, and he just said, "Do you realize how many people you have hurt?" This comment got to me like nothing had ever gotten to me before. It was then that I realized that I could never do this again.

Sherry - Victim
He's sorry for what he's done. Sorry he got caught. Anyone would be. I am sure that he is sorry.

Ben - Sex Offender
The arrest hit the papers, and it became the talk of the town. Some friends stood by me, and others couldn't believe I did this because of the positions I'd held in the community. I was on the Board of Health for four years and president for one of those years. I was a member of a civic organization for five years and was president for one of those years. This group had doctors, lawyers, and businessmen in it.

Ben - Sex Offender (cont.)
Both political parties approached
me to run for a council member
seat. I said, "No." I am not into
that. They said that someday I
could have been mayor.

> **Karen - Researcher**
> My mother tells me that this
> man, this deacon who sexually
> violated me was one of the pil-
> lars of the church. I found a
> booklet on the history of the
> southern Baptist church where
> my father was the minister. This
> man was the chairman of a
> major committee.

> > **Sherry - Victim**
> > It's scary. He's a big person. He
> > looked like a giant. I used to
> > think of him as a drill sergeant.
> > He thinks he is perfect. His phi-
> > losophy is—I may not be right
> > all the time, but I'm never
> > wrong.

> **Karen - Researcher**
> He was a big, fat man. He held
> me down on the cold, cement
> floor. The big, fat man's
> breathing gets louder and
> quicker. I can feel this. He gets
> rushed with excitement in his
> body. And so do I. I feel I am
> inside his body. My body moves
> with his. What sensation.
> Someone is unlocking the door.
> "Shut up! Stop that crying. I'm
> telling you, you better shut up!"
> He quickly pulls up my under-
> wear, brushes me off, and wipes
> my tears. "If you say anything, I

Karen - Researcher (cont.)
will get you! I will get your
father fired! And you won't
have a house to live in, and you
won't have any food to eat! And
I will kill your father if you say
one word!"

I feel the agony of his words,
but the separation of his body
and his power are more trau-
matic. He is mad at me. I must
have done something bad. He
doesn't like me anymore. What
did I do? I am sorry.

This was the last time I was
with this man, this big, fat man,
this deacon, this pillar, this man
who gave me candy and a silver
dollar.

I no longer had his affection.
I was no longer special to him.

Ben - Sex Offender
I love her, you know. You see
we really have a good relationship. She loves me, she told me
that.

Karen - Researcher
I want to believe Ben. I guess
I've always hoped that I meant
something to my abuser;
that he really did love me;
that he really did feel I was
special.

Sherry - Victim
I never felt romantic love for
him. That area disgusts me.

Ben - Sex Offender
Sherry never got mad at me.
Not really. I mean I know I
hurt her.

Sherry - Victim

Once we had a confrontation when I was separated from my husband. He asked me to be with him in a romantic way, to have an affair.

Karen - Researcher

(Yuck.)

Sherry - Victim

He was out in space somewhere that he would think I would say yes to be with him. Are you from Mars? Ben said to me, "No one cares about you, not your husband, not your mom." This is his manipulation. He is lying to me. I thought to myself, you aren't a child anymore, you are an adult. And then I started screaming and whooping and hollering. I'd never done that before because he'd hit me. I wanted him to hit me 'cos I wanted to hit him. I have felt so much better ever since I yelled at him.

Ben - Sex Offender

When they first came to live with me, they never had much before. They were eating pancakes most of the time. They ate better with us. And I took them places. Their father never did that. So I was around more, and they liked that.

Sherry - Victim

He gave us a life we didn't have. I didn't eat meat until I was 7. We lived on pancakes and eggs.

Sherry - Victim (cont.)

He gave us a home. He gave us discipline. We kids were out of control.

There is no way, shape, and form that the good he did outweighs the bad. This doesn't excuse what he did.

I've had feelings of love for him, like for a father.

Karen - Researcher

Betty Anne, his wife, says Ben and Sherry were very close. They talked about everything together. She talked with him about her period, his wife tells me. She said, "The kind of things you would think she would talk about with me, her mother."

Ben - Sex Offender

After I was arrested, my wife left me. I started seeing this other woman. She worked where I was doing community service, and she came up to me and asked me how I was doing. We had an affair. My wife came back, and I had to choose. So here I am with these two women wanting to be with me, and I didn't know what to do. This woman needed a doctor so I introduced her to my wife's doctor. And the doctor, see, knew that I was with both of them. He said to me, "What is it about you that you have so many women after you?" You

Ben - Sex Offender (cont.)

know others have said that too,
that I must have something to
attract women. Of course this
made me feel real good about
myself.

We couldn't stay in Min-
nesota. Every time we went out
to the store, people would stare.
It's a small town.

Sherry - Victim

It must be nice to just pack
your bags and leave your past
behind you.

I had people corner me in
the store and want to discuss
the abuse and the arrest with
me. They would ask explicit
details. I spent three months
not going out of the house.

People accused me of letting
him off, and I say, "Here's my
shoes. Put yourself in them.
Take a walk on the wild side."
Then I got mad, and I wiped
the word victim off my forehead!

Ben - Sex Offender

I didn't know that when I
moved here that I would have
to go to more counseling. And I
didn't really want to go at first.
But now, I am glad I did. In this
group, there are 30 people.
They don't let you get by with
lying. They know when you are
lying. And the spouses can
come. Betty Anne comes every
time. It's saved our relationship.

Sherry - Victim

I think it is sinking in. He's getting help he needed. You take responsibility.

Ben - Sex Offender

As long as we sex offenders are in denial, we can't get help. We have to admit to what we did. What I did was wrong. I know that now.

Sherry - Victim

Nobody gets well in two years.

Ben - Sex Offender

I will always be a sex offender.

Sherry - Victim

It doesn't happen that quickly. Who knows if he won't do it again.

Ben - Sex Offender

I don't ever want to offend again. So I have to remember that this is in me and to keep it in check.

Karen - Researcher

When I was divorced, for several years, I would identify myself as divorced. But now, 10 years later, I can't identify with that. I never check "divorced" on forms. I am single. And I see this as being the same with the surviving of childhood sexual abuse. I know it will always be a part of me. But I don't think I will have this need to identify with this aspect of myself so strongly that I dwell on it. Part of my healing is to get past my

Karen - Researcher (cont.)
identification as a survivor. I
have other things to do in life.

Sometimes I think the ideas
about psychotherapy keep us in
the very prison they claim to
release us from. Could it be that
alcoholics, sex offenders, and
others are sentenced by psychotherapy for life? . . . this is not
for me . . . aren't there other
ways to view this issue?

Ben - Sex Offender
I wasn't sexually abused as a
child, but my parents were
always being sexual around me.
My mother always wore a
housedress, and as it was told,
she never wore underwear. My
father always had his hands
under the dress. I started acting
out at age 5. I was being sexual
with a girl up the street.

Sherry - Victim
He needs to see it's not his
mother, father, or the alcohol.

Ben - Sex Offender
There was a lot of physical
abuse on the part of my father. I
got more beatings than the
others. One day, Dad knocked
me on the floor. I think I was
15 at the time. So I held his
hands down, and I knew I had
to live with him so I let go, and
he beat the hell out of me.

I played football as a
teenager. I played end. I got my
letters in track, basketball, and
football.

Ben - Sex Offender (cont.)

I had one year of high school and took college prep and passed, but my father didn't want me to go. I think he was afraid he would have to pay for college. So I went to trade school. I didn't finish the last year because I got drunk at school. I got my GED in 1974.

As a teen, I got into a lot of trouble. A group of us stole a car and went on a joyride. The cops would tell us to drink outside of town.

One day three cops from different towns chased me. The police picked me up later at home for speeding and peeling wheels.

I never had a dull life. Most of the time I never hurt anybody until this abuse stuff.

I got to know my step-daughter as she grew up. She is a beautiful person. I really liked her. When she was older; and we, uh, I was doing it to her, fondling Sherry, and she would ask me to put my finger in her and then ask for two fingers. Now don't tell this to my wife (Betty Anne), she would be upset by this.

Sherry - Victim

One time I was swimming in the pool. He wanted me to go in the shed and do oral sex. I swam away. He held my head under the water. Then he

Sherry - Victim (cont.)
dragged me out of the pool and
beat me with a plastic coated
wire. Then he took me into the
shed.

Karen - Researcher
(He said he loved her, that she
loved him. She said she loved
him as a father.)

Sherry - Victim
He told Mom that he beat me
because I didn't water the
tomato plants.

Ben - Sex Offender
I went to spank her one day,
and she was crying. Her pants
were down. Instead of spanking
her, you know she was crying, I
rubbed my hands all around
and under her bottom and
began to feel her. That's how it
started.

Karen - Researcher
The researcher in me wants the
details. The survivor in me is
offended by his words. My
body is aroused by his words. I
feel guilt.

Sherry - Victim
When I was 12, he raped me,
penetrated me. He told me it
was a birthday present. I started
my period the next day.

Ben - Sex Offender
I'm not sure to this day whether
it was her period or, you know.

Karen - Researcher
Yeah, I know.

Ben - Sex Offender

Most of what I did was to fondle her.

Ben - Sex Offender

My wife and I would go to adult bookstores and buy paperbacks. I'd also put a quarter in those machines and see adult movies. I'd get a few books about men with young girls. Most of them were in writing. Some foreign books had pictures with young girls and men. They were with the other books that my wife and I had. My wife never said anything.

Ben - Sex Offender

My wife was gone a lot. Every time she was gone, it was an

Sherry - Victim

He tried other times, but I was hysterical.

Sherry - Victim

He tried to rectally penetrate me. I bled, and it hurt. He tried again, but I fought him. He also used gadgets, sex toys. Candles up his rear end. He'd use vibrators. They were funny shapes. I'd put them rectally in him. Other gadgets too. I don't know what they were. Sick stuff.

I would put three sets of pajamas on, thinking he'd get fed up and leave.

Sherry - Victim

He'd make me read dirty books.

Ben - Sex Offender (cont.)
opportunity to be sexual with
Sherry. She'd leave, and I'd go
over to Sherry. After a while it
became the thing to do.

Sherry - Victim
If I stayed over at a girlfriend's
house, I'd have to pay him back
. . . with oral sex.

Ben - Sex Offender
When my wife came home, she
would go to sleep. I'd be sitting
there watching TV with Sherry
on my lap and my hand on her
breast, and we'd hear her snor-
ing upstairs. It was so natural.

Sherry - Victim
He made my brother have
sexual intercourse with me
while he watched. Sick. Sick.
Sick. Sick.

Ben - Sex Offender
It was 16 years before I abused
again. I guess I didn't have feelings about wanting to be sexual
with children because they
weren't living in the house.

Karen - Researcher
When you talk about this, with
me, about the fondling you did
with these kids, do you feel
aroused? (I am.)

Ben - Sex Offender
No. I don't feel that way
anymore.

Karen - Researcher
(I don't believe him.) You mean
you don't ever have sexual feelings for children anymore?

Ben - Sex Offender
Well, yes, but not for long, and
I don't do anything about them.

You know, you'll see a young
girl with her young body and
can't help but feel something.

It was more sexually stimulating. I liked a pelvis with no
hair. And their tight, youthful
bodies. I was about 50 when I
started with Mary. And I guess
I was at that age when I
wanted to get back my youth.
Or that's what they say. But I've
hurt enough people, and I
don't want to hurt anyone
anymore.

Karen - Researcher
(He seems to be giving the text-
book answer, and I don't think
he even believes it.)

(I am still not sure that I
believe he is being honest about
what he is doing with his sexual
feelings towards children. The
survivor in me needs to know
this. I want him to admit that
he still wants to fondle little
girls.)

Ben - Sex Offender
I have 13 weeks left of therapy.
The group decides when you
are finished though. They have
to approve it. I plan to continue
with the group even when the
group says I am finished. It
helps to have offenders in the
group who have gone through
the program because we can see

Ben - Sex Offender (cont.)
the denial in the new members.
We've been there.
    I have hurt a lot of people.
You know, it will never be over
. . . the effect. This is something
I will have to deal with forever.

Discussion
◆

Many readers have found this three-person account violent and sickening. Indeed, I respond that way as well. The tale promotes the master
narrative of abuse that centers on the offender who exerts objectifying
sexual acts on the child victim. But what gets left out by reading the
three-person account from the position of the master narrative? Are
there other ways to read and understand these accounts? A subversive
reading challenges the view of the child as exclusively a victim and
seeks to understand the child's sexuality and agency. The master narrative oversimplifies the interaction between the offender and the child
and leaves out or dismisses alternate ways that the abuse act is
perceived.

Ben and Sherry have contradictory perspectives of the abuse experience. Ben expresses a view that is not conventionally acceptable. Several times he states that he loved Sherry and that they had a good
relationship. Individuals who have read the three-person account view
Ben as a "con-artist, a manipulator," and a person who "exhibited distorted thinking." In the offender position, Ben can only be seen as an
aggressor, and his love for Sherry is considered a lie. Sherry interprets
herself through the lens of a victim, expressing the canonical story of
child sexual abuse. Respondents typically express empathy for her,
"realizing how vulnerable and powerless the child was—like all children are." But what perspective, we might wonder, would Sherry have
provided at an earlier age about the experience?

The use of the multivocal narrative and my sociological introspection (Ellis 1991) facilitate a subversive reading of abuse that

attempts to move closer to the perspective of a child's agency. By juxta-posing conflicting experiences in the three columns with myself in the center position, I found myself within the culturally mediated territory between adults' and children's bodies. As a survivor of abuse, I cannot help but be actively engaged in my research on Ben and Sherry. Researching and writing about abuse from a distance would have been misleading since I could not proceed with epistemological neutrality or moral innocence. The methodological consequence, then, was to situate my experiences of abuse in relation to the voices of Ben and Sherry and to use sociological introspection to explore these multiple interactions of perspectives. In the process, my goal became "to capture and evoke" within the three-person account "the complex, paradoxical, and myste-rious qualities of subjectivity" (Ellis and Flaherty 1992, 5). I think that had I not used this approach, valuable parts of Sherry's and Ben's accounts might be missing in my work—parts that I would be unwilling to look at face-to-face, because they challenged my way of thinking or because they were too painful for me, as a survivor, to consider.

In the three-person account, I attempt to get at the child's per-spective through the telling of my own story of abuse. I placed myself inside the characters of my abuse story and asked questions about how they might have experienced the storyline. I subsequently had bodily and emotional experiences that led me to ask questions about agency and child sexuality. I wanted to explore further Ben's "love" for Sherry, my recollection of sexual response and affection toward my abuser, and the moments when both Sherry and her niece exerted their agency in relation to Ben. I did not want to contextualize these marginal experiences exclusively within the master narrative and, thereby, dismiss feelings of love and sexual response on the part of both the offender and the victim as originating completely from the offender's manipulation.

The arbitrary boundary that society places between the sexual nature of adults and children remains intact in most studies of abuse. Research on child sexual behavior is taboo and is based on "the pre-supposition that children do not (or should not) have sharable or cred-ible knowledge of their own sexuality" (McKenna and Kessler 1985, 254). Traversing this *forbidden zone* gave me an opportunity to move beyond the socially constructed positions of Ben and Sherry to consider the perspective of children's bodies and agency.

I recognize that this study, like most, did not interview children, that there are ethical issues to be considered in doing so, and that there are pitfalls to extrapolating children's meanings from the accounts of childhood given by adults. Nevertheless, this account challenges dualistic ways of viewing agency in the abuse act and promotes the need for further study of children's agency, subjectivity, and sexuality. If offenders and survivors recall abuse events in a way that suggests that children have sexual responses and act as if they are agents in abuse encounters, then we need at least to raise questions about the importance of overcoming the taboo against studying children's sexuality. Future research that includes sensitive portrayals of child victims' perspectives of abuse and children's views of their sexuality and agency is needed to further explore the forbidden zone.

Many feminists articulate the idea that some bodies are constructed to have more power than other bodies (Bordo 1989; Grosz 1993; Hodge 1988). In particular, men's bodies define and control women's and children's bodies, which are rendered "docile" (Foucault 1979), incapable of influence or reaction. What does society lose by silencing some bodies and privileging others? More specifically, what is lost by silencing children's bodies in discussions of child sexual abuse?

Children are viewed as inherently asexual and unknowledgeable about sexuality and sexual relations. Some researchers argue that abuse is wrong on the basis that children cannot give consent. To give consent, a child must have the knowledge of what sexual contact is and must be free to refuse. Because children lack appropriate knowledge and are physically weaker than adults, they are easily manipulated (Finkelhor 1979; LaFontaine 1990; Weeks 1985). The consent argument frames discussions of child sexual abuse in terms of the preservation of children's innocence (McKenna and Kessler 1985).

Both Sherry and I felt overwhelmed by the hugeness of our offenders' bodies. We did not tell another adult about the abuse even when opportunities were available to do so. Our experiences reinforce the view that children are physically weaker and easily manipulated. But this view of children's bodies and agency also is socially constructed and needs critical review to consider whether other meanings are plausible. Ultimately, the consent argument forces discussions of abuse into a dichotomous, moral frame and stifles an exploration of the complex interactive dynamics between adults and children.

Exploring the concept that individuals and their bodies are both subjects and objects moves the abuse discourse beyond a dichotomous frame. Offenders are assumed always to be the subjects acting on children as objects. This view suggests that the solution for abuse is to fix the offenders, and the problem will go away. As Graham (1994) concluded, however, we are neither subjects nor objects, but rather we are always both, inseparably. Instead of viewing power as something possessed, as the subject/object binary suggests, Foucault (1979) provides another way of viewing modern, disciplinary power: No one possesses power, rather it circulates among individuals and institutions. The concept of dispossessed power becomes more complicated, because it is harder to point to one person or group as responsible for a social problem. Does Foucault's view of power leave us in some kind of limbo without recourse to do anything about child sexual abuse?

Under Foucault's view of power, change requires "rerouting knowledge in new directions to sustain new social relationships" (Graham 1994, 634). Black feminist thought provides a way to reconstruct the knowledge base by providing alternative perspectives from the "outsider-within" (Collins 1991, 11). In the case of child sexual abuse, children and their bodies are in a unique *outsider-within* position. When we begin to look in their direction, we may see that children can experience some degree of agency in relation to adults and even in regard to sexual relations with adults. For example, in the opening paragraph of the three-person account, Mary used her agency to tell Ben to stop touching her. Of course Ben could have forcibly abused Mary. The offender's power and agency do not, however, preclude the need to understand the part that children play in the interactional dynamics of child sexual abuse.

Although power differentials obviously exist between adults and children, there might be times when desire on the part of the child is possible. I hesitate discussing desire between adults and children. I do not want to align myself with the views of the North American Man Boy Love Association that, in general, believes that if it feels good to the child, then sex between adults and children should be acceptable. But, I am arguing that researchers need to explore the role child sexuality plays in child sexual abuse and, more specifically, how the unsexual or asexual social construction of children may contribute to a society that sexually abuses its children. Failing to do so invalidates the lived reality of children's agency.

When we bring children's agency, choice, and sexuality into discussions of adult sex with children, we capture the *outsider* voice that can produce a more open dialogue about the complexities of this issue. It is, as bell hooks says, "the silence and taboo that make coercion and exploitation more possible" (hooks 1995, 38). I think we can no longer silence children's bodies when researching child sexual abuse—to do so leads to simplistic solutions that perpetuate the objectification and exploitation of children. By including children's agency and bodies in research on sexual abuse, change can be created that reroutes "knowledge in new directions" (Graham 1994, 634) and, thereby, sustains new perspectives on understanding relationships between adults and children.

Notes

1. All names are pseudonyms.

References

Bochner, A. 1994. "Perspectives on Inquiry II: Theories and Stories." In *Handbook of Interpersonal Communication*, edited by M. Knapp and G. R. Miller. (Thousand Oaks: Sage): 21–41.

Bordo, S. 1989. "The Body and the Reproduction of Femininity: A Feminist Appropriation of Foucault." In *Gender/Body/Knowledge*, edited by A. Jaggar and S. Bordo. (New Brunswick: Rutgers University Press): 13–31.

Collins, P. 1991. *Black Feminist Thought: Knowledge, Consciousness, and the Politics of Empowerment*. New York: Routledge.

Crites, S. 1986. "Storytime: Recollecting the Past and Projecting the Future." In *Narrative Psychology: The Storied Nature of Human Conduct*, edited by T. Sarbin. (New York: Praeger): 152–173.

———. 1971. "The Narrative Quality of Experience." *Journal of the American Academy of Religion* 49: 291–311.

Denzin, N. 1992. "The Many Faces of Emotionality: Reading Persona." In *Investigating Subjectivity: Research on Lived Experience,* edited by C. Ellis and M. G. Flaherty. (Newbury Park: Sage): 17–30.

Ellis, C. 1991. "Sociological Introspection and Emotional Experience." *Symbolic Interaction* 14: 23–50.

———. 1995. *Final Negotiations: A Story of Love, Loss, and Chronic Illness.* Philadelphia: Temple University Press.

Ellis, C., and M. Flaherty. 1992. "An Agenda for the Interpretation of Lived Experience." In *Investigating Subjectivity: Research on Lived Experience,* edited by C. Ellis and M. G. Flaherty. (Newbury Park: Sage): 1–13.

Finkelhor, D. 1979. "What's Wrong with Sex Between Adults and Children?" *American Journal of Orthopsychiatry* 49: 692–697.

Foucault, M. 1979. *Discipline and Punish.* New York: Vintage Books.

Gilgun, J., and T. Connor. 1989. "How Perpetrators View Child Sexual Abuse." *Social Work* 34: 249–251.

Graham, L. 1994. "Critical Biography without Subjects and Objects: An Encounter with Dr. Lillian Moller Gilbreth." *The Sociological Quarterly* 35: 621–643.

Grosz, E. 1993. "Bodies and Knowledges: Feminism and the Crisis of Reason." In *Feminist Epistemologies,* edited by L. Alcoff and E. Potter. (New York: Routledge): 187–216.

Hodge, J. 1988. "Subject, Body and the Exclusion of Women from Philosophy." In *Feminist Perspectives in Philosophy,* edited by M. Griffiths and M. Whitford. (London: Macmillan): 152–268.

hooks, b. 1995. "In Praise of Student/Teacher Romances." *Utne Reader* (March–April): 37–38.

LaFontaine, J. 1990. *Child Sexual Abuse.* Cambridge: Polity Press.

Linden, R. 1993. *Making Stories, Making Selves: Feminist Reflections on the Holocaust.* Columbus: Ohio State University Press.

McKenna W., and S. Kessler. 1985. "Asking Taboo Questions and Doing Taboo Deeds." In *The Social Construction of the Person,* edited by K. Gergen and K. Davis. (New York: Springer-Verlag): 241–257.

Richardson, L. 1992. "The Consequences of Poetic Representation: Writing the Other, Rewriting the Self." In *Investigating Subjectivity: Research on Lived Experience,* edited by C. Ellis and M. G. Flaherty. (Newbury Park: Sage): 125–137.

———. 1994. "Writing: A Method of Inquiry." In *Handbook of Qualitative Research,* edited by N. K. Denzin and Y. S. Lincoln. (Thousand Oaks: Sage): 516–529.

Ronai, C. 1995. "Multiple Reflections of Child Sex Abuse: An Argument for a Layered Account." *Journal of Contemporary Ethnography* 23 (January): 395–426.

Weeks, J. 1985. *Sexuality and Its Discontents: Meanings, Myths, and Modern Sexualities.* Boston: Routledge and Kegan Paul.

———◆————————

Karen V. Fox received her M. A. from the University of South Florida where she conducted research on the body experiences of child sexual abuse survivors. She is currently a Ph.D. student in the Department of Sociology at Syracuse University where she is conducting research in the areas of the social construction of the body and child sex abuse. Her experiences as a Licensed Massage Therapist and body therapy instructor give her an added perspective on the body. She enjoys searching for vintage magazines in used bookstores for her collection of advertisements that she plans to use to study media constructions of menstruation.

I wish to thank reviewer Carol Rambo Ronai for her helpful critical comments and for her compelling narrative accounts of abuse. I especially wish to thank Carolyn Ellis for nudging me into adventures on the margins of sociological thinking. I appreciate the countless hours of insightful discussions with Laurel Graham, the helpful editorial critique by Sheree Wood, and the willingness of Ben and Sherry to share their experiences. I am particularly grateful for the sensitive guidance provided by Art Bochner and for his encouragement to explore the intersections of three stories of abuse.

CHAPTER FOURTEEN

Once My Father Traveled West to California

Richard Quinney

Try writing an ethnography of something very close to you. A story from the beginning of your life that takes you to the present moment. A family, silence and secrets, a few spoken words, a death, memory and love. An intimate culture, to be certain. This will take you beyond questions of participant-observation, unstructured data, case size, and interpretation. It will encompass your emotional and spiritual life, your very being. This is ethnography as the lived experience of the ethnographer.

With considerable care, I have placed these words on paper. (We imagine one another.) I work with a large fountain pen, writing with black ink on ruled paper in a three-ring binder. The writing is nearly illegible, even to me, especially after the crossing out of words and the making of new ones. After an hour, I type the few paragraphs of writing, changing words as I type. I then wait for another day. Except, sometimes, around noon, I go downtown to KJ's Tap for a beer. There, inspired, I might write a few more lines to complete the day. Not a bad life in this Midwest prairie town.

You should know that what I tell—what can be said and what can be put on paper—is hard wrought. Once writing came easily; accounts minimally related to my life poured forth. Articles and books accumulated. But as I turned to the experiences of my own life for inspiration, the pace slowed down. As I became more aware of the living of my own life, journal notes became my primary expression. My solace and salvation. A way of making sense of the daily ebb and flow, of the past's hold on the present. Occasionally I would write an essay—conceived as personal essay rather than abstract article. Collected finally as a book, *Journey to a Far Place*. Now, the living of a life—my life in connection to all life—is my field of work. A writing now and then from scattered notes. Words hesitantly committed. The play of memory and imagination. Time present.

A few paragraphs of writing each day. (Keeps the doctor away.) One binder page per paragraph. This one to set down what I might explore in the essay, this ethnographic essay. A multitude of ideas and events. How to focus? Which door to enter the house of many rooms? Begin with this: the myth of the wanderer. The hero who spends a lifetime in search of the meaning of human existence. Add to this the father, the mother, and the brother. Concretely, a farm family in the Midwest, in the first half of the twentieth century. Enter darkness, the son's treatment of the father—to become himself. Then years later the son's redress, atonement. Ethnographer in holy quest. Now the door is open. We may enter.

The inspiration for this story began with an event of a summer ago. In the fading veneer music cabinet on the front porch of the farmhouse, my mother found a packet of letters. The letters must have been placed there shortly after the California-style bungalow was built in 1929. The letters were written by my father three-quarters of a century ago on his trip to California. After making copies, I returned the packet of letters to the cabinet for safekeeping through another winter of cold and summer of heat.

My father had written the letters to his aunt Kate and his sister Marjorie. After the fall harvest in September of 1924, he and his good friend Mervin Kittleson set out in the Model T Ford. My father then would have been 24 years of age. Reaching the newly constructed Lincoln Highway, they traveled west across the plains and over the Rockies to San Francisco. They would stay in California for six months, working first in restaurants and eventually with a crew building towers for the power and light company. It was the one big trip my father would take in his lifetime. Returning to Wisconsin in March on the Southern Pacific, he settled into a life of farming. He married my mother in 1930, farmed the land, and raised a family.

The letters from the trip are filled with descriptions of adventures along the way, notes of photographs taken, and always concern about family and friends and the chores back home. In a January letter to Marjorie he writes: *Does pa water the stock in the barn and does he ever use any bedding? That cement floor is awful cold. Bet Buster is a big dog by now. Did you folks bank the house this winter? Think I'll send my shirt back the middle of the week, then if you'll change it for one with a 15-1/2 collar. There will be quite a change on farms around home this spring when people start moving.* In March he writes that he will return at the end of the month, as his father requests, to begin spring planting. But he still has things to see in the two weeks remaining. A band concert and vaudeville show at Long Beach, a trip to Catalina Island, and a week in San Diego and Tijuana, Mexico. He bought a new black cowhide suitcase for the return home.

The black suitcase rests on a bench in the dusty attic of the farmhouse. In the music cabinet on the porch is the abalone shell my father bought as a souvenir on Catalina Island. In the music cabinet also is the tattered sheet music for the song my father used to sing while we did the chores in the barn: "How 'Ya Gonna Keep 'Em Down on the Farm (After They've Seen Paree)?"

It has been 25 years since my father, on a cold and gray November day, walked into the machine shed while making a repair on the tractor, and died. The next morning, I made the flight from New York City to Milwaukee and drove in a snowstorm with my cousins 60 miles southwest to the farm. Five miles north of Delavan in the darkness of evening, my mother stood waiting. She still lives on the farm.

The potato famine in Ireland of the 1840s brought my father's grandparents to this country. John Quinney and Bridget O'Keefe both emigrated from County Kilkenny and settled in Yonkers, married there, and gave birth to two of their five children. The lure of farmland and a new life in Wisconsin inspired them to move by steamboat up the Hudson, through the Erie Canal, across the Great Lakes to Milwaukee, and finally to the village of Millard in Walworth County. There they rented a farm until they earned enough by 1868 to purchase the 30-acre homestead a few miles to the south. The site is still called the old place.

A shallow valley left by the last glacier runs through the middle of the farm. For as long as could be remembered, muskrats had built their houses on the fringes of the pond that lay at the foot of the gently sloping hills. Red-winged blackbirds returned each spring to the marsh, and cowslips sprang up among the bogs. Red-tailed hawks soared all summer long high above the giant oak trees. And on the sandbar at one end of the pond, women washed the week's laundry. In the silence of winter, an occasional field mouse made its way over the snow.

There were others on the land long before the settlers came. The Chippewa, the Ottawa, and the Potawatomi. A band of Potawatomi had summered for many years around the edge of the marsh. Among the trees they had built their circular houses of saplings, bark, and skins. They had fished in the creek that flowed through the marsh, and they had hunted in the surrounding woods. Bridget had told my father of seeing the Potawatomi walking across the fields years later, looking at the place that had once been their home. While growing up on the farm, I looked for arrowheads in the plowed fields each spring.

John Quinney, born in 1860, the son of John and Bridget, stayed on the homestead, bought more acres, and farmed the land. He married Hattie Reynolds of nearby Rock County. Hattie died a few years later of consumption, leaving John with two daughters, Marjorie and Nellie, and a son, my father Floyd, born in 1900. Little Nellie died at the age of 18 months after choking on a raw green pea. The earliest memory I have is of my father's father coming across the field from the old place to help with the morning chores. It was the last year of his life, 1939, when I was 5 years old. I heard my father say, "Here comes the old man."

My father stayed all his life on the farm. With the exception of the trip west to California.

Before the trip begins—before I attempt to recount the travels of my father and Mervin—it is important to note that among the things my father packed for the trip was the Kodak camera. The black Autographic Kodak Jr. with the folding bellows. With the packet of letters on the porch was an envelope of photographic negatives from the trip. The original prints had been sent with the letters to Kate and Marjorie. I have made prints from the negatives. The camera survives in the attic of the farmhouse.

Only last weekend, on Sunday afternoon, another discovery was made. My wife and I were visiting my mother. We drove to the schoolhouse my mother had attended 80 years ago, gathered fall apples, and had coffee together at home. I had asked my mother earlier if she could arrange a visit with Alice Kittleson, Mervin's sister. In her 90s, she lives

Beginning the trip to California, the morning of September 16, 1924. Mervin Kittleson on the left, Floyd Quinney on the right. (All photographs used in this chapter are Quinney family photographs.)

in Delavan, alone now. Mervin had lived his last years in the house of his sister. I showed Alice the prints I had made from my father's negatives and read to her portions of my father's letters. She then brought out her family album to show me a photograph. I had not known of its existence. It was the very first photograph of the trip, taken by Alice just as my father and Mervin were about to begin their journey. In the driveway of the Kittleson farm, Mervin and my father stand beside the Model T. Luggage is strapped to the running board. Mervin has placed his cap on the radiator and strikes a pose. Both are dressed in their traveling suits. Alice kindly gave me the photograph, and I have made a copy for you to see.

They were now on the road. Leaving early Monday morning, September 16, 1924. They drove southwest to Beloit, down to Rockford, along the Rock River to Dixon, and then onto the Lincoln Highway that would take them all the way west. The adventure of a lifetime had begun.

Reaching Clinton, Iowa that evening, they were 120 miles from home. The first lines home were written that evening on a postcard to Aunt Kate: *Arrived here at Clinton, Iowa at six o'clock. Are spending the night at the tourist camp. Have just gone over the Mississippi River. Had three flat tires, but didn't have to buy any new ones.* Signed *Floyd.*

Certainly Aunt Kate would be the first person my father would write to on the trip. Kate, his father's older sister, had taken over some of the duties after my father's mother died, when my father was 5. My grandfather never married after Hattie's death, telling my father, "I would never find another woman who would be as good to my children as Hattie was." Kate worked as a dressmaker and seamstress in the homes of the rich in Chicago. She had lived for periods of her life in their houses and apartments. She never married. Kate would have been 69 when my father left for California. Years later, on an April night in 1942, my father came up from the house at the old place and told us that Kate was dying. Shortly afterward, the old house was torn down. For the rest of his life, my father lamented the loss of Kate's button box. Lilac bushes from long ago continue to grow around the crumbling foundation.

My father writes to Kate after two more days on the road. From North Bend, Nebraska, a few miles west of Omaha: *Camped last night at Council Bluffs, Iowa. Crossed the river into Omaha, Nebraska this morning. Have driven 64 miles this morning. Most all pavement since we got to Omaha. Have had fine weather so far. Iowa roads were real rough and hilly.* On a postcard written the same day to Marjorie, he notes that *we seem to be crossing railroad tracks all the time. The trains go past us but don't have time to wait for us.*

Today Lincoln Highway continues to take the traveler west. It runs through the middle of this Illinois prairie town where I now live. Each day I cross the busy highway, DeKalb's main street, to get the morning newspaper, to go to the bookstore, or to make a doctor's appointment. Travel east or west in this country on U.S. 38, 30, or on Interstate 80, and you are likely to be on or alongside the old Lincoln Highway. I followed the route from DeKalb to Kearney, Nebraska on a speaking tour not long ago. You can travel on Lincoln Highway 3,300 miles from Times Square in New York City to Lincoln Park in San Francisco. The highway was built to transport us to other places.

Traveling on Lincoln Highway. *Railroad and dirt road in Nebraska.*

A highway crossing the continent was first proposed in 1912. Once the route was decided on, after great deliberation among promoters of the automobile, portions of the road began to be surfaced. The first seedling mile was completed near DeKalb in the fall of 1914. Until the great popularity of auto touring in the 1920s, travel over the highway was a pioneering experience. How the highway became an integral part of American culture—an automobile culture—is well documented in Drake Hokanson's book *The Lincoln Highway: Main Street Across America.* Enough to note here that my father and Mervin, reaching Lincoln Highway in their Model T on a September day in 1924, were riding the crest of the great tour west. Road maps, guidebooks, filling stations, tourist camps, and miles of unpaved roads, all these were part of the new life on the road.

On the fifth day of travel, after leaving Omaha, my father and Mervin had reached Laramie, Wyoming. It was Saturday night, and my father writes to his sister Marjorie. *Camped at Cheyenne, Wyoming last night. Froze ice in front of our car. Cool here all day. Went to the Methodist church this morning and then Mervin drove 53 miles here to Laramie. We had a hamburger sandwich in Cheyenne and they were only half done. Mine made me sick to my stomach. Never was so sick in my life. Fed the fish all of the 53 miles. Was so weak just couldn't sit up. Mervin went to the store and got some oranges for me and my appetite came right back.* But they have had *no tire*

Laramie, Wyoming. *Lots of tourists at the tourist camps. About 15 cars here tonight. We use our pillows twenty-four hours each day. Sleep on them at night. Sit on them all day.*

or car trouble in the last three days. And my father's hayfever left him back in Nebraska. *Am feeling fine now.*

Marjorie was 29 when my father started on the trip. She would live only 11 more years, dying of a ruptured appendix in 1935. I have a snapshot of her standing in a long dress in back of the house at the old place. A fur stole is draped around her shoulders, over a checkered coat. She is wearing a fine hat. And she is beautiful.

For most of her life, Marjorie worked with Kate, tending the homes of wealthy families in Chicago. In the summertime, she worked in the houses and cottages of the same families who vacationed around Delavan Lake. Many years later, long after her death, my father revealed to me, reluctantly, that she had owned and operated a tavern a few miles southwest of Delavan on Highway 14 during the last years of her life. Wherever I have lived, I have kept a framed photograph of Marjorie on my desk.

Over the years I have tried to learn more about Marjorie. I have talked to aging neighbors who knew her. Once I found the house of the man she had dated for some years, a house I had identified in a photograph from her black photo album. The present owners invited me in and guided me through the house. Marjorie's friend, Lloyd Latta, had operated an auto repair shop back of the house. I was told that his sister Ruby had married a doctor and lived in the big house at the far end of the street. I knocked at the door, and there was no answer. Another day I will try again. Driving back on Highway 14, I passed what once was the tavern Marjorie owned and operated. Now converted to a strip and dance establishment.

My inquiries have had a singular result: Q: "Did you know Marjorie?" A: "Yes, I knew her well." Q: "What was she like, her personality, her life?" A long silence inevitably follows. Then a fading line about not knowing her that well. I suspect that Marjorie was an independent woman in her time. Not choosing to be a farmwife, a teacher, or a secretary. She followed her aunt Kate's fashions of dress. The styles of Chicago's society women—the women Kate served as seamstress and dressmaker—set the standard. And for a woman to own and run a tavern in the 1930s must have raised eyebrows and brought censure. Marjorie was living as many women no doubt wished to live, and she paid the price for being different. To this day, the punishment of silence—to say that Marjorie did not exist.

The ghost in my life that I try to keep alive. One of my first investigations upon returning to the Midwest was to search through Marjorie's probate records at the Walworth County Courthouse. At the time of her death, Marjorie had about $400 in savings accounts and a 1930 Ford coupe valued at $30. She had half interest in the tavern on Highway 14, located 10 miles from the farm. Included in the inventory of stock were the bottles of liquor, tobacco and cigarettes, candy and nuts, glassware, the bar and four stools, two tables and six chairs, a radio, the cabin in back of the tavern, three beds and accompanying springs. Her appendix had burst on an October day, and she had been rushed to the hospital in Beloit. My father chose to tell me little. And he missed Marjorie for the rest of his life.

On the road west, the terrain had changed abruptly since leaving Cheyenne. Gone were the gently rolling plains of eastern Wyoming, and the ascent of the mountains had begun. The highest elevation on Lincoln Highway would be reached at Sherman Summit, an elevation of 8,835 feet above sea level. The Continental Divide would be crossed midway in the state. My father continued his Laramie letter to Marjorie with a description of the last day and a half of travel. *All one sees is hills on both sides covered with big boulders ready to roll down any minute. And some pine trees. Quite a lot of snow also.* But, fortunately, *have had no tire or car trouble in the last three days.* The cost of gasoline has risen from 13.9 cents a gallon to 20 cents with reports of 30 cents a little farther on.

He concludes the letter to Marjorie. *We meet cars from every state on the Lincoln Highway. Only a couple from Wisconsin. Lots of tourists at the tourist camps. About 15 cars here tonight. We use our pillows twenty-four hours each day. Sleep on them at night. Sit on them all day. We intend to get to Salt Lake City in about three days but you won't have time to write us there. And we don't know which trail we will take from there. But in case of sickness or anything like that a telegram would find us at the tourist camp. Had a chance to get a job with a threshing gang. Will close and make our bed. As ever your brother.*

Two days later, across the Continental Divide at Rock Springs, my father posts a card to Kate. *We have been traveling through mountains and deserts for the last day and a half. Haven't seen any trees or green grass in that time. Just sand and rocks. Just had dinner here for 35 cents.* The trip thus far—1,400 miles—has cost him only $20, expenses being split between the two of them. *Fine weather here. Good thing as the roads are just dirt roads.*

They reach Green River, Wyoming. My father takes a photograph of the butte at the turn of the road. Sending the photograph home, he writes: *This is the first town we came to with green trees after spending six days on the desert. Sure looks nice. Was named Green River.*

Two more cards are sent to Kate before the travelers reach San Francisco. The salt flats and the uninhabited dry desert beyond Salt Lake City have been crossed. In search of better terrain, they decide on a southern route that will take them down into the middle of Nevada. To Tonopah

Green River, Wyoming. *You will notice the large boulder on top of the mountain. Looked ready to roll down on the town anytime.*

and Mina—on what is now U.S. 95—and then up to Carson City. My father writes that they have been two days crossing the desert. The roads are awful. *Just one big hollow after another in the road and dry and dusty.* He is writing from a bunkhouse on a ranch 40 miles from any town. The next morning, as they are leaving, my father takes a photograph of *Mervin eating a pear near the bunkhouse where we stayed all night.*

The next night, now in Mina, my father reports that they are still traveling on bad roads in the mountains and desert. *Broke a spring on the car yesterday but got to town all right and bought a new one and put it in ourselves this forenoon. Every little ways we see wild horse or mustangs near the mountains. See quite a lot of turkeys. One flock of about one hundred.* They have traveled, by their calculations, 2,117 miles. *Only 460 miles to San Francisco.*

Up to Carson City, over the high Sierra Nevadas, through Donner Pass, and the descent to the valley around Sacramento. Then on to Oakland and a ferry ride across the bay to San Francisco. Extreme changes in landscape and climate certainly were encountered. Nothing is reported on these last miles of the trip west. The travelers were relieved and thankful to have successfully made the long trip from Wisconsin to

Nevada, between Ely and Tonopah. *This is a bunkhouse on a ranch where we stayed all night. Forty miles from one town and 160 from the next. It was built out of squares of stone and thatched roof covered with mud.*

California. They had been on the road for 18 days. And they were excited, I am sure, and filled with anticipation for what the next months in California might hold for them.

Growing up on the farm in southern Wisconsin, I sensed that we had been on the edge for a long time. Irish Catholic immigrants, now lapsed from the faith, in a farming community of Norwegians and Germans. Eyes turned toward the city, Chicago. For generations, a removal that comes with living on the border of a strange land. A loosening of the communal bond, but a release to the world. This is the home country to which I returned after years of traveling from one place to another. Living here and there. On a road that finally leads to home.

The ethnographer had escaped for years the life of the past, the pains as well as the joys. Returning to the farm a decade after the death of his father, he felt the past impinging on the present. He had grown up on a farm, and he knew that he could never leave it completely. His education in the rural schools of the 1940s continued to provide him with values and ideals. In all that he had learned in his years of travel, in all

Lincoln Highway, Nevada. *We have been two days crossing the desert and awful roads. Just one big hollow after another and dirty and dusty.*

that he had accomplished in his lifetime, growing up on the farm most surely gave him his identity. As time passed, he had found himself drawn to the land of his birth. More than ever, he felt himself a part of the natural landscape of the place. He would be remembered in the earth.

His flight from the home place 35 years ago had been to affirm life in a larger world. A world larger than the one circumscribed by a small farm in the Midwest. He, this ethnographer of today, traveled to know what the world might hold. But in the travel lay the contradiction and the tension: uprooted, now in need of a home. The father, no longer there, became central to the return.

When I was young, my father's age was easy to remember. Born in 1900, he was always the age of the new year. His birthday came in March as the Wisconsin winter was beginning to show signs of breaking. Farming all his life on the old place, he gradually added land until the farm reached 160 acres. He left Dunham School after completing the eighth grade, and he did not go on to high school in Delavan. His father needed him on the farm. He also worked for a time as a weaver in the Delavan knitting mills. There he learned the knitter's knot, tied so tightly that it could pass through the needle of a machine. Years later, with great pride, he taught me the knitter's knot. He also took on a milk route that would last for years, hauling cans of milk to the Bowman Dairy in Delavan. He hauled milk first with a team of horses, then with a platform truck in the 1930s.

Growing up on the farm, I heard neighbor's tales of my father's youth and good times. He had owned one of the first Model Ts in Sugar Creek township. Growing weary of the sporting life, he settled into farming after a near-fatal skid on his Indian motorcycle on the gravel road near the farm. It was after the fall harvest of 1924 that he and Mervin Kittleson set out in the Ford for California. On his return, he married my mother, farmed the land, and raised a family. After the Second World War, my father would occasionally tell me that someday he hoped to sell the farm and open a hamburger shop in town. Something that would take him to town and put him in contact with other people.

The nature of farming changed rapidly after the war. My father barely kept up with the latest farming techniques, as agriculture moved from family farming to agribusiness. As retirement neared, the farm work was reduced, and expensive changes in farming practices were avoided.

The fall of his 69th year, my father and mother visited me and my family in New York City. I was about to become a full professor; it was that stage in my academic career. My father and I walked the streets of the city. As we walked the Bowery, a man in rags lay sleeping in a doorway, and my father cried. Sitting together at Dunkin' Donuts on the corner of 3rd Street and Washington Square East, I noticed a dullness in his eyes. A dumbness, I thought at the time.

The last night of their visit, sitting around the dinner table, my father told us all that the end was not far off for him. "I take the medicine that the doctor prescribes for my heart," he said, "but sometimes my heart flutters." Immediately, I replied, "No, you're going to live for a long time." The next morning at Kennedy airport he carefully grasped my hand, for the first time in our lives. Two weeks later he died.

From the time of arriving in San Francisco on October 3rd of 1924 to leaving Los Angeles on March 23rd, 1925, my father wrote 19 letters home to Kate and Marjorie. At least these were the letters saved and eventually stored for 70 years in the music cabinet. Letters were written to others. My father mentions letters being sent to his aunt Mary, to Mary's son Howard, and to his uncle Bill in South Dakota. When he mentions sending a letter home, he is writing to Pa. These letters, for whatever reason of family history, have not survived.

Two days after arriving in San Francisco my father writes to Kate. The expenses for the trip from Wisconsin to California have been calculated. A total of $52 each, including all auto expenses, eats, groceries, and camp fees. They are now staying in an auto camp, and the fee of 50 cents a night includes the use of the laundry, hot and cold water, and a shower bath. *A slow rain all day. Jobs seem to be scarce around this city. If we don't find work here we will start for Los Angeles.*

In San Francisco, my father is impressed with *lots of nice homes or rather mansions with beautiful flowers and trees.* They buy four pounds of grapes for 15 cents, compared to 30 cents a pound paid for grapes in Delavan. *Was down to the ocean beach the other afternoon and saw some real waves.* And *there are all kinds of amusement places where one can spend money.* He closes the first letter from California with concern and advice that will set a pattern in all his letters. *I left a gallon bottle with some distilled water in it out in the garage. Will you empty it out sometime so it won't freeze and break the bottle. Don't save the distilled water for it won't be any good.* He says that he will check for mail from home at the post office in Los Angeles. *Feeling fine and hope you folks are the same.*

Later in the week a letter to Marjorie. *Got to Los Angeles at noon. Reminds me of Chicago. Buildings sixteen to twenty stories high and people galore.* They drove through Hollywood on their way into Los Angeles. *Fine homes with pretty flowers and big palm trees. Surely a rich man's city.* But nothing grows without irrigation. *Bought a ten quart pail of oranges for 15 cents today.* And signs of the old ailment: *Don't know but what my hayfever is coming back again. Have had one continuous sneezing all day and tonight my head is partly filled up. Felt fine until we got 200 miles south of San Francisco.*

This is the illness that my father will have all his life. Years of working in moldy hay was his explanation for the source of his hayfever. Often he would come into the house at night with an asthma attack. A variety of medicines would be inhaled or taken by pill. I would awaken in the night to the gaspings for breath. No doubt the heart became damaged from years of lacking oxygen. In the mix of genes, something of the immune system has been inherited from my father. But I have found some relief in occupations removed from alfalfa and the dust of the field.

My father and Mervin continue to look for work in Los Angeles. *They tell us there is plenty of work out on the ranches but can get that kind of work 365 days a year at home.* Later in the week, work is found in a restaurant downtown. *Work from 10:00 a.m. to 6:00 p.m. Get two meals. My choice of anything in the restaurant.* Mervin finds a restaurant job also, with different hours in another part of town. My father tells Marjorie that *we see lots of signs Waitress Wanted but it is hard for a man to get a job unless he wants to go on a ranch and there isn't one out of twenty-five that knows anything about a ranch. Most of them want city jobs. That's the way with us too.*

They begin to explore the city. *Sunday we went to Sunday School at the Broadway Christian Church and stayed for church also. Then we had dinner and went to Pasadena in the afternoon. When we got to the park they were just getting ready to give a concert. So stayed for that. Was very good. Have a bill of it. Will send it so you can see what it was. Got back to Los Angeles at seven o'clock and went to church again at 7:30.*

In the same letter to Marjorie, my father asks, *How is pa coming with the work? Does he still go to the corner with the milk? Suppose the nights are getting chilly now. Are the potatoes dug and how are they?* Then he reports that three cars from Illinois are parked beside theirs in the auto camp. *Saturday night we all got together and had a regular party. One woman from Chicago is surely a twin sister of Sof. Dunbar. Just kept us laughing all the time. Both of us like this city real well. My head fills up some at night.*

I have to keep reminding myself that this man I call my father is a young man of 24 as he travels and writes these letters. I was not to be born—his son—for another 10 years.

Three days later he reports in a letter to Kate that he has quit his job at the restaurant. *The Boss and I didn't agree.* But there are other things to do. *Good picture shows here for ten cents. Went to one last night. Jackie Coogan in "Robinson Crusoe." Was real good.* He observes that they *see all kinds of women barbers here. Also women selling newspapers. Anything to make a living.* They are hearing from home. *Got the papers Marjorie sent. Find lots of news in them. Seems good to read home news.* In a letter from Mrs. Kittleson, they are told that Morris Johnson was showing the silo fillers a new gun he had when it went off and the bullet went through the screen door of the house and just missed his son Arthur and two other men. My father wonders if the cows now are giving much milk, and suggests that if the chickens are fed all the grain, water, and oyster shells they want they ought to lay. *Weather is just fine. Sleep nights with our car windows open.*

By the end of October they have found jobs again. They are working for the power company putting in forms and pouring concrete. The pay is 50 cents an hour, $4 a day. They are paid even when the cement mixer breaks down and there is nothing else to do but *kill time.* They have changed their living arrangements. *We have gotten tired of sleeping in the car and eating at restaurants so we rented a two room cottage for five dollars a week here at Huntington Park. It has a real bed, tables and chairs, electric lights, water, and a two burner gas stove. Also have use of laundry and shower bath.* They will work with the power company for the rest of their stay in California.

A week into November my father sends Marjorie a letter written on a Sunday night. He and Mervin have just returned from downtown. *Had supper, got a haircut. Rained all day and still raining steady tonight. Hope it stops before morning as we want to go to work.* He plans on saving $10 a week while the work lasts. *There is an Irishman working with us by the name of Jack Brett. He is twenty-eight years old. Has been in this country ten years but has the Irish brogue. Keeps us laughing most of the time.* And then the concerns about the chores back home: *Did you folks trade drakes and gander? It would be better to trade gobbler. Ought to keep four hen turkeys. Ole Rasmusson said he would trade ganders. How many ducks did you keep? If the Ford starts hard there is a five gallon can of winter cylinder oil upstairs in the granary. Suppose it keeps pa pretty busy doing chores now. Hope you are all well.*

The next Sunday night he tells Marjorie about their day of going to the Baptist church in the morning and driving to Venice, Ocean Beach, and Santa Monica in the afternoon. *Was a dandy trip.* A perfect day with a clear blue sky and a warm sun. *Will never regret this trip as one could never tell you the sights without seeing them with your own eyes.*

After dinner we took a car and went out to Venice, Ocean Beach and Santa Monica. It has been a perfect day.

Mackerel from ten to twelve inches long were being sold from a boat for five cents apiece. All cleaned and scaled at that. At night they went to the Broadway Christian church. My father tells Marjorie that the weather of California in November is like Wisconsin's August weather. *Does pa keep all the stock in the barn now nights?*

In December they are offered an increase in pay to 95 cents an hour for putting up steel towers. The work will mean climbing on towers 90 to 100 feet in the air. They will take the examination and work the high towers.

They continue to receive letters and newspapers from home. My father requests a copy of *True Story* magazine. The Ford breaks down after two bearings burn out. *Our Ford did so much pounding everyone took a good look.* They climb to the top of a hill high above Long Beach and view hundreds of oil wells that run night and day seven days a week. *No wonder some get rich from the top of that mountain.* For breakfast they cook oatmeal, fry potatoes and bacon and eggs, have bread and butter and cookies, coffee, and fruit. During the day—pork chops, beefsteak, and sometimes veal chops. Since coming to California, Mervin has gained 13 pounds, and my father has gained 9 pounds, now weighing 178 pounds. They have moved from the rooms at Fruitland Auto Camp and are living

Went to church this morning here at Seal Beach. Are staying home this afternoon as we have been everywhere around here.

in a cottage near Seal Beach. They continue to go to the movies and have been to some vaudeville shows in Los Angeles. *Is pa cutting any wood these days and what are you burning to keep warm? How is Dick the canary standing the cold weather? Will ring off hoping you folks are all well.*

At Christmas my father receives in the mail a shirt from Marjorie and a necktie from Kate. *Many thanks to both of you for remembering me.* From a girlfriend in Delavan he receives a box of six handkerchiefs, three white ones and three with colored edges, initialed. Kate goes to South Dakota to be with her brother Tom who dies at the end of the month. Christmas day my father and Mervin are invited to dinner at the Fredrickson's. *Had a good time and a dandy turkey dinner with all that goes with it.* They play pool and go to church. On December 28th my father reports the highest tide of the year with the water coming up to their cottage door.

The new year arrives and seals come up on the beach near the cottage. My father kids Marjorie that *maybe you would like a seal skin coat. If so I'll catch you a couple. ha ha.* They continue to work from 7:30 in the morning to 4:30 in the afternoon, with a half hour for lunch, and on Saturdays they quit at 1:00. They have received a box of homemade fudge from a friend of Mervin's. They have gone to a show titled "What

Stayed at Long Beach all afternoon. Went to a band concert at the auditorium and to a show and vaudeville.

Shall I Do," starring Dorothy Mackaill. Plans are being made for a trip to Catalina Island. And my father is beginning to think about buying a suitcase for when they will have to pack and return home. *The old one is pretty well shot.*

The February days are getting longer. *Sun rises a few minutes earlier and sets later every night. Real foggy.* Oil is gushing 100 feet from a well two miles from the cottage. *Some sight.* Shows and vaudeville at Long Beach and *a glass show where a man made everything you could think of out of glass.* A fish dinner, *best I have ever eaten, all for 30 cents.* My father asks Kate, *What does pa want to buy another horse for? Has too many now to farm with.* He notices all of the auctions and the selling of farms in a copy of *The Delavan Republic,* which Kate has sent to him. *Will surely be a lot of moving around home this spring.*

The last week of February my father writes to Marjorie to tell her about the trip to Catalina Island on Sunday. From the boat Avalon he took pictures, *and if they are good will send some home. There were over 500 passengers on the boat. About ten got seasick and fed the fish. Saw a whale come to the top and gush water in the air three times then disappeared. After we reached Catalina Island we took a ride on the glass bottom boat. Just wonderful to see animal and plant life in the ocean. Could look down in the*

Yesterday we went to Long Beach to church. Stayed at Long Beach all afternoon. Believe I told you all about the amusements there.

water to the depth of 75 feet seeing the different kinds of fish, clams and weeds. One seaweed that grows to the surface of the water that potash and iodine are made from called Kelp was real interesting.

On Catalina Island, William Wrigley's mansion is seen from a distance high on the side of the mountain. *Mervin and I thought that we have helped him build it by chewing so much of his gum.* Then—*each of us bought a souvenir, an abalone shell. Has all the different colors of the rainbow.* Among the packet of letters found on the porch last summer is the *circular that I will send with this letter,* a circular titled boldly EXCURSION DELUXE TO CATALINA—THE MEMORY LINGERS.

The letter of March 2nd to Marjorie begins: *Received your letter today and as dad says to come home will work until March 11th.* Then they will go to Riverside to visit a minister who used to live in Millard—*Mrs. Kittleson said to be sure to go there*—and take a week or more to go to San Diego and Tijuana. *So won't get home until about March 25th.* The days are hot, in the 80s, and the beaches are covered with bathers. *Store windows are full of spring hats and everybody says "spring is surely here."* At home, *is the feed holding out?*

The last letter from California—written to Kate—is dated March 9, 1925, Seal Beach, California. *We went to Los Angeles Saturday*

Sunday went to Catalina Island. Was a dandy trip. Went on the boat Avalon. Took some pictures. If they are good will send some home. There were over 500 passengers on the boat.

afternoon. Went to the depots to find out about train times, fares and so forth. Think that I will come home on the Southern Pacific for anything that I know of now. I will leave Los Angeles Monday, March 23rd at ten o'clock a.m. and get to Chicago at seven o'clock a.m. Thursday March 26th, and will probably get to Delavan on the one o'clock, Thursday March 26th. While at the depot

Tijuana, Mexico. *We will take about a week more to go to San Diego and Tijuana, Mexico. So we won't get home until about March 25th. . . . Guess this is all for this time.*

he took notice of whether travelers were using bags or suitcases. *There were ten suitcases to every one bag being used. Suppose it's because most of the people were traveling a long ways and had lots of clothes that a traveling bag wouldn't hold.* Thus: *I bought a black genuine cowhide suitcase and it won't be a bit too big for all I have to put in it.* The fare home will be about $105. Mervin will be taking the train to Spokane, Washington to visit relatives. *His train doesn't leave until 6:15 p.m. so he will have a few hours to stroll around by himself after I leave.*

They go to Riverside, San Diego, and Tijuana in the days before returning home. *Will call for our last mail here at Seal Beach Saturday March 21st.* The last letter home ends: *Could plainly see the snowcapped mountains from here Sunday morning which are 50 to 60 miles away. According to the papers eight inches of snow fell in the mountains Saturday, but the weather here was just like spring. No snow. Just a little shower of rain. Guess this is all for this time. Floyd.*

The spring crops were planted in the spring of 1925. Tilled in the summer. And harvested in the fall. Seasons came and passed, one after the other in their time. My father met my mother at a dance in Delavan on a Saturday night in the fall of 1929. They were married the next year in September. I was born in May, 1934. My brother Ralph was born two years later. Mervin farmed for the rest of his life a few miles to the north. Occasionally he came to the house to visit my father.

In a gray metal box on a shelf above my desk, I have a few letters my father wrote to me after I left home. I don't read the letters often. Only when I feel that I am beginning to lose the voice, his sound, him. The return of my father. And that is just dandy with me.

How would you end an ethnography? One such as this? I could append a bibliographic essay, listing and describing all the works that have preceded this one, the research and the writings that have influenced my own efforts. My indebtedness to friends and colleagues. All this is in order, and that I choose not to add the note is indication of the endlessness of this project. To be true to the genre is to realize that the ethnography ends only with the death of the ethnographer. We write, in the meantime, to save our lives.

Rarely do I go to the grave of my father. I find him, rather, in the photographs he took, in the letters he wrote, and in the person I try to be. But I do occasionally return to the letters my father wrote on his trip to California. And I look, especially, at the photographs he took, at the particular images that he made to send home. I have reproduced, in this essay, several of the photographs for you to see. Yet, I remind myself of Roland Barthes' discussion of a photograph of his mother in his book *Camera Lucida* (1981). Barthes does not provide the reader with the photograph, writing that the photograph "would be nothing but an indifferent picture" for anyone else. Instead, he tells us of the meaning of the photograph to him. And the meaning is, essentially, in the fact that his mother existed.

The photograph—as with all photographs—is an authentication, a substantiation, that the subject in the photograph existed. Barthes writes that the photograph does not so much call up the past. "The effect it produces on me is not to restore what has been abolished (by time, by distance) but to attest that what I see has indeed existed" (82). Barthes adds, "Photography has something to do with resurrection." In the photographs of my father and the photographs taken by my father, as well as the letters that remain for my reading, I have the evidence that indeed my father existed. Each time I return to the letters and the photographs, there is the possibility of resurrection.

I share with Barthes, as well, the conviction that photographs are not to be subjected to "scientific" and "professional" discourse. Photography resists a language of analysis. The image speaks in silence. We give ourselves up to that which is beyond language and rational thought. Gift enough that a certain existence has been substantiated.

If photographs and letters are not to be "tamed" by discourse, by a "scientific" ethnography, we are left with what Barthes finally calls *ecstasy*. We stand before the image in all the wonder of existence. (This is what I hope to convey in my ethnography.) Perhaps all ethnography is about wonderment, about the ecstasy that comes in looking between the cracks, beyond the veil. We are playing in the fields of Time—and we entertain its good friend, Death. The letter and the photograph give us evidence of time past and time passing. What once existed no longer exists, except in memory, in the viewing of the artifact that is letter and photograph. In the evidence is the fact of life and death.

Does the recollection that is ethnography ease the pain of the loss evoked by the recollection? No, certainly not; ethnography is only another form of mourning. Barthes, still thinking about the photograph of his mother, observes that the gradual labor of mourning does not ease the pain of his parent's death. Only the emotions connected to loss are decreased in time. The being lost, the quality of that being, is irreplaceable. The life I see in the image speaks to me of death. My father once was, but no longer is.

Barthes also prompts us into a deeper understanding. "I am the reference of every photograph, and this is what generates my astonishment in addressing myself to the fundamental question: why is it that I am alive *here and now*?" (84). The image before us is ultimately about us. The photograph, as well as the words in the letters, opens us (no less) to a metaphysics of existence. Thus the importance of the photograph in our time. "For Death must be somewhere in society; if it is no longer (or less intensely) in religion, it must be elsewhere; perhaps in this image which produces Death while trying to preserve life" (92). A literal death in the photograph—"*Life/Death*: the paradigm is reduced to a simple click, the one separating the initial pose from the final print" (92). In each and every photograph, you and I (the living) face death. We die each moment to the image before us. A preparation; we look at photographs, we photograph what we love and hold dearly, and we entertain an ending to all of this.

Sometimes we call our efforts ethnography. What I have learned about the ethnographic enterprise in the telling this time is that our labors are without boundary. Or if we attend to boundaries of any kind (sociological or anthropological, for example), ethnography is interdisciplinary. There are many ways to do ethnography, more ways than can be imagined in any philosophy. And among the ways is the telling of tales beyond any notion of science, objectivity, or rational discourse. Time and death do not wait on the tools of any trade. Imagine wildly the possibilities of ethnography. Perhaps you will make a trip of a lifetime.

References

Barthes, R. 1981. *Camera Lucida: Reflections on Photography.* New York: Hill and Wang.

◆────────

In the course of daily life, **Richard Quinney** practices an existential, ethnographic sociology. His practice is relatively simple—a few words to the day, a photograph or two, a meditation. Eventually, he knows, not even the need for these. In the meantime, there are the productions of this inquiring mind: Professor of Sociology at Northern Illinois University, author of books and articles on social theory, crime, religion, and visual sociology. Autobiographical reflections are contained in *Journey to a Far Place.*

Open-Ending

Department of Communication
University of South Florida
4202 East Fowler Avenue, CIS 1040
Tampa, Florida 33620-7800
(813) 974-2145
FAX (813) 974-6817

March 10, 1996

Dear Readers:

We want to hear from you. You have given us ample opportunity to influence your lives. But we don't know what you thought and how you felt as you read, reacted to, and conversed about the chapters in this book. We invite you to be part of a wider conversation about <u>Composing Ethnography</u>.

It's your turn to talk back. Tell us which chapters inspired you the most and how. What did you think about as you read them? How did you feel? Who did you talk with about them? How did you connect your life to the lives of the people discussed in these works? Did your image of sociology, communication studies, or anthropology change as you read these chapters? How? Why? What kind of ethnographic writing and research would you like to do?

Feel free to express what's on your mind and in your heart. We want to hear from you.

Sincerely,

Carolyn Ellis
Professor of Sociology & Communication
cellis@chuma.cas.usf.edu

Arthur P. Bochner
Professor of Communication
abochner@cis01.cis.usf.edu

Name Index

Subject Index

Abortion, 111
Abuse, 78, 245; enjoying, 120–123; physical, 120–121, 128–129, 344, 346. *See also* Child sexual abuse; family; sex offender; sexual abuse
Activism, 167; and lobbying, 168; Civil Rights Movement, 271; feminist, 303–304; grassroots, 322; HIV/AIDS activists, 167, 168
Addiction, 78; alcohol, 78; food, 104; recovery from, 323; treatment for, 247. *See also* Alcohol; Alcoholics Anonymous; drug user; therapy
Aestheticism, 267 African, 35, 207–216, 228; ancestry, 228; professional African women, 226
Agency, 330–331, 352; of child, 350–354
Alcohol, 244; alcoholic husband, 313; health implications, 251; misuse, 244–245, 249, 259; withdrawal, 247, 249–250. *See also* Addiction; Alcoholics; Alcoholics Anonymous
Alcoholics Anonymous, 248, 253
Alienation, 325 Analysis, 30, 293; cultural, 16, 187; meta-analysis, 165; textual, 191
Anorexia, 78
Anti-Semitism, 39, 267–298; at Yale, 280, 297; blood guilt, 271–272, 295–296; denial of Jewishness of Jesus, 272; disregard of, 291; in Mexico, 273–274; Jewish problem,

287–288; multiculturalist anti-Semitism, 294; similarity to philo-Semitism, 291. *See also* Bigotry; racism; stereotype
Anthropologists, 134, 257, 268, 273, 292
Anthropology, 174, 182, 184, 188, 193, 268, 295; of religion, 292
Apprentice, 312, 315. *See also* Craft; Wicca; Witch; Witchcraft
Arts, 37; performance, 30
Authority, 49–50; control of and by environment, 67; medical, 161; of father, 231; of men, 63, 69; of personal experience, 176; of researcher, 330; principle of dominance, 67; questioning of, 161; rhetoric of, 303; scientific, 175; sociopolitical, 63
Autobiographer, 195
Autobiographic, 183, 184; genre, 184; impulse, 173; 183, 187, 195; moment, 184; situation, 184; text, 190, 192. *See also* Autobiographer; autobiography; autoethnography; narrative; writing
Autobiography, 30, 134, 184, 187–188, 193, 268, 293; as critique and resistance, 191; ethnic, 191. *See also* Autobiographic; autobiographer; autobiography; autoethnography; narrative; writing
Autobiology, 74

390